D0757649

Collections for Excellence
Assuring a Vibrant Library
John and Idamae Schack
Endowment Fund
Arts

THE LANDSCAPE ARCHITECTURE OF RICHARD HAAG

the landscape architecture of

richard haag

FROM MODERN SPACE TO URBAN ECOLOGICAL DESIGN

Thaïsa Way

FOREWORD BY Marc Treib

AFTERWORD BY Laurie Olin

UNIVERSITY OF WASHINGTON PRESS
Seattle and London

Publication of this book has been supported by generous grants from the Graham Foundation for Advanced Studies in the Fine Arts, the Foundation for Landscape Studies, the Marion Dean Ross Chapter of the Society of Architectural Historians, and the Johnston-Hastings Endowment of the College of Built Environments.

Printed and bound in China
Design by Thomas Eykemans
Composed in Minion, typeface designed by Robert Slimbach
Display type set in Futura, designed by Adrian Frutiger
19 18 17 16 15 5 4 3 2 1

UNIVERSITY OF WASHINGTON PRESS
www.washington.edu/uwpress

LIBRARY OF CONGRESS CATALOGING-IN-PUBLICATION DATA
Way, Thaïsa, 1960–
The landscape architecture of Richard Haag : from modern space to urban ecological design / Thaïsa Way ; foreword by Marc Treib ; afterword by Laurie Olin.
pages cm
Includes bibliographical references and index.
ISBN 978-0-295-99448-2 (hard cover : alk. paper)
1. Haag, Richard.
2. Landscape architects—United States—Biography
3. Landscape architecture—United States.
I. Title.
SB470.H33W39 2015 712.092—dc23 [B] 2014034911

The paper used in this publication is acid-free and meets the minimum requirements of American National Standard for Information Sciences—Permanence of Paper for Printed Library Materials, ANSI Z39.48–1984.∞

Dedicated to Marc, for making the trek to the Pacific Northwest, and my adult children, Adrian and Natasha, for becoming highly critical of their landscapes and environments

The cosmos is a park
the earth is a garden
life is a holiday
—RICHARD HAAG, *Seattle, 1964*

contents

FOREWORD by Marc Treib *ix*

Preface *xiii*

Acknowledgments *xv*

1 Growing up in a Kentucky Landscape *3*

2 A Landscape Education *13*

3 "Keep Your Eyes Open!" *25*

4 Designing the Home Garden in California *51*

5 A Teacher's Teacher *67*

6 Gardens of the Pacific Northwest *83*

7 From Modernism to Urbanism *105*

8 The Art of the Landform as Landscape Architecture *129*

9 "It Was a Gas!" at Gas Works Park *147*

10 Land Sculpting and Ecological Design at the Bloedel Reserve *169*

11 The Legacy *187*

AFTERWORD
An Appreciation of Richard Haag, an Inspiration and Mentor to Us All by Laurie Olin *189*

Notes *201*

Bibliography *213*

Illustration Credits *219*

Index *221*

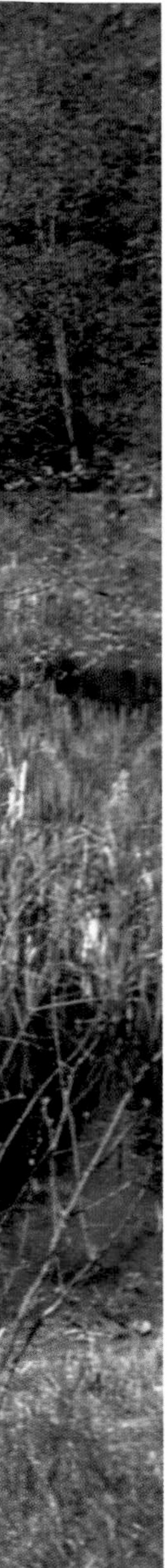

foreword

IN THE FIELD OF LANDSCAPE ARCHITECTURE, RICHARD HAAG has been known primarily as the creator of two landmark projects. The first, Gas Works Park in Seattle, on the shore of Lake Union, was among the earliest efforts to convert derelict industrial waste fields into parkland while retaining vestiges of the industry that had occupied—and polluted—the site. Rather than attempting to wipe the slate clean, here was an acceptance of the challenges of tainted land that looked forward to the potentials rather than back to the limitations. Here the landscape architect mastered political process as well as the shaping of soil and the management of vegetation. The success of the Gas Works Park project spawned a long list of landscapes reclaimed from extraction and manufacturing, and converted from private to public ownership and occupancy, in locations as wide ranging as Germany, England, and China. That is to say, Gas Works Park has been used as a starting point, and even model, for postindustrial landscapes around the world.

The second landscape, the Bloedel Reserve on Bainbridge Island, across Puget Sound from Seattle, represents the gradual and sensitive transformation of marsh and woodland into a magnificent preserve in all senses of the word. Haag's contributions followed earlier efforts by, among others, Thomas Church, but it was Haag's knowledgeable interventions that cohered the zones of the site into a linked landscape yet allowed them to remain individual in their identities. The extended reflecting pool buried within the dense forest is one of the most stunning and contemplation-provoking spaces in all modern landscape architecture, while in an area nearby, the gradual intrusions of a moss blanket over the stumps and fallen branches of what had once been woodland wraps these remains in beauty and unhurriedly marks the flow of time. Other areas of the reserve are devoted more to vegetation and fauna than to the human visitor, although they have been shaped and managed with the visitor's experience in mind. Given the specificity of Haag's design approach, the Bloedel Reserve has been difficult to emulate—unlike its sibling, Gas Works Park—although it has been uniformly appreciated as a gentle and highly personal intervention where most traces of the human hand have been subordinated to nature. Without doubt, these two projects alone would have assured Haag's place in American landscape architectural history. And yet, despite their international significance, they represent but a small fragment of a design production that has extended over half a century. Bringing a complete picture to landscape architecture, environmental, and general audiences is the principal accomplishment of Thaïsa Way's study.

Richard Haag was to the plant world born, spending his childhood on the grounds of his father's garden center in Jeffersontown, Kentucky. At a very early age, he showed a remarkable interest in plants, mastering their scientific nomenclature and use and creating gardens almost from infancy. Could we say that a life in landscape architecture, or certainly in horticulture, was preordained? His studies at the University of Illinois, the University of California, Berkeley, and Harvard may have provided a rudder for steering him through his later landscapes and urban designs, but the hull for that ship was forged in Kentucky, with its keel set in the R. L. Haag Nursery in Jeffersontown.

Stanley White, Haag's undergraduate mentor at the University of Illinois, provided increased propulsion for the voyage. Their mutual respect and friendship deepened over time and overcame any distinction between student and teacher. White's impact on Haag's thinking and emerging talent was indelible. During his Illinois years, Haag explored the midwestern landscape with White in a war-surplus jeep; later, they crisscrossed New England in their travels. From the classroom, the studio, and the actual landscape, Haag developed a sensitivity for town, farmland, and most of all the relation of part to whole. Interestingly, "while White espoused no particular style of design, his sympathies clearly lay with the Beaux Arts approach of earlier generations," Way tells us in her text. Especially interesting in that Haag held truck with neither the lessons nor the forms of classical thinking. In his teaching and practice, however, White remained a presence. Hideo Sasaki, who would leave Illinois to teach at Harvard shortly after Haag arrived there, was a second contributor to the young landscape architect's formation. Less perhaps for a greater worldview than specifically for its embrace of collaboration and landscape pedagogy, Sasaki's thinking appealed to Haag, and they became lifelong friends as well as professional colleagues. Sensing after two years that Haag had exhausted what Illinois could provide, Sasaki suggested that he complete his education at the University of California, Berkeley—which he did, beginning in the fall of 1949.

At mid-century, the San Francisco Bay area was an active hub for new thinking in landscape architecture, fueled by the postwar economic and population booms and aided by the low-interest mortgages offered to returning veterans. Thomas Church, a landscape modernism pioneer who maintained an active practice well into the 1970s, already represented an older generation, and coming into their own at that moment were his successors, often former employees of the Church office: Lawrence Halprin, Robert Royston, and Douglas Baylis, among them. As a group they were designing landscapes in a new idiom that enfolded an emerging vocabulary based to some degree on the contemporary arts with a healthy respect for the ecology of the California landscape and the families who had commissioned them.

The landscapes and the thinking that qualified these practices affected the teaching across the bay, at Berkeley, and some of these young practitioners, like Royston and Halprin, taught classes there. But even this vital and thriving atmosphere could not keep Haag in the Bay Area, and after a year, he left for graduate study at Harvard. It was perhaps less the formal coursework in the landscape architecture department there than the summers spent in the Vermont office of Dan Kiley that were of the greatest value to Haag. Simplicity, structure, and space prevailed in Kiley's work at that time, and there were lessons to be learned, most of all in terms of restraint and omission. In contrast to his Californian contemporaries, Kiley rarely utilized biomorphic forms or devices such as the diagonal. Instead, he relied on orthogonal plantings of trees in lines and bosks and fluid if rectangular spaces that could be read almost as a classical rendering of modernism—or a modernist rendering of classicism.

Sympathy for its culture, art, and design attracted Haag to Japan—his wife was Japanese American—and after receiving his master's degree in landscape architecture in 1952, he pursued a Fulbright grant to study there. His application was successful, and his stay, which began in 1953 and lasted for two years, was formative. From these travels and studies, Haag acquired an appreciation and knowledge of not only the landscape that so delighted all those with polite aesthetic tastes—key landscapes such as the garden of Katsura Villa or the stone garden at Ryōan-ji—but also the basic vernacular landscape, the traces of human efforts to make the land habitable and productive, all in response to geology, climate, and topography. But the garden, even the imperial or temple garden, was never truly detached from the land that surrounded it; in grand estates such as the imperial villa of Shugaku-in in Kyoto, productive rice fields had even been incorporated into the design. Haag's appreciation of the horticultural landscape now broadened into a vision of the cultural landscape of which the designed landscape was but a small part.

As Way tells us, Haag spent almost every waking moment in Japan acquiring experience and found tacit tutorials on restriction, reduction, and economy of means, the ability to compress designs of considerable consequence in a small space and with a minimum amount of materials. An abundance of species was rarely necessary; one should look to the site for the approach and the appropriate materials and then design with effectiveness in mind. It is commonly noted that Asian culture significantly influenced the design practices of the Pacific Northwest; however, in Haag's case, the impact was profound—less, perhaps, in how something looked and more in the way the designer thought.

Although academically attached to the University of Kyoto while in Japan, Haag's true professor was the land itself. As he had traveled in the United States with White, he now explored the Japanese countryside and small towns with the architect Norman Carver, also a Fulbright fellow. He looked, he considered, he photographed. Way tells of one humorous incident in which Haag wanted so desperately to see the structures inside the fenced compound of the Grand Shrines at Ise, a complex of Shinto shrines, that he climbed an adjacent tree in order to gain a vantage point with sufficient height. A clandestine descent proved to be far more difficult than the ascent, and the presence of guards forced him to spent the night in the branches.

Haag returned to the Bay Area in 1956 and spent a short time in the office of Lawrence Halprin, but within a year he had opened his own practice. The office soon produced a series of gardens, the most celebrated—if unbuilt—work accompanied the unbuilt Case Study House No. 19, a garden of pyramidal planes to be executed in stabilized sand. "His California gardens were meant to be more contemplative," writes Way, "more inward-looking, as aesthetically engaging as they were functional." An approach quite Japanese actually. Yet we must keep in mind that individual contemplation constitutes in itself social values and a greater milieu.

Once again, Haag's stay in the San Francisco Bay area was limited, and a year later he was lured north to Seattle by the invitation to teach at the University of Washington—first in the architecture program, to broaden the perspective of nascent building designers, and in time to establish a degree program in landscape architecture. A number of the students he taught—Laurie Olin and Robert Hanna, for example—became landscape architects as a result of his class and have enjoyed national and international reputations. He continued to draw inspiration from his contact with White, at times in joint travel but more often in letters. Haag's pedagogy, like his practice, drew on philosophy, poetry, literature, and science, values and a vision stated in an early mission statement for the program: "Here in Washington, a most important effort must be made to CONSERVE the natural resources that impart a special Northwest quality. We must recognize these qualities and RESTORE them where they have been ravaged. The landscape architect must join forces with the architect and the planner to CREATE new concepts of environment in extreme situations."[1]

In his teaching, and even more in his practice, Haag developed the idea of fusion, which might be explained as the simultaneous contrast of forms or materials in which something new and unexpected derives from the friction generated. In an article in *Pacific Horticulture*, he defined fusion in this way: "The principal idea expressed over and over again in this residential garden on Lake Washington—in the plan, the form, even the function, in the elements of space, movement, water, earth, stone, and plants—is fusion. Brick invades grass, grass captures brick, which in turn is infiltrated by moss, which merges with running stream and quiet pools of water. Stone defines edges of the water, and water impounds a mossy stone island."[2]

While hardly Haag's invention—in Japan, the mixture of formalities and the creative reenvisioning of elements was part of long-standing practice—it was more the ways in which he applied this approach, and the conviction with which he did so, that proved remarkable. Unlike Gas Works Park and the Bloedel Reserve, which are characterized by simplicity, his residential gardens explode with intricate combinations of flowers, shrubs, and trees, all set against the vertical accents of the tall pines and firs indigenous to the region.

Given the remarkable number of projects Haag realized during his career, it would be nearly impossible for anyone to produce a complete inventory and commentary in an initial study of his life and work. Instead, Thaïsa Way has taken key issues and key landscapes as the basis for structuring this book and included descriptions of landscapes and the design professionals with whom he worked, as well as insightful critique, all set against a basic biography. She has approached the book like a design project, thoroughly researched the available materials, mapped out an approach, developed a thesis, and then told the story. Feedback, which will close the loop and complete the analogy, must be left to the reader. A book on Richard Haag is long overdue, and we should be grateful that his story has been told as completely as possible in a single volume, relying on existing archival materials, interviews with Haag and colleagues, and, of course, the landscapes themselves.

MARC TREIB
Berkeley, October 2014

preface

THERE ARE MANY MONOGRAPHS ON THE BOOKSHELVES ON the practices of contemporary landscape architects and a few on those whose practices were completed in the past century. The first of these tend to be from the point of view of the designers, essentially explaining, promoting, and celebrating their work. The latter tend toward the historical narrative; when done well, they engage the social and cultural contexts and in the end can summarize a closed body of work. This book lies somewhere in between. As the author, I am a historian, neither employed by Haag nor with any intention to necessarily celebrate his work. However, it is important work and thus worthy of historical consideration, given the body of work over fifty years; even if it is not entirely finished (at the age of ninety, Haag continues to practice), it has altered how landscape architecture is practiced and understood. It is in this light that I became interested as a historian in Haag's practice. Thus what I offer here is a narrative of Haag's practice as a lens through which we might discover the emergence of urban ecological design. The intention of the book is thus to tell a larger narrative through the specific stories of one person and, to a large extent, one region—Richard Haag and the Pacific Northwest.

With this in mind, I began the project by questioning whether one could write such a history if the main protagonist was not only still alive but still in practice. Although I have always told students that history includes everything that just happened, that we are constantly becoming history, writing such a history was a different challenge. I explored the history of the department that Haag founded, the one I now teach and do research in. I visited Haag's landscapes and looked at his drawings. Only then did I decide there was the potential to write a history that could be scholarly, historical, and critical while allowing the opportunity to interview the actual people involved and visit the sites as they are being used. I had to make sure that Haag and his wife and professional partner, Cheryl Trivison, would agree to such an approach. When they asked if they would be able to read the final version and edit it, the answer was an emphatic no. I can't say they were delighted by the prospect, but over time, they grew, I believe, to trust me. In any case, they have remained faithful to that agreement. They read an early draft so that they could correct inaccuracies and suggest projects or people I might have missed. Since that time, they have not read any drafts. Haag assisted with the identification of photographs and drawings and reviewed the captions for the Japanese photographs in chapter 3. The narrative of the book is mine. I hope that Haag finds it of interest as well as challenging to his own narratives. While not every design project he completed is considered, each chapter develops important themes that emphasize his role in the development of urban ecological design in the twenty-first century.

The book is organized both chronologically and thematically. The first half of the book is chronological, as it follows a biographical narrative of Haag's youth, education, and teaching. While any biography begins with the child—for "the Child is father of the Man," as William Wordsworth wrote in "My Heart Leaps Up"—it is important for Haag, as it establishes critical threads, his interest in and deep knowledge of plants as the son of a nurseryman and farmer and his unorthodox view of the world and its politics, arts, and culture, which would be evidenced in his teaching as well as his later practice. In his debates on evolution with his parents and their efforts to combat the prevalence of racism in the South, he learned to involve the intellectual as an integral aspect of civic engagement in the public sphere.

Following the narrative on Haag's early life and education is a chapter on his experiences in Japan and the importance of the trip to the development of his practice as well as its larger role in shaping a Pacific Northwest school of architecture and landscape architecture. It includes a photographic essay composed of images that Haag took in Japan, of which only two have ever been published, providing a unique resource on Japan in the 1950s. A chapter on Haag's earliest solo work in California as he began to articulate the threads of his design practice completes this first section. Haag's early projects reflect his modernist explorations in geometry and materials, and his concern for choreography. This section thus establishes the groundwork of Haag's practice.

The second section of the book is organized thematically, emphasizing Haag's role as a designer and design activist, positioned within both regional and national contemporary practice. We turn our attention to his teaching and the development of a distinct pedagogical framework that forms the basis of his legacy as his students practiced and taught across the nation. While Haag did not write extensively, he lectured weekly for many decades. These lectures, many of which were recorded, convey the evolution of his thinking as he engaged in practice during a pivotal period in the history of landscape architecture in the United States.

The next chapter considers Haag's residential projects and their importance as sites of experimentation in ecological and cultural translations as his design process was refined and enriched during his decades of practice in the Pacific Northwest. Haag's public work is positioned within the urban renewal movement in Seattle, emphasizing that it was a response to national trends and also to specifically regional articulations including the Model Cities program and the developing environmental and ecological movements that would become associated with Seattle.

Postindustrial landscapes offered new territory in the 1970s, and Haag's work broke ground with the Gas Works Park project. As a synthesis of his contributions to disturbed sites and to the reemergence of ecological design, the Bloedel Reserve is the focus of a chapter that explores the complex narrative of this once-logged landscape. Gas Works Park and the Bloedel Reserve are Haag's best-known projects and yet are rarely considered beyond their visual impact and basic narrative. The studies offered in this chapter undertake a fuller investigation of how the projects are positioned within Haag's career and milieu. The book concludes with a chapter on Haag's legacy followed by an afterword by Laurie Olin, a leader in landscape architecture who was a student, employee, and colleague of Haag's. His essay builds on Haag's legacy while providing insights that come only from knowing someone for fifty years as Olin has known Haag. It also moves the narrative forward, as Olin considers his role as teacher and mentor and the next generation of designers.

The narrative in these pages offers what I hope is both a broader and a deeper consideration of Haag's practice and its role in expanding our definition and reading of modern space and its trajectory into what we today call "urban ecological design," a practice described as one that integrates site, landscape, and people in a design practice that is functional, artful, and engaging.

acknowledgments

THERE IS, AS WITH ANY LONG DISCOVERY, A CONSTELLATION of colleagues, friends, and well-wishers whom I need to thank. I begin by noting Richard Haag, without whom I would have no story—literally. His partner, Cheryl Trivison, was also a source of great support and assistance—my thanks to both of you. I thank Marc Treib for suggesting I take on this project as a way of learning more about this place I now call home, Seattle, and then for reading multiple drafts and marking them up assiduously. Jeffrey Ochsner was enthusiastic throughout the project, reading multiple drafts and consistently keeping me honest as a historian. John Rozdilsky is one to whom this book could also be dedicated, as his files from his master's thesis on Haag's work, given to me by his widow, started me on this project. To Laurie Olin I owe my deep gratitude for his consistent generosity, insightful comments, and enthusiasm as a "son of Rich."

There are also those colleagues whose brilliance, friendship, and wisdom were essential. Ann Huppert and Margaret O'Mara were my partners in writing as each of us struggled through our respective books. Ken Oshima, Julie Parrett, David Streatfield, Ken Yocom, and finally Daniel S. Friedman, my dean at the University of Washington, stood by and listened to me explain the point of all this research, multiple times—thank you! My graduate student research assistants included Jordan Bell, Karen Kennedy, Michael Lewis, and Danielle Pierce. Mackenzie Waller and Tera Hatfield served as exhibit designers, researchers, and creative thinkers bringing their curiosity as students and talents as artists to the projects.

The design community was also essential, as it offered not only memories but, in the case of Suyama Space and the AIA Gallery, space for me to explore Haag's work through exhibits of photographs, drawings, and designs. Peter Miller encouraged me along the way as did Marga Rose Hancock. There are also the many designers, teachers, and scholars—including Gary Hilderbrand, Elizabeth Meyer, Paul Dorpat, Barbara Swift, and Michael Van Valkenburgh—who contributed insights and thoughts on Haag's work, to whom I am grateful, as they allowed the story to go far beyond a local narrative of Seattle. Catherine Tighe, who took photographs for me, and Mary Randlett and Alan Ward who shared their photographs of Haag's work, were each instrumental. Landscape is in the end a visual, sensual, aesthetic experience, and words can do it only so much justice.

To Shannon Nichol and Jennifer Guthrie (onetime students of Haag's), and the entire staff of Gustafson Guthrie Nichol, including Keith McPeters, I am indebted, as they allowed me to hang out in the office and listen to them while they worked—all so that I could better describe design process and thinking. Important lessons from all these individuals are deeply embedded in my understanding of Haag's designed landscapes. In the pulling together of images, references, and resources, I can never thank our librarians enough. I had the gracious, consistent, and generous support of Joshua Polansky, director of the College of Built Environments (CBE) Visual Resources Collection, University of Washington. He was the one who scanned and cleaned many, many images, a remarkable feat. I would like to also thank Alan Michelson, the CBE head librarian who helped track down citations and sources. And at the University of Washington Libraries Special Collections and Architectural Records, where the Richard Haag Associates records' are being carefully cared for—thank you to Nicollette Brumberg and her staff.

There are also those who funded the research that allowed this book to become a reality. The University of Washington's Royalty Research Fund launched this project in my early years as a faculty member. The Graham Foundation for Advanced Studies in the Fine Arts made possible not only initial research but also two public exhibits on Haag's work and legacy. These were critical parts of my exploration. The Andrew W. Mellon Foundation's award to the University of Washington for the two-year-long John E. Sawyer Seminar "Now Urbanism" under my co-leadership with Margaret O'Mara funded a critical part of the research on cities and the role of design in the urban landscape. And then there are the six weeks I had to write the final manuscript while joyfully ensconced at the MacDowell Colony in spring 2013. To the leadership of the colony, the cabin in the woods, the fabulous food, and, beyond all, my fellow colonists Denise Kumani Gantt, Martha Clippinger, Leslie Robertson, Carter Pann, and Jose Carlos Teixeira—my gratitude for your steadfast quiet during the day and loud debate with laughter and music in the evenings.

For the book publication including the large number of black-and-white and color images, the Graham Foundation for Advanced Studies in the Fine Arts granted a Publication Award, and the Foundation for Landscape Studies awarded the David R. Coffin Publication Grant. The Marion Dean Ross/Pacific Northwest Chapter of the Society of Architectural Historians contributed support, and the Johnston-Hastings Endowment of the College of Built Environments, University of Washington, provided the final support for publication. Thank you to each of these important sources of support for historians, writers, and scholars.

My family has stuck by me as I finished this book, as they did for my first book. My partner, Marc, moved to Seattle so I could be a part of the design community here, and his steadfast friendship serves as a backbone for this project. My children, Adrian and Natasha, who grew from teenagers to young adults while I was writing this, are an inspiration to me and a tremendous reminder of the power of our futures.

THE LANDSCAPE ARCHITECTURE OF RICHARD HAAG

growing up in a kentucky landscape

RICHARD HAAG HAS OFTEN QUIPPED THAT ONE SHOULD "never trust a landscape architect without mud on his shoes."[1] Like children, gardens and landscapes are always growing and ever changing. Such views reflect his life and career, both spent in countless gardens, nurseries, and landscapes around the world.

Born October 23, 1923, in Louisville, Kentucky, Richard Haag grew up in a family closely knit with land and its cultivation. His mother, Luthera Owings, came from a southern family who had farmed in Kentucky since the early nineteenth century. His father's grandparents emigrated from Germany to Kentucky, where they, too, became successful farmers. Rudy Haag, Richard's father, was a farmer who had an abiding interest in ornamental and productive plants and their cultivation. During World War I, Rudy Haag used his leaves from the U.S. Army to visit gardens in England and on the Continent, collecting seeds and sending them to his sister Gertrude, who was living with their parents in the suburbs of Louisville. When the war came to an end, Rudy returned to Kentucky and married Luthera Owings. The young couple bought land from her father in Jeffersontown, Kentucky—a small town about fifteen miles east of Louisville—and established the R. L. Haag Nurseries. Rudy learned to propagate plants, and, having completed courses in accounting, Luthera managed the family business. The R. L. Haag Nurseries prospered and grew over the decades, until the couple retired in 1955. This legacy of successful farmers, growers, and propagators shaped Richard Haag's view of the world as he has described it: living and working with "nature as a lover."[2]

KENTUCKY FARMER

Jeffersontown was an agrarian community not far from the Ohio River Falls.[3] In the nineteenth century, many German American families farmed fifteen to thirty acres of red clay soils near the Ohio River, harvesting a variety of vegetables and fruits. It was an area lauded for its dairies, mills, and "fine farms in a high state of cultivation."[4] This produce fed the farming families, and surpluses were sent to urban markets in and beyond Kentucky by train and electric railway as the town was located at the terminus of the Louisville and Jeffersontown Electric Railway and along the Louisville Southern Railroad.

The Owings and Haag families were an integral part of the Jeffersontown community of farmers. Luther Clay Owings, Luthera's father, owned one of the larger farms, at 160 acres, just north of the town center. Their farm, Cedar Croft, was known for its grand home and impressive herd of Duroc-Jersey boars. When Luther died, his remaining property was divided among his four daughters, expanding the acreage of the Haag nursery. Luthera and Rudy Haag started their nursery on what one brother regarded as the worst of the four forty-acre parcels; it was watered only by a degraded stream. Nevertheless, they turned their plot into the most productive of the sections and eventually acquired a substantial portion of the original 160 acres from Luthera's siblings.

Rudy Haag's extended family included farmers as well as druggists, millers, and a few who served in public positions

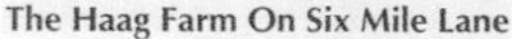

1.1 Rudy Haag and the Haag home in Jeffersontown, Kentucky.

1.2 Luthera Owings Haag with Richard (four years old) and Philip (two years old), 1927.

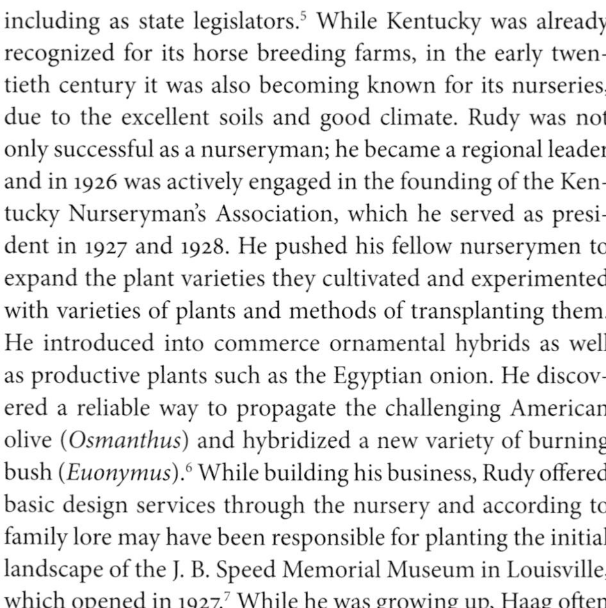

including as state legislators.[5] While Kentucky was already recognized for its horse breeding farms, in the early twentieth century it was also becoming known for its nurseries, due to the excellent soils and good climate. Rudy was not only successful as a nurseryman; he became a regional leader and in 1926 was actively engaged in the founding of the Kentucky Nurseryman's Association, which he served as president in 1927 and 1928. He pushed his fellow nurserymen to expand the plant varieties they cultivated and experimented with varieties of plants and methods of transplanting them. He introduced into commerce ornamental hybrids as well as productive plants such as the Egyptian onion. He discovered a reliable way to propagate the challenging American olive (*Osmanthus*) and hybridized a new variety of burning bush (*Euonymus*).[6] While building his business, Rudy offered basic design services through the nursery and according to family lore may have been responsible for planting the initial landscape of the J. B. Speed Memorial Museum in Louisville, which opened in 1927.[7] While he was growing up, Haag often worked with his father, and from this experience, he learned to design with an empathy for the plants.

Haag's schooling was relatively conventional. Although Jeffersontown would be absorbed into the suburban sprawl surrounding Louisville after World War II, when he was growing up, it remained a small town, with a population of less than nine hundred as late as 1940. Haag and his siblings attended the Jeffersontown School, a four-room building serving all elementary grades and an easy walk from home; a second floor was added in the late 1920s to accommodate high school students, although he remembered commuting to high school in nearby Louisville. Decades later, he credited his high school history teacher, a Mr. Knight, as an important influence for his broad explorations of contemporary literature.

Reading widely was familiar to the young Haag as his parents were avid readers and openly debated contemporary issues in science, religion, and politics. The children were expected to read and to engage in current events. They

Y EDITION OF CINCINNATI TIMES-S

FULL ASSOCIATED PRESS REPORTS

WEDNESDAY, AUGUST 22, 1928 FORTY PAGES

GHT FOLLOWING

DELEGATE TO CONVENTION OF NURSERYMEN'S ASSOCIATION

Kentucky Boy, 4, Attains Fame as Tree-Grafter

HE CAN DIG AND PLANT, ALSO CAN TRANSPLANT

Here's the bright and smiling face of the youngest practical tree-grafter in the land.

He is Richard Haag, four and a half years old, son of Mr. and Mrs. R. L. Haag of Jeffersontown, Ky., delegates at the convention of the Ohio and Kentucky Nurserymen's Association at the Hotel Gibson.

And little Richard was a delegate, too—you can see how proudly he wore the official delegate's badge on his shirt front. The badge was a well-earned and deserved honor for Richard, for he is singularly precocious in his horticultural knowledge and can already qualify as a practical nurseryman.

His father is vice president of the Kentucky Nurserymen's Association, specializing in the propagation of fine evergreens. Richard has spent all of his four and a half years amid tens of thousands of these growing trees, and ever since he has been able to walk he has enjoyed being out in the miniature forest around his home, helping his father and the workmen in planting the acres of evergreen trees. He can dig and plant and transplant—which is not especially remarkable—but he can also successfully cut and graft the evergreen trees, and that is remarkable. He has accomplished the grafting of the severed evergreen plant upon a new root system—a fine and delicate operation in horticultural surgery, and for this has won high praise. It is not known that any one else as young as Richard has succeeded in doing this.

And Richard surprised the nurserymen at the convention by his wide knowledge of the different varieties of evergreens.

Richard knows the names and can tell the many different varieties of evergreens, spruces, pines, retispora and the rest, and tupip poplars, maples, gum trees, beeches and shrubs are easy for him.

Some nurserymen tried to fool Richard the other day: "This is a Stricta Juniper" they told him.

"No, it is a Frank Meyer Juniper," the boy replied—and he was right. It takes an expert to tell the difference between the two varieties, and the little nurseryman knew.

RICHARD HAAG

"The boy has surprised nurserymen by his uncanny knowledge and skill—his conversation on technical tree matters is like that of a matured nurseryman," commented William A. Natorp, president of the Cincinnati Association of Landscape Architects that entertained the visitors.

1.3 "Kentucky Boy, 4, Attains Fame as Tree-Grafter," *Kentucky Times-Star*, August 22, 1928.

were each encouraged to pursue education beyond secondary school.[8] This childhood family background built a strong foundation for Richard Haag's future civic activism.

Haag was just about to turn six when the stock market crashed in October 1929. Initially the Haag family was not severely affected, as the farm continued to produce well, but within two years, as the Depression deepened, the Haag family faced increased economic stringency. In response, Rudy reoriented the nursery from ornamental species to productive plants and animals. The family became increasingly self-sufficient, growing vegetables and fruits and raising goats, sheep, and pigs, and managed to weather the deep depression of the early 1930s. Rudy constructed propagating greenhouses for the dual purpose of protecting young seedlings and drying fruit. For a time, the family even tried raising unusual species, such as deer, antelope, quail, and peacocks. They created a pond in a boggy area of the farm and obtained a government permit to raise wood ducks to distribute to zoos and nature shows as a means of raising income for the farm. Nearly a decade later, during World War II, Rudy helped plow the fields of the local school in preparation for growing potatoes and became a leading advocate of Victory Gardens in the region, exhibiting his own gardens as a model.

Although he was a great believer in innovation, Rudy did not take well to mechanized methods of farming. Instead, he insisted on a direct physical relationship with the land. He favored mule-drawn plows and slip scrapers for building the pond rather than new technologies. While his reluctance to employ mechanical means was not unusual, it may have been a financial decision rather than a strictly technological one, but either way, young Haag learned to work the land by traditional means.[9]

The influence of his father's interests and values on Haag's development was apparent from an early age. He learned to prune and graft trees and shrubs, construct a pole barn, dig ponds and build berms, care for animals, and perform other such tasks required to run a nursery and farm. During the annual meeting of the Ohio and Kentucky Nurseryman's

Associations in 1928, the local paper reported on the young boy's plant knowledge after a visit to the Haag nursery: "Kentucky Boy, 4, Attains Fame as Tree-Grafter."[10] The reporter quoted nurseryman William A. Natorp saying that the young Haag not only was skilled at propagation but could recite the Latin names of many plants.

Haag's early interest in design was revealed in his recollection of absconding with the gravel his grandfather had purchased for the driveway and using it to create a series of paths through the garden. He recalled spending teenage years contemplating the nature of God and looking over the family land from a perch high up in a black walnut tree. While these recollections are decades old, the stories suggest the importance the land, the outdoors, and plants, particularly trees, held for Haag—values that would remain at the core of his design practice.

First from his father, and later from the landscape architects who visited the nursery, Haag learned the role of drawing in the design process. His father was a sign painter and also created oil paintings of rural scenes and landscapes as a hobby. When he was twelve, his father bought him a drawing board and drafting tools to aid him in presenting designs for clients. Haag later recalled this period of his youth as the time when he learned that, through drawing, he could visualize not just what existed but his own ideas of what might exist. The eclectic range of his father's activities, from farmer to nurseryman, to landscape designer, to sign painter, certainly provided a creative foundation for Haag's later career as a landscape architect.

THE PROFESSION OF LANDSCAPE ARCHITECTURE AND THE NURSERY BUSINESS

As Richard Haag was learning about landscape architecture, the profession was becoming increasingly focused on a scientific understanding of ecological processes and how these might inform design. This was not entirely new, for, as Catherine Howett has suggested, ecological values had been a part of practice since the "primitive fence" defined

TRADE LIST

SPRING, 1932

The R. L. Haag Nurseries

JEFFERSONTOWN, KENTUCKY

MEMBERS

American Association of Nurserymen
Kentucky State Association of Nurserymen
National Association of Propagating Nurserymen

TERMS

Usual terms to purchasers of approved credit.

Prices apply F. O. B. Freight or Express Offices at Jeffersontown or Louisville, Kentucky, and are subject to change without notice.

Packing will be charged at cost.

LIABILITY

We are not liable for injury to stock from frost, hail, fire, or other causes beyond our control. Plants become your property on delivery to transportation company and we are not responsible for loss, damage, or delay in transit.

1.4 R. L. Haag Nurseries catalog, 1932.

1.5 Aerial photograph of R. L. Haag Nurseries, Jeffersontown, Kentucky.

a zone of human control, likely before the "primitive hut" that is believed to be at the root of architecture.[11] In the last decades of the nineteenth century, however, such interest in the environment and the ways in which humans shaped it grew significantly.[12] The term "environment" can be found in at least one hundred articles published in *Garden and Forest: A Journal of Horticulture, Landscape Art, and Forestry*, reflecting an educated understanding of Darwin's theory: "In other words, the species which most abound and have most successfully accommodated themselves to such artificial conditions, have, in the geologically brief period of man's pre-eminence, acquired advantages over species which have not been submitted to such environment."[13]

The use of the term "ecology" arose only at the end of 1890s as a framework for the study of natural processes and relationships.[14] The excitement around this relatively new study was reflected again in the journal *Garden and Forest*, which used the new term four times in its last year of publication (1897–98), sometimes to refer to the new science and other times to reference what was becoming a fashionable hobby. In a review of the book *Flowers and Their Friends*, the writer applauded Margaret Warner Morely's efforts: "To give children some notion of the ecology, physiology and histology of plants as understood to-day [was] no easy task, and we can forgive the pursuance of some rather cheap methods if the end is really attained, as it has been, we believe, in this case."[15] In an article on the botanical garden at Smith College in Massachusetts, published in *Garden and Forest* later that same year, William Ganong wrote: "It is plain to all who read the signs of the times that the present trend of botanical activity is toward the study of the phenomena of the life of plants. . . . For the systematic pursuit of physiology and ecology, however, a botanic garden with a well-proportioned greenhouse system is essential; and it is rapidly coming to pass that a college must provide these if it is ambitious to keep abreast of the general advance."[16] Thus, discussions of ecology and environmental science were being published alongside those on landscape design, shaping the design practice as it emerged as a profession at the turn of the twentieth century.

While many landscape architects pursued these scientific trajectories, others held firmly to the description of the practice as an art first and foremost. The discourse dated at least as far back as Frederick Law Olmsted and was evident in historian and critic Mariana Griswold van Rensselaer's (1851–1934) essay "Landscape Gardening—A Definition." Van Rensselaer defined the practice as grounded in art, and her descriptions of the role of nature were intended only as inspiration and guide. Nature provided "vitality, light, atmosphere," she maintained and, especially, "what no other artist ever gets—perfection in details." But "composition . . . is the chief thing in art[,] . . . and the landscape gardener's compositions are and must be his own."

What Van Rensselaer did not acknowledge with clarity was that Olmsted's initial investigations into the progressive agricultural movement known as "scientific farming" laid the groundwork for a more self-consciously scientific approach to the design of landscape. As Anne Whiston Spirn has observed, Olmsted's approach to landscape architecture was to make physical and biological natural systems function in accord with social and political contexts.[17] Olmsted wrote of "organizing a landscape in increasingly naturalistic forms [with] an emphasis on preserving the local character of a place."[18] He firmly believed that landscape design should embrace a "delicate balance, a synthesis of aesthetic, environmental, and social goods."[19] Olmsted, H. W. S. Cleveland, Frank Waugh, and, later, Wilhelm Miller, Jens Jensen, Elsa Rehmann, Warren Manning, and Ruth Dean, among others, designed with careful attention to plants, horticultural requirements, native vegetation, and the influence of local conditions on plant growth and health.[20] Haag's approach to landscape architecture, although decades later, was similarly both exploratory and grounded.

By the 1920s, the American Society of Landscape Architects (ASLA), established in 1899, had become a national organization, and many of its first members trained in nurseries, farms, and gardens, including Warren Manning, Annette McCrea, and Haag. While the ASLA did not allow professional landscape architects to act as nursery agents, given the close relationship between the two fields, many designers developed a network of nurseries to which they frequently returned. Such designers valued horticultural knowledge and took care to construct their designs with the best plant specimens. For their projects, they regularly visited local nurseries to select plants and learn from the nurserymen and gardeners of new cultivars and varieties available. By the 1920s and 1930s, it was common for landscape architects from New York, Washington, D.C., and Chicago to travel to Kentucky to discuss plants with Rudy Haag and inspect his specimens for possible purchase for a particular design, sometimes in the Ohio Valley region or sometimes farther away.

By the 1930s, the R. L. Haag Nurseries had established a solid reputation among landscape architects.[21] As Jeffersontown was at the end of the interurban train from Louisville, it was not unusual for professional clients to spend the day working and then stay the night with the Haag family. A memorable visitor, around 1934, was the landscape architect Annette Hoyt Flanders, whose firm had offices in New York City and Milwaukee. Flanders was a respected designer whose clients included some of the wealthiest families along the Eastern Seaboard. She was known for her deep knowledge of plants and her insistence on selecting mature plants as well as overseeing their planting with last-minute instructions for siting and orientation. She regularly provided horticultural guidelines for her clients so that they might maintain the gardens at an appropriately high standard and in many cases visited for annual on-site consultations.[22] Flanders arrived at the Haag nursery from New York City and spent the day reviewing the plants she required for any number of projects, primarily the trees that would structure her landscapes. With no evening return train to New York, she was a houseguest for the night and, according to Haag, discussed planting, plants, and design with his father far into the night. Haag, who was about eleven at the time, was duly impressed, and during one of these visits, he began to think he might want to be a landscape architect when he grew up.

1.6 Cherokee Park, Louisville, Kentucky, postcard, 1912. Park designed by Frederick Law Olmsted, 1887.

Landscape was also the focus of Haag family trips, including one to Cherokee Park in nearby Louisville at the end of each school year. Designed by Olmsted, the park included a natural creek with stone bridges, shaded areas, and sunny lawns for picnics and active recreation. The park also featured a breadth of plant materials, particularly trees, which were the young Haag's favorite. The family went as far as Cincinnati, Chicago, and even Florida to visit parks, botanical gardens, zoos, and arboreta, with, as Haag recalled, his father intent on meeting and talking with the gardeners. Such visits brought together Haag's interests in visual arts, horticultural and agricultural sciences, and design.

The future landscape architect was also an avid reader. Haag recalled that, as a teenager, he read Joseph LeConte's *Elements of Geology*, a textbook on geomorphology, and Somerset Maugham's *Of Human Bondage*. His father treasured his leather-bound copy of Charles Darwin's *On the Origin of Species*, which Haag read multiple times. Darwin's theory of evolution was a source of heated debate in Haag's family, as his mother was a devout Southern Baptist, while his father was a "hard-core Lutheran" and an agnostic. The celebrated 1925 Scope's Trial had taken place in nearby Tennessee, and the arguments still echoed across the region. Appreciation for argument would follow Haag into the military, where, he would later reminisce, "we had a royal bull session which ended, as bull-sessions often do, with a heated debate about religion."[23] He also recalled that his family was known for its liberal social views—including hiring black men and boys to work on the nursery and to do the landscape work as well as inviting the black domestic help to share the dinner table, an act of generosity rarely seen in the South at the time. In later life, Haag would often be described as a renegade, yet even his detractors would acknowledge his ability to fight for what he believed was right and moral, a quality that was encouraged within his family.

WORLD WAR II SERVICE AND THE ARMY AIR CORPS

In December 1941, when the United States entered World War II, Richard Haag was still in high school, but he was old enough to serve in the armed forces.[24] He enrolled in the Avon School of Electronics in Lexington, Kentucky, in May 1942, rather than completing his last year in high school, then went on to basic training at Fort Crowder, Missouri, and training school at Robin Field in Macon, Georgia. Thereafter, he transferred to the U.S. Army Air Corps and studied radar technology in Boca Raton, Florida, and advanced to the program at Smokey Hill, Missouri, subsequently serving as an electronics technician for an airborne radar unit. Corporal Haag completed his tour of duty in Calcutta, stationed with a B-29 bomber squadron in the China-Burma-India theater. He received an honorable medical discharge in spring 1945.

During the war, Haag not only learned cutting-edge technology; he also gained new perspectives on the world around him. While he went by ship to Casablanca, Morocco, he was able to travel by airplane to both Delhi and Calcutta in India and to Tripoli, Libya, and Alexandria, Egypt; he also flew supply flights inside China throughout much of 1944. Air travel gave Haag the opportunity to see landscape in a larger context and make connections that are often hard to imagine from the ground. For a rhetoric class at the University of Illinois a few years later, he wrote about his first flight with the Air Corps—from Casablanca to Tripoli on a C-54—describing his musings on landscapes and cultural histories:

> I shall always remember how Casablanca looked from the air that morning. I forgot about the houses of vice, the crowded cabarets, and the reeking medina, or native section. The city looked immaculate and organized, and no sin seemed possible there. . . . The land lay full in the sun, and barren, with outcroppings of stone and occasional dunes. . . . I remember thinking about the rise and fall of the Carthaginians, and then about the Battle of Tours. I contemplated that I might now be a Mohammedan had not Martel's forces been stronger. I remembered that the Arabs had devised the term for zero, which is the basis of our numerical system.[25]

On-the-ground visits were also enlightening. Haag visited the Taj Mahal in India and, in Egypt, the great pyramids at Giza and the temple at Karnak, building an understanding of the relationship of architecture to landscape, enriched by the experience of viewing the sites from both the ground and the air. The visual power of contrasting landscapes, such as the Nile Valley winding like a green thread through the largely barren desert, offered much more than what he had learned from photographs and texts. In 1951, in an opening essay in the new journal *Landscape*, "The Need of Being Versed in Country Things," J. B. Jackson wrote, "It is from the air that the true relationship between the natural and the human landscape is first clearly revealed. The peaks and canyons lose much of their impressiveness when seen from above. What catches our eye and arouses our interest is not the sandy washes and the naked rocks, but the evidences of man."[26]

While stationed in Kharagpur in Bengal in 1944, Haag tried his hand at experimental gardening as a means of demonstrating American methods of diversifying edible plants for Bengali farmers. Having observed traditional village life and farming techniques, and aware of India's periodic famines, Haag wrote his father requesting twenty kinds of vegetable seed from Bunton Seed and sowed them with the farmers. He would recall decades later that the garden "was a dismal failure." In the process, instead of teaching the Bengali farmers, Haag learned to respect traditional means and methods, an approach he would later label "non-striving."[27]

Three years of world travel exposed Haag to an extraordinary array of places, cultures, and experiences. One can see in these years the beginning of his inquisitive and creative view of the world. His wartime experiences informed and framed a holistic perspective of landscape and its role in culture and society, shaping his future as a landscape architect.

2

a landscape education

HOME FROM THE WAR, HAAG RETURNED BRIEFLY TO JEFFERsontown, where he decided to take advantage of the GI Bill and pursue a college degree. Interested in landscape architecture, he sought programs that offered a professional degree, which was increasingly required for practice. He was accepted into the undergraduate program in landscape architecture at the University of Illinois; as a land-grant college, it was a place a young man who had grown up on a farm might find most familiar.[1] He arrived in time for spring semester 1946.

A STUDENT AT THE UNIVERSITY OF ILLINOIS

The University of Illinois was one of the original land-grant colleges to offer courses in landscape gardening and design. The university had launched the Division of Landscape in 1912 under the leadership of Ralph Rodney Root and had appointed Charles Mulford Robinson, whose interests turned increasingly toward urban-scale landscape architecture, as professor of civic design. In 1929, Illinois was one of the first of eight schools to meet the new standards for accreditation by the American Society of Landscape Architects (ASLA), a process then just being established by a committee of professionals. The university created the College of Fine and Applied Arts, composed of the Department of Architecture, the Division of Landscape Architecture, the School of Music, and the Department of Art and Design, in 1931. Its faculty was admonished to address the " cultivation of esthetic taste on the part of the student body at large . . . and development of general artistic appreciation."[2] Repositioning the landscape architecture program within a unit devoted to art and design was increasingly common as many landscape degree programs realigned with the professions of architecture and engineering as a means of emphasizing the professional character of landscape practice. For Haag, it was likely an ideal position, as the program grew out of the agricultural sciences and was now concerned with engaging the arts, not unlike his own investigations.

Although the number of students that would enroll under the GI Bill would certainly strain the programs, by 1946 the University of Illinois landscape faculty was well established and included respected members of the profession such as Stanley Hart White (1891–1979), Florence Bell Robinson (1885–1973), and Karl B. Lohmann (1887–1963). The year before Haag's enrollment, a graduate degree had been added. The department was recognized for its strengths in horticulture, planting design, and an emphasis on city planning under Lohmann's direction. Robinson's text *Planting Design* was required reading in many programs across the country.[3] Haag entered a program recognized for its leadership in professional education and the success of its alumni.

American universities sought to accommodate the influx of GIs with great flexibility; Haag was no exception. Not only was he able to pass an exam to make up for not completing high school, but he also earned fifty-eight credits based on both his military service and his earlier work on the family nursery and farm. With the freedom he achieved by placing out of a series of required courses,

Haag shaped his curriculum to fit his interests. Although he already knew his plants well, he took the opportunity to learn from Robinson and became familiar with the plant palette of central Illinois. He took a planning course from Lohmann. He enrolled in an industrial design course with Professor Shifflet, whose lectures on the "Zen of economics" and the role of design Haag would later describe as a memorable experience. During his studies in Urbana, Haag also met two of his most influential teachers and colleagues: Stanley Hart White (1891–1979) and Hideo Sasaki (1919–2000). These mentors helped lay the groundwork for his development as a teacher and a designer.

White was a professor of landscape architecture at Illinois from 1922 to 1959. He was a well-recognized leader in the profession and served on many of the ASLA committees. White graduated from Cornell University in 1912 with a bachelor of science degree in agriculture. At that time, a solid grounding in horticulture or agriculture was considered ideal for a successful practice in landscape architecture. White subsequently enrolled at Harvard, where he completed the master in landscape architecture program in 1915. As this was one of the earliest programs to offer a graduate degree in the profession, he immediately joined an active, and rather elite, community of landscape architects.

2.1 Stanley White (left) and Richard Haag, c. 1948.

White initially worked in the offices of Fletcher Steele, John Nolen, and Harris Reynolds, and then for the Olmsted Brothers in Brookline, Massachusetts.[4] He began his teaching career while working at the Olmsted Brothers office, at the Lowthorpe School for Horticulture and Landscape Architecture for Women (established 1902), where many Harvard faculty taught part-time. He frequently recalled this experience as a major influence on his teaching, particularly the school's alternative instruction in design, planning, and horticulture.[5] In 1922, White accepted a teaching position at the University of Illinois and over the next thirty-seven years taught many students who would eventually become leaders in the field, including Stuart O. Dawson, Hideo Sasaki, Peter Walker, and Richard Haag.

White described teaching as "something between magic and philosophy."[6] Students recalled his active embrace of new ideas while he inculcated them with an intellectual framework that described landscape architecture as a high art, requiring a liberal arts education and a curious mind. Sasaki described White as "one of those unforgettable educators, witty and exuberant, for whom teaching remained a high-wire act, mysterious and unfathomable."[7] White engaged his students in the study of poetry, music, philosophy, and science, interests that were reflected in his commonplace books, a series of daybooks, that he wrote in for decades.[8] Another student described White as a teacher from whom you could expect the unexpected, from playing the violin—as it happens, not particularly well—to making a point by draping an unsuspecting student in cloth.[9] Later, as Haag developed his own approach to teaching, he, too, would become known for his ability to surprise students with his breadth of knowledge across the arts, humanities, and sciences—all part of his devotion to teaching as an art.

In addition to his teaching, a defining element of White's legacy was the Landscape Exchange Program, a series of national competitive design problems. Instigated in 1924 at the urging of members of the National Conference on Instruction in Landscape Architecture (now the Council of Educators in Landscape Architecture), White and Ohio State University professor W. R. Sears established one of the longest-running competitions in the nation in which students in any landscape architecture program were invited to participate. White served as secretary of the program from its inception until 1953. Haag would use the program in 1963 to generate ideas from students for the development of Gas Works Park in Seattle.

White's influence on Haag was evident in both the classroom and the office. Years later, Haag became known for his course "Theories and Perceptions of Landscape Architecture," which was based, to a large degree, on White's "Heinz 57" course, in which students explored diverse ways of thinking and perceiving landscape. White's intention, like Haag's, was to inspire students to think critically, see clearly, and only then to begin to design. White thought of teaching not as a matter of providing facts or filling students with knowledge but as a means of exploration and study. When he appeared in class wearing roller skates, it was to call attention to time, movement, and place and the interrelations among the three. His lectures and demonstrations were acts of storytelling. Haag, too, would teach by personal storytelling, although his approach was more suited to the radical nature of the 1960s and 1970s, as he would talk of civil disobedience and making love with the earth.

Haag and White explored the region together incessantly. Whenever the weather seemed promising, the two would head out in Haag's army surplus jeep for little known landscapes of the Midwest, perhaps discovering a pothole lake good for swimming or a particularly poetic scene. When White heard that Haag had received an army bonus payment at the end of the 1948 school year, he suggested a grand tour of New England. Such a trip east to visit canonic landscapes by Olmsted and others was normally a part of the curriculum, but Haag had not been able to afford the expense. By the end of his second year, however, with the extra money and the jeep, Haag set out for Olmsted's Central Park in New York City and the park system in Boston thereafter. He met White at his family home in Lowell, Massachusetts. From there, the two toured New England, including in their itinerary Massachusetts, New Hampshire, and Maine. As White described it in his commonplace book: "Dick Haag showed up in the jeep and I got about locally for three weeks, finding the Weston Nurseries, the Arnold Arboretum, Sargent's old garden where Dick photographed the historic old yews and *Cericidiphyllum* in the garden of Weld."[10] In addition to the Olmsted landscapes, they visited works by Fletcher Steele and others, with White sharing everything that he knew all the while. In his daybook, White wrote:

2.2 Richard Haag at Cape Cod, 1948. Photograph by Stanley White

> To Maine in the jeep early in August going through the Winnepesauksee landscape and up the toll road to the top of Mount Washington where it was very cold by sunset. The great valleys were tremendous and the rocks so archaic in effect we felt out of scale. . . . By nightfall we ran along the Androscoggin and picked a place to sleep in a clearing off the road. Spread . . . out canvasses and quilts. Hard ground and mosquitoes kept us awake. The better to enjoy one of the most beautiful nights of my life. Frogs kept going: a fox barked off in the hills. . . . Dick who suspected first a bear, then a man and found a big raccoon![11]

White and Haag traveled from Boston to Maine where they were hosted by E. B. White (Stanley's brother) and his wife, Katherine White, who wrote extensively about gardens and gardening. Haag was introduced to the architect and inventor Buckminster Fuller, who lived across the field from the White home. With the Whites, Haag was ensconced in a milieu that recognized landscape design as a significant cultural practice grounded in intellectual frames of reference that spanned the arts, humanities, and sciences. The trip offered important lesson in the legacies of American landscape architecture and the Olmsted office's hold on much of the Northeast.

Despite their many affinities, Haag and White could disagree, particularly on the modernism in landscape architecture. Whereas White believed that the modern approach was merely a passing trend too focused on form, Haag believed it offered a more radical shift, an opinion closer to that of their colleague Hideo Sasaki. While White espoused no particular style of design, his sympathies clearly lay with the Beaux Arts approach of earlier generations. White articulated his position in his description of landscape architecture as inherently contemporary and thus inherently modern at any point in time. Writing on teaching decades later, in a manuscript intended to be a primer on practice, he remarked, "Landscape Architecture as theory emerged (1850–1899) as a protest against what gardeners, engineers and architects were doing to the American scene. It is therefore an *essentially critical theory*. And since criticism always appears as a contemporary phenomenon the thought follows that landscape architecture is imbued with contemporaneousness."[12] Thus, White maintained that there was no new need to become modern per se and what was being proposed was merely form-based. Haag, in contrast, was more persuaded by Sasaki's argument for a modernist framework that might alter the paradigms of practice. Unlike White, Sasaki was excited by the modern movement and argued that landscape architects should seriously consider how ideas being discussed by contemporary artists and architects might inform landscape architecture.

Hideo Sasaki grew up on a farm in the San Joaquin Valley in California and discovered landscape architecture while studying city planning at the University of California, Berkeley. During World War II, he was briefly incarcerated at the Poston War Relocation Camp in Arizona. After the war ended, he completed his degree at the University of Illinois. Like Haag, he studied under White, Robinson, and Lohmann and graduated with a bachelor of fine arts in landscape architecture in 1946, his final year overlapping with Haag's first.

Sasaki subsequently studied at Harvard, receiving his master of landscape architecture degree in 1948. After graduation, he worked in the New York and Chicago offices of Skidmore, Owings & Merrill and taught at various times at both his alma maters, the University of Illinois and Harvard.[13] Of Sasaki's teaching at Illinois, White noted: "The students have responded to him with lively enthusiasm and turned out to evening meetings on the subject of Modernism every month."[14] In his daybook, White considered his own role as a member of the older generation: "The change is hard to realize and harder yet to adjust our minds to. We start to question whether we are adequate. We both embrace and resent the change. We tear down old customs, re-arrange the drafting rooms while Sasaki fills the screens with screwball emanations."[15] This wistful journal entry reveals that White, although he imagined himself to be a renegade, had soon

2.3 Hideo Sasaki with Haag's army surplus jeep on trip west, 1949.

realized that by then he had to a large extent become part of the past. Haag, based in Illinois during those years of transition, witnessed the changes and benefited from both White's and Sasaki's thoughts and approaches.

Haag met Sasaki in his first semester at Illinois, when Sasaki, who had not yet graduated, was teaching in the first-year design studio. Haag was drawn by Sasaki's call for professional collaborations to effectively address the challenges of housing and urban renewal. Sasaki's skill in grading and site planning impressed Haag. He soon came to realize that this knowledge supported Sasaki's ability to collaborate with architects. In addition to these skills, Sasaki believed that students needed to become knowledgeable in art and architecture, among other disciplines. His students visited buildings designed by Ludwig Mies van der Rohe at the Illinois Institute of Technology in Chicago, only hours from Urbana. Sasaki showed images of works by Frank Lloyd Wright, Jens Jensen, and Roberto Burle Marx. In school, Haag had the opportunity to work with Sasaki on a competition for the Junior Chamber of Commerce headquarters to be built in Kansas. They worked nights at a small office Sasaki had rented in the courthouse in Champaign with a local architect, J. Edward Luders, and won the competition, though the project was never built. Haag later claimed that he spent his life balancing his belief in Sasaki's forward thinking with White's respect for tradition and the past.[16]

After almost three years at the University of Illinois, Haag became restless, increasingly finding the program limited and with little sense of adventure. Sasaki encouraged him to complete his education at the University of California, Berkeley, where he might find others exploring new territories in the profession. With the decision made and his application accepted, in summer 1949, Sasaki and Haag headed west in Haag's army surplus jeep. They camped, hiked, and toured the landscape, sleeping under the stars and talking design the entire way.

2.4 Thomas Church's garden for the Martins in Aptos, California, 1948.

UNIVERSITY OF CALIFORNIA, BERKELEY

In the 1950s, the University of California, Berkeley, offered a landscape architecture program that differed dramatically from that at Illinois. Unlike the midwestern setting of Urbana-Champaign, Berkeley was part of a large metropolitan region that was then in the midst of massive growth. The mild climate of the San Francisco Bay area meant that gardens served as year-round outdoor rooms, often separated from the interior of the house by the thinnest of planes. In this context, local architects and landscape architects pushed the possibilities of form and materials. Small-scale gardens for people of modest means became an area of practice for the offices of Thomas Church, Garrett Eckbo, Robert Royston, Lawrence Halprin, and Theodore (Ted) Osmundson. As friends and as a loose-knit professional community, these firms shaped the emerging "California School" of landscape architecture.[17]

In 1948, just a year before Haag arrived, the San Francisco Museum of Art had hosted the *Exhibition of Landscape Design* with a display of works by the Association of Landscape Architects. The exhibit featured garden designs by regional firms, many of which were associated with the University of California, Berkeley, as alumni, visiting critics, and teachers.[18] Church's Martin garden, which was just being completed, and the new Donnell garden in Sonoma, along with projects by Eckbo, Royston, and Williams, were included, as they defined a new California modernism. In addition to design trends, the exhibit's catalog featured essays by William Wurster, then dean of architecture and planning at the Massachusetts Institute of Technology (MIT) but soon to return to Berkeley, and Christopher Tunnard, head of the new city planning department at Yale; they wrote, respectively, about the importance of collaboration among the design disciplines and the need to value open space. Royston would also examine the theme of collaboration in his 1949 article "Is There a Bay Area Style?" in the *Architectural Record*, writing that "what characterized Bay Area work was the spirit of collaboration, unity of purpose and free interchange of ideas, not only among members of each professional group but between individuals in all groups with a common objective—improvement of the working and living environment, private and public, for the majority of the people."[19] This thinking about style, collaboration, and the role of design would influence the young Haag, as it reflected his interest in exploring new ideas and his conviction that the objective of landscape architecture was to improve the lives of the people for whom it was designed.

The University of California, Berkeley, was an epicenter of studies in the emerging California school. Still located in the College of Agriculture, the landscape architecture faculty included Geraldine Knight Scott (1904–1989), Burton J. Litton (1918–2007), H. L. Vaughan (1905–1974), and Harry W. Shepherd (1890–1965). Like Sasaki, these teachers offered alternative perspectives on landscape design that considered modern design an art, with social and horticultural sciences shaping the practice.

By the time Haag arrived in September 1949, Vaughan had already led the curriculum away from nineteenth-century practices and the Beaux Arts method. In 1947, Vaughan had been appointed to chair the Department of Landscape Architecture, which would become part of the new College of Environmental Design in fall 1949. Royston was appointed an assistant professor and tasked to build the program and ensure that practitioners were on the teaching faculty, with others serving as visiting critics and lecturers. The school's curriculum also changed with the new leadership and faculty, who emphasized socially responsible design. As a result of this thinking, the school, like the Bay Area in general, was increasingly known for its tolerant bohemian character, a description that attracted Haag.

Haag attended the University of California only for the 1949–50 academic year, but he took full advantage of what it offered, in terms of both formal classwork and ambience. It was there that he discovered and read Christopher Tunnard's 1938 *Gardens in the Modern Landscape*, a book that would influence his work as it did many other young landscape architects at mid-century. That fall, the ASLA held its annual national meeting in Ojai, in Southern California, and Berkeley students, including Haag, attended the meeting, coming away impressed by the work presented and the discussions in which they had engaged. Haag noted years later that "it was everyone who was anyone—that was the profession then."[20]

Haag took Sasaki's advice and compiled a list of faculty and design instructors from whom he could gain the best education. He enrolled in Royston's studio and was impressed by his personality and teaching. Haag does not recall being as impressed by Royston's design approach, as he remained under the influence of White (who had seriously criticized modern California design). However, Haag thrived in the openness of the curriculum as he sought to shape a personal design philosophy. He was intrigued by Church's work and appreciated Church's sense of history and clear design approach. Haag took Burton Litton's introductory

2.5 Ludwig Mies van der Rohe visits the University of California, Berkeley, 1950.

course on California landscape provinces in which students toured landscapes and learned to use watercolors in plein air sketches. He took a plants course from Harry W. Shepherd and enrolled in a planting design studio with Geraldine Knight Scott. When Haag visited Scott at her home in the hills above San Francisco Bay, he took a photograph of her holding a cup of tea while looking out the window at the bay and commenting that the level of the tea was parallel to the surface of the bay. He would use this photograph later in his own course on theory and perception.

Haag also spent time with fellow students, including Don Carter, later a partner in Lawrence Halprin's office. On field trips, Haag and Carter visited projects designed by Church, Halprin, and Royston, all new or under construction, and so were experiencing the leading edge of emerging landscape modernism in California. They visited art projects and museums, adding fuel to Haag's developing philosophical musings. Haag was an eloquent speaker, and many of the students, Carter later recalled, would listen to him attentively.[21] The next fall, with an undergraduate degree in hand, Haag enrolled in the Harvard University Graduate School of Design (GSD) and pursued a master's degree in landscape architecture.

While at Berkeley, Haag had met Maryo Natsuhara (1922–2008), a second-generation Japanese American who had grown up in Auburn, Washington, and then enrolled as an art student at the University of California, Berkeley. During World War II, she was interned at Manzanar with her family, as were many of the Japanese living in central California. While at Manzanar, she began nursing studies, which she completed at the University of Kansas in 1944. She met Haag in the university infirmary when he was a Berkeley student. The two married after a brief courtship.[22]

2.6 Geraldine Knight Scott with a cup of tea in her garden, Berkeley, 1950.

HARVARD UNIVERSITY'S GRADUATE SCHOOL OF DESIGN

Haag's enrollment in Harvard's master of landscape architecture program in fall 1950 reflected his determination to obtain a graduate degree even though it was not required professionally, but it also indicated his continuing search for an individual approach to design. White and Sasaki had been his most influential teachers, and yet they advocated distinct perspectives on design and contemporary work. Haag was still shaping his ideas, and Harvard offered an opportunity to explore landscape theories and concepts in more depth.

The summer before starting graduate school, Haag worked with Sasaki designing a large country estate for the Gibson home in Greenville, Michigan.[23] Sasaki had recommended Frank Lloyd Wright as a possible architect, but Gibson selected a local firm to work with the landscape architects. Sasaki was responsible for siting the house and designing the landscape. Haag was not really excited about the project, but Sasaki persuaded him that it would be an easy job. One afternoon, Sasaki tried to get Haag more engaged by suggesting they treat the project like a game of "playing landscape architects." They would take the elements of the project, the topography, the house, and other required elements, and then imagine what different landscape architects might do. They developed an Eckbo scheme, a Church scheme, even a Sasaki scheme. The latter featured the chevron (V-shaped) walls Sasaki liked to use. In this way, the two began to build a repository of design ideas that they combined into a final proposal. Sasaki used this approach to explore a wide range of design responses, asking others how they might solve a design problem or approach a dilemma, and then, in trying to imitate the process, would learn to see in a new way, much as White advocated seeing a project through "new eyes."[24] Haag would use this game with students, suggesting they pretend to be someone else in the design process, to consider how someone else might design. Such an approach, he argued, opened the imagination and allowed the hand and mind to explore new design ideas with a great sense of freedom. He would also build on Sasaki's collaborative approach in his own practice, often bringing in artists, planners, technicians, and others to contribute to the design of a landscape.

Haag's decision to attend Harvard was a last-minute choice, and he had to ask Sasaki to arrange a late admission into the graduate program in landscape architecture. He started three weeks after the quarter had begun in fall 1950. The Graduate School of Design was at the end of nearly two decades of tumult in both architecture and landscape architecture.[25] The Harvard faculty, like Berkeley's, had moved away from the Beaux Arts traditions. Dean Joseph Hudnut had established the Graduate School of Design as a separate school of Harvard University in 1936; he subsequently hired Walter Gropius (1883–1969) to teach architecture and later appointed other Bauhaus architects who had come to the United States to teach. The discipline of city planning was emerging as a new program at Harvard. Collaboration across disciplines was increasingly encouraged if not often successful, as was the application of scientific methods and research findings to design and planning.[26] However, there were no new appointments of modernists in landscape architecture, and, to a large extent, the new city planning program pulled faculty away from landscape architecture. In the late 1930s, Garrett Eckbo, James Rose, and Dan Kiley led a rebellion, arguing that landscape architecture needed to radically embrace the modernist movement. The students laid out their manifesto for a new approach to design in a series of articles in the national journal *Architectural Record* in 1939 and 1940.[27]

In the following years, due to the war, the landscape architecture program at Harvard had dwindled to just a few students until 1944, when the university decided to admit women to the program. The following fall, students at the Cambridge School of Landscape Architecture for Women were invited to apply for admission to the Graduate School of Design landscape and architecture programs, and the Cambridge School was closed.[28] One of these women was Cornelia Hahn Oberlander, whom Haag would later meet at Daniel Urban Kiley's office. By 1948, the expanding program needed new instructors and designers, and Sasaki was among the faculty members hired.

The year that Haag arrived, Sasaki had begun what would become two decades as a GSD faculty member while simultaneously developing a multidisciplinary practice of architecture planning and design. In 1953, Sasaki was hired as a full-time faculty member, and in 1958, he was named chair of the department. His focus was on developing a program that emphasized "critical thinking—a process of understanding, then solving, a problem of planning and design."[29] This approach embraced the teaching of research, analysis, and synthesis in the design and planning process while seeking to balance environmental, social, and cultural concerns and purposes. In particular, Sasaki enriched the ecological and environmental areas of study within this framework, drawing on White's teachings as well as his own farming background.[30] The Graduate School of Design offered the perfect setting for Haag to round out his design education and would frame his approach to urban ecological design.

INTERNSHIP WITH DANIEL KILEY

During the summers of 1950 and 1951, Haag interned for Dan Kiley, who led a practice in Franconia Notch, New Hampshire. Kiley would later move to Shelburne and then to Charlotte, Vermont, where he would stay until his death. As was true each summer in the Kiley office, it was an informal arrangement of interns, most of whom lived at the Kiley home while they worked in the office. Cornelia Hahn (Oberlander), who was working in the office in summer 1951, recalled sleeping in the bedroom with Kiley's daughter, and Haag remembers a cot in the back room and family meals.[31] Each of the interns was assigned household tasks; Haag was responsible for stoking the potbelly stove in the morning to prepare the office for the work of the day.

Sasaki had introduced Haag to Kiley at the end of the school year in hopes that Haag might be able to intern in the office. Haag was interested, as he wanted to learn Kiley's minimalist approach to design. Kiley's main message," he recalled, "was simplify. Why is everything so complicated? Life is simple. Why shouldn't design be simple?" Haag had been inspired by Kiley's use of a single plant palette for a housing project in Philadelphia that was being rehabilitated for the Society of Friends by the architect Oscar Stonorov. Accented by the paulownia trees that are popular in Philadelphia, the design was straightforward and elegant, uncommon attributes for a housing project. Haag noted that he "learned a good thing there . . . Kiley did these backyards with one type of plant. . . . The whole thing was done in barberry." Haag was also frustrated occasionally including when one of his first projects was nothing more than an elaborate fountain for Dr. Benjamin Fein in Philadelphia that seemed to defy all the values Kiley espoused. "It was a plumber's nightmare. . . . I thought . . . all he [Kiley] needs is a spigot and a basin."[32] In the Kiley office, Haag worked on a new town project in Kitimat, British Columbia, built by the Aluminum Company of Canada, as well as helped to finish the Stonorov project.

In addition to their appreciation of simplicity and clarity, Kiley and Haag shared an interest in the history of design. Kiley, however, was drawn to the legacies of European design, while Haag would become more engaged with Japan and Japanese culture, differences that in large part reflected their East Coast and West Coast practices. Nevertheless, students later recalled that Haag frequently invoked Kiley's name when talking about remarkable design and brilliant designers.[33] Decades later, Kiley would write Haag a note congratulating him on the design for Jordan Park and noting, "You are the very *best* of my alumni. Excellent & fresh work."[34]

Haag's time as a student at Harvard's Graduate School of Design was not limited to the landscape architecture program but included hours exploring design work by the architecture students. In particular, Haag was intrigued by Walker Gropius's architecture studio. He would, with other landscape architecture students, offer to help develop designs for landscapes that were settings for the architectural projects being completed by graduate architecture students. Such collaborations were typical in the programs as younger students assisted senior students, offering drafting, rendering, or other services to complete a project. At Harvard, with both programs in the same building, students were able to interact and collaborate in ways that were not as easy in schools whose programs were located in different schools or colleges.

In Haag's final year at Harvard, he participated in a team design project for Block Island. Students from the design programs as well as those in business, law, and city planning were invited to submit initial concepts for a Block Island development that would identify the highest and best use of the land. Six concepts were selected by the jury of faculty. The teams that would develop the proposals were allotted four hundred dollars for supplies, and students joined the teams of their choice. Haag's idea for a camp and retreat for the United Garment Workers was among the final six, and five students, two from MIT, chose to join him. Over the next two weeks, they worked on the proposal for a bare-bones retreat and camp with communal eating and gathering spaces. They based their proposal on the idea of carrying capacity, arguing that the island dunes were fragile, as the area had been logged, and therefore any plan needed to lie lightly on the site. They used railroad boxcars and identified sites for tents. At the final presentation, Gropius commented that the plan led by Haag "could only have been imagined by a landscape architect," which Haag considered the highest compliment.[35] His team did not win the competition, but the project was evidence of his growing interest in the ideas of carrying capacity, ecological fragility, and, as he would term it, socialist ideas of community.

Faculty member Walter Chambers decided that Haag had not yet developed an appropriately complex final project or, more important, demonstrated his ability to prepare construction documents, a standard part of a professional design program. Haag had been expecting to graduate easily but agreed to prepare the documents for a proposed addition to a green town plan by Elbert Peets. He worked hard on the project and produced a substantial set of construction documents, all carefully drafted and hand-lettered using the Leroy system of mechanical lettering. Haag recollects that only then did he fully understand the importance of breaking a project into smaller parts and then putting the pieces back together. This became an approach to design that he would develop throughout his career. So although he grumbled at the time, he came to appreciate the project's learning moments.

Haag completed his MLA degree in April 1952 and moved back to Jeffersontown, to live on his family's farm, this time bringing his wife and two children. Moments before Haag left the Graduate School of Design, Lester Collins, the acting head of the Department of Landscape Architecture, had suggested that he apply for a Fulbright grant for travel to Japan. Haag had already developed an interest in Japanese aesthetics and culture. He didn't initially submit an application, but after a few months of working, he decided to give the program a try. To his delight, his application was accepted for fall 1953. In the interim, Haag worked briefly for the architectural firm of Sherlock, Smith, and Adams of Atlanta, commuting to Georgia from Kentucky. He then secured work with the firm of Miller and Whiry, whose offices were in Louisville, much closer to home. He was responsible for completing feasibility studies for shopping centers and subdivisions, most of which he determined would fail. This work was not of much interest to Haag, with the possible exception of a Burle Marx–inspired landscape for a hospital courtyard that may never have been built. In any case, he was ready for his sojourn in Japan, an adventure that would be one of the most powerful influences on his career as a designer and teacher.

"keep your eyes open!"

> Going to Japan changed my whole life . . . conservation and economy—Zen, borrowing and using parts of what was there . . . working with what you have.
>
> —Richard Haag

PREPARING FOR HIS FULBRIGHT FELLOWSHIP IN JAPAN, HAAG wrote to George Nakashima (1905–1990), the Japanese American furniture craftsman living in New Hope, Pennsylvania, to ask him for advice on how best to plan his studies. He had met Nakashima briefly a year earlier when he and Sasaki had embarked on a winding driving tour of architecture in the Northeast and visited Nakashima's studio. (During this epic drive, they also stopped at Philip Johnson's glass house, but Johnson came out in his bathrobe and shooed them away when the two young designers started photographing the house.) Haag recalled that Nakashima had responded to his inquiry by scrawling with a broad pen "Keep your eyes open!" and remarked, "It was the best advice he could have given me."[1]

In 1951, the Japanese and U.S. governments established the Fulbright-Hays Exchange Program. The program was launched in 1952, with the first applications accepted for 1953. Thirty-one Japanese arrived in the United States as Fulbright fellows. A smaller group of American Fulbright fellows arrived in Japan, the first after the war to travel to that country, including Norman Carver, graduate of the architecture program at Yale; Lester A. Collins, chair of the landscape architecture department at the Harvard Graduate School of Design from 1950 to 1953; and Richard Haag.

Haag's fellowship in Japan lasted from fall 1953 until summer 1955 and served as the foundation for his career as a landscape architect and as a teacher. Years later, he would awe students with lectures accompanied by hundreds of photographs of Japanese gardens and landscapes, inspiring many young designers to travel broadly and to study landscape architecture. He would draw on his images of Japan to describe a culture deeply engaged in aesthetics and intimately connected to nature.[2] His design practice was equally shaped by his two years in Japan.

Haag was not alone in his interest in Japan. With the cessation of hostilities after the war, curiosity about Japan and its arts and crafts was revived. In 1954, the Japanese Exhibition House opened at New York's Museum of Modern Art.[3] It drew more than 120,000 visitors before the building and garden were moved for permanent installation at Philadelphia's Fairmount Park. Intellectuals, artists, and designers traveled to Japan with increasing frequency in the following decades. However, as a member of the first group of Fulbright fellows to go to Japan after World War II, Haag was seeing the nation at a very particular moment and through a unique lens.

Haag prepared for his trip by perusing Loraine Kuck's *One Hundred Kyoto Gardens* (1935), a book that established an important source for Japanese gardens, especially with its discussion of the Zen garden as an identifiable style of garden design and experience.[4] Jiro Harada's *The Gardens of Japan* (1928), a companion volume to Percy Cane's *Modern Gar-*

dens, British and Foreign (1926),[5] was one of the first books to have significance in modern landscape design practice in the West and remained influential through the mid-century. Haag used Harada's book in Japan and in 1958 wrote a review of the second edition of the book (1954), noting the quality of the two hundred photographs of 116 gardens.[6] For Haag, Harada had summarized the Japanese garden in both image and text.[7] Relevant books were available at the University of Illinois as well as in the Harvard library, and Haag had sampled them, although he maintained that he was not particularly interested in traditional architecture or garden designs, a viewpoint he would come to regret.

FULBRIGHT FELLOWSHIP IN JAPAN

It is hard to know when Haag developed an interest in Japan. Perhaps it was when he first tasted sashimi in Chicago with Jobo Nakamura, a journalist, whom he had met in Chicago in 1949 through Sasaki.[8] Sasaki had befriended Nakamura in the Manzanar internment camp during the war, and the two remained in contact even after Nakamura returned to Japan. Haag had read a few books but does not recall an aha moment. However it happened, by the time he had completed his Harvard degree, he was open to the suggestion from his adviser, department chair Lester Collins, to apply for a Fulbright grant. Haag's wife was Japanese American, and she very much wanted to visit the country, which she had never seen, and introduce their children to her family's cultural heritage. The pieces came together, and Haag applied for the 1953–54 academic year.

Haag proposed to study the role of urban planning in shaping the future of cities and was interested in evaluating the carrying capacity of land in the urban context. Carrying capacity, Haag explained, would be determined by the density of the urban development, taking into consideration the need to provide food, water, and infrastructure. He believed that Japan had developed urban land use practices in an ideal manner over more than a thousand years and thus warranted intense study as a model for urban development.[9] He proposed narrowing his studies to neighborhoods of single-family homes, thereby hoping to learn how Japan met the housing needs of its dense urban populations without the high-rises Western nations relied on, reflecting his ideas for his Block Island student project. He agreed to study under the auspices of the University of Kyoto's College of Agriculture and the faculty of landscape architecture in the School of Forestry, chaired by Professor Eitaro Sekiguchi (1896–1981).[10] Haag emphatically stated that he was not going to consider, or even visit, any traditional gardens, as they had already been sufficiently studied.

And so in September 1953, Haag, with his wife, Maryo Natsuhara, their two children, and seventeen other Fulbright scholars, sailed to Japan on the passenger ship *Hikawa Maru*. Will Alex, a curator at the Museum of Modern Art, was traveling to Japan in preparation for the museum's exhibit of a Japanese teahouse. During the trip, Haag met Norman F. Carver, Jr., and Joan, his wife, and reconnected with Lester Collins, who was traveling with the landscape architect and GSD faculty member John Ormsbee Simonds. Simonds had traveled in Japan and Asia in 1939 and was in the midst of writing his textbook *Landscape Architecture: The Shaping of Man's Natural Environment* (1961).[11] Carver, who had been stationed in Kyoto from 1946 to 1948, was anxious to return to study Japanese architecture. He and Joan, both 1953 graduates of Yale University's architecture program, had set off to Japan on a Fulbright honeymoon, where they would work on what would become the first of seven books of architectural photographs from around the world.[12]

The University of Kyoto provided housing for the Haag and Carver families in apartments located in the working-class district, offering unanticipated opportunities, unusual for foreigners in 1953, for immersion in the local culture.[13] The immersion was immediate. No sooner had the Haags moved in than a typhoon hit and the electricity went out. Haag ventured out in the rain and wind and eventually found an older woman from whom he purchased matches and candles. On his way back to the apartment, he heard footsteps behind him, and when he turned, he found the woman hurrying to catch up to him in the pouring rain as he had overpaid by a few coins. It struck him at that moment that he was in a very different culture and would have to become familiar with the local culture if he wanted to learn anything about carrying capacity. Maryo helped make the transition to the new culture, although she spoke a more formal dialect of Japanese than was spoken at the time, something that was not uncommon among second-generation Japanese Americans. The Haag children attended a Japanese school, and Haag initially learned Japanese by listening to his son, who was attending kindergarten.[14]

Although the university had "Westernized" the apartments, the families lived much like the Japanese families around them, with tatami floors for sitting, sleeping, and eating. The Haags adopted Japanese cuisine quickly and taught their children the habits and traditions of their neighbors, while the Carvers recalled being more circumspect about the food and local rituals.[15] Haag also adopted Japanese dress, donning the attire of farmers and craftsmen. Jobo Nakamura gave this description on meeting up with the six-foot-tall Haag in Japan:

> With a bag over his shoulder he took to the roads leading from one village to another. Most of the time, he bedded in some old farmhouses or inns and lived off the land. He would get off a train and in some remote places if he saw an interesting house or village, he would get off and explore the area. He was on his way back from one of his trips up in the Tohoku district when he dropped in to look me up at the Tokyo billet. Rich came clonking in wearing a pair of wooden geta. The desk clerk gaped when he saw him. His shirt was made out of the kasuri material usually worn by farmwomen. In a number of places we took bath together in the community bath houses; back in Chicago we would have never dreamt that we would be tubing [*sic*] ourselves in a furoya in Nagoya.[16]

With the combination of his clothing, stature, and genuine interest, Haag made friends wherever he went. While he never learned to speak Japanese fluently, he learned enough to converse with farmers, gardeners, scholars, and anyone else who caught his attention.

After getting settled in Kyoto, Haag sought out Professor Sekiguchi in the landscape architecture program, and the professor arranged access to university resources for Haag. He was not required to enroll in any courses and soon realized that he was less interested in formal education than in a ground-up investigation focused on exploring the rural and urban landscapes. Haag intended to learn about Japanese culture and develop his research by immersing himself in every way possible. He never was one for the formalities of structure.

To facilitate their intended explorations, Carver purchased an old Dodge automobile, and the two, sometimes with their families, took off to explore. Initially they avoided the temples and formal gardens, believing these had already been well studied and there was nothing left to learn about them. However, on a chance visit to Ryōan-ji, a well-recognized garden in the dry landscape style, their stance was completely undone. Rather than having nothing to learn, they realized that they knew nothing of what these gardens offered. Years later, in lecturing to students, Haag would chide himself for being so ignorant of what the Japanese gardens had to offer.[17] After that first visit to Ryōan-ji, Haag and Carver interspersed famous gardens with their meandering walks through farmland, visits to small villages, and explorations of *minka* (literally, "houses of the people"), the traditional Japanese farmhouses.

Photography was an essential tool for exploration and discovery. Haag had intended to bring an Argus C-3 camera with him to Japan, but it froze just as he was leaving Seattle. Thus, when he arrived in Yokohama, his first purchase was a Nikon camera, and soon thereafter, he bought a Rolliflex as well as a set of Japan Travel Bureau publications on the country and its culture. He would use the Rolliflex for his black-and-white photographs and the Nikon for his color slides. Haag and Carver competed informally for catching the perfect image, whether it was the shadows on a set of steps or

3.1 Courtyard in a Japanese home, Kyoto, 1954.

the moss at Saihō-ji, a garden in Kyoto famous for its mosses. In an interview in 2013, Carver recalled that Haag "was able to get some things on film that I couldn't. I remembered some of his photographs of the moss garden at Saihō-ji and trying to get some of the same feeling he had gotten."[18] The two men were fascinated with the materials and implements used both every day and for special events. The kimonos, the fishing nets, the tatami mats, the river stones, the farm tools, and the costumes and sets created for special festivals and celebrations all intrigued them. On their return, their photographs would contribute to a larger re-casting of traditional Japanese design. Carver's book *Form & Space*, published in 1955, features the photographs of Japanese architecture and landscape he had taken during his Fulbright fellowship. The book also includes Carver's ideas about how Japanese architecture developed that Haag thought were "cockamamie," as he would later recall.[19] As a teacher years later, Haag would present an annual lecture on Japanese landscape, architec-

3.2 Shadows on the wall of a Japanese home, Kyoto, 1954.

ture, and aesthetics lasting three or four hours for his theory course, during which he showed more than 320 slides illustrating his theories of the development of Japanese crafts, arts, and architecture.

While Haag and Carver were discovering Japan, they were also visited by colleagues and friends. Walter Gropius visited during summer 1954. The seventy-one-year-old former director of the Bauhaus, whom both knew from Harvard, had been intrigued by Japanese art and architecture for a long time. When Gropius arrived for his three-month tour, he set out to experience the full range of Japanese architecture and urban development. Learning that Haag was living in Kyoto, Gropius sought him out. While Haag was willing to adopt the domestic traditions of the Japanese, including sitting on the floor, Gropius was less enthusiastic. Haag recalled that Gropius initially declined a dinner invitation. Only after being assured that he would be offered a Western chair and not have to sit on the floor did Gropius accept the invitation.

3.3 Women in kimonos, Kyoto, 1954.

3.4 Shoji Hamada (1894–1978), master potter, laying out his pottery, Kyoto, 1955.

Haag had to find chairs and a table and then persuade the owner of the small shop to sell them to him with a guarantee that he would buy them back—at almost full cost—two days later. Renting or leasing furniture was not a familiar practice in Japan at the time.

A tour of the city's craft markets followed the dinner. Haag and Gropius wandered through the pottery neighborhood of Kiyomizu, marveling at the array of ceramics on display. Haag recalled a visit to a fabric shop where they found a remarkable collection of kimonos made from fabric with polka dot patterns, "'Three thousand different kinds!' Gropius exclaimed. 'This is what I've been preaching, uniformity and diversity. Why didn't I discover Japan 40 years ago!"[20] Japanese culture confirmed Gropius's interest in "endless variety within a fundamental unity."[21] Back in the United States, Gropius wrote about the significance of the trip to Japan and his interest in its traditional arts as models for contemporary architecture in the West: "You cannot imagine what it meant to me to come suddenly face to face with these houses, with a culture still alive, which in the past had already found the answer to many of our modern requirements of simplicity, of outdoor-indoor relations, of modular coordination, and at the same time, variety of expression, resulting in a common form language uniting all individual efforts."[22]

Gropius's response to Japan echoed many of Haag's emerging concepts and ideas. Both men appreciated the use of repeated patterns, the subtle variations of colors, the focus on details and craft. Haag collected the pottery by local craftsman, often walking from potter to potter, learning from the villagers about individual production. Through these visits, he befriended the highly respected craftsmen Kanjirō Kawai (1890–1966), a Japanese potter, artist, and founder of the Kawai Factory; Bernard Leach (1887–1979), a British potter who practiced and taught in Tokyo from 1909 to 1920 and traveled there regularly until 1972; and Shoji Hamada (1894–1978), a leader of Japanese potters and a Living National Treasure. These men were part of a larger movement to reas-

3.5 Rice paddies, near Nara, 1954.

sess traditional crafts while blending modern methods of manufacture with older designs. In their work, Haag found a sympathetic approach to art and beauty in everyday life. He also became friends with the philosopher Sōetsu Yanagi, who founded the Japanese Folk Crafts Museum (Nihon Mingeikan) in Kanazawa in 1936. The two shared an appreciation for the beauty in everyday and functional objects created by local craftsmen. In these encounters, Haag sought an "authentic Japan," as he traveled to the farms, temples, and rice terraces, although it was always through the lens of a foreigner. He was interested not in negating the prevalence of modernism but in understanding how the arts, crafts, and aesthetics of the Japanese could be preserved in and shape the future.[23]

Cultural Landscapes and Vernacular Architecture

Of the agricultural landscapes—what we today call "cultural landscapes"—Haag was most interested in the productive rice terraces. He recognized the economical use of land for rice production in the terracing and irrigation methods as well as the ethic that governed the development of rural landscapes. He believed this agricultural production supported a culture that used land efficiently and sustainably, not unlike his father's values and practices. The emphasis on traditional farming methods paralleled conditions on his father's Kentucky farm and may well have allowed him to see more deeply, as the underlying values were at least somewhat familiar. At the same time, some elements, such as the presence of Shinto shrines, were unfamiliar. His experience both confirmed and challenged his ideas about Japan and about landscape and design.

In an effort to further explore the rice culture, Haag donned a farmer's hat and clothes and set off to document the rice fields and farmers. Along the way, he observed laborers in the countryside, from craftsmen to gardeners. He took note of the agricultural practices in small home gardens and larger farms. He witnessed gardeners and farmers discussing what they were planting and noted the materials they used. He watched workers weaving straw and planting or harvesting the rice. His course lectures would later include narratives from these explorations, which he used to demonstrate a particular design principal, aesthetic practice, or understanding of cultural traditions.

It was in the rice paddies that Haag began to reconsider the links between historic gardens such as Ryōan-ji and Saihō-ji and agricultural traditions. Along country roads, he and Carver found temples and Shinto shrines set in rice paddies, suggesting a local relationship between agriculture and the cosmos or spiritual world. Haag sought to extract principles of design from these cultural landscapes. It was in these investigations that he "began to get to look at the non-striving kind of methods that were used there. I started to put some of these theories together about the importance of rice culture on all of the . . . art forms, as something derived from that act."[24]

Haag identified an aesthetic and craft embedded in vernacular practice that he believed was a critical characteristic of Japanese culture. In reviewing Harada's book *Japanese Gardens*, Haag wrote that "'tradition' is not credited with a fair share of the responsibility for shaping Japan's gardens. By tradition, I refer to agrarianism—the basic man-to-earth relationship as best exemplified by rice culture. Was the designer of the famous rock and sand composition, Ryōan-ji, inspired by divine revelation or was he merely an astute observer of the pattern made by a paddy farmer plowing around stones?"[25]

Haag argued further that design was an essential link between traditional garden practices, agricultural practices, and natural landscapes, suggesting that design practice could articulate a reciprocal relationship between the two cultural inscriptions and their setting. From this understanding of the potential of relationships, Haag would develop his concept of fusion. As he noted further in his review: "All of the gardens can be explained by being an astute student of natural and agricultural process—all these things are related—fusion, relativity—this is a borrowed landscape—it is man made in the foreground but it develops into layers and layers of mountains, . . . even here I can see the derivation of pattern and form. Japan's coastline of shore rocks and trees—examples of that in nature and controlled—relationship between painting and stonework."[26]

Haag's investigations of agricultural landscapes would also significantly inform his ideas about an edible landscape, or "nutrimental design" as he called it. He believed that garden design should draw on the breadth of edible plants, simply merging design and productivity.[27] Throughout his career, Haag would keep a home garden that featured a variety of Japanese vegetables alongside a range of berries and fruits. His explorations of Japanese farming and gardens placed what was familiar to him in unfamiliar contexts, allowing him, as Stanley White had recommended in his lecture "New Eyes for Old."

In addition to landscapes, Haag explored vernacular architecture. *Minka* were the dwellings of farmers, merchants, and craftsmen. They were built with traditional carpentry techniques that reflected the transference of skills and craft from generation to generation. Adapted to their landscapes, they offered examples of how Japanese traditions were grounded in place.[28]

Haag carefully observed the rituals around the building of a *minka*, an experience he and Carver specifically sought out. They sketched and photographed the wooden structures, made of bamboo and clay with a roof of thatch and straw. Haag noted the three kinds of floors, one of earth, one of wood, and one covered with tatami. He observed the living styles and traditions, adopting many for his own family. The tatami impressed him, and he collected articles on its manufacture and use. In the notes that would become resources for his lectures on Japan, Haag wrote that the soft feel underfoot of the tatami, its resilience, the small, repeatable size and scale all contributed to the warmth and comfort of the Japanese home. He remarked, "Who does not like to remove shoes at home?" He thought the tatami offered the dwelling an efficiency, as one could "sit, read, talk, eat, lie down, etc. Without shifting location or even getting up."

3.6 *Sinkentiku*, February 1955, with Haag's photograph of a farmhouse and rice field on the cover.

Haag appreciated how it brought the eye level down, offering "a strange visual connection with the exterior." The *minka* and its details reflected the persistence of traditional modes of living, which intrigued Haag. Carver would recall many of the same experiences and responses.[29]

When Haag took Gropius to see the Junjokan (Pure View Hall) at the Sanpo-in of Daigo-ji, the architect exclaimed that Mies van der Rohe must have learned from this architecture.[30] Haag admired how the architecture "floated over the landscape," and Gropius was equally excited by the regular geometry. Modern Japanese architects had much to learn from these traditional houses and their agricultural settings, both men argued.

Enamored of the vernacular landscapes, Haag submitted the essay "Memo to Japanese Designers" to the Japanese journal *Sinkentiku* (later published in English as *Japan Architect*),[31] which published it with his photograph of a farmhouse and rice field on the cover. Haag wrote: "Throughout Japan, the domestic architecture exhibits many forgotten but important lessons. . . . There are two major forces which shape architecture. These are the cultural and the environmental determinants or more simple, the people and the land. Until recent times in Japan, these were so interwoven and so reciprocally responsive that only a great architecture could have evolved. Under the impact of industrialization this delicate balance has been upset."[32]

The essay challenged contemporary Japanese architects to reassess their historic narratives and suggested what might be learned from traditional crafts and building practices. In particular, Haag proposed that the multiple uses of space, the minimal use of furniture, and the extensive use of local materials were attributes that should shape modern architecture. Years later, Japanese architects and historians would argue in favor of saving Japan's vernacular architecture, particularly its farmhouses.[33] This movement found some of its earliest support in the observations and writings of international visitors such as Haag.

Gardens and Garden Design

Haag appreciated Japanese gardens for more than their long history and traditions. He recognized that the design and construction addressed the local climate (wind, sun, rain, and so forth) and that the arrangement of spaces integrated indoor and outdoor spaces. He was drawn to the choreography of movement through the garden. There was the sculptural use of stones or gravel to form objects, such as the cone of sand at the Ginkaku-ji. Haag noted the subtle use of raked gravel at Ryōan-ji that provided a relatively flat yet undulating setting for the fifteen moss-covered stones. At Shugaku-in Rikyū, he recognized how the gardens were integrated with the agricultural landscape, much of which was productive rice fields.

The entrance sequence of many Japanese gardens also caught Haag's attention. At Katsura Rikyū, also in Kyoto, the path moved along a bamboo-edged roadway and then through a series of gates that set the tone for the garden experience. In other gardens, he perceived the play of different scales of the spaces through which one moved. At Entsu-ji, which Haag visited repeatedly, the experience was more intimate, as it was a far smaller garden that seemed designed for the individual. Seated on the veranda, he experienced the framed view of the distant Mount Hiei, the borrowed landscape. In each of these gardens, Haag recalled exploring the relationships between the garden spaces and the surrounding landscapes. This relationship between the architectural and the landscape, between the cultivated and the indigenous, can be found in many of Haag's designs, including the Bloedel Reserve and the Battelle Research Center.

Of the Japanese gardens he visited, Haag most admired three sites: the Grand Shrines at Ise, Ryōan-ji, and Saihō-ji. These sites featured the quintessential gardens for Haag, both in their design and in their stewardship. In those and in the gardens at Katsura Rikyū, Nijō-jō, and Sanbō-in, he would sit for long hours trying to understand what he saw. Haag later spoke of his fascination with the minimalism of Sanbō-in, particularly the moss landscape, while noting that Gropius, who came with him on one visit, was more taken by the forms of the stones and their placement. Haag looked at, walked through, sat in, and thought about the gardens, contemplating the essence of each place. He photographed and drew. He talked with gardeners and monks whenever he could.

Haag recalled the lessons learned from one conversation about gardens. He asked a member of the University of Kyoto faculty to list the traditional garden plants. In this way, he hoped to learn the Japanese names of some common plants. The faculty member obliged and provided a list of twenty-three plants. Haag asked if these were the most common and to his surprise was told that these were the plants, not some of the plants. Haag realized that the gardens were composed of a small palette of plants and yet were experienced as diverse and distinct. The gardens represented endless variety within a fundamental unity, similar to modern design as Gropius had described it. Haag had already discovered this principle in Japanese ceramics when he visited the shops of small craftsmen and realized that while each focused on a particular type of pottery, often a small color range, and even a nearly constant scale, the manifestations of creativity possible with these limited resources seemed endless.

Haag also learned about the role of time and the process of aging. While a limited palette of plants might seem to produce a static design, changes in season, and even hourly changes in sunlight and shade, created a dynamism in the gardens. Aging shaped the aesthetic, whether it was a piece of cracked pottery, worn tatami, or a tree that grew into its maturity. The moss at Saihō-ji might appear constant, but it was always changing. Haag visited the garden in both winter and summer, seeking to understand the essence and full potential of the place. As he did, he observed and often photographed how the seasons, weather, and times of day altered the perception of wetness and dryness, of shade and light, of hard and soft.

The mythical and spiritual narratives of the gardens were also significant to Haag. He believed that the Ise Shrine, one of his favorite landscapes, revealed core values of Japanese

3.7 Saihō-ji, near Kyoto, spring 1954.

Shintoism and its connections to agricultural practices and nature. He was particularly interested in Pure Land (Jōdo) and Zen Buddhism, not in the practice of religion per se but in understanding the philosophies and associated aesthetics. He would draw on his understanding of Japanese ways of thinking to develop his concept of "non-striving"—the idea of being open to design inspiration and working with a place at multiple levels, from the vernacular to the metaphysical. In essence, non-striving is the foundation of Buddhism—to seek beauty where it is.

For the Ise Shrine complex, the most sacred of Japanese sites, Haag very much wanted to know its spatial structure as well as its construction details. He wanted to fully comprehend the site, not merely walk around its edges, yet, as a sacred precinct, it was surrounded by high fences, and little of the shrine buildings was visible to the visitor, who was not allowed to enter the inner sanctum. Despite the rules, Haag climbed a tree and took photographs of the central compound, the sacred space of the shrine. Unfortunately, while he was trying to position himself in the tree, he dropped a film canister, and when the guards converged on the spot, Haag had to remain still so that he would not be noticed. He was there past dark, and although this had not been part of his plan, he took the opportunity to imagine what it might be like on the inside. A year or so later, he loaned his best image of the inner shrine to friend and writer Bunji Kobayashi. The image was used as the frontispiece for Kobayashi's book *Japanese Architecture*.[34] Inside the book was Haag's photograph of the Treasure House, an unusual view capturing the new buildings with the old temples in the background (see fig. 3.17). Gropius later published the image in *Architecttura Cantiere*.[35] As such intimate images of this sacred site had never before appeared in print, Haag recalled that publication was not received well by Japanese authorities, and he speculated that it may have been a reason for the increased security at the site. He claims it was out of curiosity as well as deep respect that he sought to more fully understand what he saw. He would assert similar prerogatives when visiting Ryōan-ji,

3.8 Ryōan-ji, Kyoto, winter 1955. The vantage point is from the edge of the garden, where only the monks are allowed.

when he ventured up the edge of the garden, where one is not supposed to walk, so that he could take photographs of the rocks from "unseen" perspectives (see fig, 3.8)

Haag visited Saihō-ji, one of his "most esteemed landscapes,"[36] at least eight times over his two-year stay. He was enthralled by the physical and spiritual experience of active meditation enacted by strolling through the garden during a variety of seasons and times of day. The present-day garden was created in the fourteenth century, and an earlier garden likely predated it by three centuries. While it was initially composed of water, sand, and rock in concert with a limited plant palette of maple, pine, and bamboo, the garden flooded twice during the Edo period, and mosses began to cover it. In the twentieth century, it became known as the moss garden, and that is the garden that Haag admired.[37]

"Bathed in shadow or dappled light, sheathed in moss, the full limits of its four and half acres are explored along two axes: experiential and religious"[38] is how the author Marc Treib describes Saihō-ji. Haag recalled moving through the garden, his eyes focused on the intimate scale of the mosses, bending over to touch the miniature forests and admire the subtle forms of the earth. At the same time, the pond and three islands made up a middle-scale topography that could be easily traversed on foot, though one could never see all of it in its totality (see figs. 3.7, 3.22). The passage of time was evident in the slow growth of the mosses that had taken centuries to cover the ground as well as in the seasonal changes. For Haag, Saihō-ji exemplified relationships between nature, culture, place, and time. When he returned to practice, he used the photographs of these gardens to both shape and reveal his design philosophy. These influences can be identified in Haag's designs for the Broz (1957–58) and Zollinger (1957–60) gardens, the Case study house (1957), and, most clearly, his moss garden at the Bloedel Reserve (1980s).

Ryōan-ji also ranked high in Haag's pantheon, and he visited and photographed this garden numerous times. Most memorable to him was its initial impact, created not by its limited dimensions but by its intensity of experience: "You walk or climb up this hill," he explained, "go into the forecourt, and then you are led through and you look down on your right—the garden is about as a large as this classroom. Your breath is taken away."[39] Haag became familiar with the monks caring for the garden and was allowed to count the stones as well as photograph it from different points by moving around its edges. Photographed in a variety of lights and captured from oblique angles, including from the side and back, the garden served as a conduit to explore Japanese aesthetics. Haag's Ryōan-ji photographs remained at the core of his teaching and practice. When Gropius visited, Haag brought him to this garden where the two men sat in silence for a long while.[40]

There were also both recent and more contemporary gardens that Haag could visit. Mirei Shigemori (1896–1975), whose work centered on gardens in and around Kyoto, had been responsible for both reinterpreting older gardens and creating more modern gardens of contemplation. Shigemori's garden designs and writings shaped Japanese garden design by providing an alternative vocabulary that still fit within a traditional language. Tōfuku-ji in Kyoto, designed in 1939 by Shigemori, drew on traditional gardens but was expressed in a modernist language. Haag visited Tōfuku-ji numerous times, and the garden may well have been an inspiration for his design of the Garden of the Planes at the Bloedel Reserve.

While Haag professed less interest in the contemporary discourses of Japanese architects and artists, he did visit the work of Isamu Noguchi (1904–1988), the Japanese American sculptor whose designs, both built and proposed, offered ideas about how one might design a garden that draws on both modern and traditional materials and reflects both past and future.[41] Noguchi's landforms served for many as a synthesis of Japanese and Western approaches. Haag visited Noguchi's garden for the Reader's Digest building in Tokyo (designed by the architect Antonin Raymond in 1950). Noguchi's sculpted earth resembles the biomorphic forms that had become increasingly characteristic of Mid-Century Modernism in the West, particularly California.[42] Haag initially criticized the garden for its utilitarian water channels, which seemed to him out of place, too technological and too modern. At the time, he appreciated more traditional aesthetics, although he would later come to appreciate the channels' clarity of form.[43] His enduring interests in landforms and mounds suggests that he, too, was intrigued by the possibilities of earth sculpting. He would translate and expand such ideas in his gardens for the Wong House in Palo Alto, California; the Zollinger Garden in Oakland, California; Jordan Park in Everett, Washington; and the Bloedel Reserve on Bainbridge Island, Washington.

While "influence" can be a slippery term, it is clear that Haag's experience in Japan framed his later practice and teaching, his design process, and his design forms. He would repeat to his students the lessons he had learned, informing them, for example, that the Japanese designer "will bring you very close to the water, so you will stop and then see your reflection in the water to have a relationship with the water and the garden."[44] Or he would remind students that water provides a plane of reference and then show an image of a reflective surface in a garden such as Saihō-ji. Haag contrasted still water with other forms, such as a waterfall, in which the water's movement rather than its reflective quality shapes the experience, or the rippling pattern inscribed into the sand garden of Ryōan-ji. He reminded students of his Zen teaching: to develop an infallible technique, then wait for inspiration. And he shared the teaching of his friend Sōetsu Yanagi: "Repetition is the mother of skill."[45] Haag maintained that if "you are really going to get into one of these gardens, you stand there or sit there, and finally, when you go through the seven steps of Buddhist meditation, you will hear the surf in your ears."[46] Students were enthralled by these descriptions.

Haag's investigation of Japanese aesthetics had an even larger influence on what would become his design philosophy. The clearest application of Japanese aesthetics was using what he called a "non-striving approach" as a framework for the design process, an approach that he likened to Zen practice. The non-striving process was a way of articulating a search for the essence of a place, a spiritual as well as a scientific reading of a site. He would tell students that the design process should begin by "know[ing] the site—sleep on it, muse with the genius loci."[47] This statement framed his belief on how one should proceed with a design, by paying attention to what might be recognized as the seven steps of Buddhism or Zen: mindfulness, calming down, insight, trance, objectless inwardness, wisdom, and emptiness or nirvana.

Haag was, like his peers, interested in modernism, and specifically in modern concepts of space. His photographs of Japan, its gardens, architecture, and landscapes, coupled with his descriptions reflect his ideas of space and time.[48] Japanese gardens and architecture suggested a particular characteristic of space for Haag—that of movement and experience through sequential space. After his return to the United States in 1956, Haag wrote "Space," an article in which he drew from his Japanese experience to describe an increasing interest in designing space.[49] "Spaces are understood by the sequential development of the simultaneous image, i.e. multisensory perception involving the ability to see, to feel (kinetically), to hear, to smell, to touch, and to taste."[50] Spatial experience, for Haag, was grounded in sequential movement, reflecting his experience of Japanese gardens and landscapes as well as their urban contexts.

In a similar manner, Haag considered how the Japanese described negative and positive spaces—or voids—and "filled-in" spaces, what he would consider female and male spaces. In describing them, he wrote

> Ryōan-ji, the famous stone and sand garden in Japan impels a high order of psychical participation and penetration into its infinite timelessness. The spatial mechanics develop a sequential experience ranging from the geometric precision of the man-measured rectangle through the transient tensions of the space-field implied by the stone groupings and to the ultra-dimensional void beyond. The implication that the void or negative space is as equally important as the "filled-in" or positive space is a profound contribution.[51]

In this rather complex view, Haag linked his observations of Japanese gardens and arts to his design practice.

CONCLUDING OBSERVATIONS

In his request for a second year in Japan, which he submitted in the spring of 1954, Haag reported that he had already completed "a survey study of National Planning Problems and Policies as formulated by the central government and implemented by the Ministry of Construction."[52] He had also made, he claimed, a generalized study of the hydrography, topography, and climate of Japan and their resulting influences on the people. He noted that the national "balance sheets" had been examined with particular attention given to population and the production and consumption of foodstuffs, fibers, and natural resources. The notes in his files give little indication of his formal research. Instead, it is clear that his real interests lay in Japanese landscape: "I have observed the reciprocal relationships of human response to environment and the conclusion is being drawn that *culture* in a very real sense, also sets rigid limitation on the area any ethnic group can inhabit. The land sets up opportunities or obstacles for human settlement and whatever the mode of occupance, it must maintain a biotic balance with the land, if it is to endure."[53] Those observations derived from walks through the countryside, explorations of cultural and vernacular landscape and architecture, and a reconsideration of the role of traditional gardens in the larger culture.

Based on his initial work, Haag argued that renewing the fellowship would allow him time to develop "a more intimate understanding of and fuller sympathy for the Japanese culture and its occupance features, i.e. agricultural patterns, settlement forms (urban and rural) and even dwelling types." He was articulating what would become principles for his design praxis, as he believed that design must address "more humane population controls." "Positive population controls," he continued, "may result from changing the attitudes, objectives and technical abilities of man in respect to his *total* environment and may help to negate our past reliance on Malthusian controls."[54]

The extension was granted, and Haag, along with Carver, remained in Japan for an additional year. At the end of 1955, following the completion of his fellowship, Haag found employment in the city-planning firm of John Lord King in Tokyo (on Carver's recommendation). He continued to explore and still recalls the night Carver arranged for a dinner with the architect Kenzō Tange. When the electricity went out, and with the streets dark, Tange insisted that Haag and Carver remain until morning. They drank the night away, deep in the discourse of design, inspired by the spaces of Tange's house.

Immersions in Japanese culture form significant points of influence on Haag's work as a landscape architect and teacher. For his clients and students, these influences were revealed as shared wisdom, an approach to a particularly vexing question, or encouragement to be patient. Remembering the poetry, Haag wrote in his class notes:

Sitting quietly, doing nothing
Spring Comes
and the Grass grows by itself

Haag sent boxes of slides to his mentor and friend Stanley White, who was delighted to use the materials in his courses at the University of Illinois. On receiving the last shipment of photographs, White wrote Haag, "I have been using your slides for teaching . . . the subjects are largely the great pieces from the Kyoto area and are a very complete representation of the high period of very old history. Thanks and thanks again."[55] The two teachers and explorers were again sharing their experiences of land and landscapes.

The following photographs, with captions from his lectures, have been culled from those Haag used for teaching for fifty years. They describe his experience of Japan during his stay there in 1953–55, only a decade after the end of World War II. This is the Japan that he shared with his students.

3.9 "The angle of repose pervades the countryside / harmony from the mundane to the sacred."

3.10 "The cultivation of rice is the mother of Japanese Culture. It informs the land, architecture, drama, dance, visual arts, customs, and manners."

3.11 "Rice paddies are the national gardens of Japan, a landscape of extraordinary beauty and bounty."

3.13 "Master carpenter consults specifications to prepare structural skeleton. This remarkable system evolved through the centuries for building a farm house."

3.14 "The greatest lesson that we can learn from domestic architecture is derived from the fact it faithfully echoes the changing attitudes, aspirations and abilities of the people in respect to their total environment."

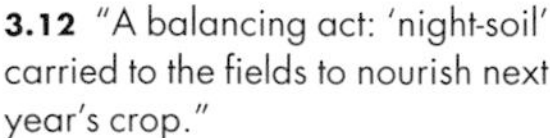

3.12 "A balancing act: 'night-soil' carried to the fields to nourish next year's crop."

3.15 "The ubiquitous rice-drying rack (inagi)—the first act of architecture, the forbear of the shrine?"

3.16 "Shinto shrine, neglected because of WWII, perhaps it will be reclaimed by the Hinoki Cypress forest?"

3.17 "The main sanctuary of the Grand Shinto Shrine at Ise, awaiting the ceremony to receive the 'spirit.'"

3.18 "Spiritless, these structures will be removed, and the precinct will be fallow for a generation awaiting the reincarnation and rededication of its former self."

3.19 "The sheds of the Grand Shinto Shrine at Ise are gilded with fragrant leaf fall from the katsura trees."

3.20 "Ryōan-ji: Do islands define the sea or do stone outcrops interrupt the rice planting? Meditate."

3.21 "Katsura Villa where guests gather on the viewing rock, waiting to trace the night fall and the moon rise."

3.22 "Saihō-ji: Study the silent bones of the earth, listen to the noisy trees, the quiet moss. Buddha is in the concept, his followers in the detail."

designing the home garden in california

IT WAS IN RESIDENTIAL GARDENS THAT MANY LANDSCAPE architects developed a modernist language in the mid-twentieth century.[1] They drew on what was by that time almost a century of design practice. As the profession of landscape architecture was coalescing in the early twentieth century, progressives and professionals concurred on the significant influence of residential design on social behavior and character. Landscape architects such as Frederick Law Olmsted and his successors the Olmsted Brothers, Thomas Church, Marian Cruger Coffin, Jens Jensen, Beatrix Farrand, and Warren Manning designed residential gardens. However, with increasing interest in the modernist movement, landscape architects had the opportunity to use the residential garden as a place in which to experiment with new forms, new materials, and new programs.

The residential garden held possibilities for those interested in pursuing radical design investigations of modern life and art. As Haag launched his career, he took full advantage of these circumstances to use residential-scale projects in the unfolding of a distinct design approach engaging modernist forms and ecological processes, the arts and the natural sciences.

LANDSCAPE ARCHITECTURE IN CALIFORNIA

Upon returning to the United States after two years in Japan, Haag initially considered relocating to the Pacific Northwest both because his wife's family lived nearby and because the region intrigued him, with its close links to Japan. Searching for a place to land, he visited Portland, Oregon, and Seattle, where he met members of the small community of landscape architects, including Glen Hunt and William Teufel and one of the region's leading architects, Fred Bassetti. However, there were few jobs outside of city planning positions. The late 1950s would see the start of exciting projects in Seattle, but they would not have been visible quite yet. During the same period, Ian McHarg offered to hire Haag to teach at the University of Pennsylvania. Haag did not wish to move east and was not ready to commit to teaching, as he wanted to practice first.

In contrast, California was one of the most exciting regions to practice in the decades after World War II. Of the early firms, Thomas (Tommy) Church (1902–1978) had established his office in 1929 and would remain in practice for forty years, during which he designed nearly two thousand gardens and mentored many landscape architects, including Robert Royston, Douglas Bayliss, Mae Arbegast, and Theodore Osmundson. Of the firms that were launched in the 1940s while Haag was a student at the University of California, Berkeley, one of the more influential, both regionally and internationally, was Eckbo, Royston, and Williams, founded by Robert Royston, Garrett Eckbo, and Edward Williams in 1945. John H. Staley, who had been in practice since 1939, joined with Theodore Osmundson to establish a firm in 1946.[2] Lawrence Halprin worked for Church and then, in 1949, opened his own office and remained in active practice until his death at the age of ninety-three in 2009.

The mid-century saw the emergence of informal modern

living, ideal for the California climate and landscape. California's *Sunset* magazine promoted modern living and the houses and gardens that would nurture such a new lifestyle. Landscape architects were at the leading edge of this movement. Garrett Eckbo's *Landscape for Living* (1950) describes how house and garden together would support contemporary lifestyles and aspirations. In a similar vein, Church's 1955 book *Gardens Are for People: How to Plan for Outdoor Living* expanded the recognition of what landscape architects might contribute to modern life.[3] The landscapes featured easy access to the outdoors, a relatively low-maintenance plant palette, and an emphasis on the recreational spaces in the garden including those for swimming, tennis, and lounging. The garden encouraged informal living with the addition of the barbecue, deck chairs, tables, and swings, "more social than horticultural in its intentions."[4] It was an experimental approach that sought to articulate a new, modern language of design that would meet the ambitions of those promoting modern art and modern living. Thus, by 1956, when Haag returned from Japan, heading to San Francisco, where he had gone to school, made sense, and chances were good that he could land a position in a growing firm.

Once settled in San Francisco, Haag interviewed with firms, including Church's, and then accepted a position in the landscape architecture firm of Osmundson & Staley in Oakland. Theodore Osmundson had opened the firm in 1945, and John Staley joined soon thereafter. When Haag was employed, the firm was working on the Kaiser Center Roof Garden with associate David Arbegast, who had also recently joined the firm. This would become one of Osmundson's most important projects. It was also significant for development in the design of landforms used to obscure the gridded nature of the tree plantings, an approach that would become part of Haag's repertoire.

Haag did not stay long, however, and by the end of 1956, he was working with Lawrence (Larry) Halprin (1916–2009), who would be responsible for well-recognized design projects such as the Franklin Delano Roosevelt Memorial in Washington, D.C.; the Sea Ranch community in California; Freeway Park in Seattle; Heritage Park in Fort Worth, Texas; and Lovejoy Plaza in Portland, Oregon.[5] Halprin's office was in the same building as two other practices, one of which was Marquis and Stoller, and Haag recalled years later that if an important client was coming to visit a firm, staff from the other firms would set up desks so the host firm's office looked busy and at capacity. They would also help draft projects when the need arose. Haag was joining an exciting community of designers as he launched his professional career.

Don Carter, who worked in the Halprin office for twenty-five years, recalled that it was an office where employees enjoyed discussions and debates as they helped Halprin forge alternative paths in landscape architecture practice. Carter believed that, while retaining a strong hand in the process, Halprin encouraged his employees to accept the opportunities residential projects offered to develop their own approaches, experiment with new ideas, and pursue design concepts as a means of learning as well as pushing the boundaries of practice.[6] Designers were also encouraged to explore the arts in multiple forms and media, and the office space featured works of art as well as craft objects.

Haag had heard of Halprin's work before coming to the office and was acquainted with a number of the employees from his days at the University of California, Berkeley, including Richard Vignola and Satoru Nishita, in addition to Carter, his colleague from Harvard University's Graduate School of Design. He had worked on a Halprin project, the Whitesburg Memorial Hospital in Kentucky, just before going to Japan. In the Halprin office, Haag collaborated on a range of projects, from small residential gardens to public parks and the campus plan for the University of California, Davis. He was also exposed to a variety of project types while participating in contemporary debates within the design and planning communities.

Halprin's experimental approach to landscape design likely encouraged Haag to pursue a similar path. The two shared a willingness to take risks and explore alternative avenues of investigation and design. However, there were also differences in their approaches. Halprin's experiments were more socially based than Haag's would be. Halprin was interested in what he would call the "RSVP cycle" and his Experiments in Environment project with Anna, his wife, as investigations of human and social responses to site and environment. He was most interested in the choreography of people's movements through a site. Ecology and environmental processes would play a part in Halprin's designs but were often secondary to people and programs. For Haag, however, social and cultural programs were essential, but he would increasingly come to believe that they were to be designed into the site in ways that nurtured its natural cycles and systems.

Both Halprin and Haag were willing to engage in politics and advocacy on behalf of their landscape visions. As they embarked on their lives as professionals in the 1950s and 1960s, both were active participants in the emerging environmental and civil rights movements. Haag, however, was also a teacher and expanded his advocacy to include students as well as colleagues, a sphere of influence that would extend much further than Halprin's. Both designers included the public in their advocacy, Halprin writing books on cities and freeways describing an alternative vision of the future and Haag focusing on letters to the editor and public meetings.[7] Despite the shared viewpoints, Haag did not fare well for long in the office. Halprin's temper was provoked when Haag insisted on developing a design in the direction that interested him rather than following Halprin's lead. Seeing the work on Haag's desk, and noting his displeasure, Halprin knocked Haag's desk over and told him to design as he had been instructed. In the following decades, Haag and Halprin collaborated on only a few projects and competed on far more as they both remained on the West Coast.

Later, after leaving Halprin's office, the two continued to cross paths. An important early project for Halprin was the design of the Century 21 Exposition, the 1962 World's Fair in Seattle, and in 1972, he was commissioned to design Seattle's Freeway Park, the first highway-lidding project. Haag's office served as the local firm for the fair project and was an active leader in Seattle in the 1960s and 1970s, serving on Seattle's Municipal Arts Commission for many years. Halprin also worked on a master plan for the University of Washington, where Haag was then teaching and was responsible for collaborating with Halprin.

In 1957, Stanley White visited Haag in Berkeley when he traveled to the National Conference on Instruction in Landscape Architecture conference in Ojai, California. White's description of the meeting reveals the dynamism of the period:

> The California Landscape Architects notably of the "modern school of design," Eckbo, Royston, Halprin, Church and others, were introduced into the discussion and made a showing that was forceful and substantial in a critical way. . . . During the day we appreciated the stimulation of impromptu remarks by several excited speakers: Ian MacHarg in his eloquent defense of Landscape Architecture as the "noblest" profession, carrying the weight of the world, as every one of us believed it should if it could, Church, in a quite petulant tone, insisting on the common sense of his whole attitude (and offering a slight slight to Harvard, where presumably he had wasted his time), Halprin using strong language effectively to gain his points, Bob Royston in a gay mood that I had not anticipated and Eckbo who was always sincere, effective, and thoughtful, rather than startling like the others, . . . clamoring for the fresh approach as a nucleus of our salvation in a profession in the modern society.[8]

With regard to Haag, White remarked that he seemed to be adjusting well to the region. He wrote that "Rich's present house is a section of some old temporary housing soon to be torn down. The community now consists of people from the dust-blow, with their local customs brought along, a special group. Rich had done a garden (bed) of beach pebbles and a clump of tall native grass, very fitting." They enjoyed a Japanese dinner, which White thought fun, and then debated late into the evening:

> We dwelt on the effects of man on the habitat and the meaning of landscape in the culture where novelties such as the architects are producing are vulnerable to the changes brought about as whim supersedes whim when the ideas come only off the drawing board. The Neolithic is still the low bas from which tastes arise with fancies and sentiments that are always earthy, not sophisticated as the architect hopes to make them. Vanity erases the more solid values. In the international scene, he says that we are making huge mistakes by not understanding the tragedy of the Japanese culture under foreign urges.[9]

In 1957, barely a year after joining the Halprin firm, Haag opened his own practice, Richard Haag Associates, on San Francisco's Embarcadero at Pier 18–20.[10] He attained his California landscape architectural professional license the same year and quickly developed a solid private practice, focused on residential design.

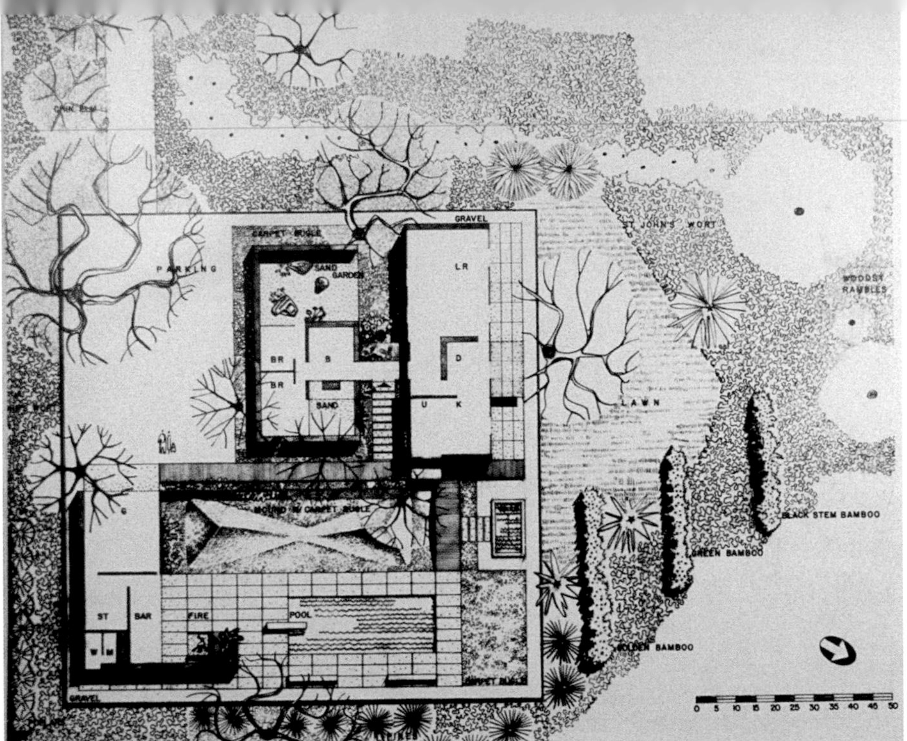

4.1 Case Study House plan as published for the Case Study project.

CASE STUDY HOUSE AND GARDEN NO. 19

Among Haag's projects in California, a selection of his residential gardens and one commercial landscape describe his early design approach. An early project for the Case Study House Program brought attention to his work. The program in California, funded by *Arts & Architecture* magazine, was launched in 1945 and lasted until 1962.[11] *Arts & Architecture* initially commissioned eight firms to provide the designs for eight distinct houses. In 1957, Haag joined architects Richard Neutra, William Wurster, Donald Emmons, Theodore Bernardi, Charles Eames, and Eero Saarinen on a list of potential designers. Within weeks, Haag was asked to provide the landscape design for the steel-framed Case Study House No. 19 designed by Don Knorr of Knorr-Elliot in San Francisco and intended for a location in Atherton, California.[12] The project originally had a real client, but by the time Haag joined the team, it had become a proposal only, allowing Haag, with Knorr in agreement, to design as he chose without the need to accommodate a client's demands.

Haag sited the Knorr-Elliot steel house in two parts on a 120-foot-square terrace a few inches above grade in the midst of an old orchard and native oak landscape. As few trees were cut as possible; thus, the house and garden appeared carved out of a natural clearing. As Knorr wrote, the landscape was "a continuation of volumes, planes, and surprises."[13]

Haag created a sequence of gardens defined equally by the geometry of the architectural spaces, the trees, and the topography. Existing oak and apple trees were retained, and together they contributed a sense of stability and age. In this project and many that followed, Haag used rows of Lombardy poplars to define larger spaces. They form the northeastern boundary of the garden rising above the garage and, with the pine trees to the north, underline the horizon from the terrace. In addition, he used lawn and Saint-John's-wort to create freestanding horizontal planes within the landscape, in active dialogue with the adjacent architectural spaces.

In a design detail that echoed the work of Eckbo, Haag established vertical walls of bamboo that led the eye from the foreground of the pool terrace to the wooded ravine beyond. The bamboo wall cut through the plane of Saint-John's-wort and intruded upon the lawn, adding a dynamism that played against the placement of the architecture on the raised terrace. To accent the visual effect of the bamboo walls, he used a progression of color and texture, from brighter yellow bamboo with coarser leaves and stems nearest to the terrace and moving to darker black-stem bamboo with finer foliage at the edge of the ravine. This created not only a dynamic and seasonally responsive landscape but the illusion of more distance than was actually available.

The house was placed on a terrace that included smaller courtyard gardens. One of the two interior sand gardens was meant for contemplation, while the other served as a scenic backdrop. A third court garden to the north was initially composed of twin pyramids of white sand, echoing a correspondingly smaller-scaled sand pyramid. These sand forms flanked the bridge that linked a swimming pool to the house. In the final design, a spray pool replaced the smaller of the sand pyramids and the larger pyramids became two asymmetrical tetrahedral mounds covered with carpet bugle. The forms were reflected in the swimming pool, multiplying their form and geometry and thus heightening the experience of the pool and its terrace. (While with Halprin's office, Haag used a similar mound in a design for a school courtyard in South San Francisco.)[14] Beyond the pool were a fire pit and dressing rooms, essentially an outdoor living area that resonated with the indoor living room and its fireplace at the opposite corner of the terrace. The composition as a whole, as John Rozdilsky noted, was bold and spare in form, color, and texture.[15] While future designs would increase the simplicity, this one was characteristic of Haag's early modernist designs that focused on shaping space and creating forms in the landscape.

As a Case Study House project, published in 1957, the design was innovative. Haag investigated alternative forms in the vegetation and made the first of what would be a number of sand pyramid proposals. It was, however, also the work of a young designer, with a forced geometry and too many ideas filling the voids. Over the next decade, Haag would learn to edit his work and find an appropriate expression for each landscape.

CAMP GARDEN

While the Case Study House was never built, Haag's design for Harry Camp's house and garden in Hillsborough, California, was constructed between 1957 and 1960 in collaboration with the architects Marquis and Stoller.[16] The architects set the modernist home at the front of the site, giving significant space to a backyard, where the Camps wanted a swimming pool and putting green. As with the Case Study House, Haag wanted to site the pool at a distance from the house, surrounded by earth mounds, and to place the putting green to one side as a landform. He recalled that "the big problem there was getting them (Camps) to accede, or consent to the idea of removing the swimming pool from the house. All those . . . California people, they want to jump out of, spring out of their beds, and pop right into the pool. . . . Camp was a good client, he was educable."[17] Clearly, early in his career, Haag wanted to build on his ideas rather than what the client might have in mind, and he persuaded the Camps to site the pool away from the house, framed by two earthen berms. Camp would remark that the mounds were there to interrupt the view to the pool "so we won't feel we're living in a beach club."[18]

Looking out from the living room's large, plate glass windows, the mounds were seen as garden sculptures, spatially defining and directing the view to the trees in the background and, indeed, obscuring the view of the pool.[19] Privacy was important, as Camp wanted to be able "to go anywhere on the grounds, unseen, clad only in shorts."[20] The larger mound was eventually modified and became two asymmetrical mounds, and the landforms were covered with English ivy, which created a rough texture that contrasted with the smoothness of the lawn and the reflective surface of the pool. The shadows of the trees moving across the ground as the sun crossed the sky heightened the visual character of the mounds, appearing to move in opposition to the horizontality of the house.

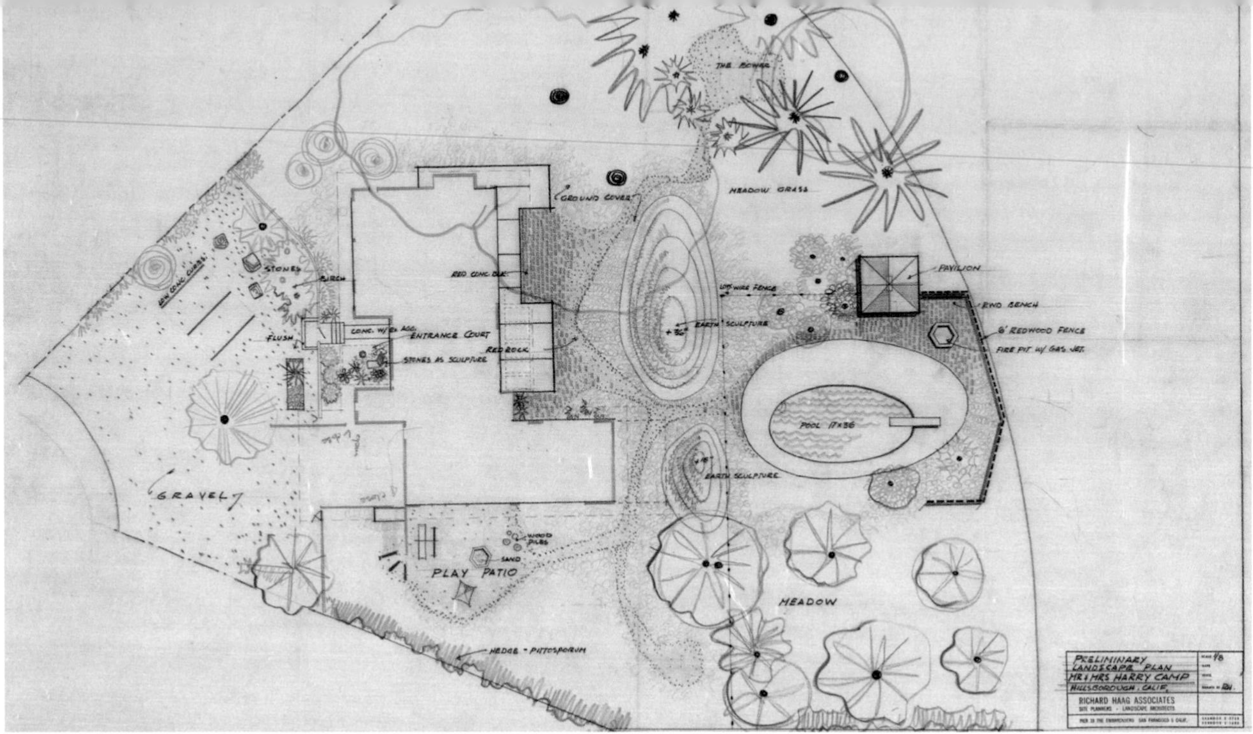

4.2 Preliminary landscape plan for the Camp house, showing the influence of mid-century California modernism.

4.3 Camp house and garden, Hillsborough, California, 1958.

Realizing that he might be trying to merge too many forms and materials, Haag specified that the pool's coping should be a continuation of the paving around the pool, simplifying its appearance so that the forms would be read without the distraction of "jamming all these materials together."[21]

Haag also looked to modern technology to highlight the modern forms of his garden. The Camp garden featured modern light fixtures that accentuated the effects of light and shade, which in turn emphasized the form and texture of the materials. Lights located behind each of the three stones at the threshold between the forecourt and the entry courtyard, for example, drew on the darkness of night to accentuate the form of the stones juxtaposed to the white wall. The feathery shadows of the silk trees (*Albizzia*) also contrasted with the solidity of the stones. Lights were used to create shadows on the mounds in the backyard. Thus, this early garden design was modern in its use of modernist forms, its articulated geometry, and its use of modern technology. Although Haag used plants, this design did not make the natural processes or ecological systems particularly evident.

There are subtle references to Haag's interest in Japanese gardens in these early designs. The sand and rock gardens were relatively direct translations, while the earth mounds appear to be more abstract interpretations. In neither garden did Haag suggest that he was creating a Japanese garden; rather, the aesthetic infused his approach. He used local plants and stone while drawing on compositional principles of Japanese garden design. In the entry garden, he used gravel, stone, and selected shrubs as specimens rather than foundational plantings. Finally, subtle Japanese references could be found in the architecture of the Camp house: the vertically divided wall panels that form the threshold between the entry garden and the house read as screens in the photographs, while the shadows of the trees and shrubs against the white walls suggested shadow play.

It was also in these early projects that Haag further developed his concept of fusion as a design principle. Fusion called for the merging of humans and nature, order and randomness. In design, it meant the blurring of boundaries, from programming to materials. Fusion was a means of treating the elements of a design in relationship to other elements and the whole rather than as a series of objects sited in the larger landscape. As he described it, this approach allowed "these [pavers] to escape into the graveled area and the graveled to escape into the [paving area]."[22] The sequencing of movement through the landscape was critical to his idea of fusion. Through movement, the human experience of the order of an architectural path might merge with the apparent randomness of a woodland or meadow. Fusion called for integrating the architecture with the landscape, creating indoor-outdoor spaces that were tightly choreographed to respond to one another. The Camp garden was more focused than the Case Study House project, but it, too, had a number of distinct spaces and objects that suggested the need for further editing and clarity of design.

WONG GARDEN

In May 1957, Haag was commissioned to design a small garden for the house of Mr. and Mrs. Elwood Wong in Palo Alto, California.[23] His goal was to create the sense of a larger space, a more generous spatial experience. The garden was only fifty by sixty-eight feet, composed of three sequential spaces organized around an iconic Eichler house, with the fourth side of the house functioning primarily as a boundary and for utility circulation.[24] The street side of the site was centered on a red rock path for pedestrians and a driveway leading to the garage. These were flanked by beds of Algerian ivy, with each space featuring a specimen tree—a magnolia, a silk tree, and a zelkova, respectively. The front path led indirectly to the front of the house, although without as many turns in direction as at the Case Study House project. A pair of vertical fences defined a series of thresholds. Haag used bamboo to give definition to the scale of the enclosed space as well as to create porous edges. A sunken lawn sat to one side of the entry courtyard, with the entrance to the house lying straight ahead. A second space in the garden was encountered by means of a checkerboard path that merged the concrete of

4.4 Perspective sketch for Mr. and Mrs. Elwood Wong.

4.5 Wong garden with landforms, Palo Alto, California, 1958.

the house with the grass of the lawn in a form reminiscent of the geometry of the grass squares Haag had seen in the gardens at Tōfuku-ji. This was a transitional space that moved the individual from the front, more public area of the site to the back and its more private garden.

For the garden behind the house, Haag used topography as the primary design element and selected only a few plants for vertical accent points. In the far corner, the view ended at two small earthen cones juxtaposed with a small Chinese angelica tree. These cones were eventually covered in blue fescue, although the original plans called for carpet bugle. Closer to the house, just off the patio, a sunken terrace paved with small red-rock framed a honey locust tree that would eventually provide dappled shade. The garden was a mix of social space and contemplative setting. At the far edge was a small raised bed where the family could grow vegetables. A small reflecting pool in the form of two adjacent triangles could be covered with a wooden deck for safety when not in use. The perspective sketch of the pool and mounds with the sunken terrace and a barbecue in the foreground suggests Haag's steady merging of his Japanese interests with the language of northern California materials and programming.

The characteristics of Haag's early gardens increasingly included Japanese references, earthen mounds, and clear explorations of modernism as it was being expressed in the Bay Area in the 1950s. In the drawings for many of his California gardens, Haag used a sketching style similar to that of his Bay Area colleagues, among them Garrett Eckbo, loose, almost cartoonlike. The drawings show families engaged in the outdoor activities that were so popular in the Bay Area, barbecuing, enjoying the swimming pool, lounging in the sun, and gardening. The drawings often include children, as the gardens were intended as places of active recreation for families. Haag completed more than thirty-six gardens in California between 1957 and 1960, and the vast majority of reveal a similar approach.[25] His work was acknowledged professionally in magazines, including *House & Garden*, and the Western Home Awards contest sponsored by the

4.6 Wong garden with sunken terrace, Palo Alto, 1958.

American Institute of Architects (AIA) and *Sunset* magazine, among others.[26] The sketches and descriptions place the gardens within the trends of 1950s modernism and reflect Haag's ability to adopt and adapt.

JAPANESE GARDENS

For the most part, Haag was not interested in designing Japanese gardens, but he did work with a few clients who were deeply interested in Japanese aesthetics. Mr. and Mrs. James Broz were one such couple. They had lived briefly in Japan before moving to San Francisco and wanted a small garden and deck for the Japanese soaking tub (*ofuro*) they had installed. Haag used the redwood the Brozes provided and Japanese joinery methods on the deck and bench. He had the ends of the wood painted white, as Japanese craftsmen did in order to prevent rotting, although such protection was unnecessary for redwood. With small shrubs, Haag created

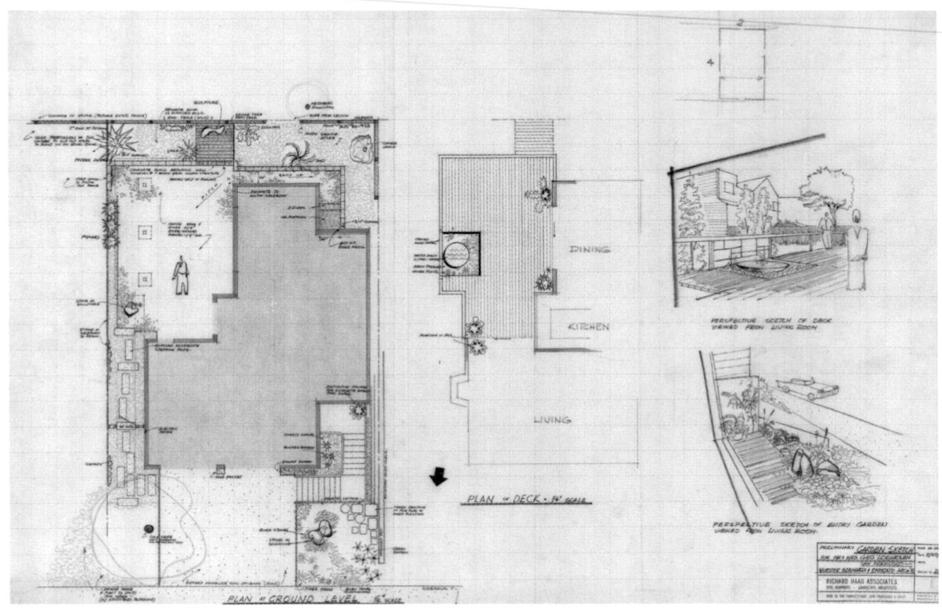

4.7 Loehner garden plan, San Francisco, 1958.

a meditative garden around the small deck. His design was a regional response yet was also aesthetically inspired by Japanese gardens and crafts. As he would later recall, this seemed an appropriate project for drawing directly on his knowledge and experience of Japan.

Another Japanese-inspired design in California came to Haag in May 1957, this one for Mrs. Lee Zollinger.[27] An avid fan of Japanese gardens who had visited Japan, she wanted to bring the experience to the hillside garden that surrounded her Berkeley home in the Uplands neighborhood.[28] Zollinger had called the landscape architecture department at the University of California, Berkeley, to ask if they knew of a Japanese gardener who might design her garden. The secretary, according to Haag, did not know of such a person but instead recommended that she consider hiring Haag, who had recently studied in Japan. Zollinger contacted Haag and hired him initially to help lay out the driveway. She assumed they would move the garage to sit next to the house and then cut into the slope in order to bring the drive directly up the slope. Haag argued that they should leave the garage where it was and not allow a driveway to cut through the slope. Instead, he designed a walking path along the hillside, which focused on the entrance experience of the pedestrian rather than the driver. A bosk of birch trees created a woodland around the path, accentuating the experience of the landscape.

With the path established, Haag was asked to design a teahouse and garden in the backyard. Using the hillside, Haag designed a series of terraces, abstractions of rice paddies planted with thyme at the bottom and carpet bugle at the top. The teahouse was tucked into the top corner, surrounded by Japanese maples, rhododendrons, bamboo, and pittosporums. The simple wooden post-and-beam structure faced a composition of three boulders reminiscent of the garden at Daisen-in in Kyoto. Although suggestive of a Japanese teahouse, its form was more mid-century functionalism, resembling an open wooden tent.

As the project's landscape architect, Haag initiated a request for contracts from three construction companies.

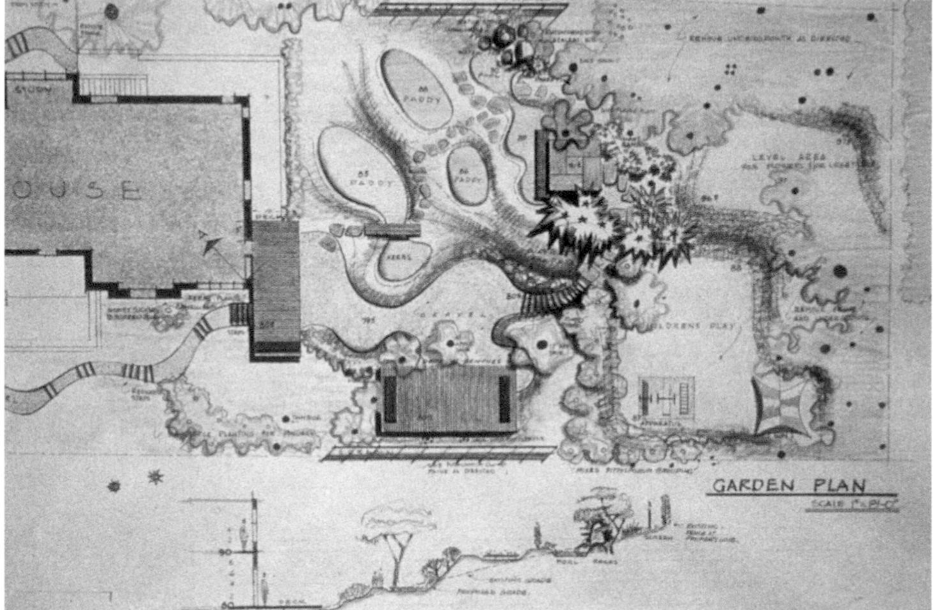

4.8 Broz garden,
San Francisco, 1958.

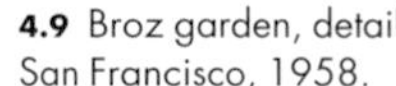

4.9 Broz garden, detail,
San Francisco, 1958.

4.10 Mrs. Lee Zollinger
garden plan.

4.11 Zollinger garden with boulders and teahouse, Berkeley, California, c. 1960.

Haag and Zollinger believed that Sakanashi Construction was the only contractor of the three with experience with Japanese gardens. They selected the company to build the teahouse as well as obtain and plant all the plants, working under Haag's close supervision. Russ Riley, who had been hired by Haag while a student at the University of California, recalled that Haag "had such a feel for the rocks" and the siting of driveways and paths. Riley remarked on the "Japanese feel in [Haag's] private life and landscape design."[29] The Zollinger garden was not a Japanese garden but a means of remembering the experience of a Japanese garden, and that satisfied Mrs. Zollinger.

DUX FURNITURE PROJECT

Haag's collaboration with Knorr-Elliot on the Case Study House project led to others, including a garden for the Lidy couple as well as a very different design project for a commercial landscape in 1958. Knorr-Elliot had been commissioned to design office, warehouse, and factory facilities for DUX in Burlingame, California.[30] Furniture maker Folke Ohlsson had moved to the United States from his homeland, Sweden, in 1953 and established DUX in San Francisco. In 1957, Ohlsson moved the company to Burlingame. He desired architecture that would reflect his furniture, noting: "Quality architecture is to us a symbol of quality furniture. . . . Realizing that the building must perform more than the function of an industrial operation, the goal here is to achieve an architectural environment that will promote interest in one's work."[31] In addition, like many new corporate headquarters, the structure would need to fit into a residential neighborhood, requiring zoning variances and a low horizontal profile.[32] The landscape would play a critical role in fitting the building into the neighborhood and providing a place where employees could enjoy their work.

For this project, contracted on November 18, 1957, Haag drew on his knowledge of Japanese design as well as the materials and design approach of DUX furniture. The buildings became the backdrop to Haag's landscape. The landscape was portioned into geometrically clear ground planes of either mineral or vegetal character. The mineral forms were gravel or black slab granite with concrete paths linking them to the buildings. The vegetal forms were grass lawns or grids of birch trees. Water was present in the form of fountains.

Haag combined the materials at distinct points, contrasting pebbles with mondo grass or horsetail (equisetum). In the central court, a small stone fountain provided both vertical dynamism and a cooling effect. Haag claimed that the form of the white stone fountain was based on lessons he had learned from Japanese crafts with concentric rims emphasizing the bowl's roundness, reflecting the Japanese focus on the inherent character of the form. The granite reflected the sky, fusing sky and ground in a manner Haag appreciated. The play of mineral and vegetal media was complex in its diversity but could be clearly read and understood, neither overwhelming nor acquiescing to the architecture.

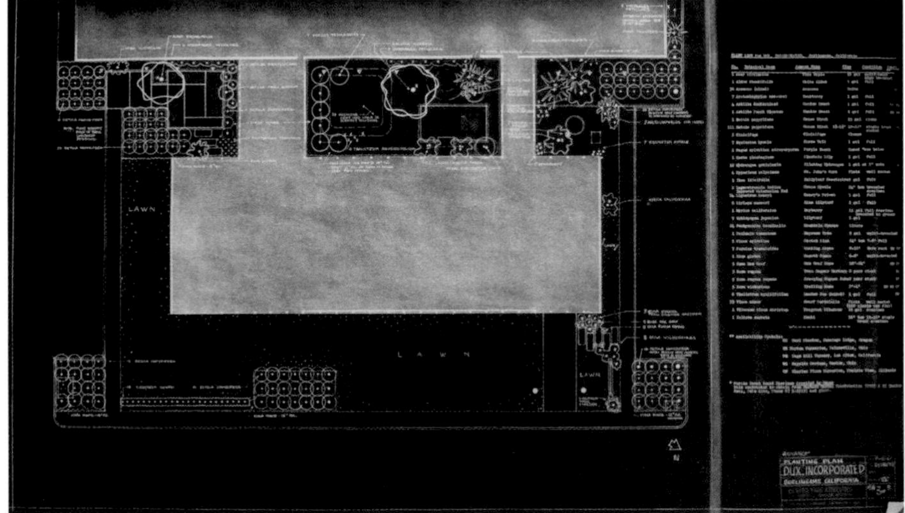

4.12 DUX building and courtyard with birches, Burlingame, California, 1960.

4.13 DUX planting plan.

Using birch, a favorite material for the furniture line, as a theme, Haag created a series of rectilinear tree compositions defining the spaces while expanding the perceived space of the main offices. The birch grids flanked the parking lots to the northwest and southeast of the main structure and created small rooms around the terraces to the south. A final cluster of birch was set at the sidewalk edge in the front near the southeast parking lot, defining the entranceway and altering the apparent scale of the expansive lawn.

Haag's use of the birches was subtle and bold. The clear geometry and the density of the four-feet-on-center planting created a confident verticality in the landscape that balanced the horizontal character of the architecture. The tree trunks echoed the architectural columns and the vertical timber slats of the exterior walls, with the trees reaching higher into the sky. Rozdilsky has suggested that this design might have been a tribute to Dan Kiley, in whose office Haag had interned.[33]

Inspired by the DUX furniture, Haag designed a platform bench for the landscape that he believed reflected a similar approach to design. The bench was defined by the proportions of two tatami mats, a six-by-six-foot square.[34] The placement of the benches emphasized the geometry of the larger design and provided surfaces where people could gather in addition to the more traditional rectangular benches that were also offered in the courtyards. One of Haag's employees, Ilze Jones, later named these platforms "keblis," a term that was later inserted in the city codes for furniture in public spaces for the city of Redmond, Washington, where Haag would again use the bench.[35] Haag would use them in other designs as well, including for the Battelle Research Center in Seattle.

The DUX project was one of a few corporate designs that Haag worked on. This was a new area of landscape architecture design, one that was growing much faster in the suburbs of New York, with corporate headquarters, including those of Avon, Chrysler, and Westinghouse, moving into suburban neighborhoods. In California there was moderate growth of corporate headquarters in the suburbs joined by substan-

4.14 DUX, detail of mineral, vegetal, and water elements in the landscape, Burlingame, 1960.

4.15 DUX, birch trees and courtyard, Burlingame, 1960.

tial civic and governmental projects. Haag provided designs for the Marin Professional Center off Highway 101, a project designed by the architects Marquis and Stoller.[36] It was a modernist structure surrounded by a landscape of lawn and trees that echoed the rolling landscapes of northern California. He also provided designs for Commodore Aviation in Marin, the Whelan Professional Building in Palo Alto, and the Napa Medical Dental Building in Napa between 1957 and 1959. Nevertheless, this area did not become a major part of Haag's design practice.

CALIFORNIA EXPERIMENTS

Each of these California projects exhibited elements of what would become characteristic of Haag's experiments and designs: the juxtaposition of the geometry of hard materials such as stone and concrete forms with the softer lines of shrubs, trees, and earth forms, the use of trees as spatial and character determinants, and the use of landforms. Haag drew on diverse regional plants, not necessarily native but regionally associated, along with local stones and boulders that grounded the gardens in place. He used plants as specimens to mark an edge or create a focal point, rarely massing them to serve as foundation plantings. A birch grove was an insertion that was simultaneously spatial and temporal, sculptural and horticultural.

Haag had absorbed much from Japan, and yet his California designs were not Japanese per se. Even his design for the Zollinger project, for which he was asked to create a Japanese garden, referenced elements of Japanese gardens such as the teahouse but used the vocabulary of mid-twentieth-century California. He did not replicate the tea garden's sequence of thresholds and movement, and yet movement and thresholds were important elements of the design. He did not design paths to lead directly to the entrance or the pool but configured indirect paths that were sequenced so as to engage participants in a richer experience. His use of stones reflected the belief that such elements could initiate memories of distant landscapes or long-ago stories and in that way carry "the whole mystery of the earth and waters"[37] to the observer.

The gardens clearly reflected Mid-Century Modernism in landscape architecture in California. They were nonhistorical, neither of the Beaux Arts tradition nor specifically Japanese. The design for DUX was the most recognizably modern, with a bosk of birch trees planted on a dense grid that echoed the columns of the architecture in a modernist manner. As did designers such as Garrett Eckbo, Haag eschewed primary symmetries in his designs, even when using the grid as a layer. Also similar to California modernist gardens was the fluidity of indoor and outdoor spaces. Joseph Hudnut, in describing the modern garden, proposed that "gardens, like houses, are built of space. . . . The space of house and that of garden are parts of a single organism . . . the new vision has dissolved the ancient boundary between architecture and landscape architecture. The garden flows into and over the house. . . . The house reached out into the garden with walls and terraced enclosures that continued its rhythms and share its grace."[38]

Haag also responded to functional needs, providing equipment where children would play while planning easy access to the barbecue and vegetable garden. He differed from his California colleagues in his limited use of lawns or swimming pools with spacious patios. For him, such spaces were not aesthetically interesting—they were monotonous to the senses and to be used only when necessary. His California gardens were meant to be more contemplative, more inward-looking, as aesthetically engaging as they were functional.

Haag's early residential work in California set important trajectories for his design practice. Although he would later complain that he was not able to approach design as he wished in these early projects, they reveal his experimentation and development of an attitude toward design, particularly at the intimate human scale. Following his brief practice in California, Haag moved to Seattle in fall 1958 to launch a university landscape architecture program and establish a new practice. He left the Dux, Camp, and Zollinger projects to be completed by Russ Riley in Haag's San Francisco office and other projects for landscape architect Peter Walker, who took over the office space in San Francisco.

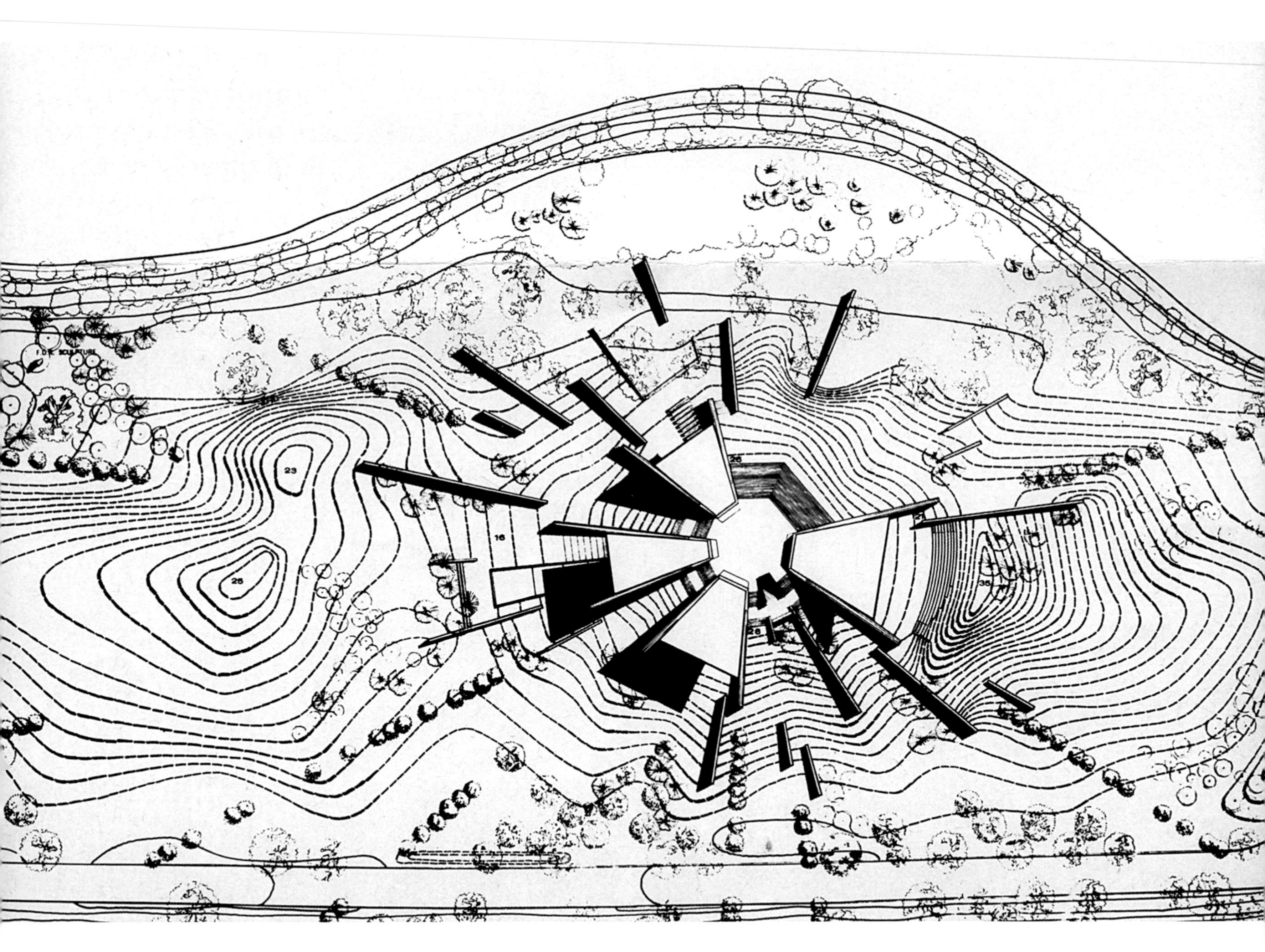

F.D.R. SCULPTURE
23
25
16
26
28
35

5

a teacher's teacher

IN SEPTEMBER 1958, AS HAAG ARRIVED FOR HIS FIRST FACulty meeting at the University of Washington's College of Architecture and Urban Planning (CAUP), Victor Steinbrueck, a professor in the college, remarked, "We have been waiting a long time for you."[1] This was not a fanciful welcome so much as a statement of the faculty's commitment to including landscape architecture in the design curriculum.[2]

As early as 1914, there had been discussion of a "landscape designing" option in the proposal presented to university regents by local architects David Myers, Charles H. Bebb, and Carl F. Gould. The earliest program curriculum described courses in landscape designing as well as city planning;[3] however, with no one likely to champion the idea and extensive work required to launch the architecture curriculum, the inclusion of landscape architecture would not become a reality until the College of Architecture and Urban Planning was ready to expand in 1957.[4] By then, competing schools already had such programs, including the University of California, Berkeley, and the University of Oregon in Eugene. The State College of Washington (renamed Washington State University in 1959) also offered courses in landscape design as the first step toward its undergraduate program.[5] Arthur Hermann, the college's first dean, understood its importance and began the process of launching the new program.[6]

Although he might have turned to landscape architects in Seattle, Hermann asked architecture professor Robert Dietz to identify a leader from outside the region. Dietz approached Thomas Church in San Francisco and Hideo Sasaki, by then chair of landscape architecture at Harvard's Graduate School of Design, for recommendations. Sasaki suggested Haag, as he was young and forward-looking and had already established himself on the West Coast. In addition, Sasaki noted that Haag had been in Japan with Norman Carver and would thus be a good addition to the faculty in Seattle, whose members were already interested in Japan and the East.[7] Church concurred, as did Ian McHarg, a member of the faculty at the University of Pennsylvania.[8] With these recommendations, Dietz contacted Haag, proposing that he move his firm to Seattle and start the landscape architecture program at the University of Washington. He promised that Haag could also open a practice in Seattle as a faculty member, as others in the college had done.[9] Haag accepted, and in September, he left the Bay Area to launch his careers as a practitioner and a teacher in the Pacific Northwest.

THE COLLEGE OF ARCHITECTURE AND URBAN PLANNING

In fall 1958, the College of Architecture and Urban Planning greeted Haag with a faculty of twenty-three members, including Lionel Pries, Victor Steinbrueck, John Rohrer, Jack Sproule, Omar Mithun, Wendell Lovett, Keith Kolb, Robert Dietz, and Daniel Streissguth, with Myer Wolfe heading the urban planning program and Herrmann serving as dean. Many were active design or planning professionals, and a number would become engaged in civic outreach and activism beginning in the 1960s.[10] Haag thus found a congenial community.

The university approved the bachelor of landscape architecture program in 1960 and in the same year promoted

LANDSCAPE ARCHITECTURE

JEAN BEARDSLEY
MARGARET BLACKBURN
MARY EDSTROM
WILLIAM RICE
LLOYD THORSON

A NUCLEUS OF PEOPLE ARE NOW ENROLLED IN THE RECENTLY FORMED SCHOOL OF LANDSCAPE ARCHITECTURE. THEIR FIVE YEAR CURRICULUM LEADS TOWARD A DEGREE AS BACHELOR OF LANDSCAPE ARCHITECTURE. THIS PROGRAM IS BUILT AROUND A CORE OF DESIGN COURSES AND STUDIES IN RELATED FIELDS. EMPHASIS IS PLACED ON THE CONSERVATION, THE RESTORATION AND THE CREATION OF MAN'S NATURAL ENVIRONMENT.

IN ADDITION TO THIS GROUP, WHO ARE PRESENTLY ENROLLED IN GRADE 1 AND GRADE 2 DESIGN COURSES, EACH ARCHITECTURE STUDENT IN GRADE 3 DESIGN IS GIVEN THE OPPORTUNITY TO WORK ON A DESIGN PROBLEM RELATED TO LANDSCAPE ARCHITECTURE IN SOME MANNER. THE WORK ON THE ADJOINING PAGE SHOWS SOME EXAMPLES OF THE PROJECTS UNDERTAKEN BY THIS GROUP.

5.1 Richard Haag teaching "Poetic Response." Drawing by Laurie Olin for the College of Architecture and Urban Planning yearbook, 1960–61.

Haag from acting associate professor to associate professor with tenure. Haag's appointment proved an immediate success, and it did not take him long to develop a following among the students. The first group of students to declare landscape architecture as a major included Jean Beardsley, Margaret Blackburn, Mary Edstrom (later Booth), William Rice, and Lloyd F. Thorson.[11] The first to graduate with a BLA degree were Thorson in December 1963, Robert E. Holtman in March 1964, and Blackburn in June 1964.[12]

Accordingly, Haag needed to identify a demand for landscape architects outside the college if he was to argue for a whole new program. While there had been significant growth in the profession in the eastern United States—between 1957 and 1966, the membership of the American Society of Landscape Architects doubled and the number of landscape architecture students tripled—the Pacific Northwest was home to a relatively small professional community. Haag saw potential in the region.[13] He later commented that "the non-striving attitude is based on a healthy natural environment. So this [University of Washington] was the place to bring that message to . . . and not California. I tried in California but California is a desert . . . without water. Everybody wants their little Eden down there. So the Japanese experience couldn't easily be translated in the California landscape."[14] In the Pacific Northwest, however, appreciation for "the beauty of [the] environment" and the potential of architecture and landscape as intimately engaged had already emerged.[15] Haag envisioned an expanding role for landscape architects and the programs that educated them, one that would address the large scale of the Pacific Northwest's environmental challenges and opportunities.

TEACHING LANDSCAPE ARCHITECTURE

Haag had been interested in teaching since his student days with Stanley White. He had served as a jury member and, for the fall semester of 1957, an associate faculty instructor at the University of California, Berkeley, while practicing.[16] In summer 1957 he co-taught a landscape architecture workshop with Hideo Sasaki, William J. Johnson, and Peter Walker, sponsored by the Sasaki office in Watertown, Massachusetts.

Seeking advice on how best to frame the new program, Haag wrote to his good friends and inspiring mentors, White and Sasaki. White's advice built on his ongoing correspondence with Haag as well as Haag's experience as his student. Over the years, Haag adopted many of White's approaches and habits. Both men were well read and could quote from a broad range of references, and they shared values regarding social and environmental issues. Where they parted ways was White's commitment to teaching and Haag's insistence on developing a practice, with teaching as a secondary activity.

White's commitment to landscape architecture as a high art demanded a broad education in the humanities, arts, and natural sciences; this grounded Haag's approach to teaching and practice. White advised Haag to teach from the heart, to explore widely, and to avoid debates on style: teach idea, not ideology. White's rather famous course "Mixed Pickles" (later "Heinz 57") was a powerful manifestation of this framework, and Haag drew on it in developing his course on landscape architectural appreciation and theory.[17] Accordingly, he argued for a broad education across the disciplines of ecology, economics, sociology, and political science in order to address the "whole environment." He also embraced the making of art, as White described landscape architecture in the preface to his manuscript "A Primer of Landscape Architecture": "Landscape architecture is one of the great arts. It is the superb handling of the land by the creative artist who engraves upon the face of nature those expressions of the culture we need to set the stage of our ordinary lives."[18] Haag shared White's belief in nature as a source of inspiration, asserting that "we in the United States have become so machinized and so denaturized that our very instincts and emotions have somewhat atrophied. . . . Consequently, modern man has forgotten that nature is the life-giver to all creation, to all ceremony and to all symbolism—is the law-giver to all system—is the form-giver to all structure."[19]

While Haag had experienced White's curriculum firsthand, his correspondence with Sasaki was based on more recent critiques of design pedagogy. In 1950, Sasaki published "Thoughts on Education in Landscape Architecture: Some Comments on Today's Methodologies and Purpose," reflecting his interest in how modernist ideas might frame design teaching.[20] In particular, he argued for increased emphasis on research and theory in design pedagogy. This thinking must "be bold enough to question and to re-evaluate many of its precepts, and to change them for new ones if necessary to compete successfully with the other disciplines in the field of environmental planning."[21] Sasaki was less concerned with how design was taught than with encouraging and developing critical thought, a skill he considered essential. Such a framework began with research in multiple forms (verbal, visual, and experimental), proceeded to analysis, and resulted finally in synthesis.

Haag, like Sasaki, was intrigued by technologies and the potential of modern engineering, although his interest was moderated by his concern for the environmental consequences. "Herein lies a significant difference between medieval man and modern man," he wrote in his program proposal. "In fact, our processes and projects must now be considered as the New Nature-force. Previously occupance patterns were dictated by topographic form, by water sites, by climate, etc. This has changed within our life-time."[22] In other words, the potential of science and technology was not merely in efficiency or modernism per se but in how they would alter the relationships of culture and nature. While technology would be detrimental if abused, landscape architects, Haag argued, could respond to the challenges of previous mistakes through science and technology. He maintained that the "vast regional systems of dams, reservoirs and channels supply inter-regional electrical grids, . . . control floods, conserve natural resources, restore biotic balance between man and the land and create a recreational wealth." However, he wrote, "the conception, design, and implementation of projects on the West Coast have too often been lost through the single-minded 'efficiency' of the engineer with his 'success' rated only in kilowatts rather than life-values." He even went as far as to note that society had to address the "cumulative results of radio-active pollution of our total environment." He continued, insisting that we could build on our advantages, as "the U. S. has reached an unprecedented point of material wealth and technical know-how, where virtually nothing is impossible. . . . If we decide to send a man to Venus, he will be sent.[23]

In addition to his mentors, Haag looked to the emerging countercultures that were an important part of Seattle in the

5.2 Richard Haag at wedding reception for Laurie Olin and Anne Ricker, Washington Park, Seattle, 1963.

1960s. In the 1940s, the Northwest School, an art movement composed of Mark Tobey, Kenneth Callahan, Guy Anderson, and Morris Graves, had created a distinct regional style in painting and sculpture. Graves and Tobey no longer lived in the Pacific Northwest, but their art remained influential. Building on their strong associations with the region's environment, activists and artists introduced alternative musical forms, explored the creative power of poetry and prose, and embraced civil rights and feminism. The 1960s was the era of Students for a Democratic Society and the *Helix*, Seattle's first underground newspaper.[24] Tom Robbins's radio show *Notes from the Underground*, played on the alternative Seattle-based FM station KRAB and featured the Doors, Jefferson Airplane, the Grateful Dead, and local musician Jimi Hendrix long before they became mainstream. The focus in Seattle also turned to the environment, eventually leading to the first Earth Day on April 22, 1970, marked with teach-ins at the University of Washington and Seattle Center. Haag's belief in the importance of caring for the environment, his interest in poetry and music, his interpretations of Zen, and his references to "making love to the land" reflected such countercultural movements.

But Haag also held his own positions within the larger movements. Unlike many activists, Haag did not intend to "go back to nature" but wanted to move forward without losing the past. Nor did he share the counterculture's suspicion of science and technology, instead seeing in science a means of devising alternative practices that might improve rather than disrupt human and natural environments. With his students, Haag sought to bridge the professional and countercultural worlds by teaching them the skills required of professionals while encouraging openness to the creativity of those outside the system.

A CURRICULUM

As Haag formulated the landscape curriculum at the University of Washington, it was expected that he would build on existing courses. Design studios were at the core of any design curriculum, and associated course work developed an understanding of architecture as it shaped human culture and habitation, building on a liberal arts education. Related courses in architectural history and sociology as well as physics, mathematics, structural engineering, building technology, and construction courses were also required.

Haag's first inclination was to offer undergraduate students an educational foundation that would enable the best ones to pursue a graduate program in landscape architecture as a profession. In his opinion, if one developed a solid undergraduate curriculum with a focus on landscape design but not solely oriented toward the profession, the best students would proceed to complete a master's degree program in landscape architecture. Those who did not go into professional practice would become knowledgeable critics of built environments in whatever careers they eventually selected.

Haag considered proposing a graduate-level professional program. Harvard's Graduate School of Design and the University of Pennsylvania had chosen this route, arguing that a good design education required an undergraduate liberal arts education. Haag soon dismissed this approach as unfeasible, however, because the program would be difficult to build, graduates might not measure up in competition with graduates of the landscape program offered by Washington State University, and, finally, the college was not interested in professional education at the graduate level.[25] Haag had been asked to develop a comprehensive professional program for undergraduates and needed to complete that task.

While remaining committed to broadly educating students, Haag next proposal would integrate architecture and landscape architecture courses rather than offer separate degrees. The new track could be called "urban design" or "environmental planning." Landscape architecture courses could be offered within the existing architecture curriculum, advancing landscape as a directed track. A third-year course would introduce the history and theory of landscape architecture as well as the principles of site analysis. Landscape criticism would be available for third-, fourth-, and fifth-year students, and those who chose the landscape track would be presented with landscape studio design problems. In the fifth year, students would take a more advanced course in landscape architecture focused on "cultural and social consciousness and responsibility, a perception of environment, and man's reciprocal relation to it."[26] Haag concluded his proposal for the new program by returning to the enormous challenges ahead and calling for the education of future designers:

> There will be problems engendered by population increase on an ever diminishing base of natural resources . . . [and] increased mobility, . . . resulting in the scatter-ated suburban slums. . . . The problems of pollution—both physical and visual—of our atmosphere, our water, and our land, are all inter-related. . . . While many of the symptoms of our biotic-breakdown are readily observed in the "open country," it is nevertheless true that they are generated by essentially urban disorders. . . . It is our responsibility to train designers in these directions if we would best serve the community of man.[27]

Haag preferred this proposal; however, it met with opposition from the architecture faculty members who wanted a distinct professional program in landscape architecture.

BACHELOR OF LANDSCAPE ARCHITECTURE

The five-year curriculum leading to the degree of Bachelor of Landscape Architecture is listed below. Richard Haag is in charge.

PREPROFESSIONAL REQUIREMENTS

First Year

AUTUMN QUARTER	CREDITS	WINTER QUARTER	CREDITS	SPRING QUARTER	CREDITS
Arch. 100 Appreciation	2	Arch. 101 Appreciation	2	Arch. 105 The House	2
English 101 Composition	3	English 102 Composition	3	English 103 Composition	3
Math. 104 Plane Trig.	3	Math. 105 College Algebra	5	Sociol. 110 Survey	5
Health Educ. 110 or 175 Health	2	Approved electives	5	Approved electives	5
Approved electives	5	Phys. Educ. activity	†	Phys. Educ. activity	†
Phys. Educ. activity	†	ROTC	‡	ROTC	‡
ROTC	‡				

Second Year

AUTUMN QUARTER	CREDITS	WINTER QUARTER	CREDITS	SPRING QUARTER	CREDITS
Arch. 124 Design Gr. I	6	Arch. 125 Design Gr. I	6	Arch. 126 Design Gr. I	6
Biology 101J-	5-	Biology -102J	-5	Art 272 Sculpture	3
Approved electives	4	Art 258 Water color	3	Bot. 113 Local Flora	5
ROTC	‡	Approved electives	2	ROTC	‡
		ROTC	‡		

10 credits in a physical science may be substituted for Biology 101J-102J

Electives should be approved by the adviser of the College.

PROFESSIONAL REQUIREMENTS

Third Year

AUTUMN QUARTER	CREDITS	WINTER QUARTER	CREDITS	SPRING QUARTER	CREDITS
Arch. 200 History	3	Arch. 201 History	3	Arch. 202 History	3
Arch. 224 Design Gr. II	6	Arch. 225 Design Gr. II	6	Arch. 226 Design Gr. II	6
La. Ar. 230 Theory & Perception	2	La. Ar. 231 History	3	Urb. Pl. 400 Introduction to Urban Planning	3
Art 426 Origins of Modern Art	2	Anth. 250 The Nature of Culture	2	Art 129 Appreciation of Design	2
				Gen. Engr. 121 Surveying	3

Fourth Year

AUTUMN QUARTER	CREDITS	WINTER QUARTER	CREDITS	SPRING QUARTER	CREDITS
Arch. 303 History	3	La. Ar. 335 Construction	4	La. Ar. 336 Construction	4
La. Ar. 334 Construction	4	La. Ar. 351 Landscape Design Gr. III	6	La. Ar. 352 Landscape Design Gr. III	6
La. Ar. 350 Landscape Design Gr. III	6	Geog. 370 Conservation of Natural Resources	5	Bot. 331 Ornamental Plants	3
Urb. Pl. 479 The Urban Form	2			Geog. 302 The Pacific Northwest	3

Fifth Year

AUTUMN QUARTER	CREDITS	WINTER QUARTER	CREDITS	SPRING QUARTER	CREDITS
La. Ar. 460 Landscape Design Gr. IV	6	La. Ar. 461 Landscape Design Gr. IV	6	La. Ar. 462 Landscape Design Gr. IV	6
Sociol. 430 Human Ecology	5	La. Ar. 465 Planting Design	4	La. Ar. 470 Off. Procedure	3
Geog. 477 Urban Geography	3	Urb. Pl. 482 Community Facilities	2	Anth. 201 Physical Anth.: Man in Nature	5
For. 356 Forest Recreation	3	For. 301 Survey of Forestry	3	Approved electives	2-3

† See Page 32 for Physical Education Activity requirement.
‡ See Page 31 for ROTC requirement.

5.3 Landscape Architecture curriculum, 1961, from the *Bulletin of the College of Architecture and Urban Planning, 1961–63.*

In March 1959, Haag submitted his final proposal to the university. It was approved, and the program became an official offering in fall 1960.[28] What emerged was a curriculum that shared content with architecture and urban planning while clearly establishing its own niche both professionally and pedagogically.[29]

The approved proposal for landscape architecture shared two years of common courses or preprofessional requirements with architecture (including sophomore-year courses in representation, technology, and human behavior) followed by three years of professional training that progressively emphasized landscape theory, design, and construction, as well as ecology and natural systems. A solid architectural foundation provided the fundamentals, and advanced courses addressed the sciences distinct to landscape architecture. In the fourth and fifth years, the landscape design studios took on large-scale landscape problems, primarily in urban contexts.

Haag's curriculum also drew from disciplines across the university to include courses on anthropology, sociology, and forestry. The geography course in the natural history of the Pacific Northwest and Puget Sound taught by Professor Arthur Kruckeberg became a requirement for landscape architecture students. Recommended courses included philosophy, art, and poetry. The program offered the opportunity to study more broadly than many professional degree programs and allowed architecture majors to cross over to landscape architecture without losing credits, as a number of students chose to do.

Although the program was approved, Haag still needed to promote the practice of landscape architecture to students and reached out to those who had never even heard of the profession. In an effort to engage students in his mission to improve the world through landscape architecture, he published his vision for the program in the February 23,1960, issue of *The Daily*, the university's student newspaper. This statement addressed popular interest by emphasizing increased focus on social activism together with stewardship of the environment:

> Landscape Architecture is the art-science of planning land for human use and enjoyment. It is the only profession concerned with the entire problem of relating man to his environment. Here in Washington, a most important effort must be made to CONSERVE the natural resources that impart a special Northwest quality. We must recognize these qualities and RESTORE them where they have been ravaged. The landscape architect must join forces with the architect and the planner to CREATE new concepts of environment in extreme situations.[30]

With its emphasis on conserving, restoring, and creating, Haag's description was grounded in values that meshed with what his students recall as a growing desire for civic engagement.[31] As Haag wrote in an early draft of the *Daily* article, "One hears a great deal these days about the social man, the economic man, etc. . . . good, fine—but let's not forget the natural man."

LANDSCAPE ARCHITECTURE AS MAGIC

Haag's teaching in the studio and the classroom emphasized the role that landscape architecture might serve not only as a profession but also as a life perspective.

> Nature is my life force, the processes, the beauty, the transcendental transient qualities. That is my main force, my life force. . . . I have a farm and I grow a lot of trees, etc., and that to me is like my parents are to a lot of people. . . . The farm fills that role. My practice is like a good wife. It has certain constancies to it, . . . but certain unexpected things happen too. You have new sites, new processes, different clients, etc. It's an exciting thing to do. My professing here at the UW is like my mistress. . . . You should fall in love this time of year every year.[32]

Haag defined landscape architecture for students as offering three unique services: grading plans that treat the earth as

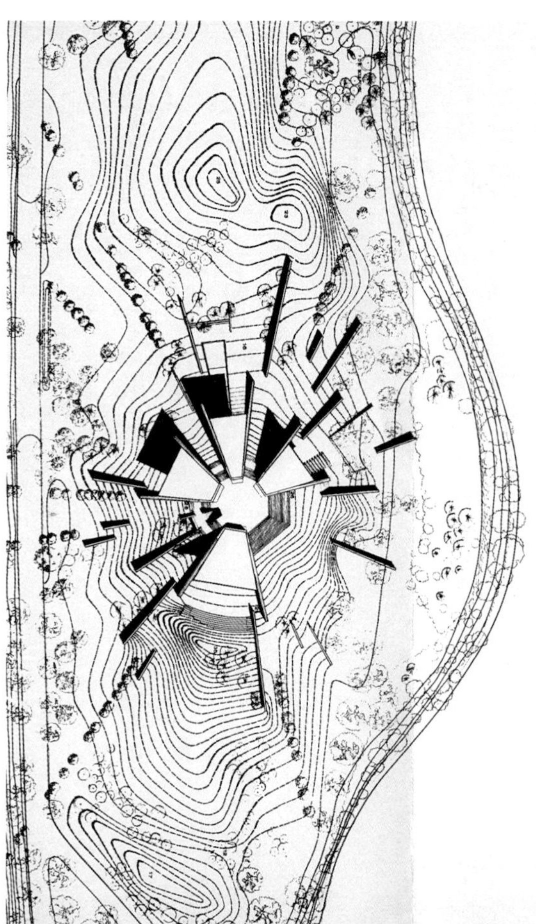

LANDSCAPE ARCHITECTURE

LANDSCAPE ARCHITECTURE is a young and growing profession combining the arts, engineering, social sciences, and natural history—a career with a challenging range of possibilities

LANDSCAPE ARCHITECTURE deals with the out-of-doors—
conserving the natural, restoring the ravaged, and creating a favorable environment for man

LANDSCAPE ARCHITECTURE involves comprehensive design for construction of an engineering nature—grading, earth sculpture, surveying, drainage, designing highways—
and a knowledge of plants, their performance and function in the landscape

LANDSCAPE ARCHITECTURE IS THE ART AND SCIENCE OF PLANNING LAND FOR HUMAN USE AND ENJOYMENT

THE LANDSCAPE ARCHITECT'S WORK

Through the working out of his own creative design and through working with allied professionals, the landscape architect attempts to satisfy man's desire for beauty and purpose in his environment.

He presents preliminary plans, sketches, and reports followed by precise drawings, including general site plans, grading plans, construction details, road profiles, planting plans, specifications and cost estimates. Bids are called and contracts issued and construction work begins, usually with personal supervision.

THE LANDSCAPE ARCHITECT'S OPPORTUNITIES

The increase in population, living standards, and leisure time here and in foreign countries ensures a challenging career for the landscape architect. There are employment opportunities with architectural or engineering offices; with landscape architectural and city planning organizations; with the United States government in urban renewal, conservation, park and recreational work; and in the field of education; or the graduate may open a private office, serving clients as does a lawyer or doctor. Beginning salaries range from $350 to $400 a month. Age or sex have little to do with success in this profession.

THE CURRICULUM IN LANDSCAPE ARCHITECTURE

Design courses in the curriculum are intended to aid the student in using his increasing knowledge.

Problems are given, ranging from the layout of home and school sites, parks and subdivisions, to city and regional land problems. Professional visitors are consulted. Lectures, movies, and class discussion concern problems in landscape architecture, and organized field trips allow inspection of a wide range of projects.

BACHELOR OF LANDSCAPE ARCHITECTURE

The University of Washington five-year curriculum leading to the Bachelor's degree provides students with basic competence within the areas of land planning and design but also with the sound liberal education essential to future development.

FACILITIES

The Department of Landscape Architecture is housed in the Architecture Hall on campus, where drafting, lecture and seminar rooms are provided. Shop facilities provide basic woodworking tools. The nearby arboretum serves as an outdoor laboratory for planting experiments.

5.4 Brochure for the University of Washington Landscape Architecture Program, with Haag's Franklin Delano Roosevelt Memorial competition submission to the left, 1963.

sculpture rather than as an inert material; planting plans that arrange living and growing plants to contain space and catch light; and synthesis, the high-wire act of the profession, the magic, the mystic. Grading as a means of sculpting land was considered a primary tool. Haag criticized land artists such as Robert Smithson and Michael Heizer, describing their work as treating land as if it were cardboard, an inert material. Instead, he suggested, one could use land, soil, and water as dynamic elements and shape experience over time and space. Land was an active agent of experience as well as a design medium.[33]

Design was not merely the sum of the parts, but, as Haag described it, a kind of magic that offered dynamic experiences, supported healthy and thriving environments, and narrated a mythical relationship between culture and nature. In the 1960s, the practice of landscape architecture as a civic engagement that addressed growing concern for the environment and cultural practices offered one of the most exciting opportunities in any design field.

One course that specifically built on this potential was "Theory and Perception" (LA 230), which Haag taught as a two-credit seminar for architecture students. The course eventually became the core theory course for landscape architecture students.[34] Haag taught the course from 1959 to 1996, using it to articulate his vision of landscape architecture as a melding of the humanities, the arts, and the sciences, a means of stewardship of the earth and its cultures.[35] Officially, the course content was a "general survey, orientation, and introduction to basic theory of landscape architecture";[36] in reality, it was a complex investigation of theory and practice. It quickly became one of the most popular courses in the college.

Haag's lectures were notorious for being enthusiastic calls to action as well as stream-of-consciousness talks about the earth and his personal land ethic. He challenged students to consider important philosophical dialogues and scientific discourses by requiring reflection essays.[37] He encouraged them to become familiar with the avant-garde in painting, sculpture, literature, and design by visiting the local museums and galleries and taking courses in contemporary art. Such an education would be grounded in critical thinking.

Haag modeled engagement in intellectual exploration by sharing the influence of theories on his thinking. He was known for paraphrasing Charles Darwin's concepts of the connectivity and relativity of all nature—"There is no loosening of one thread in the blanket without stressing every other thread or unraveling it"—explaining that the blanket is a metaphor for nature.[38] He considered Henry David Thoreau a high priest for landscape architects and his *Walden* "a poetic description of a man possessed by and therefore possessing his environment."[39] In the introduction to his course, he told students,

> *Walden*, reread it every spring. Take it out in the woods with you, to a pond, a lake. Look at other people's farms, enjoy them. . . . Loren Eisley—he's kind of a nature freak, poet, writes in a very lyrical poetic way about earth history, earth drama, man's evolution and attitudes. Loren Eisley, *The Immense Journey*, we're going to take part of that journey here. . . . Another book, if you can find it, by Paul Shepard, . . . *The Tender Carnivore*, . . . I guarantee . . . will shake you up. When I read that, I began to question a lot of precepts, a lot of ideas and attitudes that I had down pat to my own satisfaction.[40]

Haag introduced students to Goethe's writings, Thoreau's essay on civil disobedience, and William Strunk Jr. and E. B. White's *The Elements of Style* (1918). Ian McHarg's *Design with Nature* joined the others on the bookshelf after it was published in 1969, followed by Ann Whiston Spirn's *Granite Garden* of 1984 and *Earth in the Balance* by Al Gore in 1992, as did discussions of the Gaia theory by James Lovelock and Lynn Margulis. Students read poetry and contemplated paintings by Paul Cézanne and Leonardo da Vinci, the abstractions in the cave paintings in Lascaux, France, and the work of Chinese and Japanese painters and scholars.

Haag shared issues of J. B. Jackson's journal *Landscape* with students and explored the significance of the vernacular landscape, the everyday landscape of community and human settlement.[41] He drew on Kevin Lynch's *The Image of the City* (1960), which explains how architects might understand the ways in which the public perceives city form and how mental maps shape one's reading of city life. He added the perspective historian Leo Marx articulated in *The Machine in the Garden: Technology and the Pastoral Ideal in America* (1964), which discusses the dialectical tension between the pastoral ideal in the United States and the sweeping transformations brought about by machine technology and urban development. Yi-Fu Tuan's work, in particular his books *Topophilia* (1974) and *Space and Place* (1977), grounded Haag's emerging interest in a deeper exploration of why images and experience lead to associations and perceptions of places, particularly city and urban landscapes. Jay Appleton's *The Experience of Landscape* (1975) became required reading as soon as it was available. These books reflect almost two decades of focus on human perceptions of cities and modern spaces in the twentieth century. They reveal the evolution of designers toward an increasing appreciation of public perception and the call to engage the public in the design and planning of cities. Haag tapped all of these sources in his teaching and mentoring of his students.

Haag's visual presentations seduced students with images from around the world, most noticeably from Japan. His lectures reflected the growing interest in Japanese art and architecture among the college faculty and the architectural community. Lionel Pries had used Japanese elements such as shoji screens in his work, the local architect Gene Zema visited Japan multiple times and collected Japanese art, and Victor Steinbrueck had visited Japan and then shared his experiences with students. With the arrival of Phil Thiel in 1961, interest in Japan, as well as in human behavior and perception, expanded.[42] The Japanese architect Teiji Ito joined the college in 1963 as a lecturer in Asian studies and an instructor in the college, further strengthening the focus on Japan.[43]

Haag used his experience in Japan to encourage students to see differently by relying on alternative reference points and frameworks. He drew on the pedagogical values espoused by White, illustrating the need to develop new eyes by looking, reading, and exploring carefully and closely. His slides featured vernacular images from the Japanese countryside, of farmers, textiles, and offering poems, and displayed Japanese paintings and scrolls. He paired the slides with photographs of temples and ancient gardens such as Saihō-ji and Ryōan-ji, demonstrating how such places were intimately connected to one another in tradition, spirit, and experience. One could not fully comprehend the meditation garden without understanding the agricultural practice of rice cultivation, Haag told his students. The real experience of the garden, he explained, was located in the larger experience of a sequence of experiences and views that together form a regional aesthetic. Through photography, he choreographed the discovery of Japanese gardens for students in Seattle. In these ways, he actively connected study of the arts and cultural explorations of place to the design process, a set of relationships that excited students who envisioned themselves as global citizens. For Haag, without landscape, "life, soul, and thought are inconceivable,"[44] and through his images and readings, he infused his students with that enthusiasm.

Design studios served as another platform for modeling Haag's design praxis.[45] His studios became known for their rigorous design exploration and Haag's clear bridging of theory and practice.[46] He often began by asking students to establish a concise program of activities that were both required and possible by working with the proposed client as well as drawing from their own experience. Intuition was valued alongside formal investigation and research. Students were expected to consider who and what issues were missing from the discussions by referring to an extensive reading list. They might even question the purpose of the project and ask how it might be challenged in order to address a broader set of social, cultural, and ecological purposes. Through this work, Haag expected students to develop an attitude about the project, an attitude that he hoped would inform their future practice.

Students were tasked with analyzing the site and discovering the genius loci, or character of the place. Haag asked that they develop an extensive series of drawings alongside reports on the related ecology, geology, and hydrology of the site plus write about or illustrate its social and cultural narratives. Haag explained the long association of natural sciences with design evident in Frederick Law Olmsted's work in the nineteenth century and subsequent work by ecologists and designers such as Jens Jensen. At a time when others were just rediscovering the science of ecology and environmental design, Haag's program emphasized these areas of knowledge as the basis of good design.[47]

With the analysis and program defined, students were to search for synergies that would lead to a plan. As students made adjustments, the plan would evolve, and the whole "expression will achieve fine form in close harmony with the original terrain without serious sacrifice of important plan relationships as established by the scheme," Haag argued. He outlined the sequence of the laws of site planning for his "Theory and Perception" course in 1965:

1. develop an approach and attitude toward site planning;
2. know thy site—sleep on it, muse with the genius loci;
3. function follows form; and
4. never but never build on the best part of the site—save it for your garden!

Students were intrigued by Haag's ability to move fluidly between the abstract of a theory and the tangible quality of a rule. He modeled the transition of the abstract theory of non-striving to the rules of site engagement. They found his lectures compelling, if not always easy to follow and even harder to imitate.

Haag offered students design challenges that would require "thinking outside the box." For example, when given the opportunity soon after arriving at the school, he devised an early sketch problem, or *esquisse-esquisse*.[48] In asking students to "design a tree," he sought to have them consider the complex character of trees, nature, and the role of the designer in the dialogue between nature and culture. He wanted them to understand that a tree is a living entity, that design must have life. Instead, what he received were drawings of trees, not designs of trees. As he later wrote:

> The assignment was as vague as a line of a Zen koan, but actually, it was in line with the previous programs. Of course, a tree can be drawn, sculpted, photographed, planted, hybridized, killed, bisected, autopsied, eulogized, worshiped, etc. . . . but it is beyond human capability to "design a tree," beyond arrogance to even imagine that millions of years of testing co-evolutionary reciprocal relationships, competing (Survival of the Fittest), cooperating (Origin of Species), the process Charles Darwin named Natural Selection could be captured as a "design."[49]

Haag used such focused projects to conduct a dialogue with students about the role of representation and imagination in design as well as the role of science. While he was reportedly never asked by the faculty to devise a shared sketch problem again, he continued to challenge students to consider landscape as a spatial, temporal, and aesthetic practice that required a synthesis of nature and culture. One can't design a tree, but one can design with trees.

When Hermann retired in 1961, Robert Dietz was named dean of the college and expanded the design trajectory by emphasizing a culture of research, rather than pure design, which he believed should underpin design in the school. Haag responded by emphasizing scientific research in his studios and in his experimental approach.[50] In an advanced studio in 1964, he asked students to consider what metrics, measures, and criteria from the science disciplines might be applied to design. Students learned through projects how one discipline fostered inquiry in another as they sought to establish design criteria for parks and recreation plans, to design a subdivision as a "way of life" or a learning landscape for the Western Washington College of Education campus, and to investigate the concept of regionalism in design. Haag asked students in one studio to add energy accounting to the metrics of functionality.

Such projects were, as Haag wrote, case studies for design. They were focused on public areas and often on urban redevelopment projects. This concentration on the urban did not negate a concern for the natural in Haag's perspective. Instead, he believed, it was the role of the landscape architect to design so as to reveal natural systems and environments, to reveal the ecology of the landscape, be it urban or rural. As he noted in his curriculum description, the program focused on the "restoration and the recreation of new environments where the natural has been damaged, but a major emphasis will be on the conservation of natural landscape values."[51] In 1975, in a design studio offered a year after the oil embargo, he asked students to research what he called "symbiomsteading," for which they had to determine the minimum and optimum land and elements required to sustain a single person. The idea was to design a system that would foster a reciprocal relationship between an individual and the natural resources of the site. Haag believed in thorough research, whether it was social research on human behavior or ecolog-

5.5 Student diagram of Haag's min-max approach, LA 230.

5.6 Laurie Olin student project, University of Washington, Seattle, 1961.

ical research on the habitats of a site, as the basis for designing with nature and culture.[52]

Drawing on his experience in Japan, Haag taught what he called the "min-max approach," which required the designer to consider the minimum means of creating or instigating the maximum effect. The process involved a thorough site analysis to identify existing resources and then imagining what the desired maximum effect might be. If they were to achieve the maximum effect, Haag believed, students needed to know the basics of ecology, biology, and botany as well as geology and hydrology. With this knowledge, a landscape architect could design a minimum insertion or intervention that would initiate the maximum response environmentally, socially, politically, and economically.

Creativity was equally as important as research and analysis. And creativity meant building the imagination in response to pragmatic problems. In winter 1963, Haag's grade IV (LA 461) studio developed a garden for Architecture Hall. Haag had joined the University Landscape Architecture Committee and was interested in his students' ideas. In his studio projects on the future of Gas Works Park, Seattle Center, and other local urban sites, he asked students to propose creative responses to the challenges of real places and real conditions.

Haag also valued creativity as a purely imaginative project. In the 1964 spring quarter, he offered a design grade IV (LA 462) studio that began with an assignment to design the "secret garden of your dreams in your imaginary landscape." Mindful of Oscar Wilde's comment "If your maps do not include UTOPIA, I am not interested," his teaching emphasized mining the imagination. He did not allow students to use words on their design boards, challenging them to explore their imaginations visually and graphically. Haag believed that this approach gave the minds of visually oriented students the space to move beyond words and to formulate images, the source of imagination.

Both of these approaches to creativity—the response to pragmatic conditions and the purely imaginative—were essential to Haag's balance of creativity and observation, the ability to think at multiple scales. They could be combined in what he called his "theory of non-striving." The "non-striving" attitude grew, like the "min-max approach," out of Haag's experience in Japan. It was a state of mind, not a style or a method, maybe not even an approach. It meant identifying the genius loci of the place, using existing resources, recycling what was there, or in the words of his mentor, Stanley White seeing with new eyes. Non-striving was both an attitude of the designer and a character of the design. The designer was meant to simply discover the answer to Louis Kahn's question "What does the brick want to be?"[53] The design was non-striving when it could be experienced as part of the larger landscape, as an active agent in the making of a community and a place. This was one of the most challenging of ideas for students, as it became clear only with practice. Many of Haag's students would be able to claim only decades later that they had finally learned to design in a non-striving manner.[54]

A similar ability to move between abstractions and guidelines framed Haag's teaching of architectural space. Space as a modernist concept had become part of the vocabulary of the modern movement in architecture and, after World War II, increasingly a part of landscape architecture. While he was working in Halprin's office in San Francisco, Haag wrote about space in landscape, an element that would define a language of design and landscape distinct from that of architecture or planning.

> The perception of space is of a higher order than the perception of the pictorial and of the plastic, i.e. sculptural. . . . In some painting, the surface plane has been deliberately "opened" and the eye is invited to the surface to probe around "within" the painting—a curious kind of 2½ D. This begins to suggest sculpture which usually exhibits a convex surface and requires of the eyes a stereoscopic tracking to "feel" its inherent third-dimensionality. Movement and the tactile faculties may provide further insight. Architecture demands a spatial perception of a higher order, it involves a kinetic response.[55]

Haag described landscape architectural space as distinct, in design and in experience. Architectural space shaped temporal and spatial experiences, but landscape, according to Haag, was also seasonal and geographic. In this description, he addressed the issues of space and time as well as the aesthetic and sensual character of landscape.

> Over-simplified as a formula, landscape architecture $3d^2 + X$, the third dimensional is squared because the participant is monitoring varying spatial experience in going to and returning from the architecture. X equals all the unknown influences to which the participant is subjected; these may be: the underfoot feeling of cobblestones or of mud, the kinetics of climbing, turning, etc., the smell of vegetal growth or of engine offal, the sound of wind in leaves or of newspapers blowing, etc. These, too, are contributing components to the emotions of spatial sensation.[56]

Haag's focus on the experience of movement and spatial sensations was a perspective that was increasingly part of the design dialogue of the 1960s. Halprin was investigating similar ideas, although he concentrated more on improvisation and embodying the experience of being in the landscape. The geographer Jay Appleton was developing theories of landscape perception based in the instincts of prospect and refuge. Haag was interested less in how the public might imagine a space than in how his design might arouse the senses, engage the body, and alter the user's perception of place through movement.

In addition to these more philosophical investigations, plants remained a critical element in the design process for Haag. He taught students to treat plants as a dynamic medium of design rather than as a building material as noted in his notes for course in Planting Design (LA 465). They were never to refer to plants as "plant materials"; they were plants. The appropriate use of plants, particularly trees, was essential for shaping space. Always the nurseryman, Haag insisted that students know their plants by the Latin names, by growth habits, and by relationships and design character. His lectures were richly illustrated with plants in designed landscapes and in natural surroundings. He would show examples of different uses of plants, including Bernard Maybeck's wisteria at the Christian Science Church in Berkeley or Osmundson's roof garden in San Francisco, and compare the trees of Versailles with the beech bosk designed by Beatrix Farrand for Dumbarton Oaks in Washington, D.C. He derided the 1968 Ford Foundation Building courtyard garden in New York City by Roche and Dinkeloo with Daniel Kiley as a "pipe dream" because a real forest cannot be re-created inside architecture, even inside a city. "Would it thunder and rain?" he asked in the lecture on planting he presented for his landscape theory course.

While Haag celebrated a wide variety of plants, he commended the use of a limited plant palette in any single design. He called for the determination of an LCD (least common denominator) list of plants that thrived best in any given landscape.[57] "Thrived" meant not merely proliferated, nor did it necessarily require only native plants; it meant to grow vigorously and contribute to the usefulness and pleasure of the place. Once criticized for using London plane trees and honey locusts rather than native trees for Seattle Center, he responded that because of the particular soils (contractor soil mixed with Vashon till) and the microclimates of the urban campus, native maples and conifers would not thrive and thus were wrong for the site. He argued that "urban centers are so destroyed that any of the native plants would have a difficult time making it there, so if I'm after effect, I have to somehow simulate it or symbolize it and use plants that will endure."[58] Haag would remind students of his discussion with Japanese professor Kobayashi about the twenty-three plants used to create Japanese gardens. He asked students to prepare an LCD list for every design, selecting the plants that thrived horticulturally and would nourish the program. Haag concluded many lectures with a paraphrase of his favorite Japanese philosopher, Yanagi: "A thing that cannot be used has something negative about its beauty."[59]

Haag taught design as a love affair with the earth and nature. For him, design was a form of Zen practice that engaged culture and nature in a dialogue in intimate and thoughtful ways. It was not a profession so much as an art and a way of life. He encouraged students to understand a site by "making love to the earth." When he stated that they should "copulate with the land," he was conveying a deep belief in the need to engage intimately with place. It was not always easy to understand Haag, and while he inspired some students to pursue a praxis that would challenge contemporary practice, those who wanted to learn the technical skills required for professional practice were frustrated. Haag, however, was not interested in job training and the limitations of professional requirements; he wanted to teach an approach to design that embraced his values.

The Cosmos *is an experiment*
The Universe *is a park*
The Earth *is a pleasure ground*
Nature *is the theater*
The Landscape *is our stage*
Let us write *the script*
Direct *the play*
And embrace *the audience*
With compassion and joy
For Life[60]

BUILDING AN INSTITUTION

As the program in landscape architecture grew, Haag reached out to others to help teach the courses and lead studios. As early as July 1963, he reduced his teaching commitments to three-quarter time so that he could devote more time to his practice and allow himself the flexibility to work on campus projects without a conflict of interest.[61] While some in the college questioned Haag's mixing of practice and teaching, he believed it made design real and supported a more experimental approach to practice.[62] To make up for his reduced teaching, he hired practitioners for his firm who could also teach, a solution he learned from Sasaki.[63] Donald Sakuma taught construction and advanced graphics and led design studios while working in Haag's firm.[64] Over the next decade, Haag hired Laurie Olin, Kenichi Nakano, Frank James, Jerry Diethelm, and Robert Hanna to teach site planning and graphics as part-time lecturers while they were employed by the firm. They would continue to serve as lecturers through the early 1980s. In this way, Haag continued to influence the entire program even though he no longer taught all of the courses.

While he was most visible for students in his teaching role, Haag also took his role as professional mentor seriously. He would hire students as designers for projects in the office and encourage them to develop and draw alternate ideas on paper. At night, he might come in and review the work on the tables, leaving long notes or sketches on the drawings. As a mentor, he is remembered as a man of few words except when lecturing on theory or practice.[65] Frank James recalled that "Haag made mystic statements & let his acolytes loose to create with simple nudges. . . . Enabling Zen Growth and Zen PRODUCT."[66] He would engage with students over a beer at the end of the day or on excursions in the countryside. Former students still remember some of the trips as wild excursions into drugs, drink, and philosophy, with Haag oriented toward the latter.[67]

Haag continued to develop the Department of Landscape Architecture. Sakuma was the only other tenure-track faculty member from 1963 to 1969, with the rest part-time lecturers hired on a course-by-course basis. Haag likely kept the permanent faculty small so that he could retain flexibility. In 1964, the department was officially listed in the *University of Washington Bulletin* as a program in the College of Architecture and Urban Planning. In 1969, the Landscape Accreditation Review Board accredited the bachelor of landscape architecture program. It became increasingly clear that the department and program would need an administrative leader, essentially the chair position that Haag had never quite accepted.[68] In July 1970, the college appointed a new department chair, Robert Buchanan, from the landscape architecture program at the University of California, Berkeley. With Buchanan in charge, Haag negotiated to teach half-time, less than his previous schedule, leaving more time for practice and activism. The 1970 university catalog lists Haag as teaching the majority of landscape studios and courses, with Don Sakuma and Frank James teaching construction and design studios and Grant Jones serving as a guest lecturer and studio instructor.[69] By 1974, there was a growing core of landscape faculty members, including Buchanan as chair and David C. Streatfield and Richard K. Untermann, who both joined in 1971. The Master of Landscape Architecture program was initiated in 1979 and accredited in 1986, with a focus on research. Haag was interested in research but was more concerned with merging environmental sciences with an aesthetic purpose, in essence, what he had described in 1960 as a practice that was an "art-science of planning land for human use and enjoyment, . . . concerned with the entire problem of relating man to his environment."[70]

Haag was promoted to full professor in 1980 and selected as a fellow of the American Society of Landscape Architects in 1983. He retired from teaching in 1996 and was named professor emeritus in 1998. Through his four decades of teaching, Haag mentored hundreds of students and taught many the non-striving attitude and min-max approach. They recalled the importance of learning from Japanese design without needing to imitate Japanese gardens. They reminisced about Haag as a designer in dialogue with the earth, nature, and the genius loci. There were rough times, such as when he led students through value-building exercises rather than teaching them the nuts and bolts of practice. Asked to have students submit résumés for faculty advisers to review, Haag assigned essays on design philosophies. Final exams could include surprises, such as the tongue-in-cheek question "If weep holes did not relieve the wailing wall, when did weep holes become necessary? Answer: with the advent of the concrete wall." Or the question might have a political agenda: "What is bureaucratic pollution? Answer: a malodorous, toxic, word/

paper storm from politicians, bureaucrats that stifle creativity and bankrupt firms, causing frustration and mental depression and the flight of joy."[71] This unorthodox approach may well have been frustrating for some, but others found it an exciting way to think about a career.

gardens of the pacific northwest

HAAG WAS ATTRACTED TO THE PACIFIC NORTHWEST FOR reasons similar to those of many others who settled the region. The dramatic and diverse landscapes attracted people who dreamed of spending time on the lakes, rivers, and mountains, all within easy reach of the city of Seattle. These interests were evident in the choice of homes as well as in leisure time activities. Residents chartered organizations such as the Mountaineers, which formed in 1906 to host outdoor trips that also served as social gatherings. A group of wilderness advocates came together in 1916 to form the Co-Operative Campers, whose aim was to "make our mountains accessible through co-operative camps and to encourage a love of simple living in the open air."[1] There were also those who were tended toward the entrepreneurial. In 1920, Eddie Bauer opened his first store providing equipment for outdoor sports. Lloyd Anderson, a Mountaineers member, launched Recreational Equipment Incorporated (REI) in 1939. This cooperative buying organization pooled annual membership fees to purchase equipment in bulk and resell it at competitive prices. Such entrepreneurs were responding to the increasing call for specialized outdoor equipment and clothes as well as maps and guidebooks. Together, they constituted a constellation of outdoors-oriented residents and communities.

HOMES AND GARDENS FOR OUTDOOR FAMILIES

The families who hiked, skied, and camped often appreciated homes and gardens that encouraged the outdoor life. Their gardens often blurred the "boundaries with nature," as historian Matthew Klingle has suggested. Seattleites believed that in the natural landscape children would "grow straight as pines, learned in water craft and wood lore."[2] With this love of the outdoors, suburban sprawl seemed inevitable as families sought to be a near a city while enjoying the amenities of the countryside.

Seattle is on an isthmus, with the twenty-two-mile-long Lake Washington to the east and Puget Sound to the west. After 1945, suburban development spread north, east, and south. Most development projects were fairly conventional, but where the hilly topography limited conventional development, more innovative patterns of land subdivision were sometimes imagined and constructed. An early example was the Highlands, north of Seattle on land overlooking Puget Sound, which the Olmsted Brothers planned in the early twentieth century as an enclave for the wealthy. They left the natural topography largely intact, laid out narrow roads following the contours of the site, and divided the land into large irregular lots, many with views to the sound framed by large trees they had preserved from the original site.

In 1946, a group of architects and University of Washington faculty came together to create the Hilltop, a visionary development southeast of the eastside community of Bellevue. Their design retained seventeen acres of land in a central community park and a greenbelt that wrapped the development. Houses were located away from the roads and sited to take advantage of views and maximize privacy. Many were custom-designed by Seattle's best-known architects, including Bassetti & Morse, Chiarelli & Kirk, Perry B. Johanson (of NBBJ), Wendell Lovett, Lionel Pries, Tucker, Shields & Terry, and others. Landscape architects such as William Teufel and Francis Dean, from the California firm of Eckbo, Royston and Dean, and, later, Glen Hunt, Robert Chittock, and Haag also contributed. The houses and their gardens were distinctively Northwest Modern.

Even though most suburban development was not as visionary, postwar designers developed an architectural approach that came to be called "Northwest regional modernism." It included careful consideration of the landscape in siting the architecture, use of natural materials, large areas of glass, views to water or mountains or both, and an indoor-outdoor flow of space.[3] Such designs provided opportunities for the growing community of landscape architects.

SEATTLE'S LANDSCAPE ARCHITECTURE COMMUNITY

Although residents sought new homes and gardens that supported the new informal indoor-outdoor patterns of living, the landscape architecture community was still relatively small at mid-century. The first landscape architect of note, Edward Otto Schwägerl (1842–1910), who was born in Bavaria and raised in Paris, arrived in the region in 1890 and served as Seattle's superintendent of parks from 1892 to 1896. Nevertheless, the dominant landscape firm in the region in the first decades of the twentieth century was Olmsted Brothers of Brookline, Massachusetts. The Olmsted firm received many of the most important commissions, including the plans for Seattle's parks and boulevards, the early campus of the University of Washington, the Alaska-Yukon-Pacific Exposition, and major subdivisions such as the Highlands. In time, others arrived, and among those who arrived in the 1940s are Cassius Beardsley (1910–1986), who received a degree in horticulture from Oregon State University and worked for the Seattle Parks and Recreation department in the 1950s, then headed his own practice; and Roberta Wightman (1912–2011), who received her landscape architecture degree from the University of Illinois in 1938 and moved to Seattle in 1944 to work with Edwin Grohs at the Washington Arboretum before starting her own landscape architecture firm. The 1950s brought William G. Teufel (1925–2007), a 1953 graduate of the University of Oregon's landscape architecture program, who launched a successful design firm in Seattle and would work with architects Paul Kirk, Fred Bassetti, and Ralph Anderson on the Century 21 Exposition and Bellevue Community College; and Glen Hunt (1921–1994), originally from Washington, who headed his own landscape firm after 1955 but more importantly was an advocate for landscape design through his articles in the *Seattle Times* from the late 1950s to the early 1970s. The community continued to expand, with newcomers Esther Pearson, Richard I. Yamasaki, and Edward Watanabe.[4] In 1946, landscape architects in the region formed the Washington State Society of Landscape Architects; in 1962, with the group having established its stability, it was accepted as an official chapter of the American Society of Landscape Architects.[5] By the time Haag arrived, the small community had achieved sufficient critical mass to suggest that there was a productive future ahead for the profession.

LAUNCHING A FIRM IN SEATTLE

While Haag had ostensibly come to Seattle to teach, he insisted that he be allowed to practice professionally as well, choosing to be appointed a part-time faculty member. In spring 1959, he opened Richard Haag Associates (RHA) in an abandoned storefront on Fuhrman Avenue, in a primarily residential neighborhood near Eastlake. There was a small grocery and convenience store next door, and it was walking distance from school. Just down the block, halfway to the university, was Sam's Red Robin, where architects, artists, and academics gathered regularly to drink and debate.[6] Design was discussed in the midst of political, social, and cultural debate, offering a rich background to ideas about cities and the role of design.

To build his practice, Haag hired his best students, those who could draw well, those who showed curiosity, and those with good plant knowledge. Grant Jones excelled in

6.1 Richard Haag Associates staff, Fuhrman Avenue office, Seattle, 1964. Left to right, back row: Jerry Deithelm, Robert Hanna, Miles Yanick, Grant Jones, Ken Rupard. Front row: Jerry Finrow, Patti Jorgensen, Richard Haag, Don Sakuma. Not pictured: Mary Edstrom.

his knowledge of plants and was soon a part of the Haag office. In addition to Hanna, Jones, and Olin, Jerry Finrow, Jerry Diethelm, Sally Swanson, Dale Dennis, and Sherry Fike worked in the office.[7] A core group remained for years, including Kenichi Nakano,[8] Craig S. Campbell, Miles Yanick, Frank James, and Mary Edstrom (later Booth). Haag hired Donald Sakuma from the Sasaki office to design for the firm and teach at the university. Lottie Eskilsson worked for Haag in the mid-1960s before launching her own practice, one among a significant early community of women in architecture practicing in and around Seattle. This was an incredibly dynamic community of young designers, inspired by the Pacific Northwest and engaged in the arts, culture, and urban life of Seattle.[9] For the students and young graduates, the office was an atelier where they learned to practice, although it could be a chaotic, sometimes stressful learning process for some. These were also the very designers who would eventually become Haag's strongest competitors in Seattle when they branched out on their own.

A REGIONAL DESIGN APPROACH

In the decades after World War II, as the architectural and art communities grew, a distinctive body of architecture emerged that architectural historian Grant Hildebrand has labeled the Northwest School or the Puget Sound School: a community of designers who defined a regional approach to architecture, particularly the modestly sized houses and small professional offices, libraries, churches, and civic institutions.[10] The architecture was modern in its lack of historical imitations and its frequent expression of structure. The Seattle architects emphasized regional materials in a natural state or minimally treated in order to withstand the wet climate. Most of the relevant buildings were residential or small institutional structures of one or two stories and featured a remarkable level of craftsmanship. The siting within the landscape was often done in collaboration with landscape architects and featured views of mountains, woods, and water.[11]

The houses and their gardens were intimately linked to their environment. Seattle's relatively mild winters and moderate summers encouraged an indoor-outdoor lifestyle, as the rain was often only a drizzle. Decks and terraces were protected under overhanging roofs and served as active transitions between indoors and outdoors, visually and physically. Broad windows framed the view from inside to the landscape while offering a transparent boundary between the house and the garden landscapes. Gardens became literal extensions of the living area, just as the indoors became shelter in bad weather.[12]

There was also a Japanese character to both the architecture and the landscape architecture. In the Pacific Northwest, this interest was grounded in geography and local culture as well as the more general interest of modernists in Japanese aesthetics and crafts. Geographically, the city and region served as thresholds on the Pacific Rim, intermediate between Japan and the East Coast. By the 1950s, there was increasing interest locally in the Japanese use of wood in buildings, both structurally and as a craft. Additionally, there were Japanese craftsmen and artists in the city, includ-

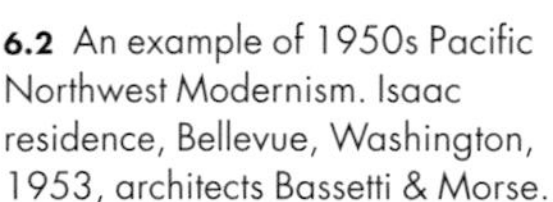

6.2 An example of 1950s Pacific Northwest Modernism. Isaac residence, Bellevue, Washington, 1953, architects Bassetti & Morse.

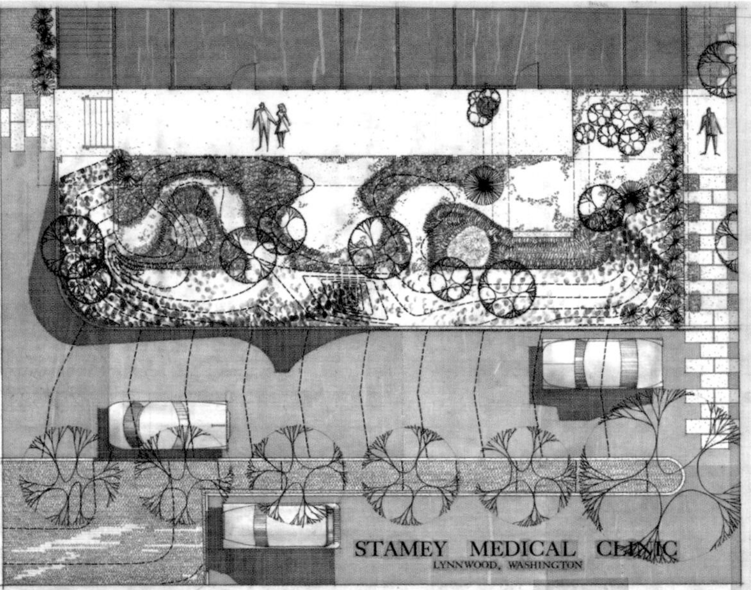

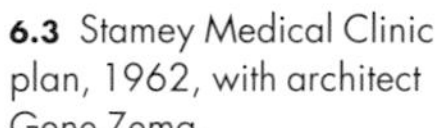

6.3 Stamey Medical Clinic plan, 1962, with architect Gene Zema.

6.4 Stamey Medical Clinic, Lynnwood, Washington, October 1969.

ing George Nakashima, a graduate of the architecture program in 1929 who left Seattle after World War II to become a renowned furniture maker; George Tsutakawa, a well-respected sculptor best known for his fountains, of which there are examples throughout Seattle; and Paul Horiuchi, known for his collage paintings and his murals for Seattle's Century 21 Exposition in 1962. There were also Seattle residents who traveled to Japan frequently, such as Gene Zema, who visited Japan more than sixty times, developing an expertise in Japanese antiquities; Philip Thiel, who had traveled in Japan extensively; and of course Haag, who had lived in Japan.[13]

Haag often worked with architects who were interested in regional design, including Fred Bassetti, Wendell Lovett, Gene Zema, Ralph Anderson, Paul Kirk, and Ibsen Nelsen. They often shared an appreciation for the landscape of the Pacific Northwest and looked to Haag to help them incorporate its character in their architecture.[14] Haag worked with Bassetti on his Hilltop house of 1962, his Maiden Lane home and garden in 1977, and his Portage Bay house of 1985–92. Bassetti shared an enthusiasm for trees and wrote to Haag that he had "walked by Steinbrueck's house yesterday morning and found a large tree growing blackberries! what the hell is it?" This was followed by "Start researching great water-loving native NW trees to succeed the dying alder by the shore."[15] The loose style of Haag's drawings for the gardens he was designing for Bassetti reveals how the two designers used sketching as a means of discussion. The gardens were functional and included play areas and vegetable gardens. Bassetti and Haag would go on to design a number of university campuses, modern homes and gardens for the Frey (1962) and Dimmich (1968) families, and the Henry M. Jackson Federal Building (1974) in downtown Seattle.

The Stamey Medical Clinic in Lynnwood, a dental surgery office just north of Seattle, was an important early design for Haag. Completed in 1962 and designed in collaboration with architect Gene Zema, the building used post-and-beam construction, an approach then associated with regional design. The wooden building featured steep pitched roofs and walls. The garden design drew on the character of the architecture

6.5 Haag on a tractor at Trees Nursery, Arlington, Washington, c. 1990.

and the surrounding landscape, merging the two into a unified whole.

Haag worked with his employee Frank James to create a design that would guide patients from the street to the building entrance as well as offer a restful and memorable garden. James was working for Haag in his final year of the architecture program at the University of Washington. He developed the concept and drew the details for the project. As James recalled, Haag "let his architectural acolytes do basic design with little interference except Zen presences, the review for drainage—the sine qua non!!—and the planting plan. None of us, except Grant R. Jones, ever went into planting understanding." The staff also relied on contractors and others to help with some details. James recalled that the contractor for the Stamey clinic project figured out how to create the concrete substrate for the stones.[16]

The Stamey Medical Clinic design reflected what was perceived as a Japanese character in its horizontal orientation,

6.6 Frank James, Princess Louisa Inlet, British Columbia, 1964.

6.7 Grant Jones and Laurie Olin, Lost Wilderness, North Cascades, Washington, September 1963.

low building height, extended eaves, and honest use of local materials, primarily wood. The garden featured an undulating line of local river stones connoting a dynamic riverbed, which was punctuated by two stone cairns as it crossed the front of the building. The stones and boulders marked the site's boundaries and guided the flow of both pedestrians and drivers parking their cars. Years later, Haag would present the project as a design problem for his Architecture 226 class. The problem description read: "The small scale wooden architecture of the Pacific Northwest is internationally acclaimed. The so-called Northwest style has reached a high state of refinement in residences and small clinics. It would seem the problem here is to provide a 'north-west' (whatever that is, let's discuss this point) landscape for this clinic."[17]

This Northwest landscape would, according to Haag, be defined by its plants, specifically its trees. When he arrived in Seattle, he wanted to purchase land for a plant nursery and began by surveying soil types in the farmlands in the region. He eventually located an area in the bottomlands along the Stillaguamish River in Arlington, north of Seattle, that he purchased from a farmer in 1962. The site had good soil, deep enough so that he could eventually transplant large trees, and plenty of water access. Haag considered his nursery, the Trees Nursery, his cathedral and has cultivated his tree collection for fifty years, some for use in his designs, others as experiments in cultivation. Possibly inspired by Harvard's Arnold Arboretum, where he had spent time as a student, and certainly by his family's nursery in Kentucky, Haag sought to introduce hardy tree species into cultivation in the Pacific Northwest. He not only specified the varieties in his plans but also grew the trees while experimenting with microclimates and soils. Haag believed that to if one is to truly know a plant, one must grow it.

In a speech for the Great Garden Vision Symposium in 1993, Haag remarked that plants were the essence and lifeblood of the garden and that landscape architects "are shaping space, modeling space with earth, water, light, time, sometimes structures, pavements . . . but plants are the design element that is unique to our compositions." He continued, "Could any artist living, dead, or yet to come imagine a more exultant medium, a more transcendental palette?" Seasonal change was a critical character of plants, although Haag considered them first for form, then foliage, then flower, fragrance, fruit, and, finally, visual or photogenic qualities. For Haag, plants were the "main space-giving, form-giving, quality-giving elements of any garden."[18] Haag told his students, for "if your vision gives form to space, to earth, water, light through the reciprocal relationship of plants, set aside a wonderful lifetime of trial and error."[19] The importance of Haag's engagement with plants and growing trees continued throughout his career, and the nursery is where he has spent most weekends from spring through fall for the past fifty years, even noting once that he wants to be buried there.

Haag did not necessarily take design staff or students to his nursery, but he led exploratory field trips to the forests, lakes and rivers, and mountains. One year, for example, he decided that instead of giving office bonuses, he would take the staff on a boat trip. They chartered an old motor yacht, the *Maureen*, and with Grant Jones in command, sailed to Princess Louisa Inlet, British Columbia, north of Vancouver. There, they hiked in the spectacular fjordland, thickly covered with wet forest, the only environment of its kind on the Pacific coast, and watched waterfalls cascading down four-hundred-foot cliffs. While the younger employees drank Molsons in a dry cabin, Haag sat cross-legged at the end of a three-hundred-foot floating dock. As James recalled, Haag "really is a zen character."[20] While the excursion was meant partly for relaxation, it was also a learning experience, an investigation of the region and its landscapes, islands, water, and forests. On another trip, the staff headed to the North Cascades to hike in the Lost Wilderness, again retreating from the firm's urban location and focus and learning about the region through deep immersion, a practice that many, including Jones and Olin, would continue throughout their careers.

These trips would become the background for many of the designs that Haag and his design staff created. For the D. L. Sprague family in Seattle, Haag designed a garden highlighting the Pacific Northwest landscape and the opportunities it offered for living in the woods as well as its rich variety of plants. Frank James worked on the project in the Haag office, from initial concepts through construction. The house was located at the center of the site and was surrounded by trees. A gravel-and-stone courtyard served as the entrance garden, with stone pavers providing a dynamic path to the front door and the garage. In the backyard, two wooden decks provided gathering space overlooking a garden of water, trees, stones, and landforms, elements that had become part of Haag's repertoire by this time. In Seattle, it was even possible to design a substantial pool with boulders and a bridge that fit the landscape in a way that Haag never thought worked in California's drought climate. The Seattle environment supported the diversity of trees and shrubs, allowing Haag to create a garden that seemed carved out of the forest. And once again there were references to Japanese gardens, particularly evident in the drawings that Haag produced for the project, such as the view from the bathroom of a specimen tree, the pavilion labeled with a "4.5 mat" geometry with a waiting bench at the end, and even the potted plant on the wooden deck that was drawn to resemble a bonsai tree. The plan itself included a Japanese stamp just above the RHA title block.

Finally, it was important to Haag that the house and gardens merge, allowing the family to move in and out as the weather allowed. Neither the house nor the gardens were ever fully revealed from any one viewpoint, similar to the houses and gardens in books by Jiro Harada and others. Instead they were woven together, offering a sequence of spaces and views that could be learned and enjoyed over time.

The project for Mr. and Mrs. Richard B. Edgar in Issaquah, located east of Seattle, which Haag accepted in April 1966, was to include an entrance court, a redesign of the drive and circular turnaround, a future pool site, an interior paved court, a vegetable garden, a fruit orchard, and woods, with little lawn area and low-maintenance gardens. The architects for the house were Ridenour & Cochran of Seattle, which brought Haag in to design the landscape after the house was

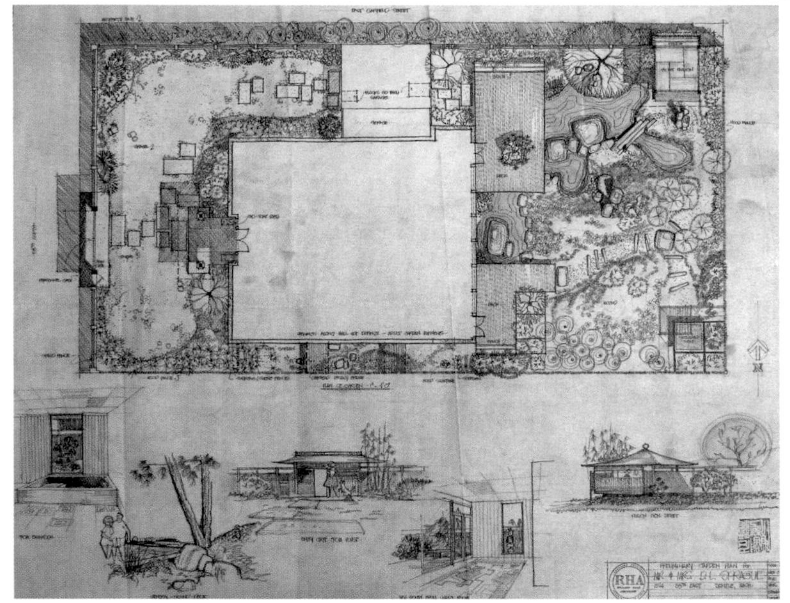

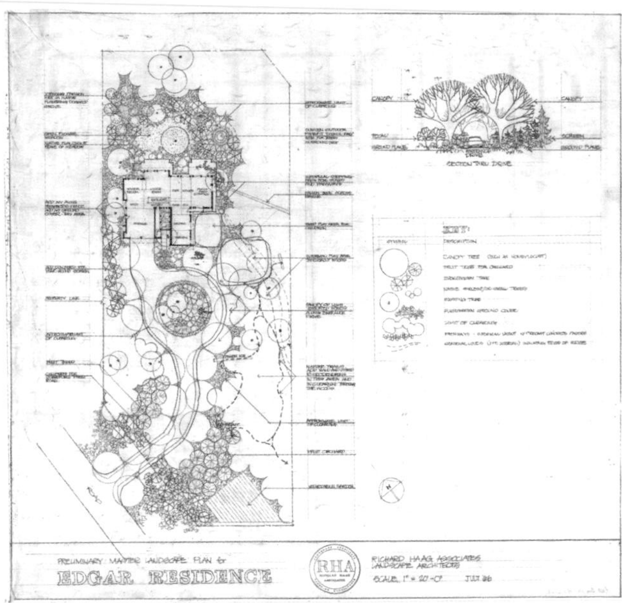

6.8 Sprague garden plan, 1965. Drawing by Frank James

6.9 Edgar garden plan, 1966.

under way. The design would win an award from the Seattle chapter of the American Institute of Architects and be featured as a Home of the Month by the *Seattle Times* in 1966.

By this time, the design process in the Haag office had become relatively established. As there were rarely more than four or five employees in the office, everyone knew every project and pitched in as needed, with one staff member in charge of the project. For the Edgar design, Haag and Mary Booth met initially with the clients on-site. They discussed the clients' needs and desires and asked them to fill out a six-page landscape questionnaire about the amount of time they expected to spend gardening, their level of expertise, their wishes for recreation, and whether they would use a vegetable garden. He asked about their childhood memories of landscapes and requested collections of magazine cutouts and travel photographs of gardens and landscapes that they liked. The questionnaire was long and detailed, and many clients chose to answer just the questions that interested them. The completed questionnaire was returned to the office, where it would be compared to notes taken during the initial meeting, and work would begin to establish program ideas.

Design was an iterative process, and Haag remained in charge while depending on his staff to generate ideas and alternatives. They began with sketches on trace paper, notes written on the sketches, a survey, more notes, and then a more concrete plan. As a form of nudging rather than dominating, Haag would comment on ideas as they progressed by writing or drawing on the sketches, adding descriptions or cartoons that might reflect alternative programs or character. He insisted that designers have all the tools they might need; thus, the office was always well supplied with pencils, pens, charcoal, paper, and drafting and drawing tools. Every drawing was taken seriously, as Laurie Olin learned when Haag snapped angrily at him for sketching an idea on a scrap of trace paper. Scrap paper suggested a scrap idea, so Haag insisted that everything be drawn as if it might be the brilliant idea that would clinch the design process. All drawings were altered and redrawn, and only after a concept had gone through multiple iterations in the office would it be shared with a client. For some projects, particularly public projects, Haag would share alternative plans, but for the most part, he presented what he thought was the strongest idea while leaving room for refinement and modifications.

The staff member in charge attended all meetings with the client and handled the correspondence between the firm and the client. For selected projects, such as the Kukes and Sommerville designs, however, Haag collaborated closely with the client and was the primary person, on paper and on-site. Office staff were responsible for producing the final construction drawings—including a planting plan, a grading and drainage plan, and any construction details that might be necessary—as well as overseeing the bidding and construction. Once the project was completed, there were rarely as-is drawings or formal presentation drawings produced.

While this method generally assured a smooth development process, there was also a certain amount of disorder. With Haag deeply involved in the design, he was stretched thin when the workload increased. The staff, particularly those leading projects, could find themselves in a difficult position, caught between clients who expected schedules and bids to be honored and Haag, who wanted to get each project "just right," even if that meant missing a deadline. Sakuma, James, and Nakano often wondered if Haag would be able to stay in business, and yet he did.[21]

The Edgar project followed this design process, with Haag developing the initial ideas and general plant palette, Mary Booth managing the project, which involved meeting with the client, developing details, and specifying plants and construction materials, and Roy Lehner stepping in after January 1968 to oversee completion. The site was a wooded landscape on Cougar Mountain with a steep slope and a ravine on one side affording beautiful views of Lake Sammamish. The design featured a framework comparable to that of the Sprague garden, but with an even stronger emphasis on native plants (Douglas fir, madrona, dogwood, and native cedar) and a naturalized landscape of rocks and ravines.[22] The site offered the advantage of existing trees, which Haag retained, even a fallen tree that lay across the ravine, and tree stumps. He located trails and a clearing in the woods. Initial plans showed Haag's intention that there should be an "informal play area throughout the woods."[23] Haag began by marking a small woodland space and, over the course of the design process, added a small circular lawn abutting the concrete patio, which served as the social space for the garden just off the family room and bedrooms. At the back, where most families would have a second lawn, Haag and Booth designed an open flower meadow enclosed by native shrubs. To the east of the meadow, Haag placed a sunken fire pit and council ring encircled by fir trees.

The design responded both to the landscape as forest and meadow and to the modern architecture, with garden spaces extending the views from within to the forest beyond. Like the Sprague garden, the Edgar house and garden merged into one, offering the family the opportunity to move between the indoors and outdoors with ease.

Residential gardens continued to be an important part of Haag's practice throughout his career. In 1986, he designed the garden for Dina and Wilbur Kukes on the shore of Lake Whatcom in Bellingham, Washington, collaborating with David Hall, an architect in the Henry Klein Partnership who was designing the house. Hall had not worked with Haag before, although Klein had introduced the two and Hall was familiar with Haag's work. The Kukes told Hall that they wanted to work with a landscape architect, as Dina Kukes wanted to have a native garden around the house and to take advantage of the existing woodland. As Hall recalled, when Haag met the Kukeses, he quickly identified features that they had wanted but had not made it into the house design, including a river rock foundation, which had been eliminated because of its expense. Haag suggested using river rocks in the garden, which would require fewer rocks than a foundation, and consequently cost much less, yet make the rocks a primary design element. His solution was persuasive, and the Kukeses gave him the commission.

Haag was not involved in the initial siting of the architecture but worked with Hall to refine the placement of the

6.10 Kukes house, Bellingham, Washington, 1986, with architect David Hall of Henry Klein Partnership.

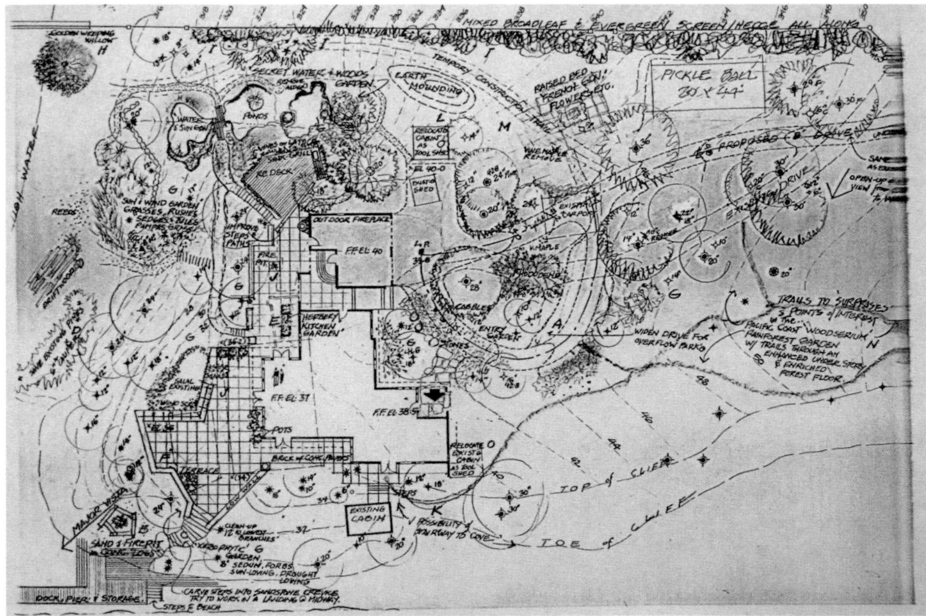

6.11 Kukes garden plan, 1986.

6.12 Kukes garden and waterfront with concrete pods as a dock, Bellingham, 1986.

house and its terraces in relation to the gardens and landscape. He designed a garden that merged with its architecture and with the native landscape of tall Pacific Coast forest on one side and shoreline on the other, interweaving nature and culture while retaining the distinctive character of both architecture and landscape.

He carved out intimate spaces such as the secret water-and-woods garden to the north and the sun-and-wind garden on the waterfront. Behind the house loomed the native forest, with bits of sky visible above the canopy. With a similar view of the trees through the windows, the site of the house within the forest was emphasized and celebrated.

On the shore, concrete pods served as an extended dock. The pods contrasted with the boulders excavated from Lake Whatcom that were placed along the shoreline. The river stones that formed a dry creek bed visually connected this waterfront to the house and its terraces. The creek bed moved from the waterfront up to the bluff, where it became a stone wall that culminated in a stone cairn in front of the house and front terrace. The undulating line of river stones is similar to Haag's garden design for the Stamey Medical Clinic. The terrace was composed of exposed aggregate concrete with edges and accents of red brick, while the steps were made of upside-down grass crete pavers. Willow trees were brought from Haag's nursery, as were a number of other trees and shrubs. It was a landscape of contrasts, of yin and yang, as well as harmony and fusion. In time, Haag and Hall would work on a design for the North Cascades Environmental Center, another project that built on their shared commitment to blending landscape and architecture. The Kukes residence, however, remains the most elegant of their collaborative projects.

In 1987, Vinton and Mimi Sommerville commissioned Haag to design their garden on Lake Washington in Medina. In the office, Robert Foley assisted Haag on the design for the gardens that surrounded the house, designed by architect Robert Small with interior designer James Halvorson.[24] The site had been essentially a bog that was exposed in 1916 when Lake Washington was lowered 8.8 feet for the construction of the Ship Canal and Montlake Cut in Seattle. The house was nestled into a thirty-foot bluff that rose to street level and looked out directly over the shore and lake; it was sited wisely, so that many mature trees were retained. The owners had a number of desired programs, including a putting green, a spa, and a crow's nest as well as fountains and a garden that would attract birds.[25]

Haag's development of the idea of fusion was central to the design. In writing about the project later for *Pacific Horticulture*, he began:

> The principal idea expressed over and over again in this residential garden on Lake Washington—in the plan, the form, even the function, in the elements of space, movement, water, earth, stone, and plants—is fusion. Brick invades grass, grass captures brick, which in turn is infiltrated by moss, which merges with running stream and quiet pools of water. Stone defines edges of the water, and water impounds a mossy stone island. And so it

goes—the yin and the yang of the lifetides of the garden echoing the ebb and flow of the seasons.[26]

The process of blending elements together started at the entry drive. Facilitating a thirty-foot drop to the house required a steep drive with a slow curve and a switchback. The surface included paired brick treads turned on their corners, offering traction for drivers and walkers. These same bricks curved with the driveway and then extended to form walking paths through the gardens. The steep drive required a strong retaining wall for which Haag specified concrete cribbing filled with liriope that merged visually with the hill and resembled a waterfall when the wind blew, suggesting the lake beyond. Trimmed yew hedges lined the top of the wall enclosing the driveway up to the point of arrival. In these ways, the entry drive fused construction materials and plants, functions and aesthetics, revealing themes carried out through the gardens.

At the back of the house were the gardens and a small terrace for family gatherings. Haag created two gardens between the house and the waterfront, both highlighting water and the abundance of vegetation. There was no one element that was quintessentially Japanese in any of the gardens, such as a lantern or a water basin, yet the character of the simple compositions suggested a Japanese influence. The first garden was designed around an old birch tree that had once been poorly trimmed. Haag asked his son, who had become an arborist, to "find the birchness" of the tree; he did, and the tree survived. There had been two large erratic boulders under the birch, but Small had moved one to the entrance, where it stood as a visual connection between the gardens and the home. The second boulder remained under the birch tree and became the central piece in the stone-and-water garden.

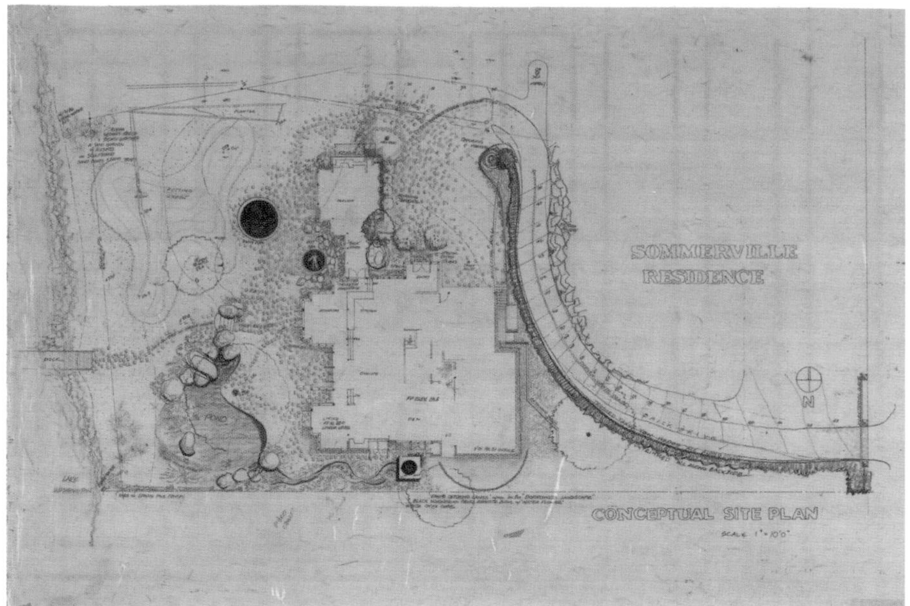

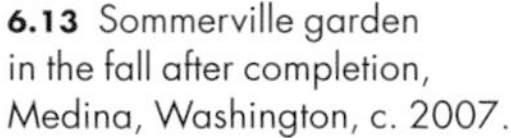

6.13 Sommerville garden in the fall after completion, Medina, Washington, c. 2007.

6.14 Sommerville plan, 1987.

Haag found a small collection of moss-covered glacial stones at a local stone yard, Marenakos Rock Center, and placed them carefully around the "mother stone." Finding the garden still too subtle, he went in search of additional stones that would strengthen the composition. He gained access to an abandoned sandstone quarry at Willkeson, in the foothills of the Cascades, where he selected stones with sawed surfaces and borings. These were integrated with the glacial granite. A wide range of plants provided exceptional seasonal color and textural interest. Amelanchiers, blueberries, viburnums, strawberries, and daphne were used for color and texture and to attract birds.

In a private and shaded space off the library, opposite the entrance side of the house, Haag placed a bronze water flower, designed and cast by Tom Small, on a shallow hemispherical basin centered in a block of dark granite. Water poured from the flower as if it was the source for the garden. The water was then carried down the hill to the pond and a waterfall designed by the sculptor Charles Greening. Although the system had a recirculating pump, the water appeared to be an extension of the larger lake just beyond, and in fact during hard rainstorms, the overflow did indeed drain into the lake through the bog on the shoreline.

Farther out past a small stone-and-water garden, the dock floated on the lake. This most private of gardens on the lakeside faced west, had excellent solar orientation, and benefited from light breezes blowing in over the water. Although the Sommervilles had requested a putting green, Haag suggested a bog garden to absorb the water, due to the wetness of the site, with a smaller lawn between the house and the bog. The bog attracted birds as well as solved the drainage problem. It was a means of acknowledging the nature of the site, in a contemplative manner, giving breathing space to the larger landscape and house.

6.15 Sommerville patio, with the idea of fusion expressed at ground level, Medina, 2005.

6.16 Sommerville rock and birch garden, Medina, 2010.

6.17 Sommerville garden with rock and step detail, Medina, 2010.

6.18 Sommerville garden with view over bog garden to Lake Washington, Medina, summer 2010.

The terrace included a small spa bordered by trees selected for their intimate details, including Japanese stewartia and the Japanese tree lilac (*Syringa reticulata*), as well as a katsura, one of Haag's favorite trees, and bayberry (*Myrica pennsylvanica*), all of which he brought from his nursery. As he told a reporter, "The bark and sculptural form of the [Japanese] stewartia and the Japanese tree lilac have an almost sensual appeal to the touch; the branches of the katsura and serviceberry display special patterns; the blue-gray berries of the bayberry are persistently striking; and the double file viburnum has admirable qualities in every season."[27] Throughout the garden, a wide variety of plants were used because of the Sommervilles' interests and willingness to maintain the gardens and also as a reflection of Haag's interests in a larger variety of plants that could be enjoyed on the lake.

Increasingly evident in these residential designs by Haag is a close attention to the natural processes, the flow of water, and what would eventually be termed "ecological design." He was interested in the long-term growth and maturation of the garden, noting that once hired by a client, he was the project's landscape architect for life. In partnership with the client, Haag was able to realize his ideals and would be engaged with the garden for the next twenty-five years.

AN URBAN PROJECT, THE MERRILL COURT TOWNHOMES

In 1982, the architect Ibsen Nelsen invited Haag to develop designs with the developer Herman Sarkowsky for a new development in the Harvard-Belmont neighborhood on Capitol Hill in Seattle.[28] Named the Merrill Court Townhomes, as they were built next to the R. D. Merrill mansion, they were in a primarily residential neighborhood. In order to best fit the townhouses into the residential neighborhood, Nelsen and Haag drew from the early twentieth-century concept of a garden suburb plan, with houses enclosing the semiprivate Grassy Common in the center that served as the front lawn. Although the project initially met with resistance, it typically is now part of the annual Capitol Hill garden tours.[29]

Haag nestled the houses into the land so that their scale would not overwhelm their context, regrading the site and laying out the buildings in an L shape set into the slope. The central gathering space, or Grassy Common, was an expansive lawn that featured significant existing trees providing enclosure for the residents while offering an amenity to the larger neighborhood. Katsuras, seviceberries, and Japanese stewartias joined the existing mature redwoods, creating a woodland garden of shade-loving plants. Benches were placed under the trees, facing away from the private entrances to the townhouses, and surrounded by shrubs.

In addition to the Grassy Common, Haag carefully designed the public realm of the streets that bordered the townhouses. Along Harvard Avenue to the east there was an ironwork fence with concrete pillars at the entrances, so that the common area was visible to all yet was clearly understood as private property. On the west front facing Boylston Avenue, Nelsen located the garages, integrated with a retaining wall topped by a balustrade. Haag then covered the wall with wisteria, creating a romantic layer. On Aloha, to the south and moving around the corner to Boylston Avenue, Haag planted katsura trees intermixed with the existing poplar trees along the street edge. At the corner of Aloha and Boylston, a mature beech tree spread out from the top of the wall.

For each townhouse, Haag designed a small roof garden built over the garage. Thus, the gardens were both a technical engineering design and a garden design. The garden for the developer Sarkowsky was typical for the project, with plants selected for form, foliage, flower, fragrance, and fruit. It contained Pacific Northwest plants, with a woodland corner, specimen plants chosen for their sculptural character, including Kousa dogwood and stewartia, and espaliered fruit trees on the garden wall. There was an area for garden furniture and pots for temporary plant displays. While this garden included an urn on a pedestal, others featured local rocks with depressions for holding water or stone sculptures. For the north-facing gardens, Haag specified brilliantly colored flowers and scented plants that would attract birds and retain interest in the winter months, including rhododen-

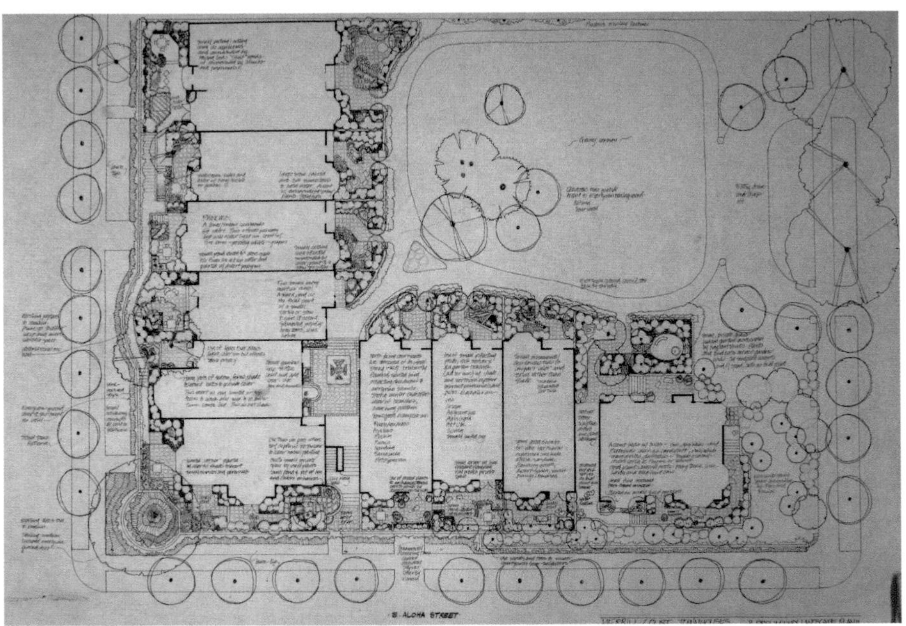
E. ALOHA STREET

6.19 Merrill Court Townhomes Grassy Common, with bench under the sequoia tree, surrounded by a garden, with its back to the private gardens, Seattle, 2014.

6.20 Merrill Court Townhomes landscape design, 1982.

6.21 Grassy Common, Merrill Court Townhomes, Seattle, 2014.

6.22 Public realm along Boylston Avenue, with wisteria growing along the wall and liriope below, Seattle, c. 2000.

6.23 Merrill Court Townhomes, garden plan for Mr. and Mrs. Herman Sarkowsky, Seattle, 1985.

6.24 Merrill Court Townhomes, Sarkowsky garden with moss and paving expressing fusion, Seattle, c. 1985.

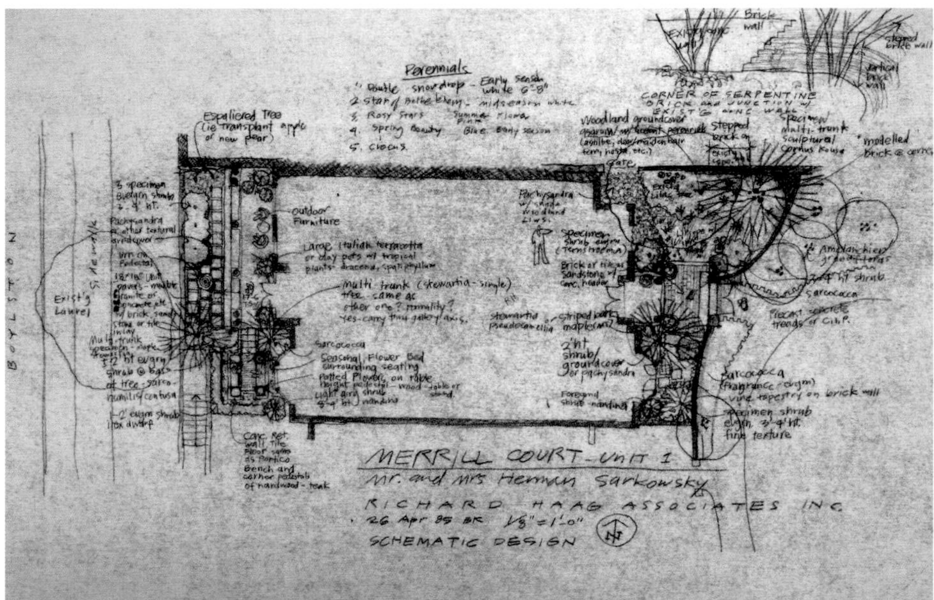

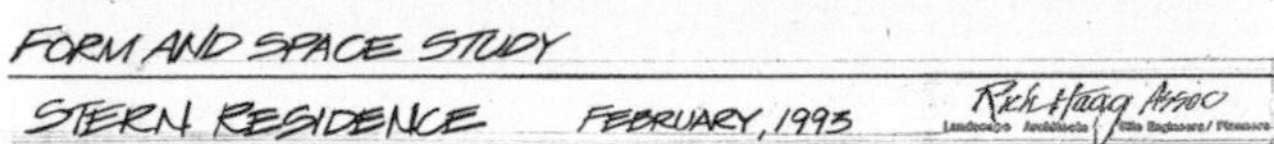

drons, azaleas, nandina, and sarcococca plants. Water fountains and stone sculptures by Richard Beyer, as well as a bird bath, were used at garden entrances and meeting points in the larger complex, where they introduced an intimate character.[30] Throughout the designs, Haag fused materials, such as grass growing over brick walkways or vines covering walls.

Residential gardens remained important to Haag's practice. In the 1980s and 1990s, he would design gardens in Pittsburgh, Pennsylvania, and Aspen, Colorado. In 1992, for the Stern garden on San Juan Island, closer to home, Haag further explored the use of landforms, the power of trees as a design element, the dialogue between landscape and architecture in form and material, and the ability of landscape to create a place for human interaction with nature. This garden featured flowering plants such as viburnums and dogwoods, emphasizing its seasonal nature and diversity. The range of plants was emblematic of the region's environment.

This focus on the richness of the existing landscape and the ability of design to nurture natural processes as well as embrace cultural narratives was an approach Haag had been developing since the 1960s and would eventually be labeled "ecological design." His residential gardens expressed a regionally grounded approach to landscape just as their architecture reflected a regional style. They were initial experiments in using ecology, natural systems, and regional plants to create works of art. Haag revealed natural processes and elements in subtle ways. The Edgar garden worked with mountain and forest ecologies, creating a space for habitation where children could launch explorations of the woods, forests, and mountain streams. The garden for the Kukeses highlighted the site's location on a peninsula, where the family could watch the weather move across the lake and the seasons alter the landscape. The Sommerville bog retained water when it was needed and then released it back into the ground and lake. The Merrill Court Townhomes brought the magnificence of large trees and lush gardens to an urban setting. In addition to the ecological sources of the designs, landforms and small-scale earth-

6.25 "Form and Space Study," Stern garden, 1993.

6.26 Stern garden, with landforms defining space, San Juan Island, c. 1996.

6.27 Stern garden, showing occult balance with center line of entrance drive, San Juan Island, c. 1996.

works were evident in many of the residential gardens, perhaps as a counterpart to the architectural geometry of the modern homes or as an intermediary between the natural landscape and the formality of the homes. The Stern garden brought these various investigations together. Each project responded to the client, the site, and, most of all, the region in its materials, processes, and experiences. In 1997, when Haag was asked to participate in a series of lectures and an exhibit on eco-revelatory design, design that made ecological processes legible to the user, he could put a name to the approach that he had already established.[31]

NUTRIMENTAL LANDSCAPES

Haag's efforts to establish edible and productive landscapes were another example of his interest in ecology, natural systems, and plants. Ecological design, or design that considered the ecological health of the biological environment, also took care of animals, including humans, according to Haag. Interest in edible plants had been a growing topic of discussion in the early years of his practice. It was a part of the back-to-the-land movement as well as an outgrowth of the World War II generation that had grown Victory Gardens. Haag's term for the selection of plants that would contribute nutritionally as well as aesthetically was "nutrimental horticulture." It responded to the call to counter the green revolution promoted by petrochemical companies and agribusiness.

Haag observed in his essay "Edible Landscape," published in *Landscape Architecture Magazine* in 1980, that China had for centuries relied on the home garden and understood the need for plants to produce, or, as we would express it today, to perform. He traced an emphasis on productive gardening in American history and quoted Samuel Johnson, the British writer: "The garden is best which produces most fruit." He further pointed out that Thorstein Veblen, a late nineteenth-century social critic and economist, had "condemned the lawn as a symbol of superfluous materialism, i.e., surplus 'pasture' uncropped by herbivores and disdainfully displayed to the less-landed and less fortunate." Haag continued, "Certainly, with today's fossil fuel crisis, maintaining lawns with fertilizers, pesticides, weedicides and power mowers is immoral." With all of this as ammunition, Haag challenged landscape architects to "break down the barriers that separate agriculture from horticulture, this senseless dualism, forever trying to disengage beauty from utility."[32]

Haag's advocacy for growing food in home gardens was well received in Seattle, where an urban agriculture movement was taking hold. This movement had started as early as the 1960s with the formation of Puget Consumer Cooperative, which brought together concerned consumers in a food-buying club. With the construction of the Danny Woo Community Garden and the Picardo Farm community garden, the launch of the P-Patch Community Gardens throughout Seattle, and the emergence of Seattle Tilth, there was an increasingly vocal community of urban gardeners and farmers.

Like many of those involved in the movement, Haag considered nutrimental design to be a social, ecological, and political act, and landscape architects were in an optimal position to do something. It was not merely the use of native plants and the preservation of a diversity of plant species and varieties that were threatened by the monoculture techniques of corporate farms, or the contemporary focus on the clean air and water acts, but attention to the multiple benefits of carefully selected plants. As early as 1957, he had proposed to the California State Highway Department that it plant the freeway with fruit and nut trees, beginning with a project to "fruitify" the rest stops. He imagined lineal orchards along the right-of-way along freeways, with special harvest days or gleaning programs. While there was initial interest from the highway department, Haag recalls, fruit growers expressed concern that such trees would spread disease and insects, and the idea died without ever being realized.

Haag brought the idea of edible public landscapes to the project to develop Gilman Village and Gilman Boulevard in Issaquah. In the mid-1970s, Haag had convinced Marvin and Ruth Mohl to invest in a series of older, mostly abandoned, small wooden houses in order to create a new commercial core for the growing town east of Seattle, what became known as Gilman Village. Haag designed the general plan, incorporating a series of gardens that would allow pedestrians to move around the core and enjoy small gathering spaces, places where they could eat together. In 1986, Haag was asked to provide designs again, this time for Gilman Boulevard, the approach road for Gilman Village. Haag adapted the idea of "fruitifying" the roads from his proposal for the California freeway system, but at a much smaller scale, making it more likely to be adopted. After doing extensive research on potential microclimates along the road and selecting appropriate species of trees and shrubs for the design, Haag laid out the four-lane roadway framed by allées that would form a landscape buffer. The plan showed four rows of trees, the third composed of plum, apple, pear, and nut trees, with grapes growing on the fences along the interstate. The fruit trees would be densest along the swale that took advantage of the drainage and would make gleaning fallen fruit easier. Haag combined blueberries, grape vines, and clover along the arterial roads. Picnic areas were marked out. While the project was not fully successful, in large part because the contractor planted whatever fruit trees he could purchase inexpensively, not the species Haag had carefully selected, and because of maintenance problems, it demonstrated the potential of a productive design approach at a larger scale than the home garden.

Haag's experiments with nutrimental design in his own gardens have been more successful.[33] The Seattle garden he shares with Cheryl Trivison, his wife, was established in 2005 in the residential neighborhood of Capitol Hill in Seattle. Located on the northwest corner of a four-way intersection, the garden and house enjoy optimal exposure to sun and water. The new house rose to capture sun, wind, and views, while the garden grounds the place to the site and region.[34]

A stone terrace with a fireplace was placed to receive afternoon sun and allows ample space for gathering with friends and family. Raised garden beds provide comfortable seating

6.28 Haag/Trivison garden with Richard Haag, Seattle, 2009.

at the right height to engage in a bit of gardening, should one choose. Here, Haag cultivates more than a dozen types of blueberries, multiple varieties of currants, strawberries, and gooseberries, and a collection of relatively unfamiliar edible plants including goumi (*Eleagnus multiflora*), jostaberries, and five different commercial amelanchier varieties. The raised garden beds hold an assortment of both traditional and Asian vegetables. Haag cultivated three udo (*Aralia edulis*) plants, and when they are harvested, he shares them with the chef at a local Japanese restaurant.

Haag's attention included the public realm of the sidewalk. The curb is planted with a variety of bush berries, fava beans, and garden peas, garlic, and shallots interspersed with a carpet of evergreen lilyturf. His experiments engage his neighbors and community, serving as a magnet for young gatherers modeling a different approach to gardens and the city.

Haag created hundreds of residential gardens in the more than fifty years that he practiced landscape architecture in Seattle and the Pacific Northwest. In addition to the projects described here, he designed gardens in Spokane and Pullman in eastern Washington, Vancouver, and Portland, Oregon. The gardens are expressive of a Pacific Northwest regionalism that is at the same time carefully responsive to the individual landscape and clients. Haag's residential designs, while not in the public realm, reflect his deep commitment to the role of the landscape architect as an advocate for a better built environment. When Haag found a client who shared his view of landscape and the environment, the design excelled.

PUBLIC
PARKING

from modernism to urbanism

> Seattle, a favored spot, haunted by memories of an Indian past, a lumbering past, a fishing past, by the ton of gold, by fire, remembering corruption and zeal of reformers, remembering Chinese riots, vigilantes and strikers, the town with guts enough to build two World's Fairs, the airplane place, with two kinds of water, with hills and trees; Seattle, the place in the upper left-hand corner is your place. ACTION: BETTER CITY
>
> Fred Bassetti, *Action: Better City*

FOR HAAG, LANDSCAPE WAS INHERENTLY POLITICAL, CULtural, and ecological. In 1957, Phil Thiel, who later came to the University of Washington, and Haag were hired by architectural critic Allan Temko to help organize the fight against the construction of the Embarcadero Freeway in San Francisco.[1] In Seattle, Haag and Thiel would join those who fought to stop the R. H. Thomson Expressway. It was only one battle in the 1960s and 1970s in Seattle. Haag, always the activist, was involved in many of the debates on the future of the city.

Seattle's urban development from 1958, the year Haag arrived, to the early 1970s was complex. The older generation was losing its hold on city government as a group of younger activists came to the fore, inspired by leaders such as Jane Jacobs, Rachel Carson, and those in the emerging preservation movement. The demise of Seattle's R. H. Thomson Expressway was emblematic of the change. Voters approved bonds to build the expressway by a comfortable margin in March 1960, but in February 1972, 71 percent voted to terminate the project. Haag participated in advocating for change, and his practice benefited from the new vision of Seattle—some of his most important projects, such as Gas Works Park, were possible only because of the transformation in how citizens and leaders envisioned their city.

Seattle in the 1960s was a metropolitan region in the midst of immense growth, particularly with the expansion of the Boeing Airplane Company. Changing demographics, the push toward the suburbs, and the growing primacy of the automobile challenged city leaders as they sought to respond to the changes, particularly suburban growth and what they perceived as inner city decline. Business and civic leaders proposed solutions based on urban renewal and urban highways. This vision of the future was echoed in the Century 21 Exposition, the 1962 Seattle World's Fair. For many city leaders, the success of the fair offered lessons that might be applied elsewhere: cleaning up the city by clearing out "blight," rebuilding according to low-density suburban models, and providing access to the city for suburbanites by constructing new freeways. Urban renewal and highway construction would be expensive, but federal funding was available. The fair would put the city on the map, leaders hoped.

There were a few young leaders, however, who argued for a different vision of the future of Seattle. Haag's colleague Victor Steinbrueck was among the first to question the leaders' plans for modernization of the city. A 1935 graduate of the architecture program at the University of Washington, Steinbrueck had joined the faculty in 1946 and developed a small practice, primarily designing modern residences. In 1953, he had become interested in the history of the city when he prepared a small guidebook to the city's architecture for the national American Institute of Architects convention in Seattle that year. In 1957–58, Steinbrueck spent a year working in classmate Minoru Yamasaki's office in Detroit, and this raised his consciousness of the impact of freeways and slum clearance for urban renewal. He returned to Seattle with a greater appreciation for the city and with more concern about plans for the future. In October 1959, Steinbrueck began publishing his sketches in the *Argus*, a local weekly newspaper, and for the next three years, he showed readers their city, revealed not by means of the major buildings but through ordinary buildings and everyday places. In May 1962, he published his first book, *Seattle Cityscape*, a volume of sketches timed to be available for the Century 21 Exposition and offering a vision of what the city might become—a vision that was very different from that of the city's leaders.[2] There can be no doubt that Steinbrueck discussed his sketches with colleagues, including Haag. Architects, artists, planners, and activists united to oppose what they saw as unnecessary destruction along with poor stewardship of public finances and resources.

Haag participated in these debates on urban development both as a citizen and as a professional. In 1962, he was appointed to the Seattle Arts Commission, which supported art in public spaces, thus bringing his professional values into play. On the commission, he argued that the design of public spaces was as important as the installation of works of art in the public domain. In a similar manner, he advocated for environmental awareness in the city. He had always been concerned with environmental issues as a landscape architect, but his focus would be strengthened by the growing environmental movement. He joined the calls for addressing the obvious degradation of the region, including the potential demise of native salmon and the scum that increasingly covered Lake Washington. In these years, Washington State benefited from the leadership of U.S. senators Warren G. Magnuson and Henry M. Jackson, who would lead Congress through the passage of key environmental laws including the Coastal Zone Management Act, the National Environmental Policy Act, the Wilderness Act of 1964, and the landmark Clean Air and Clean Water Acts. Throughout, it was a fight to determine whose vision and what values would shape the city.

Yet, even as these groups fought over the future of the city, leaders reached consensus on a number of urban investments. In 1966, James R. "Jim" Ellis, a leading downtown attorney, organized the Forward Thrust initiative. This coordinated cluster of city and county bond referenda, largely approved in 1968, was intended to fund a program of capital improvements including a rapid transit system, a major league sports stadium, low-income housing, a world trade center, and a significant expansion of parks, plazas, and greenbelts. By 1973, the Forward Thrust program could take credit for funding "$56 million of improved arterials designed to carry transit buses, eleven thousand street trees planted, 20,000 more being grown, a children's zoo, . . . 12 new indoor swimming pools, five more under construction, . . . 15 miles of pedestrian and bicycle paths, 25 street triangle landscapes, 22 neighborhood parks in process, stadium under construction."[3] Haag benefited directly from Forward Thrust, as these bonds funded several of his public projects, including Gas Works Park.

Seeking an opportunity to study alternative plans for the future of Seattle, Haag joined Bassetti and other architects, designers, and advocates in coordinated efforts that became known as Action: Better City. As president of the local AIA, Bassetti had "gathered together about 50 or so eager young architects, and we started to work, first on deciding what the most important urban needs were and how to meet them. [and] began a personal effort to raise money to pay for out-of-pocket expenses, and for the cost of a film to document what we were doing."[4] Teams of individuals selected one of seven study areas—downtown, Elliot Bay, Pioneer Square, Lake Union, Wallingford, Denny Regrade Park, and the need

7.1 *Action: Better City* cover, 1968.

for downtown housing or "in-city living"—and worked on design visions that were then collated into a proposal for the city. At the final banquet at the Olympic Hotel, attendees viewed the film *What Is So Great about Seattle?* and were presented with a sixty-four-page brochure documenting the group's plan. Eventually, parts of this visionary plan were implemented, including Gas Works Park, the Burke-Gilman Trail, and a modified version of Westlake Square. The preservation of Pioneer Square and the development of Occidental Park were successes that arose from this plan, and in the early 1970s, Freeway Park was designed by Lawrence Halprin as the first lidded highway park. All of this was possible because, as Bassetti proclaimed, Seattle was not burdened by the so-called baggage of East Coast cities or the traditional wealth and power of San Francisco or even Los Angeles.[5]

In 1968, following a different model that focused on similar issues but in different neighborhoods, civil rights leaders gained approval for Seattle's Model Cities development plan—the first city in the nation to be approved by the U.S. Department of Housing and Urban Development. The Model Cities program was intended to improve the quality of urban life by engaging residents of the very neighborhoods that urban renewal so often disregarded. The program was a crucial element of President Johnson's War on Poverty and mandated citizen participation in the planning process. Initially, Seattle's selected neighborhoods for application of Model Cities funding were the Central Area, the International District, and Pioneer Square, much of which had not been part of the Action: Better City focus. With changes to federal law in 1971, Seattle's program expanded to include neighborhoods in north, southwest, and southeast Seattle. Haag and Steinbrueck would be just two of several university faculty members and urban professionals who would contribute to the programs during the planning process and implementation.[6] Haag would work on several public projects funded by the Model Cities program, including street tree plans and a playground.

In the years between 1967, when CHECC (Choose an Effective City Council) first backed candidates in a Seattle City Council election, and 1973, city government was transformed—nine new council members were elected, and in December 1969, Wes Uhlman, the youngest mayor in Seattle's history, took office. The older council had embraced a vision of urban renewal and highways; the new members were open to preservation arguments and alternatives for urban design and would approve Haag's proposal for Gas Works Park. In 1970, the city made Pioneer Square its first legally protected historic district, and on November 2, 1971, when Seattle voters approved the measure protecting Pike Place Market, it became the city's second historic district.

The historian Jeffrey Sanders has argued that an urban environmental movement emerged from this collective work in Seattle, a label that can also describe Haag's design practice. This urban-oriented movement grew out of discourses on social, political, and economic equity in conjunction with environmental and ecological arguments.[7] It shifted the focus of urban issues to environmental justice and ecological health at the same time that environmentalists were turning their attention from wilderness to the urban landscape.

PUBLIC SPACE AND PARTICIPATION

Haag's professional practice was growing during this period. As involved as he was in city debates, he encountered tensions between his various roles—teacher, advocate, practitioner. He believed that design was inherently a civic act and saw landscape architecture as a socially and environmentally relevant practice that offered designers an opportunity to change the world around them. This was a powerful message for young students and a difficult position for a professional establishing a practice. It may have lost him a project here or there, but it also gained him a reputation as a dedicated, even tough advocate for urban landscapes.

Haag brought this activism into the classroom, often by sharing the public work that was being designed in his office with students. This allowed him to use studio teaching for design explorations and experiments. For example, in a 1961 studio, Haag posed the issue of suburban developments as an urban challenge, introducing it as follows:

> Urban planners, architects, and landscape architects have a long record of protestation against the ruthless exploitation of our landscape. . . . The sad fact is that the speculator and the highway engineer (sometimes in un-holy alliance) have been making the major "planning" decisions. If we believe in human values, values other and above short-term economic values, then we should be able to communicate our point of view and make a significant contribution.[8]

Students explored residential area development, including cluster developments and row-house groupings. In a similar manner, in spring 1963, fourth-year students engaged in an intensive study of the Sammamish River region development plans. Rather than making it a purely academic project, Haag arranged for students to present their work to the planning commissions of Redmond, Bothell, and King County.

As early as 1960, Haag had focused his teaching on the idea of recycling landscapes. He assigned the same studio project, designing a park for Seattle's gasworks site, in 1960 and 1967. In fall 1964, he posed the question of appropriate uses of Fort Lawton Military Reservation, a demilitarized landscape. Students produced a site analysis and research report, followed by proposals. This work would eventually make its way into Haag's submission to an invited competition for Fort Lawton when the reservation was turned over to Seattle to become a public park. The subject continued to interest him, and in 1985, he offered the seminar "Recycled Landscapes," which explored creative approaches to converting the "graveyards" of the industrial era into alternative forms of public space. As he noted in the syllabus, "This course shall aid you in defining a creative 'adaptic' approach to the conversion of obsolete industrial plants and military bases, etc., into parks and recreation centers."[9]

In another studio, students considered the plan to build a ring road/highway around Seattle's downtown. The plan was the epitome, Haag maintained, of the poor decisions engendered by urban renewal and the Federal-Aid Highway Act of 1956. After debating the project in the studio, he sent students to advocate against the project door-to-door, describing it as a noose around the city. Other faculty members also involved students in their advocacy and activism, including Steinbrueck, who had much earlier sent his students to do measured drawings of buildings that would be lost with the construction of Interstate 5 (I-5). Haag and colleagues argued that politics was an essential element of practice for the design professions.

In each of these real projects, Haag described a broader role for landscape architects in public and civic discourse. He argued for the long-term partnership that each site and its client ought to have with the landscape architect. As Halprin once remarked, landscape architects spend the first part of their career designing and constructing and the second part fighting to save what they have designed.[10] The ASLA, Haag suggested, could develop a contractual form that would link the landscape architect with the growing landscape over its lifetime, to help guide the changes and, of course, to argue against the destruction of the projects. While he understood that not every project should be preserved, he argued that decisions about the future of designed urban landscapes were frequently made without consultation with professional landscape architects or even a full understanding of the role of design in the urban context. In 1966, Haag sent a letter to the *Seattle Post-Intelligencer*'s "Northwest Today" outlining how landscape architects might work directly with state leaders to preserve the region's natural resources, specifically in developing a statewide landscape policy. This policy would work, he explained, at multiple scales: from enforcing antipollution legislation, to allowing scenic easement rights, to using federal aid for the arts, to providing funds for planting shade and flowering trees.[11] He sought to model this approach not only in his teaching but through his work to save Pike Place Market, his battle against the highways, and his design for Gas Works Park, among his many public projects. The landscape architect was a critical leader in creating the city both today and in the future, according to Haag.

THE PUBLIC REALM

The Model Cities program and Forward Thrust were sources of primary funding for projects in the public realm, and Haag found ways to contribute as a professional and an advocate. He frequently worked with Seattle's Central Area Motivation Project (CAMP), the first community-inspired program in the country to receive funding from the Office of Economic Opportunity and a crucial leader in the Model Cities efforts.[12] Haag developed plans for introducing street trees in neighborhoods that had been ignored by the city's parks and improvement departments. He oversaw the planting of more than 1,200 street trees in 1966 and 1968, as part of the CAMP Beautification Program, with the Citizens Planning Task Force that then became a model program in the city.[13] He redesigned intersections to privilege pedestrians through the use of pavers and the careful placing of trees in planting strips that would allow adequate root growth. A decade later, he worked with the Solar-Assisted Low-Income Housing project as the landscape architect.

With Kirk, Wallace, McKinley & Associates, Haag designed Center Park (1967), which provided living accommodations in Seattle's Rainier Valley for physically or mentally challenged individuals and their caretakers, one of the first such facilities in the nation. He set the building back from the street, buffered with large sycamores, and tucked the parking lot into the corner. Haag partnered with the architectural firm Wallace, McKinley & Associates on Jefferson Terrace for the Seattle Housing Authority between 1965 and 1968. The project, located at the edge of First Hill overlooking downtown Seattle, was the housing authority's first new low-income housing since Yesler Terrace, built in 1941. Haag buffered the residents from the highway, again setting the building behind a landscape of grass and trees, this time on the top of the slope, further distancing the residents from the highway and busy streets surrounding the complex. Haag also worked on a number of King County Metro projects including plans and designs for bus stations at Rainier, Renton, Belvoir, and Dexter Avenues. Each of these projects was important to Haag's vision of the role of landscape architects. However, the craft of the designs was rarely evident to the uninformed eye; it never demanded attention but instead served its users quietly and efficiently.

A project that Haag and Bassetti found challenging was the East Pine Street Substation, a utility site for the publicly owned Seattle City Light, completed between 1965 and 1971. The substation was located in an underserved community,

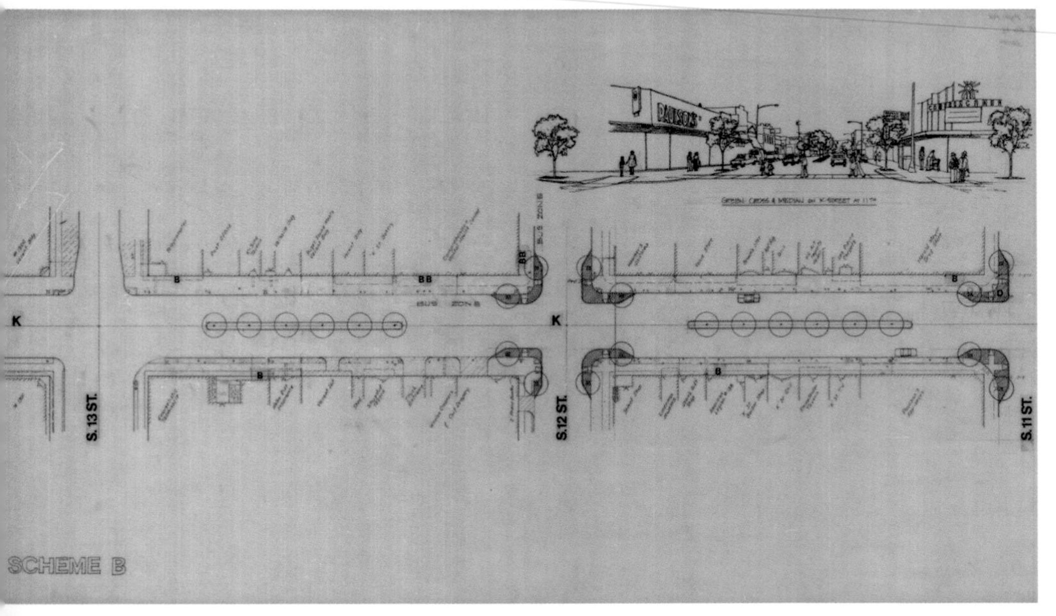

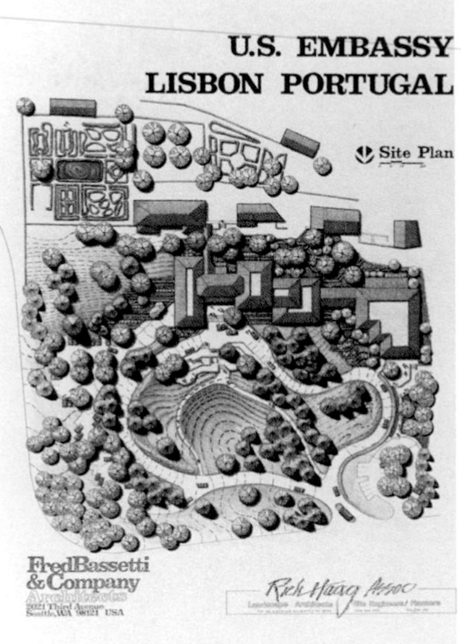

7.2 K Street Farmers Market proposal, 1979.

7.3 U.S. Embassy and Consulate site plan, 1974–83, with architect Fred Bassetti.

and the two were asked to design a site that would not insult the neighborhood.[14] The substation was a utilitarian structure surrounded by tall brick walls on all four sides of a full block. Bassetti designed the brick walls to have interest and elegance, while Haag specified a variety of Pacific Northwest trees and shrubs that would provide seasonal color and soften the structure. This project demonstrated the potential of good design, not only for utilitarian infrastructure but in communities where the city did not traditionally invest many resources. The project, which won an AIA Seattle Honor Award in 1967, was important both as a design project and as a public statement of values.

Haag was also involved in what are today called "green infrastructure projects," including the Seattle Commons. Bassetti, in collaboration with *Seattle Times* columnist John Hinterberger, proposed the project in 1991; however, it failed to win approval from voters in 1995.[15] Imagined as a sixty-one-acre park stretching from Lake Union to Elliott Bay and downtown Seattle, the Seattle Commons was to be an immense civic space bordered by the growing high-tech industries as well as housing and urban amenities. Haag served as the lead designer for a portion of the proposed park that would extend from Westlake Center in downtown Seattle to the southern tip of Lake Union. His design addressed storm water management with a series of terraced wetlands, clearly an example of urban ecological design. As Richard Brooks wrote to in a letter to the *Seattle Times*, the proposal would "reduce water pollution in Lake Union and Puget Sound, it will increase the city's potable water supply, will make a salmon run a distinct possibility, will give us bird and small-animal habitat and will cleanse the water for free instead of in a costly mechanical process."[16]

Haag also worked in the public realm for cities outside Seattle. Olympia and Tacoma hired him for public projects, including planning studies. In Olympia, he provided initial plans for the capital landscape in 1966 and then for the Capitol Lake Recreation Plan in 1977; he also worked on designs for the K Street Farmers Market in Tacoma in 1979. In the early 1970s, Haag contributed waterfront, recreation, and parking studies as well as designs for the Blaine Street parklets for the City of Blaine while at the same time working on plans for the city of Everett, including for Colby Mall and downtown streetscapes. The Army Corps of Engineers commissioned Haag to provide plans for the visitor center at the Little Goose Dam, in Walla Walla, Washington, in 1974–75, and in 1990, Haag submitted a master plan for the urban waterfront in Port Townsend.[17]

In 1975, Haag had another opportunity to work with Fred Bassetti, this time on one of his only projects in Europe, the U.S. Embassy in Lisbon, Portugal.[18] Their design had to both address security concerns and represent the United States to the public. Bassetti used the steep grade of the land from the Avenida das Forças Armadas and the existing villa, the Quinta do Pinheiro, to cascade the buildings across the top of the ridge, just like the siting of a traditional villa. This left the northern half of the site, which slopes downward, open for lawn and trees. Haag carefully graded the hillside so that it would provide generous space for walking and sitting and permit the tree canopies to conceal the buildings. Between the buildings, Haag inserted small garden beds that echoed the formal gardens of the villa in the southern corner of the site. And as with most of his work, the drive does not enter on center or become a primary element of the design but was carefully graded into the site to create an elegant entry sequence by car, not visible from elsewhere on the site. For those arriving on foot, a path led through a woodland landscape and up the hill to the front entrance. A small stream bordered by colorful flowering plants flowed down the center of the site. It was a design that responded to the historical site and to the modern need for security and privacy, with traces of history woven in through such elements as the tiles, the architectural materials, and the woodland.

PIKE PLACE MARKET AND STEINBRUECK PARK

The effort to save Pike Place Market marked a pivotal moment in Seattle's history. In the early 1960s, as the market had increasingly suffered from neglect and with the city seeking to redefine itself through urban renewal projects, leaders proposed the Pike Plaza Redevelopment Project.[19] The plan called for replacing existing buildings with high-rise apartments, hotels, and a seven-level parking garage—a fairly typical plan for the 1960s from a city that wanted to reenergize its downtown and counter suburban spread. Meanwhile, city council member Wing Luke quietly talked with civic leaders about organizing a public protest.[20] In 1964, the Friends of the Market was launched with Steinbrueck at the helm. Steinbrueck, one of the founders of Allied Arts, of which Haag was also a member, wanted to save not only the market buildings but associated public uses. He developed a powerful visual argument by publishing collections of sketches of the market and Seattle sites that residents knew well. These images, as architectural historian Jeffrey Karl Ochsner has suggested, grew out of the emerging critique of modernist urban planning and

7.4 Richard Haag at Pike Place Market, Seattle, December 1964.

7.5 Victor Steinbrueck Park, view to Puget Sound and the Olympic Mountains, highlighting Seattle's natural setting, c. 1988.

emphasized the experience of urban space over time to create a strong sense of place.[21]

By 1969, the public was increasingly suspicious of urban renewal projects. Friends of the Market invited Laurie Olin to return to Seattle to be the organization's vice president, with Steinbrueck as president. In 1971, they launched Initiative 1 to save the market, and it passed in November, although not without a fight. By 1974, the nine-acre Pike Place Market Historical District was undergoing renovation as a major attraction and market space. Haag was not at the forefront of the public discourse but participated in informal debates, many at the Red Robin near his office. More important for Haag, however, was learning from those efforts how to frame his own advocacy for future projects, including Gas Works Park and Steinbrueck Park.

The Washington State National Guard Armory stood just north of Pike Place Market, built around 1909 and partially destroyed in a fire in 1962. While focused on the market itself, Friends of the Market opposed plans to develop the armory for commercial uses while acknowledging that some type of parking area might be necessary. They quickly understood that this triangle of space could be an important extension of the market and a public open space in downtown Seattle. Steinbrueck wrote, "One of the grandest downtown lookout places is at Western Avenue where it meets Pike Place and Virginia Street. It has been neglected by the city and its possibilities for enjoyment are ignored except by a few habitués and passing pedestrians."[22] Steinbrueck produced a series of sketches of the sights that might be viewed from this small piece of land, suggesting that one could see what amounted to a microcosm of Seattle and its urban and natural assets.[23] The city purchased the land in 1968, demolished the remnants of the armory, and transferred ownership to the parks department in 1970. It was a power move on the part of city leaders who opposed the Pike Place Market preservation efforts, but Steinbrueck and Haag devised an effective response.

In what seemed an extension of the market preservation efforts, Steinbrueck and Haag proposed a community devel-

7.6 Victor Steinbrueck Park plan, completed in collaboration with Victor Steinbrueck, 1982.

7.7 Victor Steinbrueck Park perspective sketch, 1981.

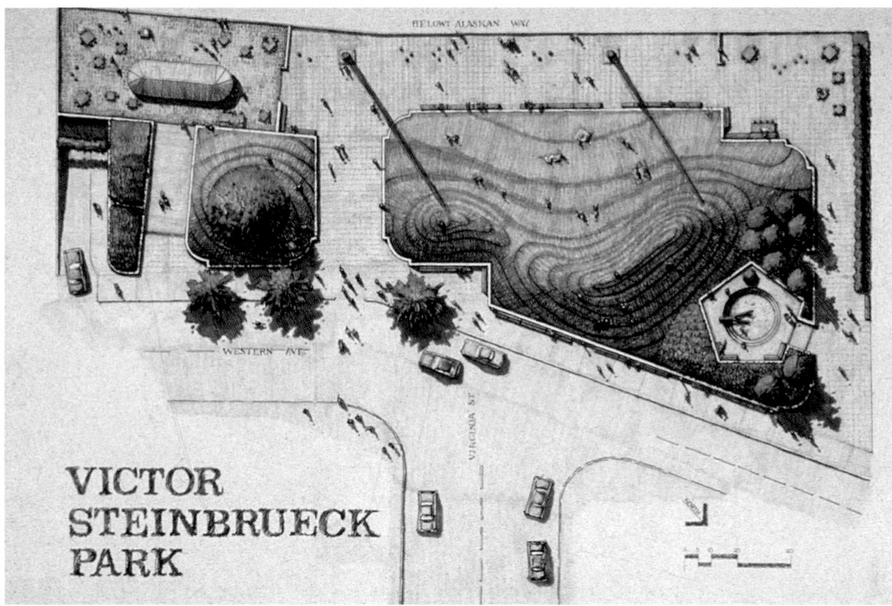

opment project to make a temporary park out of materials from the demolished building site. In July 1972, the Seattle Department of Community Development approved a temporary park at the armory site, which was dedicated on June 4, 1973. Steinbrueck and Haag joined forces again to advocate for a permanent park on the site and were approved to develop the park as part of the Pike Urban Renewal Project on April 12, 1978. Thus, the temporary armory park eventually became the Market Park, which opened on May 28, 1982; after Steinbrueck's untimely death in 1985, it was renamed in his honor.[24]

The three-quarter-acre site, a cantilevered terrace over a parking garage, featured a view of Elliott Bay and the Olympic Mountains. As Haag remarked, the park is "essentially a belvedere to honor the view, to increase the street life, and continue the sociability of the Market."[25] Haag, Peggy Gaynor, and Steinbrueck designed two earth forms to center the space. On the west side of the park was a railing so that visitors could get as close as possible to the edge and look down on the Alaskan Way Viaduct—Seattle's elevated highway, built in 1949–53—and the view of mountains and water. Against the southwestern edge was a pergola that appeared an extension of the market stalls that made up Pike Place Market. Stools and small tables were placed throughout the park, including benches marking the edges of the park.

For the northeastern corner, Haag designed a depression that offered a protected place for a playground. Buster Simpson was commissioned for a piece that would serve as a play structure. The idea for the play structure came after Simpson and Haag applied to designate Post Alley as a right of way, and Simpson tried to save a cherry tree that had been on the site for years. When they lost both fights, they saved the trunk of the cherry tree and recycled it as a play structure and sculpture. Neighborhood artists including Robert Hendrickson, Lawrence Ulaaq R. Ahvakana, James Harmon, and Buster Simpson carved the tree. Ironically, one night when Hendricksen was carving the tree trunk, the police arrested him for vandalism. Simpson bailed him out for $400, and the carving continued. Children enjoyed the cherry tree and

7.8 Victor Steinbrueck Park, with landforms giving space to the movement of people, sun, and wind across the landscape, Seattle, 2014.

7.9 Victor Steinbrueck Park, playground with cherry tree sculpture by Buster Simpson set in the sandbox, Seattle, 1982.

sandbox by climbing and exploring the carvings for years. Steinbrueck and Haag went into the forests in the Cascade Mountains and selected trees to be carved as totem poles for the park. Artists Marvin Oliver and Jim Bender designed and crafted the two tall totem poles, one for Native American peoples and the other for farmers. Steinbrueck and Roman E. Torres designed and fabricated the delicate ironwork that casts an intricate shadow on the overlook's terrace.

Steinbrueck had argued about the importance of preserving public views as early as 1960–61 and again in his *Seattle Cityscape* of 1973. Haag, too, understood the power of views for the city. Together, the two men created an iconic public space in Seattle from which a visitor could see the breadth of Seattle's assets—from Pike Place Market to the mountains and water vistas.[26] Today, it remains an iconic place in Seattle as well as contested territory. In this park, tourists at Pike Place Market meet workers on lunch break, and both overlap with homeless individuals, youth, and communities of Native Americans who have few other gathering places in the public realm. This has caused concern for some, and yet the park's design continues to encourage these disparate groups to occupy adjacent spaces, perhaps because of the different modes of seating available—from benches, to stools, to the lawn—the distinct spaces, the focus of the view toward the mountains, and the site's location in the middle of a downtown that does not have many open spaces. Unfortunately, the playground fell into disrepair and was replaced with a sculpture intended as a remembrance for the homeless who have died in Seattle. The parks department also made other changes in the past two decades, including lowering the berms and removing the shelter. Haag originally designed an eighty-foot hedge of blueberry plants for the public to forage, but this was changed to an evergreen hedge that would be easier to maintain. These alterations frustrated and often disheartened Haag as he continued to argue for a more powerful and authoritative role for landscape architects in the public landscape, as advocates for the public.

SMALL PARKS AND VIEWPOINT PARKS

Between 1965 and 1995, Haag was commissioned to provide plans for street trees and streetscapes as well as multiple small parks across the Seattle metropolitan area. He also worked extensively with the King County Department of Highways on the Urban Arterial Improvement Project, as the firm's records include a list of twenty arterial streetscape projects ranging in scale from one avenue or street to county-wide projects. The firm, in collaboration with the architect Victor Steinbrueck, also provided designs for a number of Seattle's viewpoint parks, including Betty Bowen Park in 1977 and the Capitol Hill Viewpoint Park between 1966 and 1975. The parks were a concerted effort by Steinbrueck and Haag to take advantage of points throughout Seattle that afforded spectacular views of the mountains and the sound. The Capitol Hill viewpoint stands at the top of the Louisa Boren Park, created in 1913. In the 1970s, as Steinbrueck and Haag identified their viewpoint parks, this site was an obvious candidate for improvement, as it had fallen into disrepair. Its views took in Lake Washington and the Cascade mountains, and its triangular shape between intersecting roads meant that a small park was an ideal use.

The plan was composed of simple elements: a path that skirted the edge of the slope, separated from the street by grass-covered berms and a row of linden trees along busy Fifteenth Avenue. A sculpture by Lee Kelly was installed, and the lighting fixtures were designed to echo the rusted steel sculpture. Looking north towards the city, on the right is a magnolia tree that featured a bench wrapped around its trunk, and to the left is a big-leaf maple. It is a park for viewing the landscape, protected from the street and yet still a part of of its urban landscape setting.[27]

The Firehouse Mini Park, on Eighteenth Avenue in the Central District of Seattle, featured a small open lawn and trees as well as a substantial playground. It was created in 1971 in a neighborhood that had not had such amenities. The CAMP headquarters were located at the restored firehouse next door, which would become a historic landmark and

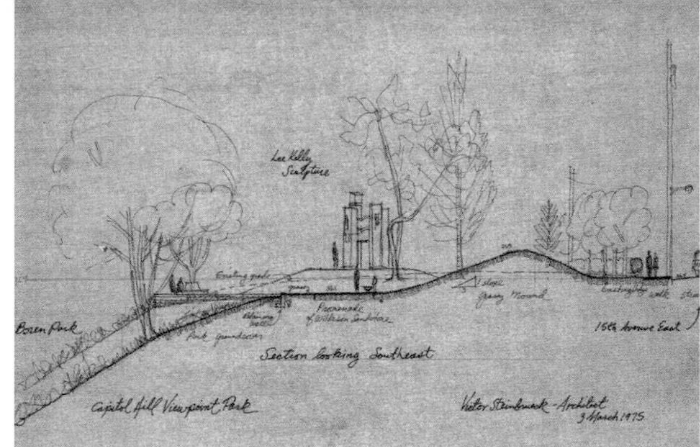

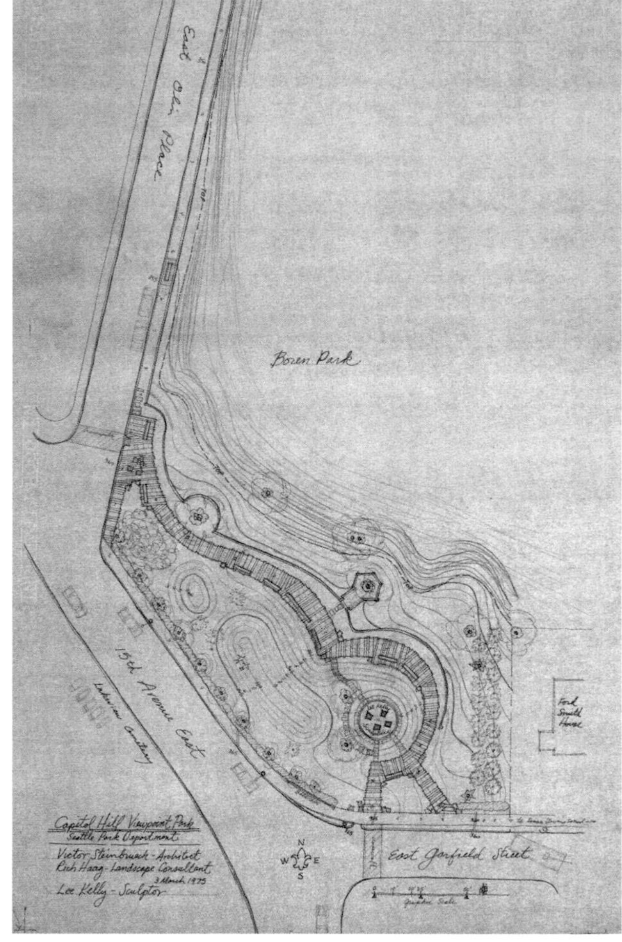

7.10a, b Capitol Viewpoint Park site plan, 1975, with architect Victor Steinbrueck.

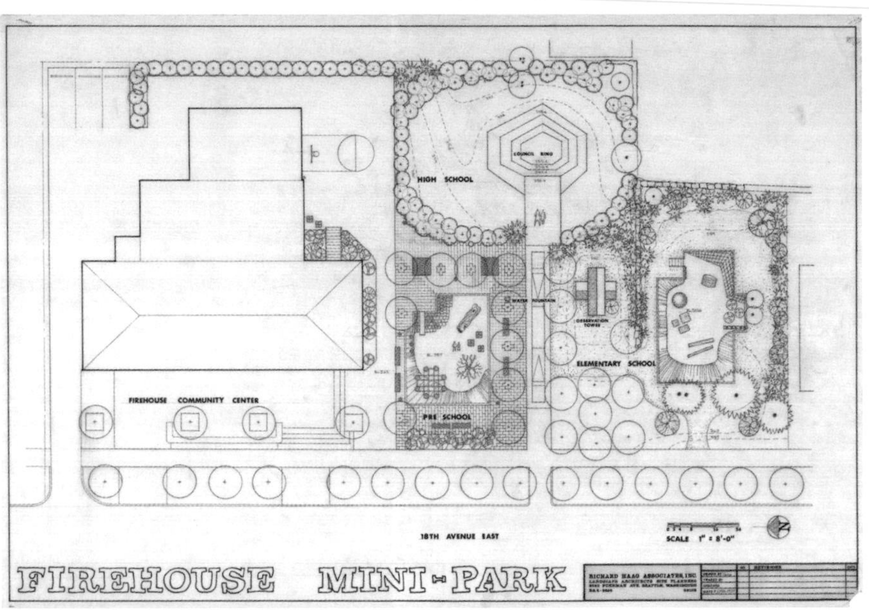

7.11 Firehouse Mini Park design, Seattle, 1971.

7.12 Firehouse Mini Park, lookout tower, Seattle, c. 1982.

7.13 Firehouse Mini Park, playground, Seattle, c. 1982.

community center. Initially, Haag had persuaded the city to purchase adjacent houses, in one of which he hoped to create Seattle's first adventure playground and offer classes on the construction trades. His idea was to gut the house and then teach the electrical, plumbing, and carpentry trades inside the structure. Outside the house would be construction materials that children could use to build their own structures. He brought students from his course on recreational planning and design to develop ideas for this innovative proposal. However, it did not appeal to the neighborhood, as many residents wanted a playground similar to those in other neighborhoods. Adventure playgrounds and a house that was always under construction did not meet their expectations, so Haag withdrew the plan and proceeded to develop designs that were closer to what the community wanted.

Within these constraints, Haag created distinct spaces for each of the groups that were expected to use the Firehouse Mini Park. The council ring, for example, was surrounded by a double row of trees planted on earth berms that allowed the seating to be sunk into the ground, forming a safe and secure space for teenagers to gather. The preschool playground was defined by a paved courtyard with widely spaced trees and benches so that parents could mingle on the edges while the children played in the center. The playground was equipped not with the standard structures but with logs, a tree, and simple landforms. A water fountain separated the preschool children from those in elementary school, and a lookout tower established a vertical marker in the landscape. Unfortunately, of the programmed ideas, only the tower was built, while other ideas were lost as construction costs mounted. Nevertheless, the 17,600-square-foot park was installed for less than $38,000 and still serves the community.

Playgrounds remained an important part of Haag's practice, and he would design play areas for other public projects, including the Arboreal Adventure for Island Park Elementary School on Mercer Island, near Seattle. This project was created within a second-growth forest that had not been logged for more than thirty years. Haag created a series of clearings in the woods connected by a path that wound through the

7.14 South Passage Point Park plan, 1977.

7.15 North Passage Point Park plan, 1977.

7.16 Marymoor Park master plan, 1973.

entire park. He headed up the efforts of local residents who volunteered to thin out the dead trees and create stumps for climbing and sitting. Haag added just a few rhododendrons and ferns as underplants. This park was used by the elementary school as well as by other schools in Seattle for field trips and by the Seattle Head Start program.[28] While *Landscape Architecture Magazine* covered this project, it was the first adventure-type playground it featured, Haag was never able to design the true adventure playground he had envisioned.

North and South Passage Point Parks, built under each end of the I-5 bridge over Lake Union, were the result of space left over between the bridge's enormous pillars after construction of Interstate 5, a project Haag had opposed—and Forward Thrust bond funds were available to develop them into a public amenity. Haag's design for Point Parks, each under an acre, focused on the views from the waterfront. He placed seating in the spots with the best views, adding a weeping willow for shade and seasonal interest in the park to the south and red maples in the park to the north. The trees mediated the scale of the pillars and gave each tiny piece of land the character of a park.

In addition to his work on the smaller parks, Haag also designed many of the large parks in the Seattle area. In the 1970s, he provided plans for Carkeek Park, a restoration and renovation project in northwest Seattle, and Westcrest Park, a new park wrapped around the West Seattle Reservoir. Haag worked on rehabilitation plans for Volunteer Park between 1970 and 1975. As the park was being overused, he initially proposed enlarging it, but when that did not work, he realized that another solution would be to slow down movement through the park and proposed banning cars. He persuaded the city to remove some of the roads and to turn others into one-way streets, thus improving the park for its many pedestrians.

For Marymoor Park in Redmond, a King County project, the placement of roads was again a focus of argument. It was the largest park Haag worked on, designed in phases between 1969 and 1975. The 486-acre park featured a wide variety of programmed space, including a velodrome, ball fields, and an archaeological shelter. Haag became involved when he was invited to a general meeting to discuss the plans completed by landscape architects William Talley and Cassius Beardsley for farmland that was to become a county park. Partway through the meeting, however, Haag realized that the plan included an extension of Interstate 405 and a series of parking lots cutting through the park. He objected quietly, and when challenged to come up with a better plan, he agreed to try. His alternative plan was eventually approved, and although it was not fully implemented, due to significant increases in the construction bids, the general configuration reflects his vision. In the Seattle suburbs, Haag provided designs for Bellevue parks, Cougar Mountain Park, and Kenmore Park, the latter two for King County. Thus, Haag has shaped many of the parks that locals came to use on a daily basis.

Of the public parks, Haag's design with Steinbrueck for Steinbrueck Park remains his best known next to Gas Works Park. As an extension of Pike Place Market, the park makes a statement about not only the beauty of Seattle's views of

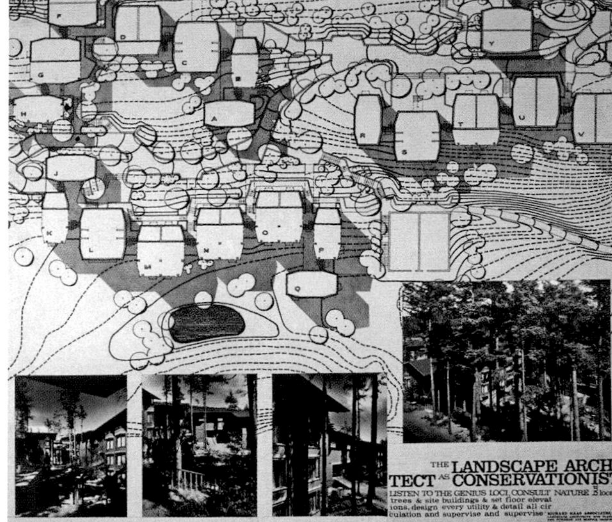

7.17 Western Washington State College residence master plan, Richard Haag Associates and Fred Bassetti, 1959–64.

7.18 Ridgeway dorm, with boulder showing the steep slope on which the campus was designed, Western Washington State College, Bellingham, c. 1970.

mountains and water but also the important role of preservation and civic advocacy. This is the lesson Haag passed on to his students and young employees. Few of his designs stand out as Design; many of the parks seem to blend in with the larger landscape, and people often have no idea the parks were designed. That was Haag's intention. He believed that good public space was most important, not the designer's apparent brilliance.

COLLEGE CAMPUSES

One of Haag's first projects after arriving in Seattle was the design for the dorms at Central Washington State College in Ellensburg, with his colleague Fred Bassetti of Bassetti & Morse. The project began in 1959, received an AIA Seattle Honor Award in 1961, and continued through 1974. Bassetti & Morse, with Bassetti as lead, was also commissioned for the Ridgeway dorms at Western Washington State College in Bellingham. Bassetti brought Haag onto that project as well, and once again the AIA Seattle recognized the project with an Honor Award in 1963.[29] Originally, the administrators leading the project had imagined that the Ridgeway dorms would be built on a flat piece of land adjacent to the playing fields, but Bassetti and Haag explored the forested slope above the fields and proposed dorms nestled into the slope and among the trees. They designed the dorms in a cluster, like a small village. At the time they were working on the project, their employees included Bob Hanna, Grant Jones, Jerry Diethelm, and Frank James in the Haag office and Olin in Bassetti's office, all classmates and friends, which made collaboration productive and congenial.

The two principals, Haag and Bassetti, set the framework: essentially, the dorms were to be sited in the landscape to meet contours and allow as many of the existing trees as possible to remain. Haag remarked that architects are uncomfortable with a site that is not flat, so he began the project by designing stairs. In that way. he had already started to define the spaces for the buildings. Bassetti and Haag together

7.19 Ridgeway dorms, path, and terrace in the woods, Western Washington State College, Bellingham, c. 1970.

7.20 Fairhaven College of Interdisciplinary Studies, Western Washington State College, Bellingham, 1995.

7.21 Rainier Vista, looking southeast toward Mount Rainier, University of Washington, Seattle, n.d.

then oriented each dorm in these spaces so as to maximize sun and wind advantages. The dorms were nestled into the undulating landscape and woodland, with the stairs providing circulation through the site. Using the topographic form of the land, Haag designed the paths to move through the native habitats, appearing to wander from building to building. This emphasis on the existing landform and native plants celebrated the experience of the campus as set within a hillside forest at a human scale. The result was a series of dormitories that appear to emerge from the site, each with its entrance threshold sheltered by honey locusts. The design as constructed reflects the close collaboration between architecture and landscape, with the academic village appearing to grow out of the hillside. Students ascend and descend by means of multiple stairways, always surrounded by forests, with openings like glades at the entrances to the buildings. It was a landscape that expressed the nature of the region.

Bassetti went on to design many of the campus buildings as well as the sculpture *Alphabeta Cube* (now at Fairhaven College of Interdisciplinary Studies, Bellingham). Haag developed plans for the central library plaza that included the use of his favorite benches, the platform-style keblis. In 1962, he was invited to join Paul Thiry on the commission for the design of the library addition and to revise the landscape around the president's house extension, which Thiry had completed in 1958. Thus, the school, although significantly enlarged, remains grounded in Haag's regional design response to the landscape.[30]

In 1968, Haag was again commissioned by Western Washington State College to design the landscape for Fairhaven College. Fairhaven was to serve as a new type of campus located in a hidden valley, as Haag described it. With a planned enrollment of six hundred and a faculty of twenty-five, it would be designed as a small community cluster. Haag recalled this project as a highlight of his early design work with Bassetti as did his Richard Haag Associates (RHA) employees Sakuma and Lehner. Together they designed a community that would foster a sense of place and purpose,

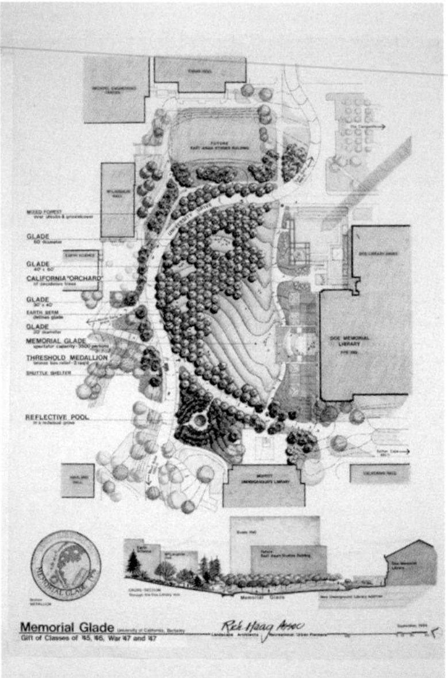

with a large central space that provided places for gathering, gardening, and lounging. They used red maple, birch, aspen, and dogwood trees, with rhododendrons serving as a middle-scale plant. The design also featured Haag's favorite tree, the katsura, along with hemlock and Scotch pine. The college became a community carved out of the site.

Haag also worked as a landscape architect for the University of Washington's Seattle campus. As a faculty member, he was invited to serve as a founding member of the University Landscape Architecture Committee in 1962. The first meeting was held on Thursday, November 1, 1962, with members Brian O. Mulligan, Arthur R. Kruckeberg, Frank C. Brockman, Varro E. Tyler, university architect Eric W. Hoyts, and Haag. The committee soon came to the conclusion that it needed a master plan for the campus landscape and asked Haag to lead the effort. By 1968, Hideo Sasaki was serving on the university's Architectural Review Commission as an outside professional, and he would be involved in reviewing the proposed plan as would the office of Lawrence Halprin on specific projects.

Haag saw the master plan as integral to his development of the landscape architecture degree program and department. For this reason, he began his report on the university campus with a description of the educational objectives for the curriculum he was leading, implying that the two roles, teacher and professional, would be grounded in the same set of values:

> The objective of the Landscape curriculum at the University of Washington Seattle: The objective is Competence in establishing a design of balance for the human environment. This competence:
> - Recognizes the primal import of nature systems as supreme giver of form, giver of life, giver of ceremony
> - Insists on an ecological approach to design—in time (history), in space (dwelling to dwelling, dwelling to street, to neighborhood, etc.) and in human/economic values.

7.22 Grieg Garden, University of Washington, Seattle, designed by Hanna/Olin and Robert Shinbo, landscape architects, 1990.

7.23 Eastern Washington State College, path showing fusion of brick and grass, Cheney, c. 1990.

7.24 Memorial Glade plan, University of California, Berkeley, 1994.

- Acknowledges the reciprocal relationship between the design specialties
- Presupposes and understanding of structural systems, tools and techniques
- Suggests a strategic attack rather than tactical
- Cuts across temporary barriers of individual "style" etc.
- Demands an enlarged role in community affairs
- Is bound in compassion for the human condition

Respectfully submitted, RH

With the framework described, Haag turned his attention to the details of refining and enhancing the campus. A primary concern was the health of the trees and the definition of the campus perimeters. Haag explained where trees needed to be added and how the campus edges might be strengthened as thresholds. He also laid out the areas that showed potential for further expansion, as the university was in the process of building up its campus facilities. Haag recommended that existing landscape spaces be preserved and existing buildings expanded rather than new buildings built. He listed what he considered the sacred areas of the campus: Rainier Vista, the Sylvan Theater, Madrona Grove, Governor's Grove, and the woods along the edges of the campus, areas that most still consider special. Subsequent plans outlined suggestions for each area and focused heavily on the addition of trees, the insertion of pedestrian paths, and definition of the edges and entrances. Haag's plan offered an analysis of the campus at the time and did not engage a particularly new vision for the landscape.

In the following decades, Haag would design campus landscapes for the University of Washington Bothell, Eastern Washington State College in Cheney, and Washington State University in Pullman. For each landscape, he drew on his design tools of fusion; the min-max approach, which considers the minimum means of achieving the maximum effect; and, most important, the character of the Pacific Northwest's landscape of forests, water, and mountains. His firm also received commissions from community colleges in the state, including Big Bend Community College in Moses Lake (1962–65), Everett Community College (1970–71), Highline Community College in Midway (1974), and Walla Walla Community College (1969–70).

7.25 Frye Art Museum expansion, view from sidewalk, Seattle, 2014, with architect Rick Sundberg of Olson Sundberg Kundig Allen Architects.

In 1994, RHA was commissioned to restore the Memorial Glade at the University of California, Berkeley, Haag's alma mater. This significant landscape within the urban campus served as both a public gathering space and a memorial to those who had served in World War II. With the expansion of the library (designed by SOM), the university committed to reserving a four-acre landscape to be transformed into a memorial and central campus element. The landscape echoed nearby groves and lawn, creating a series of spaces of varying proportions and character. As the war memorial committee noted, the limited use of any architectural materials was a strength of the design that celebrated the region's trees and views. At a time when college and university campuses were expanding dramatically, Haag played a critical role in providing the master plans and landscape designs for West Coast and Pacific Northwest campuses.

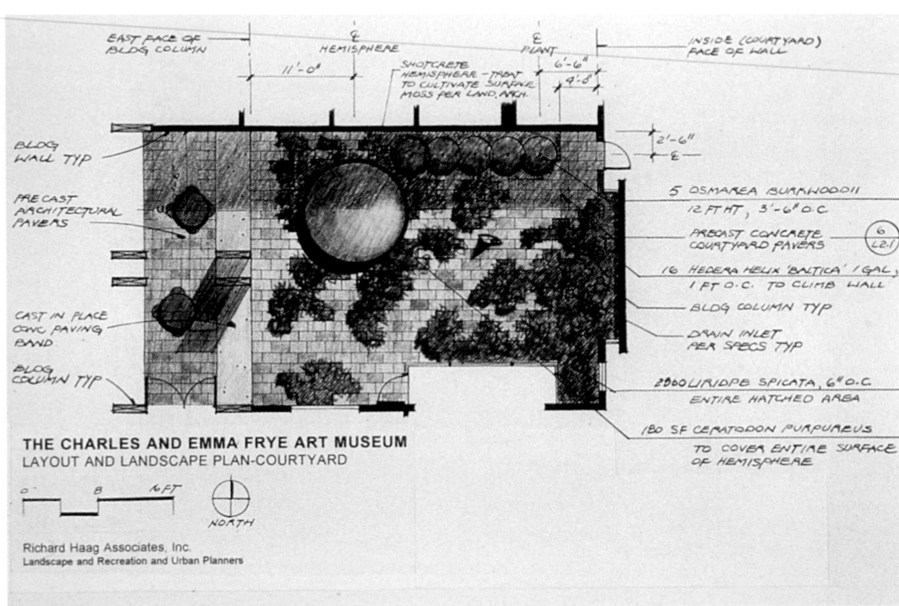

7.26 Frye Art Museum courtyard with moss hemisphere, Seattle, 1997.

7.27 Frye Art Museum courtyard plan, with Richard Haag's notes, 1997.

MUSEUMS

While college campuses served a particular public role, museums were another important public learning space. Haag worked with architect Rick Sundberg of Olson Sundberg Kundig Allen to design a significant expansion for the Frye Art Museum in Seattle (1994–97). Haag's initial requirement was to mark the entrance as well as design the setting as a visual asset to the neighborhood. He accomplished this by establishing a screen of street trees that created a rich threshold for the museum site and obscured the parking lot across the street. A ramp ran parallel to a long, reflecting pool at the front of the building. Once inside the building, the axis ended in an open-sky courtyard. Through these intersections of inside and outside, Haag and Sundberg created a fluid sense of engagement in the site. The courtyard took this one step further by featuring a large moss-covered hemisphere that served as a piece of sculpture as well as part of the vegetation.

Haag again used fusion as a concept for the Frye Art Museum design, merging architectural materials with plants and mixing indoor and outdoor, structure and nature. He placed a large rough-cast concrete hemisphere emerging from the ground and covered in moss (*Certodon purpureus*) in the courtyard, just off center, creating a dramatic focal point. In this urban courtyard, Haag did not sculpt the land but used architecture to create space for a sculpture reminiscent of the earth: a concrete boulder made by an artist rather than by geologic processes. He considered other design ideas, most significantly a form of the Bloedel Reserve's Garden of Planes, with pyramids of white gravel, experimenting in drawings with single and double pyramids of a variety of scales.

Given the enclosed character of the courtyard, however, many of these concepts would seem to overwhelm the space. Over time, Haag moved from the form of the square or rectangle to the circle and sphere—in one sketch, he paired a circular mound with a pyramid. Eventually, he simplified the design and placed the moss-covered hemisphere off center in the courtyard, with osmanthus softening the back wall. This combination of the vertical, lacy trees with the moss-covered hemisphere responds to the space in a more dynamic manner than other concepts considered. In another reading, the hemisphere echoes the domed entrance space, as if the two were nested in each other. In a review of the museum's new landscape and renovations, *Seattle Post-Intelligencer* art critic Regina Hackett wrote, "The mound's weirdness is oddly comforting amid the chic of the building."[31] This characterizes Haag's approach well, especially when compared with many modern designs by today's architects. And yet, the minimalist character of this project moves beyond the weird or odd, or even expressive. The moss-covered hemisphere is a minimalist expression of the land, nature, and character of the Pacific Northwest. It is an abstraction of the wetness, lushness, and roundness of the region's landscape and environment. Haag remained fascinated by a search for the essence of a place, both at the site and at regional scales. His work offers an expression of a design minimalism focused on the essence of a place defined by basic geometric forms, such as the sphere and the plane. This is the power of the Frye Art Museum courtyard, far beyond the mere presence of garden courtyard.

LIBRARIES

Haag defined his approach to design primarily in his residential work, but with his increased focus on public work, a few small projects composed in collaboration with local architects gave him the opportunity to translate his residential design into a more public design language. The Magnolia Branch library, completed in 1965, is one such example. Haag was commissioned to work with noted Seattle architect Paul Hayden Kirk of Kirk, Wallace, McKinley and Associates. The project is recognized today as "a quintessential example of Northwest design with distinct influences of Japan."[32] Seattle's Landmark Preservation Board would designate the library as a landmark in 2003.

7.28 Magnolia Branch library, front entrance, just after planting around existing madrona tree, Seattle, 1966.

7.29 Magnolia Branch library, Seattle, 1966.

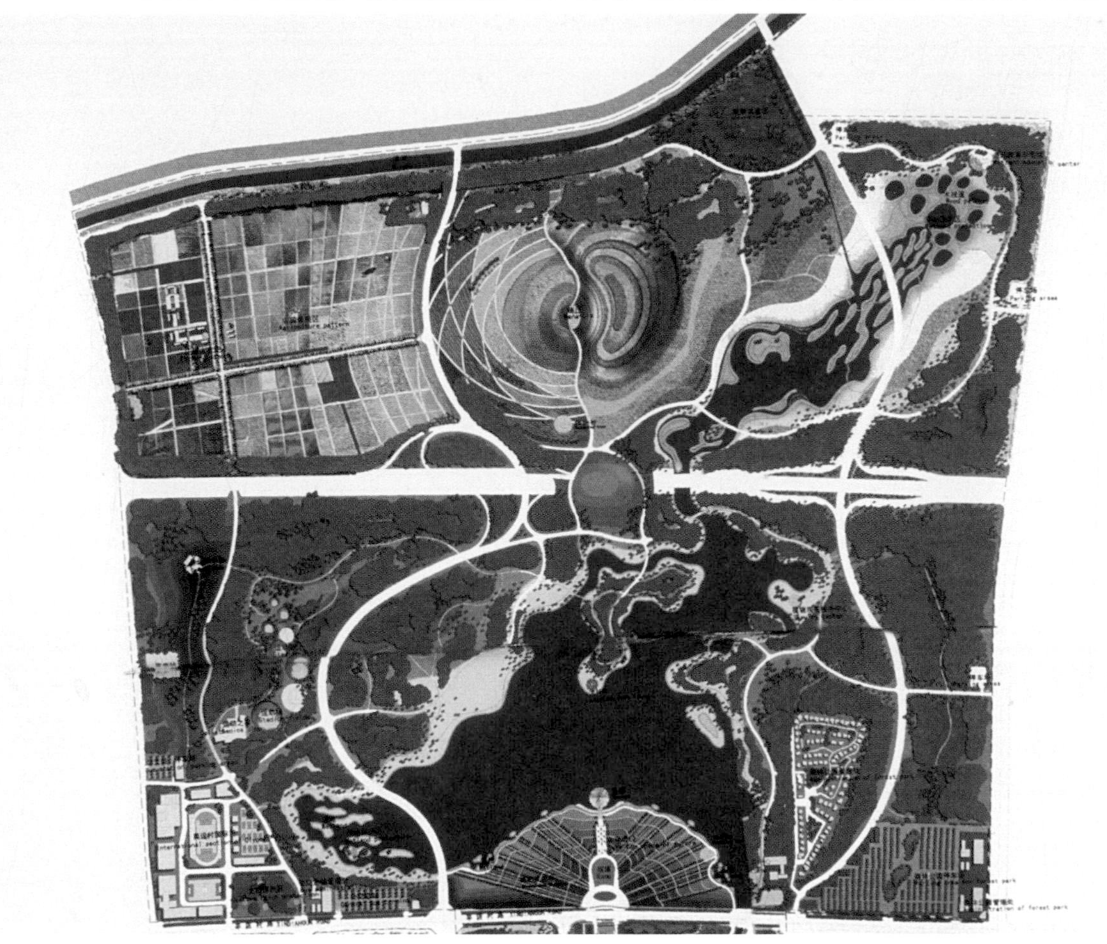

7.30 RHA submission to the Peoples Park Competition for the 2008 Summer Olympics in Beijing, 2004.

Haag's design, with its use of the madrona trees, salal, viburnum, and ferns, reveals his attachment to the flora of the Pacific Northwest. The brick entrance path starts at the edges of the sidewalk and spirals gracefully up the stairs and around the corner to the library door. The whole area was in dappled shade, and the library's large windows reflected the trees and shrubs, thus doubling their presence. Visitors have a similar experience from inside the library, where the large windows reveal a Pacific Northwest woodland landscape, giving the effect of being nestled in the woods. Kirk's interior use of wood emphasized the experience: one small child is rumored to have commented that the place clearly was not a "branch library" but a "tree library."[33]

COMPETITIONS

Haag also enjoyed the competition for public projects. While he did not receive significant recognition for his submissions, they were important for developing ideas and representing his experimental approach to design. His firm submitted designs for Fort Lawton (a commission Kiley won), the Bellevue Downtown Park in 1984, and the Washington State Department of Ecology Building in Lacey in 1991 and won first place for the design for Kirkland's Panorama Park. His submission to the 2004 Peoples Park Competition for the 2008 Summer Olympics in Beijing was voted the public's favorite. The design, completed with Cheryl Trivison in the RHA office and the architects Studio Ectypos, was again a public favorite in the 2005 Blue Green Park, Orange County Great Park Competition, for a park to be built over the runways of the former El Toro Marine Corps Air Station.

Haag competed for more distant projects, including the Copley Square competition (1965) and Spectacle Island competition (1983), both in Boston; the international Bridging the Gap competition (1991); and the Parc de la Villette competition in Paris (1985). The latter was an important moment in landscape architecture, as Bernard Tschumi, an architect, won the competition. Haag's submission explored the idea of evolving and successional natural habitats. He designed the park to reflect the evolution of the garden, from the kitchen garden to the ecological garden, narrating the story of humans moving from nature to culture and from country to city.[34] He wove in the course of water as an inherent part of that history. Finally, he layered a series of investigations within the details of the garden that focused on the garden, labor input, and energy output. It was as much an intellectual proposal as an ecological design.

As he became increasingly widely recognized, Haag was invited to serve on competition juries across the country. Among these were the Washington Roadside Council Awards (1978) and the Design Arts Commission in Denver, Colorado (1980). He was appointed to the National Endowment for the Arts First Presidential Design Awards jury (1984), participated on its Design Arts Program Design Communication panel (1985), and was a delegate for its Landscape Architecture Retreat in Virginia. He has served as a juror for the AIA Seattle's Honor Awards program (1988), the National ASLA Awards (1988, 2004), and the Taipei "Central Park" Competition (2008). He was an invited juror on the Oklahoma City Memorial International Design Competition in Oklahoma City (1997) and the Flight 93 Memorial, Pennsylvania (2005). More recently he has served on juries for the Vancouver Connector Competition in Vancouver, Washington (2009); the Environmental Design Research Association International Competition—Great Places (2012); and Design Waller Creek, Austin, Texas (2012).

Throughout his career, Haag has offered his expertise as he advocated for a leadership role for landscape architects. In 1962, he was an adviser to the U.S. Department of Agriculture on farmer's markets and the United Indians of All Tribes Foundation in Seattle. Also in Seattle, he was a founding member of the Friends of the Duwamish (Citizens' Watch Dog Committee) and a member of the selection committee for the Rome Fellowship Program of the Northwest Institute for Architecture and Urban Studies in Rome. In these and other roles, Haag has actively advocated for design to engage in supporting the improvement of society and the built environment. As he would teach his students, "Landscape architecture is criticism. . . . Its importance will increase as man's occupancy increases and is magnified by increasing demands on the diminishing earth base. Landscape architecture is in. The environment is a political issue."[35]

8

the art of the landform as landscape architecture

PUBLIC PLACE AS A DEMOCRATIC SPACE WAS AT THE CORE of Haag's design values, but equally significant to his practice was the art of form making with earth and land, to shape spatial experience and ecological process. His experimentation with form making and the medium of landscape could be traced to his childhood play with his grandfather's gravel. It carried through to his garden designs in California and the Pacific Northwest. It was inspired by the use of stones and earth in the Japanese gardens he visited. And his imagination would be expanded on trips in 1957 and 1960 to Mexico, where he found dynamic landforms at the archaeological sites of Mitla, Chichén Itzá, Uxmal, and Teotihuacán.[1] Finally, Haag's shaping of land reveals a minimalism that evokes the art of the 1960s and 1970s, the search for the essential nature of a site through its topography.

At the Mesoamerican sites, Haag walked through landforms of an immense scale, the opposite of those in Japan. The pyramidal mounds set within an imposing geometry of axes made an immediate and lasting impression. As many of the areas, including the Pyramid of the Moon at Teotihuacán, had yet to be fully excavated, they appeared literally as large mounds. He imagined these forms describing a social composition with high priests and leaders at the top and people filling the volume of space in the ground plane and between pyramids. The Japanese gardens were at a human scale, ideal for contemplation or attuned listening. In the Mesoamerican sites, the immense landforms created large social spaces that served as bridges between the human world and the cosmos. It was in comparing Japanese and Mesoamerican landscapes that Haag came to fully realize the range of approaches to the forming of space with land, that the sculpting of earth might engage any scale, intimate or immense, and that the narratives conveyed by such forms were infinite. He would experiment with these ideas beginning with the small pyramids he designed in the early California gardens to the ziggurat-like form at Jordan Park in Everett, Washington, in the 1970s.

THE LAND ART MOVEMENT

As Haag was developing his experiments with mounds, cones, and other landforms, artists such as Herbert Bayer were exploring landforms as an art medium, one that engaged place and time. In his 1955 work for the Aspen Center, one of the earliest modern earthworks, he shaped the land into a circular form and then allowed climate and time to continue the process. Ernst Cramer's *Poet's Garden*, created for the 1959 Garden Exhibition in Zurich, featured a series of steeply edged grass mounds enclosing an open space at the center. As Robert Smithson has observed, however, interest in shaping land dates back to Frederick Law Olmsted at Central

8.1 Ernst Cramer's Poet's Garden, Garden Exhibition, Zurich, Switzerland, 1959.

Park.[2] The Back Bay Fens by Olmsted and Charles Elliot was another type of land sculpting. At Harvard University, landscape architecture faculty member Walter Louis Chambers,[3] who taught site engineering, encouraged students, including Haag, to sculpt the earth as designers, giving them the skills to design and engineer the landforms.

By the middle of the twentieth century, sculpting land was increasingly of the avant-garde. In October 1969, the year Michael Heizer's *Double Negative* was "unearthed" and a year before the completion of Smithson's *Spiral Jetty*, *Landscape Architecture Magazine*'s editor Grady Clay featured the articles "Dirt Art" and "Light Art."[4] As Clay noted, there was growing interest in shaping earthen mounds as works of art and landscape, from practitioners such as Lawrence Halprin as well as the earth artists.

The environmental art movement of the 1960s and 1970s ushered in a new wave of art that utilized the landscape as both medium and site.[5] Landscape architects were influenced by the strong formal gestures and conceptual proposals of environmental artists. They took notice of how Smithson, Heizer, Walter de Maria, Nancy Holt, and Robert Morris used their work as a means of calling attention to land reclamation. Although they were intrigued, and Smithson remained a significant inspiration, even cult figure, Haag and others also criticized the work for its thin approach to site and landscape. Haag described it as treating the land as cardboard rather than a living medium, one that, as Clay had suggested, has yet to capture "the full potential of all the plastic media (earth, masonry, concrete, metals or industrial plastics) which are available to be designed as an organic system of materials to express a unified esthetic concept."[6] And yet that was not the intention of these artists, many of whom were more interested in rejecting museum cultures than in taking an environmental stance; however, the manifestation of their work often challenged the public to distinguish between land art and landscape architecture.

Haag's play with landforms both precedes and coincides with the environmental art movement; it also draws on his Japanese and Mexican experiences. In the early residential projects, he experimented with the construction of earth forms—sometimes pyramids of sand, sometimes mounds of clay—while other projects were more about spatially defining the area within or between. He covered some mounds in plants, as for the Harry Camp Jr. project, built others of sand and left them in the sun, as with the Case Study House, and investigated the possibility of sunken spaces in the Elwood Wong garden. Later, he would use landforms to create spaces in his public places.

Haag was interested both in sculpting and in the means by which such shaping might reveal a site-conditioned design. He entered one of his first large-scale designs for sculpted earth in the competition for the Franklin Delano Roosevelt Memorial in Washington, D.C., in 1960. For this project, he worked with his students Laurie Olin, Frank James, Elaine Day Latourelle, Jerry Diethelm, Herb Seablom, and Frank Lockfeld. The design proposed a three-hundred-

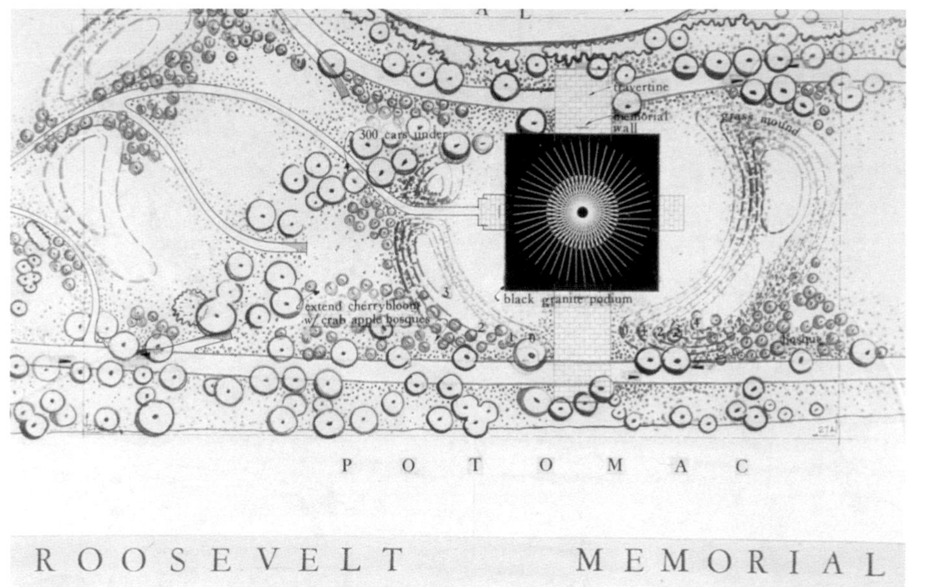

8.2 First submission to the Franklin Delano Roosevelt Memorial competition, Richard Haag Associates, 1960.

8.3 Staves sculpture model for the Franklin Delano Roosevelt Memorial competition, Richard Haag Associates, 1960.

foot-square black granite plaza enclosed by earthen mounds. At the center of the plaza was a sculpture in the form of a North American tipi or, as Haag recalled, the form created when a Japanese farmer stacked poles in the field. The tepee was composed of fifty-one bronze staves, each two hundred feet long, erected over the center of a sunken council ring one hundred feet in diameter. The council ring was sunk five feet below the surface and surrounded by concentric circles that served as seats or stairs. The scale of the project was immense, recalling the Mesoamerican mounds. In addition to the sense of scale and grandeur, the staves represented the founding members of the United Nations, which was, according to Haag, Roosevelt's crowning achievement. It was a far-reaching design that likely had little chance of being selected but rather provided an opportunity for Haag and his students to develop their ideas in an experimental manner.

The jury did not select Haag's entry, but the design interested architect Abraham Geller, who invited Haag to collaborate on a second-round submission. Haag and Lockfeld joined Geller in his New York office, while students in the Seattle office kept a close eye on their progress. The revised submission, "Four Freedoms, Four Courts," was awarded second prize, the first time one of Haag's designs received national recognition. The project's concept was based on an exploding star representing Roosevelt's influence and leadership. It was composed of four folded steles (or cantilevered planes) that shot outward and were echoed in the landscape by radiating rows of poplar trees. All of this was centered on a large hill with undulating slopes that allowed walkers to wander through the site rather than arriving too early and formally at the center. Earthen mounds flanked the paths; in their round form, they appeared to contrast with the steles and the strict grid of poplars. The walkways, which contained pavers set in a wave pattern that countered their architectonic nature and then dissolved at the edges into the grass lawn, were also a play between architecture and landscape, reflecting Haag's idea of fusion. The drawings for the design demonstrate an architecture that appears to be in opposition

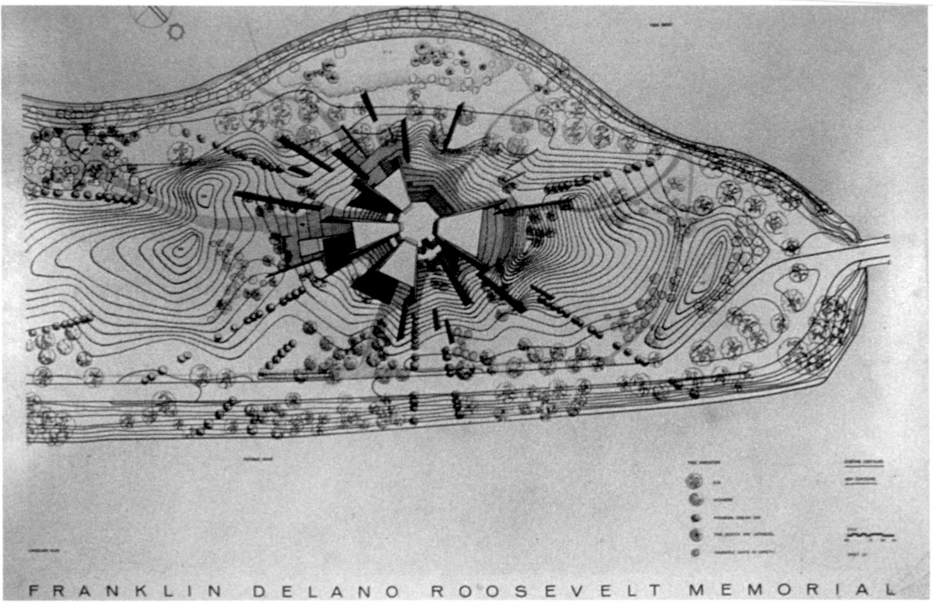

8.4 Plan submitted to the Franklin Delano Roosevelt Memorial competition, Geller + Richard Haag Associates, 1961.

to the landscape. As Haag's first attempt to take his sculpting of land to a much larger scale, it is an ambitious project. Neither submission was built, and these early attempts to employ a larger-scale landform remained conceptual schemes.

SEATTLE CENTER

In 1959, Haag was given an opportunity to construct his landforms in Seattle. Leaders in the city were planning a celebration of the fiftieth anniversary of the Alaska-Yukon-Pacific Exposition, although the event was postponed until 1962. Presented as the Century 21 Exposition, it would look forward rather than backward in time. The fair, featuring a futuristic science narrative, was intended to establish a new civic center for the city, Seattle Center. The city chose a site just north of downtown that had been deemed a derelict neighborhood—known as the "Warren Avenue slum"—not only reenvisioning the district but extending downtown northward. As discussed by Seattle historian John Findlay, the fairgrounds reflected suburban planning principles.[7] The lead architect was Paul Thiry, with prime landscape architect Lawrence Halprin. Halprin selected Haag's office as the local firm to attend to the details of the design and oversee construction. With less than five years since Haag had left Halprin's office, this collaboration may well have been a sign of Haag's growing recognition in the Seattle area as an important landscape architect.

In addition to those parts of the fair on which he was to collaborate with architects hired to design pavilions and exhibit spaces, Haag was responsible for developing portions of the fair. One such area was Flag Plaza. With Grant Jones and Robert Hanna, both of whom were working in his office, he designed a council ring of sorts, a place where the public could come together in a communal fashion. It was composed of a sunken seating ring surrounded by a row of locust trees. The ring was created with pavers and had three levels, which provided flexible seating and allowed standing and talking. It was a clearly a constructed space, and yet with

8.5 Artist's rendition of Century 21 Exposition fairgrounds, with Mount Rainier in the background, 1962.

the locusts growing in the outer ring and the rough surface of the pavers compared to other path materials, the ring had a natural character, similar to that of outdoor amphitheaters.

Haag's office also designed the space in front of the United Nations Pavilion, shaping a bowl by surrounding the center with earthen mounds. Trees wound across the mounds. This provided both a clear space in which to gather on the fairgrounds and a more intimate, green space where visitors could find respite from the excitement of the fair. It was not a meditative or quiet space; however, it was separate from the grandeur of the rest of the fairgrounds. [8] The mounds provided seating areas as well as potential space on which to perform. The performative nature of the space was further enhanced by the shadows of the trees moving across the mounds. The space as a whole—earthen mounds, grass, and trees—was simply articulated and yet offered an alternative to the apparently natural landscapes of public parks, where artifice is made invisible. In this space, artifice in the form of earthen mounds and the lines of trees was clearly defined.

In addition to his travels in Japan and Mexico, a trip to Sweden in 1963 expanded Haag's ideas on the use of landforms. While in Stockholm to attend a conference, he made the trip to Woodland Cemetery, designed by Gunnar Asplund and Sigurd Lewerentz (1915–1940). He was impressed by the landscape's scale and siting, describing it as an "evocative, powerful powerful place." He recalled the vivid topographic experience of ascending the steep meditation mound at the core of the cemetery, on the deep-set paths, "like river channels and you get up to the top and there's that low wall and then there are trees, and some gravestones and just some benches. It's really prospect, and yet refuge at the same time."[9] Haag returned to Seattle more confident of his new experiments in land sculpting at a larger scale.

And he soon had another opportunity to implement his ideas. In the fall of 1963, Haag was commissioned to transform the Seattle Center landscape into a civic and cultural center. He subtly altered the landscape, while leaving many

DFPA Home of Living Light Century 21 Exposition
Liddle & Jones architects

8.6 Home of Living Light sketch, Century 21 Exposition, showing a subtler version of landforms, 1961, with architects Liddle & Jones.

8.7 Council ring, Century 21 Exposition, Seattle, 1962.

8.8 Woodland Cemetery, Stockholm, designed by Gunnar Asplund and Sigurd Lewerentz, 1963.

8.9 Landform planted with trees emphasizing the movement of the space, in front of the Pacific Science Center, Seattle Center, Seattle, 1964.

8.10 Landform and trees defining spaces and walkways, Seattle Center, 1964.

of his first landforms in place. He also looked for a place where he might expand on his ideas for shaping environmental spaces with landforms. The area at the base of the Space Needle was being prepared for a large fountain designed by Halprin, and Haag had the excavated soil that would have been dumped into Lake Union deposited at the northeastern corner of the fairgrounds where, rumor had it, a parking lot was being considered. With this one clever move he questioned the construction of the parking lot, arranged for free removal of the excavated soil, saved the city money, and secured the medium for his experiments with earth forms. He persuaded the city to let him experiment with the excavated soil and created a line of architectonic landforms enclosing an open lawn on three sides with more mounds at the southern end. As the forms were approximately six feet high, perhaps reminiscent of the Mesoamerican pyramids on a smaller scale, they shaped the interior space at a human scale, forming an intimate place of engagement. They were not unlike those he had created elsewhere on the fairgrounds. Haag called the site the "Indian Shell Mound Park"; thus, through shaping and naming, he made the leftover site a new place. The project caught the attention of the public, as noted by the *Seattle Times*:

> Things must be quiet around town. The Seattle Center is catching what for again. This time it's "the mounds" that are causing the fuss and furor. The mounds are flat-topped mounds of earth on the site of the Seattle Worlds' Fair's Show Street, the southwest corner of 5th Ave N and Mercer St. Eventually they'll be covered with grass and hither and thither, mostly thither, will be flowers and a few trees. This is called "sculptured landscaping." Richard Haag, landscape architect and member of the Municipal Arts Commission, is the man behind the plan. And the Seattle Center Advisory Commission, which has been informed on the landscaping of the Center, approves. Matter of fact, it thinks it's ginger peachy. There's one strange thing: Similar grass-covered mounds in the Pacific Science Center [United States Pavilion] never have occasioned a complaint, nor have the mounds on the mall near the Horiuchi mural or around the Flag Plaza.[10]

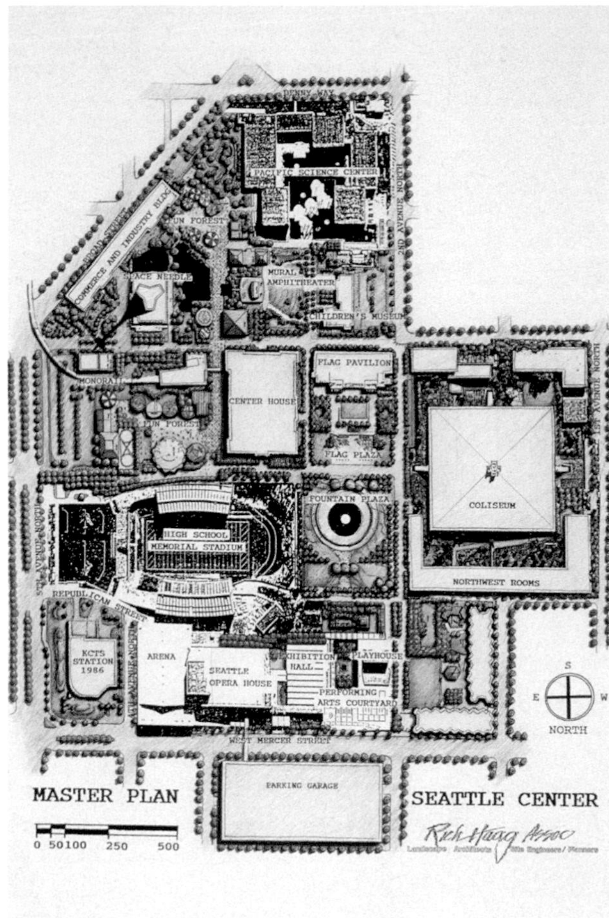

8.11 Seattle Center plan, with landforms, including those surrounding the KCTS building (lower left), 1964.

Despite the protests, the mounds were retained as a public park until the area was redeveloped in 1986. Haag was brought back to consult on the siting and was able to retain a series of landforms along the edge of the street. While he lost the park itself, he had played a role in helping the city to

8.12 Seattle Center alder allée, c. 1968.

8.13 Seattle Center allée, c. 1970.

reimagine the site as something more than a flat parking lot. Today, his mounds blend in with the neighborhood, having become in many respects a characteristic of the larger civic and cultural campus.

Trees also played a significant role in the design of Seattle Center, both during and after the fair. They defined edges and axes, provided vertical thrust to horizontal landscapes, and helped ameliorate the scale of the buildings so that the structures blended in with the scale of the site. They also provided shade, color, and texture for a landscape that had few flowers or gardens per se. The palette was relatively limited, with pines and London planes as the primary trees used to define the main spaces.[11] Maples, Lombardy poplars, honey locusts, Kentucky coffee trees, katsura trees, and plums were used where their forms or colors could be highlighted. Rows of Lombardy poplars defined important walkways and axes, while other trees gave individual character to specific points in the landscape. For the mounded space at the corner of the fairgrounds, Haag thickened the edges and gave scale to the earth forms with a series of bosks and allées using sycamore and alder trees. He specified single rows of trees in front of buildings, creating thresholds and gathering places.

Haag was called back to Seattle Center in 1967 to refine the design and respond to new buildings. He sought to strengthen the links between the programmed spaces of the large civic campus with groves of trees and framed vistas. His inscriptions on this urban landscape were both subtle in the choreography of connections and fluid movement and bold in their use of earth and trees as primary media of spatial formation at this large scale. In 1992, he received the Distinguished Service award from Seattle Center in honor of its thirtieth anniversary and for his work to make it "such a remarkable regional gathering place."[12] While Seattle Center today serves even more disparate functions, the places where one space flows into another reflect the details that were the focus of Haag and his firm.

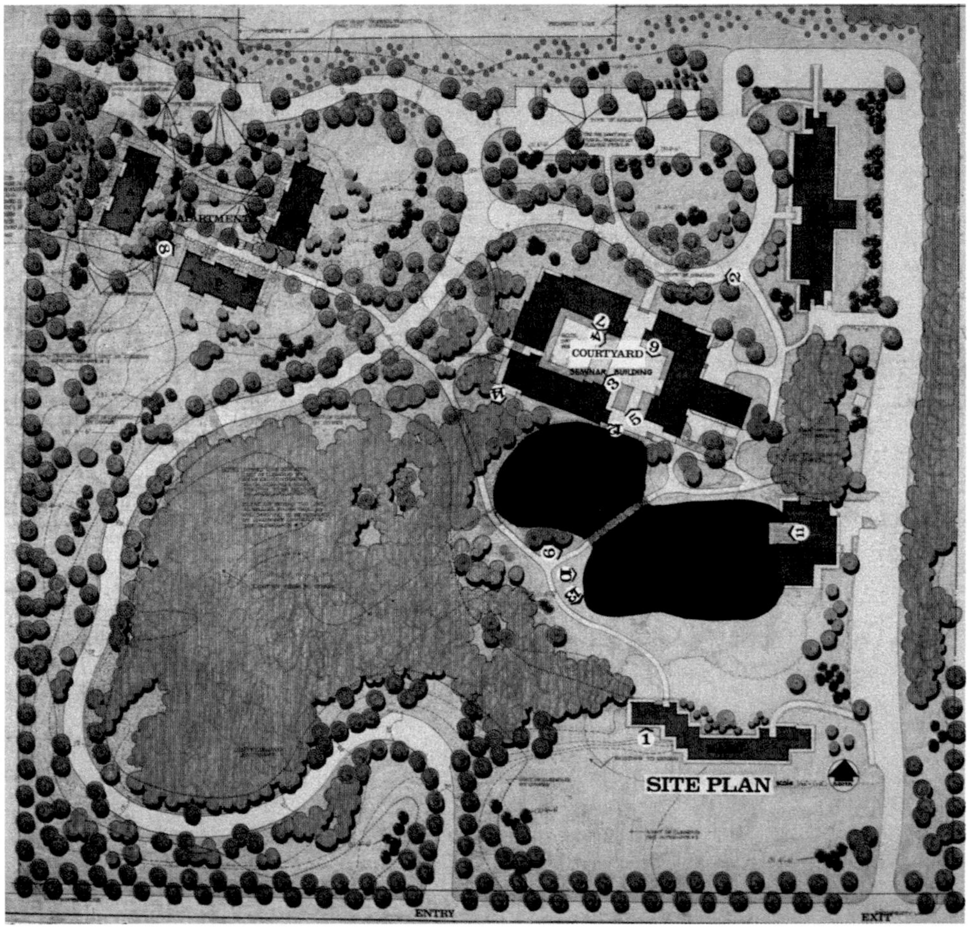

8.14 Battelle Memorial Research Institute plan, 1968.

BATTELLE MEMORIAL RESEARCH INSTITUTE

In 1962, Haag found another opportunity to use landforms and trees, this time for the grounds of the Battelle Memorial Research Institute (now the Talaris Conference Center) in Seattle.[13] The wet, eighteen-acre site lay just northeast of the University of Washington. Working with Bob Hanna and Miles Yanick, Haag defined the place through the sculpting of land and the movement of water. With sculpting, he was able to shape space and make visible the natural processes of the landscape. The dynamic series of sweeping rises and falls guided water and people through the site, experientially, aesthetically, and physically. He sited a pond at the lowest point of the meadow where water naturally settled and clarified its edge with a rock border that separated the grasses from the water. It was a minimalist approach to design that emphasized a baring of the essential character of the site and the relationship between the landscape and the architecture.

8.15 Battelle Memorial Research Institute, pond and willow tree, Seattle, 2014.

8.16 Battelle Memorial Research Institute, main buildings with pond, Seattle, c. 1966.

8.17 Battelle Memorial Research Institute, courtyard with keblis, Seattle, c. 1966.

8.18 Battelle Memorial Research Institute, housing courtyard with small gardens, Seattle, 2014.

A willow tree at the corner of the pond provided a vertical accent as well as seasonal character and obscured the landscape from the adjacent terrace. In the woodlands, existing trees were preserved and new ones planted. The density of the trees varied depending on the functions of the space, from the courtyards to the open meadows to the thick woods. The courtyards offered spaces for social gatherings framed by a regular arrangement of trees. The woods were imagined as intimate spaces for walks and wandering, with the density of trees evoking a place entirely distinct from the city of Seattle.

The firm of NBBJ (Naramore, Bain, Brady, & Johanson) was originally commissioned as the architect in 1961, with Dave Hodemaker as the project architect for the cluster of low buildings nestled into the undulating landscape. Built of stained wood with pitched metal roofs, the buildings reflected the Japanese character of Pacific Northwest architecture. The dark browns of the siding and roofs integrated the buildings into the woodland setting. These were not imposing buildings but small clusters of simple one- and two-story structures communally sited.

At the core of the institute were the offices and meeting rooms with an enclosed courtyard at the center for gathering and resting. Within a generally geometric plan, paths of concrete pavers intersected squares of moss-covered gravel juxtaposed with squares of pachysandra. Haag blended pavers and gravel in the edge spaces, enhancing the evidence of craft. The limited plant palette included groundcovers, several flowering plants for seasonal accents, and small flowering trees with branches that spread delicately across the gardens. Low concrete walls enclosed the trees and offered seating. Haag also installed a keblis, the platform bench that he had developed for the DUX furniture project—another square, another seating area, another use of concrete. The courtyard, with its shady corners and areas of dappled sunlight, was intended for small gatherings, private retreats, and lunch breaks.

In a second cluster of buildings, primarily temporary housing for researchers and smaller offices, the landscape was composed of lawn and flowering trees, with edges that were more porous than those in the central courtyard. The landscape moved across the site horizontally and vertically by means of short runs of steps leading to generous landings and enclosed gardens for each resident. The design integrated the architecture into the landscape and provided graceful thresholds between indoors and outdoors.

The landscape defined the character of the Battelle Research Institute, and, in turn, the design was site-conditioned, both revealing and shaping the place. The woodland separated the site from the city, revealing the natural phenomena in place. The pond offered refuge, a place for reflection, with its dark green depths, emphasizing, even celebrating, the lowest point in the landscape and the movement of water through the site. With no paths other than the primary walkways visitors were encouraged to wander through the undulating landscape, as if discovering the place for the first time.

With the initial project completed by 1965, in 1969, Haag was asked to help with an expansion plan, and he then appointed Craig Campbell, who worked for RHA, to assist him. They refined the courtyard plantings and restored the shoreline of the pond. Haag was commissioned again in 1991 to increase the density and thickness of the edge grove by replacing lost and weak trees and adding trees as needed. Although it was a relatively large landscape, the place continued to provide the experience of a quiet enclosed garden.[14]

JORDAN PARK, EVERETT, WASHINGTON

Jordan Park (initially Everett Marina Park) provided Haag with the opportunity to create a large landform.[15] Commissioned in 1970, he would design this new park for the Port of Everett. It was located in the midst of a large, flat landfill formerly the site of extensive docks and numerous warehouses. Haag developed the design with his employee and former student Dale Dennis and the architectural firm Environmental Concern.

The design for Jordan Park would be Haag's most dramatic use of landforms before the Great Mound at Gas Works Park. Designed within a few years of the first exhibitions of land art at the Dwan Gallery in New York City and at Cornell University and at the same time that Robert Smithson constructed *Spiral Jetty* at Great Salt Lake, Utah, and Robert Morris created his *Observatory at Ijumiuden* in the Netherlands, Haag's design was of the moment. Yet he had been exploring landforms as an art for almost two decades. This park, more than any of Haag's designs, reveals the influence of the Japanese, Mexican, and Swedish uses of landforms. In addition, John Rozdilsky has suggested that Haag may have been inspired by Mount Baker, which would have been in view from the top of the largest mound if the tallest warehouses were gone.[16]

The waterfront site for the park was almost a perfect square acre in a zone of light industrial commercial and marine activities. To the west was Puget Sound and the Olympic Mountains, and the bluffs of Everett formed the eastern border. In order to create the park and restore optimal access to the waterfront, the marina was dredged. Haag

8.19 Jordan Park plan, 1971.

at once stepped in and persuaded city officials to allow him to reuse the five thousand cubic yards of dredged sand instead of paying to load, haul, and dump the materials in tidal flats (an environmental hazard). He had used the remove-and-reuse process for Seattle Center and would refine it at Gas Works Park. "One man's waste is another man's treasure" was the approach. As Haag wrote, "This waste sand was utilized to give form to one of the earliest modern public earth sculptures."[17] It not only was an eco-

8.20 Jordan Park in summer, Everett, Washington, 1996.

8.21 Jordan Park in winter, Everett, 1998.

nomical decision but, because the material had a very low slump characteristic, would allow him to explore steeper slopes than would normally be possible. (In the case of the interior slopes, he constructed them at 1:1 rather than the normal 1:3 maximum for the remaining sides.)

The design centered on four truncated pyramids—the highest about twenty feet tall, and the lowest four feet—loosely oriented to the cardinal directions. Each mound formed a flat ridge at the summit from which people could enjoy views of the waterfront or watch performances on the central plaza. The mounds varied in length, with the Great Pyramid 110 feet long and 110 feet wide (including the approach mound) and the other three mounds at 80 feet long and between 25 to 40 feet wide. The mounds were graded with an apparent bilateral symmetry, although the inside slopes of each mound were steeper (1:1 vs. 1:3). The steeper slopes created the illusion of more height when viewed from the central courtyard. The steeper slopes were further stabilized with Baltic ivy, while the other slopes were planted with athletic turf. As Haag described the park:

> A sequence of interlocking spaces on the ground plane are formed by the multi-facetted series of earth sculptures, each levelled into a ridge along each summit. . . . The Plaza Plane is a sun pocket and pavement is a thermal mass, storing the sun's energy during the day to fend off the coolness of the evening. The morning Plane earth sculpture offers protection from the Northwesters, inviting those who assemble to celebrate, to give witness, to party, to play games. The Great Pyramid, mother to her children sculptures, rises more than 20 feet. Here set into the summit is a "secret" redoubt, the Watch Tower, a heightened expression of the primal landscape's values of prospect and refuge simultaneously, Long views of the sea and mountains, view of the yacht basin and industrial yards, and close-up views of the earth sculptures and public events staged on the Plaza Plane are offered from the great Pyramid, the Morning Plane, and the High Noon Plane.[18]

Haag described the border of Lombardy poplars on three sides as "a landmark to returning seafarers as well as to land-lubbers searching for the yacht basin."[19] On the edge with the parking lot, he planted a more diverse palette of flowering trees and pines, creating a softer and more land-based threshold. Most of these trees had been salvaged from the existing site, once again underscoring his attention to materials and a site-based approach.

The landscape appeared straightforward while at the same time offering a complexity of spaces, and it was not all immediately legible. The largest of the pyramids, sited at the southern edge, comprised two mounds, a smaller step form abutting the pyramid. The ascent was a process of approaches, thresholds, turns, and finally arrival at the top. At the summit was a watchtower, where one could look for the incoming boats. To the west was the Morning Plane, protecting the plaza from storms off the ocean, while the High Noon Plane stood to the north. Haag imagined that people coming to watch the boats from the marina would come and go or wait for the ferry or for someone to return.

Between the pyramids, sited to the west, was the main plaza, or Plaza Plane, as Haag labeled it, protected from the winds and in full sun, with its exposed aggregate pavement acting as a thermal mass storing the heat from the sun, a much-needed attribute on the Washington coast. Picnic lawns were located in the south half of the park, with lawns at the base of each mound. The details of the park, including the light fixtures and the faceted curbing, drew on the pyramid concept. In the case of the stairs ascending the larger pyramid, the shadows cast across them recall photographs Haag and Carver had taken in some of the temples in Japan. Haag commissioned Mary Randlett to photograph the project, and her images evoke this character.

Years later, Haag would refer to Jay Appleton's theory of prospect and refuge. While Appleton did not publish his book *The Experience of Landscape* until 1975, he had lectured at the University of Washington, and he and Haag had engaged in long discussions about the theory. Haag had a similar theory about the universal human desire to both climb to the top, "the will to surmount," and find shelter in an enclosed site, "the desire to encave." Jordan Park offered both: places to surmount and protected shelters.

Over the following decades, Haag photographed Jordan Park mounds in different seasons, some of the strongest taken when they were blanketed with snow. These photographs reveal the ways in which slopes, aspect, and climate inform and shape the spatial experience of a place. Dan Kiley wrote Haag in 1992, "Jordan Park looks good. . . . I love geometric earth forms."[20] The park remained a significant public design project until it was demolished around 2008, with the intention to redevelop the site for mixed residential use.

HENRY M. JACKSON FEDERAL BUILDING

At the same time that he was working on Jordan Park, Haag was invited to partner with John Graham & Associates and Fred Bassetti & Company on the design for the Henry M. Jackson Federal Building in downtown Seattle, commissioned in 1970 and completed in 1974. Bassetti served as the primary architect, working closely with Haag to develop a design that would best use the urban site and contribute to the public space of Seattle. In addition to the challenges of designing an immense government building, this complicated project involved the demolition of an older and revered building as well as being sited on a very steep slope between First and Second Avenues.

To placate community protesters who were angry that the skyscraper would replace the Richardson-Romanesque Burke Building, Bassetti incorporated parts of the older building into the public landscape. Connecting the two ends of the plaza that rose forty feet from First to Second Avenue presented a larger challenge. The designers explored a wide range of possibilities, from siting the building in the center of the block with plazas dug to the lowest level, to tucking the building in a corner and building up the edge spaces.

With the building finally sited to the northwest, Haag divided the public space into sections, the Morning Terrace, the High Noon Terrace, and, on First Avenue, the most west-

8.22 Henry M. Jackson Federal Building at the top of Morning Plaza, Seattle, c. 1976.

8.23 Henry M. Jackson Federal Building plan, 1970, with architect Fred Bassetti.

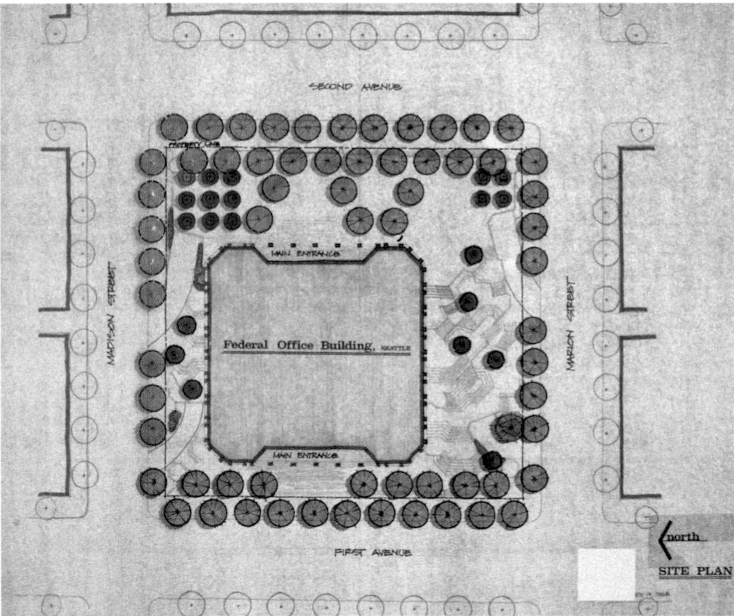

ern edge, the Evening Terrace. The Morning Terrace was an open plaza framed by trees, with the remains of an extant entrance arch to the old building on the corner. Shallow steps brought the plaza and sidewalk together, making the whole into a public space. It was a formal plaza that gave a governmental presence to the federal building.

The Spanish Steps in Rome inspired Bassetti and Haag to use the drama of the street levels in their approach to the steep slope of the High Noon Terrace. The wide steps would allow the building to nestle into the opposite corner. Architect Steven Holl, then a student in the University of Washington's Architecture in Rome program, was asked to provide measured drawings of the Spanish Steps. Haag and Bassetti used the drawings to establish a rhythm for the steps that would take the visitor from First to Second Avenue while offering a variety of gathering spaces and viewpoints.[21]

The descending stairways were constructed of brick and concrete, "a river of red tumbling between parapets that just manages to maintain its shifting course."[22] Alternate views of the urban waterfront opened up with each change in direction moving downward. Fragments of the Burke building were inset in corners and landings. The stairs featured simple metal railings and equally simple light fixtures.

For the Evening Terrace along Second Avenue, an allée created a formal edge and offered a more pedestrian scale for the street front. This project used bricks, terra-cotta tiles, and concrete to create an urban landform that wrapped the building with public space. The slopes recalled the pyramids of Jordan Park, the Mesoamerican ruins, and the Spanish Steps. It was the first time Haag had translated his design into a purely urban landform. After the project was completed, Isamu Noguchi's sculpture *Landscape of Time* was commissioned for the morning terrace in front of the building's entrance.

As designed by Bassetti, the building was to have been clad in red brick as well, which would have produced a much softer texture than the concrete used. The brick plazas and stairs reflect Bassetti's original intention and remain a popular spot for lunch on summer days. The composition can be read as architecture that acts as landscape, and landscape

8.24 Henry M. Jackson Federal Building, High Noon Terrace with stairs, Seattle, 1976.

that serves as architecture. It was an urban design that fully engages its public space as part of the larger city.

FROM MODERNISM TO URBANISM

Initially interested in moving earth as a landform within an intimate garden, Haag increasingly used this approach to create urban spaces, whether with soil, as in Jordan Park, or through structure, as with the Jackson Federal Building. This evolution from a focus on form as an investigation in garden design to what would become a platform for urban design reveals a change in scale and intention. The landforms in Haag's early garden were for the most part primarily objects that signified modernism in design. One observed them or walked around them. The landforms of Haag's large parks and urban plazas shaped space and defined the place, establishing an integrated urban design where the landform was the landscape rather than in the landscape. This use of topog-

8.25 Henry M. Jackson Federal Building, High Noon Terrace stairway, Seattle, 2014.

raphy to define the landscape was not new; Olmsted did the same at Central Park in the nineteenth century. Yet in the urban spaces Haag designed, the forms were never intended to connote natural landscape but rather were meant to bring attention to the urban topography of the ground and skyline. The dramatic forms that Haag designed competed directly with the dynamism of the urban architecture, a stance that positioned landscape architecture as not merely a servant to architecture but an equal partner in creating the city.

PARK

"it was a gas!" at gas works park

IN SEATTLE, AS WITH CITIES ACROSS THE NATION, THE period after World War II saw significant transformations of the urban landscape, from industrial and manufacturing cities to postindustrial service-oriented metropolitan regions. The shift was not merely economic; it redefined the city's image locally and nationally. Despite the natural beauties extolled by Seattle residents, the city was also home to the polluted Lake Washington and Lake Union and the degraded Duwamish River. These problems stemmed in large part from rapid expansion, which led to infrastructural decisions that did not always consider environmental health a top priority. By the 1950s, both lakes were too toxic for swimming, and there was increased concern about the safety of the drinking water. A group of Seattle residents under the leadership of Jim Ellis organized to establish the Municipality of Metropolitan Seattle, or Metro, as a means of regulating public issues throughout the region. The argument was that the organization could advocate for a regional transit system, sewage and pollution control, and regional growth planning. While the larger plan did not make it past a public vote, a scaled-down agenda of establishing a sewage treatment and transport organization passed with an overwhelming majority in 1958. Lake Washington was subsequently cleaned although Lake Union remained polluted. Metro and the cleaning of Lake Washington was just one manifestation of the emerging activism of Seattle residents and leaders when Haag arrived in Seattle.

A second event in the city that would become significant in Haag's career was the 1956 closing of the gasification plant that lay on the northern shore of Lake Union. Sitting on a small promontory once known as Browns Point, the plant had manufactured the gas that supplied the city for fifty years. It had also been the source of immense pollution in the soil, water, and, most visibly, air. When it closed due to new sources of gas and energy, it was a toxic wasteland, and yet, because of its central position in the city, many considered it potential park space. Money was available for such a transformation, but the question was how to address such a disturbed and toxic site. From these conditions, Gas Works Park evolved as one of the first postindustrial landscapes to be transformed into public place.

FROM BROWNS POINT TO GAS WORKS PARK

Ever since his arrival in Seattle, Haag had been dreaming of what to do with the abandoned site. It would take until 1975 to open the park to the public. Today it includes 20.5 acres of land projecting 400 feet into Lake Union with 1,900 feet of shoreline. It features the 45-foot-high Kite Hill, preserved gasification towers called "cracking" towers, a boiler house converted to a picnic shelter complete with tables and grills, and a former exhauster-compressor building transformed into the open-air Play Barn housing a maze of brightly painted machinery for children. It inspired projects across

9.1 Gas Works Park, Seattle, 2013.

the nation and around the globe, from the work of Julie Bargman in Vintondale, Pennsylvania, to the work of Peter and Annelise Latz at Duisburg Nord, Germany.

Gas Works Park sits near the geographic center of Seattle. The lake was known by native peoples as Tenas Chuck (Small Water) and grandly renamed Lake Union by its first white settler, Thomas Mercer, in 1854, as he assumed (correctly, as it would turn out) that it would link Puget Sound with the larger Lake Washington to the east. This freshwater lake, gouged out by glaciers, covered more than six hundred acres in its pre-urban state. Steep hills surrounded it on the east, south, and west. The relatively shallow body of water teemed with life, surrounded by dense evergreen forests and ringed by cattails and waterweeds, its waters teeming with perch, crappie, and bluefish, its "mirror-like surface" skimmed by wild ducks.[1] Native Americans considered the northern promontory a special place, calling it "descending from the ridge," as the land sloped down to the marshes. With the settlement of Seattle, however, the landscape would be dramatically altered.

As the city of Seattle grew, Lake Union rapidly became the city's industrial hub. The lake provided a critical means of transportation for a hilly city where road transport was tremendously difficult. Beginning in 1872, the Seattle Coal and Transportation Company ferried coal across the lake for portage across to Puget Sound. Canals with locks were cut in 1885, and a more massive system of locks and the Montlake Cut opened in 1916, linking Lake Washington to Puget Sound with Lake Union at the center. The arrival of the Seattle, Lake Shore and Eastern Railway in 1887 further strengthened the Lake Union's industrial development. The water was both a source of power for the sawmills and kilns that filled the shores over the last decades of the nineteenth century and a convenient dumping ground for effluents and trash. And yet the northern promontory remained a picnic destination by boat and foot for Seattle residents.

In 1900, the Seattle Gas Light Company began purchasing selected lots on the northern promontory in the neighborhood known as Edgewater and Browns Point. In 1903, John

9.2 Gas plant, Seattle, c. 1950. Aerial photo by Floyd Naramore

C. Olmsted, commissioned by the city of Seattle to develop a park and boulevard master plan, reported that "the point of land between the northeast and northwest arms of Lake Union and the railroad should be secured as a local park, because of its advantages for commanding views over the lake and for boating, and for a playground."[2] Nevertheless, in 1906, Seattle Gas Light Company commenced building an industrial plant to convert coal and later oil into manufactured gas. The American Tar Company (ATCO), which manufactured tar from coal by-products, also operated a tar refinery at the site. The Seattle Gas Light Company's towers spewed black smoke for fifty years while providing Seattle residents with gas and then oil for heating. And eventually, wastes from the gasworks and tar production, as well as serious leaks from the facilities, led to some of the most serious contamination of the soil and groundwater.[3]

While the smoke-spewing gas plant closed in 1956, small-scale manufacturing and maritime industries continued to ring the lake and send effluents into its waters and shoreline soils. A changing industrial mix reflected a changing city; commercial operations serving pleasure boats replaced those supporting commercial shipping, and tanneries and kilns gave way to laundries and garages. The city was growing, and along with new industries there was a renewed call for public amenities. Lake Union seemed an obvious place to develop new facilities. The gasworks site, even polluted and degraded, was a large space that many quickly identified as a site for a new public park, one that would in fact realize the Olmsted Brothers' Seattle park system plan.

A POSTINDUSTRIAL WASTE LANDSCAPE

The gasworks site did not look like much in 1956 when the facility closed down. It held fifty years' worth of industrial waste, and in the years following its closure, the site was used to store equipment for Puget Sound Energy (formerly Washington Natural Gas). Many found the industrial site an obvious blemish on the city. It was a vivid reminder of the excess of production and the disregard for the natural environment that was in fact at the heart of Seattle's success (e.g., logging, quarries, fishing). In 1962, a letter to the editor in the *Seattle Times* complained that "with all the rush to beautify our city before the Century 21 Exposition . . . , a large black eyesore has been overlooked: The abandoned gas works . . . stands out—a huge blot on an otherwise interesting and beautiful waterway. Can't this be converted into a park, with walks and benches for observation points so that our visitors and residents alike may view this jeweled city by day and night?"[4] The first impulse, expressed by the writer, was to clear the land, to wipe away evidence of past pollution.

Nevertheless, there were individuals who imagined a very different future for the landscape, one that would serve the public in a manner different from that of the earlier industry. As early as 1946, artists were dreaming of what the place could be. Painters, poets, and intellectuals described the black towers as dramatically sited on the promontory in Lake Union, suggesting a significant city landmark.[5] In 1962, in response to some of these dreams, but without committing to fulfilling any, with the leadership of Seattle City Council member Myrtle Edwards, the city of Seattle agreed to a ten-year purchase contract for a total of $1,336,352, which would be due in full in March 1973.[6] Thus began the debate about what kind of park the site might host and how to treat the pollutants that were still leaking into the water and oozing from the mud.

To compound the challenges, unsourced pollution was recognized as a serious health problem for the entire lake. In spring 1962, Seattle newspapers reported the appearance of a small island that erupted from what was assumed to be chemical sludge at the bottom of the lake.[7] The city banned further dumping into the lake and infill from the interstate (I-5) construction project; when the ban was lifted a few months later, the island reappeared. The emergent environmental consciousness, the lake-bed eruptions, and the visible pollution of the shoreline spurred debate among Seattle journalists, academics, and planning professionals. With the 1965 passage of the federal Clean Water Act, it was clear that something needed to be done.

NEW EYES FOR OLD

Haag saw the dramatic site for the first time by rowboat on an autumn night and was immediately drawn to the somber black towers of the gas plant, set on the promontory surrounded by water on three sides and the Olympic Mountains visible in the far distance. He continued to explore the place and over time developed an attitude toward the remains of the gas plant. As he described it:

> When I get a new site, I always want to know, figure out, what is the most sacred thing about this site? Well, this site, without the buildings, there was nothing sacred about it. It did have a shoreline, but it would have a shoreline with or without the buildings. So I decided that this big tower, the one right behind me, was the most sacred, the most iconic thing on this site, and that I would go down to the wire to save that structure. Then as I got into it more, I thought, that's kind of silly. Why wouldn't you save the one behind it? You know, husband and wife? And then you start thinking, wait a minute, there's four more: those are the kids. So it would break up a family. So I began to think bigger and bigger about saving more of these structures.[8]

As Haag explored the site, he would become increasingly enamored of its character and its potential as a new type of public park, specifically, a new kind of historic preservation effort, this one focused on an industrial past. As he later recalled:

> I haunted the buildings and let the spirit of the place enjoin me. I began seeing what I liked, then I liked what I saw—new eyes for old. Permanent oil slicks became plain without croppings of concrete, industrial middens were drumlins, the towers were ferro-forests and the brooding presence became the most sacred of symbols. I accepted these gifts, and decided to absolve the community's vindictive feel towards the gas plant.[9]

Haag began to engage architecture students and young landscape architects, including Kenichi Nakano, who worked on the project for ten years in Haag's office. In October 1961, the *Seattle Times* reported that designs had been created by University of Washington students and the Committee of 33 for the gasworks site.[10] Architecture students Rod Knipper, Rod Clarke, and Paul Pierce made a student video about park development at the gasworks and showed it in class. In fact, one could argue that students understood Haag's concept better than anyone, as evident in their letter: "Dear Mr. Haag: . . . The Gas Plant and people should be involved in the park. Not structured involvement, but free, spontaneous activity. . . . The park must become a technological environment encouraging new forms of human association, perception, and participation."[11]

As head of the landscape architecture program, Haag submitted the gas plant site for the National Landscape Exchange program, a student design competition, in 1963. He pro-

9.3 Gas plant site with dirty water and tower ruins, Seattle, 1969.

9.4 Aerial view of the gasworks site, Seattle, c. 1969.

vided aerial photographs, plan views, and site photographs to thirteen participating schools with landscape architecture programs. Of 130 student submissions, not a single proposal retained any of the structures or history. Each submission proposed carting the toxic soil to external landfills and creating a park on a blank new space. Haag's students, however, were excited by the potential of alternative approaches. They generated ideas and garnered notice when landscape architect Glen Hunt wrote to the city suggesting it consider the student proposals in its plans for the site.[12] However, the ideas were initially too radical for most of Seattle's more traditional citizens.

Plans in 1962 were for city staff, likely landscape architect Cassius Beardsley, to design the new Lake Union Park, the assumption being that all structures would be removed to a landfill.[13] An interdepartment memo to Edward Johnson, superintendent of parks, noted:

> In view of the above unknowns or uncertainties the basic elements of the plan would seem to boil down to large open areas of lawn and trees surrounded by a seawall at the water's edge. This approach could accommodate a large open air swimming pool, picnic and toilet facilities, children's play area and wading pool. Incidental to these would be the Harbor Patrol facilities and generous parking areas, but would preclude recreation facilities such as softball, tennis, and other hard surfaced play areas.[14]

In October 1962, Haag, working with Frank James in his office, was one of a handful of landscape architects who offered proposals for a park. Haag's differed from the others in that he planned to use of the relics of the site rather than carting them to a landfill at a cost of only $3,000.[15] The next month, Franklin Lockfeld, an employee of Richard Haag Associates and trustee of the Citizens Planning Council, wrote an article calling for a park on the northern promontory . Within weeks, the Seattle Board of Park Commissioners (commonly referred to in correspondence as the park board) was discussing hiring a landscape consultant to consider the potential of such a park.

Opponents of Haag's ideas for the park included Elizabeth Cary Pendleton Miller, a local philanthropist and member of the Seattle Garden Club, and Myrtle Edwards, Seattle City Council member since 1955 and leader of the initial efforts to acquire the gas plant site for a city park. They advocated removal of all of the toxic materials and creation of an Olmstedian park, similar to Volunteer Park. Edwards worked with the Wallingford neighborhood on a survey as late as 1970 that reported the gasworks structures were "undesirable" for the community.[16] Many who wanted the structures razed viewed the site as a reminder of the pollution of Lake Union and preferred a waterfront park of beach, grass, and trees.[17]

Other groups had their own ideas for the park. The Lightship Relief Guild and the Puget Sound Maritime Historical Society proposed a maritime museum and historic boat center.[18] They were well connected to city leaders, including City Councilman Wing Luke as well as supporters at the *Seattle Times* and other media outlets, and so the idea received significant press. Miller supported the boat center and offered the assistance of the Seattle Garden Club in planting the future "Gasco" Park. [19] The maritime concept garnered attention until concerns were raised that it was too costly. In November 1963, the Seattle Parks and Recreation Department announced that it would be holding off on the historic ship concept.[20]

Meanwhile, the parks department continued to debate whether it needed to hire a landscape architect instead of using city staff to complete the job. The Municipal Art Commission voiced its support for hiring a professional, a choice the architects in particular favored. Haag followed these conversations carefully and in spring 1965 wrote again to administrators for the parks department, asking it to announce a call for a Lake Union Park development plan. In May, the city informed AIA Seattle that it would accept proposals for the site, and the park board suggested a competition. Debate continued, however, as constituencies advocated for what they thought would be the best use of the site. On March 18, 1966, the parks department wrote to ask if Haag's firm would be interested in a Lake Union Park Development master plan project. Haag's response was affirmative. Nevertheless, in January 1969, the city and members of the park board and the Seattle Design Commission were still debating the merits of a competition for the park design.[21] In October, Hans A. Thompson, superintendent of the parks department, wrote to inform the Washington Natural Gas company that a competition was being planned and that no demolition should take place before the design was selected, as "it has come to our attention that one or more of these design proposals might recommend certain portions of the existing superstructure of the gas works be retained and integrated into the design of the park, perhaps as a form of industrial sculpture."[22] By late February 1970, Thompson reported that plans for a competition had been put aside, and that Richard Haag Associates or Ian McHarg would likely be awarded the project.[23] Excitement about a new type of park was building, with reports and letters being published across the Pacific Northwest.[24]

While Haag was focused on Gas Works Park, Fort Lawton, an immense military zone on the western edge of Seattle, was being decommissioned, and the city decided to purchase it with the intention of creating a large public park. Haag teamed up with Okamoto/Liskamm for the limited competition.[25] The team was shortlisted along with three others, including Dan Kiley, to present to the Seattle Design Commission. The commission initially sought to award the project jointly to the Kiley and RHA, but neither principal relished the idea, and Al Bumgardner, president of the Design Commission, announced that the Fort Lawton project would be awarded to Kiley, working with Seattle architect John Morse, and that Haag would be awarded the gasworks site with no competition required.[26]

With Forward Thrust funds in hand, in spring 1970, Thompson reported to Haag that the park board had decided to award RHA the authority to develop a master plan for the new Gas Works Park.[27] Advocates on the park board included Calhoun Dickinson, chair of the board, who was taken with the idea of the towers, claiming they reminded him of an "Émile Zola novel" with its depiction of an "oppressive, industrial atmosphere."[28] Thompson, another important ally for Haag, supported saving the gasworks structures and hiring a landscape architect to advise the city. He did not get in the way when Haag requested a hold on demolition so that he could photograph the structures and requested his own hold when the design competition was suggested.[29] During the initial phases of negotiation, Thompson indicated to Haag that the parks department staff were having trouble writing up the specifications for the contract for Gas Works Park because so much was unknown and unclear. Haag suggested that Thompson allow his office to create a first draft of the contract. Thompson agreed, and Haag worked with a University of Washington law student to write the contract allowing the firm to control the site analysis, programming, and planning of the park.

POWERS OF PERSUASION

While Haag's political strategies were critical to his eventual success, his efforts to persuade the public engaged distinct strategies. He did not rely on his professional credentials but spent a decade educating the public and its leaders on the importance of seeing with new eyes. At the suggestion of colleagues, Haag met with University of Washington philosophy professor Frederick Adrian Siegler and took him on a tour of the site, which included climbing the cracking towers. Upon reaching the top of one of the towers, Siegler exclaimed that Haag was absolutely right about the genius loci and that he needed to get everyone on the site. That idea was immensely appealing to Haag. He proceeded to take students, colleagues, and artists to the gasworks to walk through it and around it, experiencing the views from it as well as to it from afar. In an effort to promote his views further, beyond the design community, Haag made himself available to give talks to any group that could get at least three people together. And soon he would be able to invite those who were interested to his office on the site itself.

9.5 Gasworks blacksmith shop during renovations, Seattle, 1970.

9.6 Haag leading meeting in the rehabilitated blacksmith shop that served as his office, Seattle, 1972.

In December 1970, Haag secured "free access" from the gas plant owners and permission from the city to convert an obsolete blacksmith's shop into an office. Haag and his employees cleaned the space of machinery, fire-hosed the grit and grime out, added a skylight, and painted the interior bone white. They hosted a celebratory party and invited city leaders and community groups. As Haag later recalled, the "Cinderella" transformation of a derelict eyesore into a bright office was a startling demonstration of seeing potential where others saw only waste.[30]

Haag did not merely move his office onto the gasworks site; he moved from one derelict building to another with a sleeping bag, acquiring a deep familiarity with the landscape. Later, he would tell students that he "made love to the earth" as a way of reading the genius loci. While this was part of his design process, it was also a public relations strategy. By doing so, he was suggesting that the site was not as toxic or derelict as it might appear. He also brought in allies such as Mary Randlett, a photographer, and Victor Steinbrueck of Save the Pike Place Market fame to support his efforts.

9.7 Gas Works Park as a concept, 1971. Rendering by Dale Jorgensen

Realizing that members of the public wanted their favorite forms of recreation included in the program, Haag made sure that renderings of the park showed a wide variety of activities. He included everything from kite flying to picnics and music events, to boat museums and restaurants. Picking up on the momentum of the boat enthusiasts, Haag tried to capture that community as an ally. Bob Ashley, a leader in efforts to create a center for wooden boats, wanted to see a dock for historic boats, and so Haag had one included in the drawings. He worked with the head of state parks (a supporter of Save Our Ships and a gourmet) to develop a plan that would include a dock for the *Wawona* with a restaurant on board.[31] There was a group interested in preserving railway history, so Haag added this to the conceptual designs. He admitted to students that this approach, depicting all kinds of program activities in the park so that most people could imagine themselves in the image, was "a real visual swindle." But, he argued, it was a means of opening the minds of the public.

In preparing for a meeting with Mayor Uhlman, who was worried about the plan, Haag commissioned Dale Jorgensen to make a rendering of the park design concept that would appeal to the mayor and city leaders. The rendering colorfully idealized activities at the site with the towers holding the center. Haag showed the renderings to Mayor Uhlman and won him over.

While it was a clever move, it was not an irresponsible one, as Haag argued that his designs would "challenge and direct the emerging recreation energies into creative expressions. The site is well-suited to harness these energies, and to encourage a freedom of play-style not found in the established settings of existing Seattle parks."[32] Thus, to some extent, he was claiming that one could imagine anything in this park, as long as preserving the industrial past and its artifacts was part of the plan. This would draw residents into the design process, as each could imagine being engaged in a favorite activity. For Haag, the community design process was a matter of persuading audiences to expand on his ideas, becoming allies of a larger vision.

9.8 Cracking towers and drums at the gasworks site, Seattle, 1971. Sketch by Victor Steinbrueck

9.9 Stairs from the waterfront to the Prow and cracking towers, 1971. Sketch by Laurie Olin

By May 1970, the site was set for demolition, requiring Haag to work fast. In June, he requested a stay of demolition so that he and Randlett could photograph the landscape and its structures for posterity.[33] They documented and photographed the dramatic skyline of the towers against a backdrop of sky and water and then turned their attention to the tar flows, the joints of the gasification plant, the oil slicks, and other apparent detritus at the site. This documentation gave Haag ammunition for a second strategy, which he had been building over the past decade: to present the structures and the site not merely as industrial artifacts or historical objects but as works of modern abstract art, a new type of art.

Laurie Olin and Victor Steinbrueck sketched the site, suggesting new uses for and new ways of seeing the landscape and its history. Their drawings would be shared with public audiences as rough ideas for the site's possible development. Haag could also use the dramatic photographs to present the gasworks site to audiences not as a place of waste but as a new form of art. Haag elaborated on the potential of merging this artistic character with technological awe to create a new type of public space. He compared photographs of architectural structures with modern sculptures, abstract paintings, and modern art. He suggested that the "generator towers offer a testimony to 'Rube Goldberg' engineering and at the same time an 'Iron Gothic' sculptural experience. The contrast between the timeless grandeur of these structures and the softness and the temporality of the landscape will set the design theme of Myrtle Edwards Park."[34] He compared the colors and textures of oil slicks to the works of Mark Rothko, the tower structures to the sculptures of Jean Tinguely. Slowly, the community began to consider how these ugly artifacts might be seen differently. They began to imagine not a toxic wasteland but a curated exhibit of modern sculpture and landscape. This significant reenvisioning of landscape came on the heels of a reappraisal of urban renewal and the emergence of the environmental movement. The leaders in the movement questioned the basis of what had been promoted as appropriate for public space, particularly around the judgments of beauty and of the effects of human and environmental health.

9.10 Cracking towers as modern sculpture, gasworks site, Seattle, 1970.

9.11 Oil slick as art, gasworks site, Seattle, 1970.

9.12 Mayor Uhlman surveying the site while Haag explains his plans, Seattle, 1974.

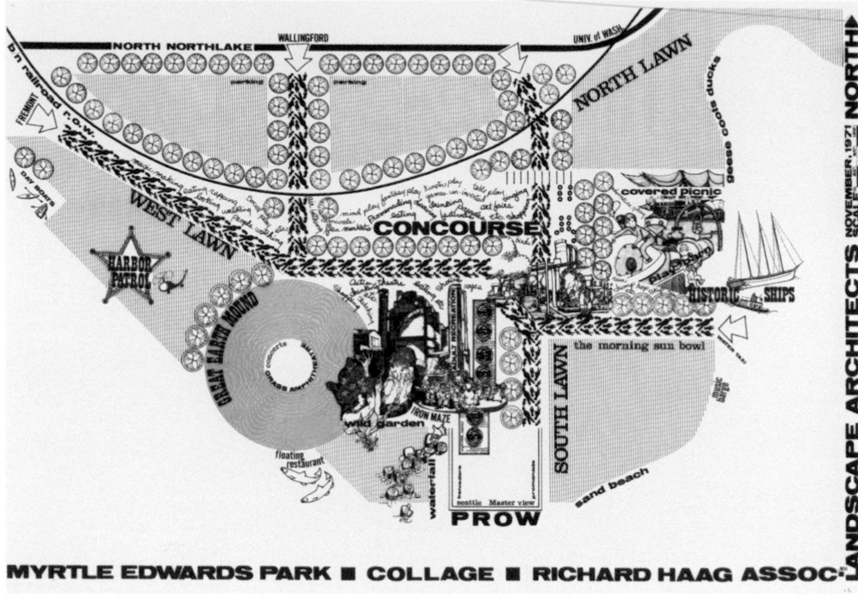

9.13 Myrtle Edwards Park master plan collage, 1971.

These public meetings and presentations were critical to Haag's strategy for the park. Public support was essential. Thus, at each meeting, having presented his ideas, Haag carefully watched and listened to his audience, as he needed to time his next request with precision. When the tenor of the meeting seemed positive and the majority appeared to be enthusiastic about his idea, he would urge the group to take a vote and pass a resolution in support of the master plan. Thus, through multiple small meetings, he slowly opened the imaginations of residents, encouraging them to think of new ways of using the site.[35] And he would leave each meeting with a majority of attendees in favor of his proposal if not unanimous approval. By the time he presented his master plan to a full house on March 1, 1972, at a public meeting in the Eames Theater, the public was for the most part persuaded.[36]

A third approach to promoting preservation of the gasworks, the one most grounded in the pragmatics of the project, was to debate the relative costs of the different proposals. The original contract between the gas company and the city stated that the latter was not to take ownership of the property until the structures were removed "to grade." Haag met with the gas company directors and pointed out that this wording was legally unclear in terms of what it meant for the concrete foundations of the rusting towers and machinery on the flat waterfront site. He asked demolition contractors for bids on the price of removing the structures and concluded that the gas company could save $70,000 by not removing the structures from the site. This cost, when compared to the possible income from selling the scrap iron from the site, suggested a reasonable balance of risk versus return. Haag presented the idea to city officials, arguing that they could always remove the structures later but could never replace them. An engineer reviewed the structures for safety and deemed them usable. In spring 1971, the idea of not removing a good portion of the structures and moving the soils around rather than off the site was given more open consideration than before. Haag continued to argue for this approach, as

9.14 Gas plant site shoreline soils, c. 1973.

9.15 Gas plant site soil drills showing water tables and shorelines, 1973.

it was more environmentally sound and would cost both the industry and the city less.

These "guerrilla tactics," as Haag called them, came from all angles—the aesthetic, the economic, the historic, and the nostalgic. Through these tactics, he inspired a diverse group of supporters.[37] Olin, Steinbrueck, Lottie Eskilsson, and Nakano participated in charrettes, or intensive design sessions, to reimagine the site, while Nelsen and Bassetti argued for the site in public meetings and in letters to the editor in Seattle newspapers.[38] Steinbrueck, just as he had done for Pike Place Market, published sketches of how the park might be experienced as children and adults came to play within and on the towers, the machines, and in the landscape.[39]

On September 4, 1970, a fire destroyed a portion of the structures, raising new concerns about the safety of the site. It took another year of advocacy, many meetings, and many debates, but in December 1971, the *Seattle Times* reported, "The proposal to retain some of the generator towers and other paraphernalia from the old gas works for the new Myrtle Edwards Park at the north end of Lake Union has been approved informally."[40] And in March 1972, weeks after the public meeting at the Eames Theater, the city council, under Bruce Chapman's direction, unanimously approved Haag's concept plan.[41] In January 1973, the Arts Commission followed with a vote of support. The members of the council and many in the public had come to see the disturbed site with new eyes, to see potential in a new kind of site.

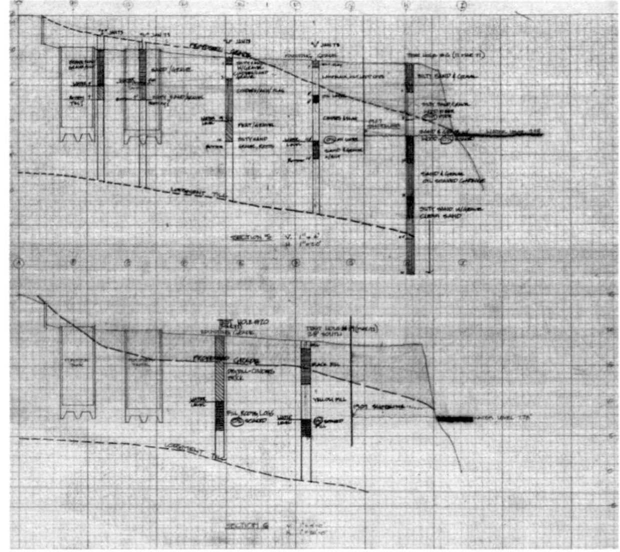

REMEDIATION AND RECLAMATION

Although the community had come to see with new eyes, the challenge of toxic and polluted soil remained. More than a decade had passed since the site had been abandoned, but essentially no vegetation had grown, indicating the level of pollutants in the soil. Haag described the site as "a composition of rubble-fill capped by a 50-foot high mound of subsoils filled with industrial afterbirth: oil, tar and so-called 'exotic' toxicants: erratic ground water tables caused layers of oil-filmed water to perch within two feet of the ground

9.16 Doug Tuma (left) and Larry Leland look over sawdust and organic matter to be incorporated into contaminated soil, Seattle, 1971.

9.17 Gas Works Park grading plan, 1973.

9.18 Gas Works Park master plan, 1971.

surface."[42] Furthermore, when excavators dug a series of fifteen pits to explore how the soil was layered, the layers of industrial wastes and residue were visible. The smell confirmed the problem.

In 1971, Seattle's parks department brought in Dale Cole, a faculty member in the University of Washington's Department of Forest Resources, to determine the extent of the pollution. Cole had been using the site in teaching a course on soils and land use, in which students assessed and mapped the soils and their contamination. As Haag had already excavated portions of the site, Cole collected test soils from these pits. The high level of pollutants became evident when he lowered himself into the first pit only to become ill from the fumes and had to be assisted to safety. He completed his assessment, reporting that there were major zones of contamination below the soil surface as well as heavily contaminated groundwater, both due to earlier use of the site for the production of various organic products and a subsequent major oil spillage that occurred when a huge storage tank emptied its entire contents. The oil spill had been superficially covered over with about twelve inches of soil fill material. The city proposed that the top six feet of soil be taken to a landfill in Arlington, Oregon, and replaced with 180,000 cubic yards of new soil. Another proposal was to "cook" the soil with steam.[43] However, any of these would have left little funding for the actual park. At the same time, Haag and his colleagues were working on a proposal to preserve the soil and treat the toxins in situ.

By 1970, having heard of the project through friends, Richard J. Brooks, a chemical engineer from Boeing, was collaborating with Haag on the project. They both agreed that in addition to the expense, replacing the contaminated soil would only relocate the problem, making the plan an unappealing solution. So they needed to develop an alternative. They knew that the Shell Oil Company was breeding bacteria that had the potential to digest hydrocarbon molecules and began to explore how they might experiment with a similar process. They contacted Willis Lebo, a farmer, businessman,

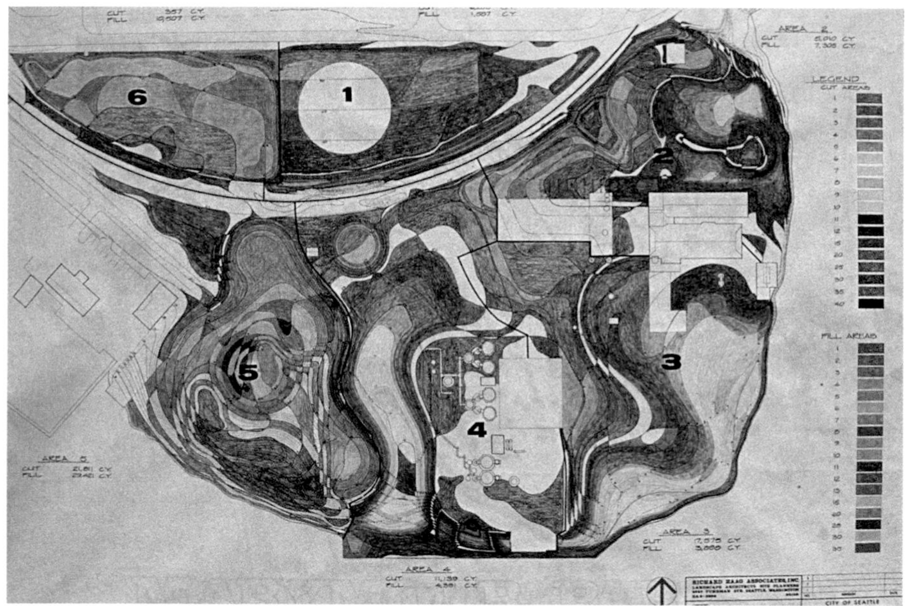

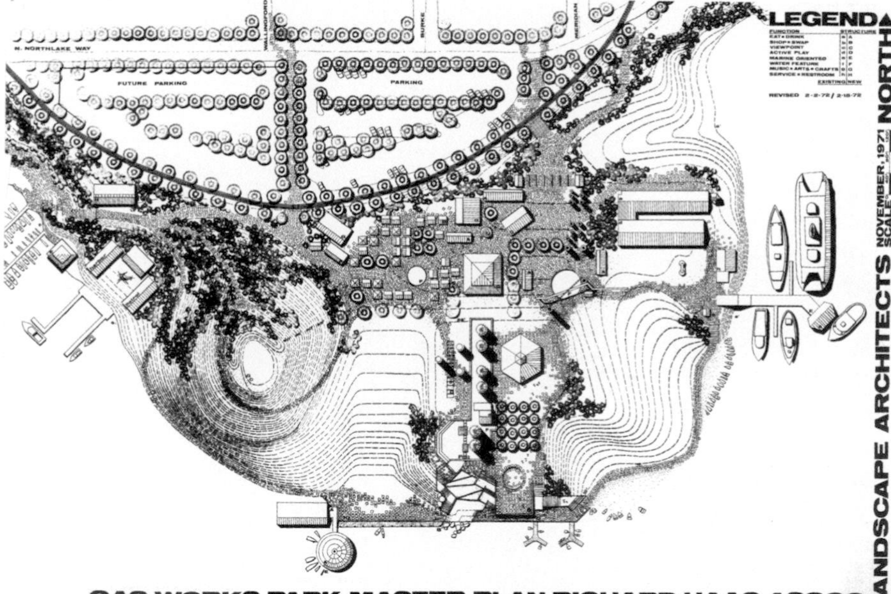

and inventor who sold fertilizers and technology to farmers in the Kent Valley and was known locally for his experiments with soil. Lebo suggested that the soil could be cleaned up in situ. He told Haag and Brooks to till the soil deeply, in order to get oxygen below the surface, as it was in an anaerobic (no oxygen) condition. Working with Lebo, they prepared demonstration plots in the most contaminated soils. Haag directed the bulldozers to break through the layers of clay and sand and mix the soil layers.[44] They added sewage sludge, biomass, leaf litter, and fly ash donated by a cement factory for the acidic areas. By the end of the first year, eighteen inches of sewage sludge and sawdust had been added throughout the site. According to Brooks, after "allowing the bacteria to work for a few months, the treated soil germinated rye grass where none would sprout before. Even the oil lake succumbed to this treatment in an amazingly short time."[45] Haag took the soil to his greenhouse and by growing plants showed that soil that had not hosted any vegetation in decades had become fertile in one summer. Nevertheless, there were detractors, including Miller and Cole, both of whom were at the very least cautious about what plants could actually grow on the site and whether trees could thrive. It was, in fact, determined that trees would not tolerate the subsurface toxins and high water table, killing the idea of a park of grass and Northwest forest.

For Haag, on-site remediation of the soil reflected his non-striving approach as it drew on natural processes to recycle and neutralize contaminants and allowed humans to engage with the site in multiple ways that, like the soil, would change over time.[46] Engineers and city leaders were astounded and delighted by the potential of such an approach, although they remained skeptical.

Once the potential of bioremediation had been demonstrated, Haag focused on creating a design for the whole site. Not all of the soil could be treated in-situ—at least not in the simple manner demonstrated. Therefore, Haag needed to set aside the most polluted soils as well as the construction rubble that could not be recycled. In the final design, the most toxic soils and rubble were moved to a large pile to form

9.19 Aerial view of Gas Works Park soon after it opened, c. 1975.

the Great Mound. Haag covered the mound with an eighteen-inch clay cap and fresh topsoil, so that water would not penetrate and flow through the toxic soils and carry the pollutants into Lake Union. The mound was a perfect cone, and water ran down the surface too fast to penetrate the hillside.

For the rest of the site, Haag designed a grading plan that would best support the dynamic process of water movement and bacterial agency in the soil. The land was graded to form a landscape of gentle rolling hills and valleys that allowed water to move slowly and steadily from the northern urban edge to the shoreline on the south, mixing with the soils and providing the appropriate environment for a healthy bacterial ecology. The hills moved water faster, while the water infiltrated the valleys slowly, so that soluble pollutants could break down along the way. In this way, both the rain that fell directly on the site and the storm water from above the park helped cleanse the soil. The landscape became a working system that constantly cleansed and changed itself.

There were setbacks to the project. In the first summer, tomato and marijuana plants covered the site. Clearly, they had come in with the sewage sludge and other organic materials, a public contribution to the new park landscape. The city's engineering department administered quick tests on the tomatoes, and, although they turned out to be as clean as the San Joaquin Valley tomatoes that were used for comparison, the public was warned not to eat them.

Along with all the controversies, there was also the dilemma of what to name the park, which was initially called Lake Union Park. In October 1969, the park board voted to name it Myrtle Edwards Park in honor of Edwards's leadership in the effort to purchase and transform the site into a public park. But with the controversies surrounding the type of park it would become, in June 1972, following Edwards's death, her family requested that her name not be used. On October 31, the *Seattle Times* announced that the Edwards name had been officially withdrawn. Initially named Lake Union Park, it soon became known simply as Gas Works Park.[47]

In spring 1972, with the grading completed, the soil was

9.20 Barn and machinery with dancers and filmmaker, Gas Works Park, Seattle, c. 1975.

9.21 Children swimming off Gas Works Park using the remaining infrastructure as a dock (no longer allowed), c. 1975.

ready to be seeded in grass. The city's parks department required that an irrigation system be installed if a lawn were put into a public space. The project had no funds for the irrigation system, nor did Haag want one, as it would not allow the natural processes and systems of his non-striving plan to fully engage. Seattle's engineering department, however, was concerned about the possible erosion of the soil if it were not seeded. The two agencies battled, and in the end the city hydro-seeded the whole site with grass without the irrigation system. Haag's ability to know when to step back and let others fight their battles served him well in this case.

OPENING THE NEW PARK

For the public, the first visible act on the site was the planting of a barrier at the north end—evergreen plants, primarily western red cedars—which defined a threshold for the park. Creating an inside and outside for a site, and thereby defining a place physically, was a technique used in Japan, Haag noted. The next step was to reshape the landscape by mounding the most toxic soils and construction debris that could not be reused. Haag had learned this approach in Japan as "dig here, pile there."

On August 30, 1973, the Great Mound was opened to the public as an observation station from which to oversee the transformation of the park and enjoy the views of Seattle's skyline. It was soon a popular place for flying kites and became known as Kite Hill. It was a steep hill with a path spiraling from bottom to top, providing both easy access and full 360-degree views of Seattle, from its fishing industries in Ballard, across Queen Anne Hill, to the Space Needle and downtown skyscrapers, and then around the lake with its houseboats, and, finally, the I-5 freeway. The Great Mound was both a place of reflection and an icon. It continues to serve as a repository for the industrial waste of the past, a place of contemplation, an experience of movement through the landscape, and a reminder of the remarkable landscape of the Pacific Northwest.

The barns were the first structures to be rehabilitated and opened to the public in September 1975. The original pump house and exhauster-compressor building constructed of wood and steel were cleaned, stripped, and painted under the supervision of the architect Michael G. Ainsley with the assistance of Haag's office. Brightly painted murals cover the trusses, creating a fantastical space for the imagination. The boiler house was converted into a picnic shelter with tables, fire grills, and sinks to be used by homeless or indigent individuals as well as by families. This was to be a community gathering place.[48] The floor was left wide open for dancing, games, or musical events. The former exhauster-compressor building became the children's Play Barn. This area featured a maze of Ingersoll-Rand machines arranged as a "brightly painted garden of ironmongery."[49] A sand play area and outdoor climbing structures ran alongside the barn's southern edge. All of the machines, building, and spaces were remnants of the former factory refashioned into a life-size play area filled with huge colorful toys.

A playground was installed outside the barn to the south, incorporating industrial tanks and pipes as well as the only surviving smoke arrestor hood, which became a climbing structure. An amphitheater and benches were added as well as a wooden deck area. Children were invited to climb, clamber, and yell to one another across the barn, creating a cacophony of squeals and a whirlwind of action.

The lawn areas were fully opened to the public in spring 1975, although a fence had been erected around the towers after two children were injured in falls. Ten concrete rail trestles framed the entrance to the north lawn, once part of the railroad siding. The trestles mark the places where coal was delivered to fire the steam-powered generators in the boiler house, which became a picnic area.[50]

In 1976, the Prow, the infrastructure that once served as an oil-loading platform, became a gathering space at the tip of the park's promontory with $290,000 of funding from the Department of Housing and Urban Development's Community Development Block Grants. It had been built in 1936 for unloading tankers and thus was sturdy enough to withstand the weight of a crowd and provided remarkable views of the city and the lake. Benches and handrails were added and, later, steps to the shoreline. This is where the city's elite are hosted for the annual Fourth of July party.

9.22 Aerial view of Gas Works Park, Seattle, 2012. Photograph taken from seaplane

In 1978, a twenty-eight-foot sundial created by two Seattle artists, Chuck Greening and Kim Lazare, was placed at the very top of the Great Mound. Formed out of concrete and delineated with rocks, shells, glass, bronze, and many other materials, the sundial tells the time of day and the season by using the visitor's body as a gnomon.

The park was a dynamic and dramatic rolling landscape, punctuated by the towers and the Great Mound. Its plan described seven areas or programs in the landscape: the north meadow, the Play Barn, the Prow, the towers, the Great Mound, the swale, and the north field. It was bounded on the north by earth berms and the thick border of western red cedars with water on the south, east, and west edges. The visitor arrived in the parking lot, entered the park through the dark hedge of trees, and then stepped into the light of the open landscape with a long view of the city. The industrial remains were evident in the cracking towers that stood majestically in the center of the park, juxtaposed to Kite Hill to the west and the machinery barns to the east. The towers did not block views but offered frames of distant views as well as foregrounded the industrial past of the site and the city. While the industrial remains stand on their original soil, the swales and mounds were created around them for the purpose of moving water and people.

While challenged by controversy, the park was quickly acknowledged as a success once it opened. Awards of excellence were noted by the Seattle–King County Board of Realtors (1975) and the Washington chapter of the American Society of Landscape Architects (1979). Nationally, the park was awarded Special Mention for Open Space Project Design Award by the U.S. Department of Housing and Urban Development in 1980 and the Presidential Award for Design Excellence by the American Society of Landscape Architects in 1981 (the highest award for landscape architecture). On January 2, 2013, the park was listed on the National Register of Historic Places.[51]

ONLY IN SEATTLE THEN

Haag's argument for the new park emerged at an opportune moment in Seattle's history. The early 1970s were exciting years for the city as it began to re-imagine itself as a post-industrial metropolitan region and refocused efforts on the challenges of constructing a healthy city. Action: Better City, the fight for Pike Place Market, and the preservation of Pioneer Square all contributed to the Gas Works park project by creating new eyes for old, opening minds, and establishing an innovative and experimental approach in Seattle's urban design and planning efforts. Planning, design, and construction of parks was facilitated by H.U.D. and a large public bond, called "Forward Thrust" that included funds of $1.617,000 for development of an urban park at the Gas Works site. The project also benefitted from the efforts of hundreds of individuals, most in Seattle, some in distant corners. City leaders in government assisted, as did the Army Corps of Engineers and the National Park Service, particularly staff member Eric DeLong. The engineering consultants Arnold, Arnold and Associates helped as did photographers John R. Ullman and Mary Randlett as well as Joyce Copeland of Vaughan / Architects. While Haag is credited with leading the project, it was a team effort that included students, employees, and colleagues, a truly collaborative re-thinking of what a city might do with a toxic waste site.

In 1984, Haag met Cheryl Trivison, who became his office manager and eventually a principal in RHA. Trivison was a community, political, and environmental activist who had worked with community services in the Seattle region. In 1996, Trivison and Haag, along with Connie Bain, John Rozdilsky, Patrick Waddell, Peter Cohan, Carole Fuller, and Diane Simpson met at the RHA office on Eastlake Avenue to establish the Friends of Gas Works Park (FoGWP).[52] The group has advocated for the opening of the towers (Free the Towers) and stewardship of the park, including the replanting of trees. In 2004, its work was honored with the Cultural Landscape Stewardship Award for Excellence. The Friends of Gas Works Park also led in nominating the park for City of Seattle Landmark (1999) and the National Register of Historic Places in 2013.

In the time that Haag was working on the Gas Works Park project, the RHA office moved from Fuhrman Avenue to Northlake, then Eastlake, and finally settled on Tenth Avenue in Seattle's Capitol Hill neighborhood. The firm has

9.23 Gas Works Park, Seattle, 2014.

never had more than a handful of permanent employees, much as in the early 1960s, and yet its projects have been located around the globe, from Italy, to China, to Seattle.[53]

Haag has proposed and designed other postindustrial sites, including Jordan Park in Everett, Washington; a proposed project for the Port of Seattle grain terminal; and the North Waterfront Park in Berkeley, California. These projects reflect his ongoing experimentation with landforms, ecological systems, and cultural approaches to the reimagining of urban spaces and public places. His proposal for the North Waterfront Park master plan presented an alternative to the cap-and-cover approach to solid waste landfills, developed in collaboration with Richard Brooks and Berkeley landscape architect John Roberts, beach dynamics engineer-scientist Willard Bascom, and environmental artist Agnes Denes. They described how the ninety-seven-acre site at the edge of the marina could be made into a public park that would break down the waste by means of bioremediation. The project was not approved, because it conflicted with California state law requiring that polluted soils be capped and because, despite all the experimentation, there was still a conservative culture when it came to treating pollution and other toxins.

Some forty years later, there are other postindustrial projects and remediation designs, yet landscape architects around the globe reference Gas Works Park as a precedent for the research and practices of the twenty-first century. Methods of bioremediation and phyto-remediation are being tested in a wide range of landscapes and spaces and are taught in landscape architecture and ecological design programs in many universities. What was once considered terribly risky by Seattle is now considered appropriate and necessary at many sites around the world. Haag's groundbreaking work opened that door, and he continues to advocate for the park, for adding a camera obscura in one of the towers, for building a tower museum, for opening the towers up to climbers, for developing "new eyes for old."

9.24 Richard Haag Associates office employees, c. 1992. Left to right: Cheryl Trivison, Bob Foley, Nancy Rottle, and Corice Farrar.

10

land sculpting and ecological design at the bloedel reserve

10.1 Garden of Planes, The Bloedel Reserve, Bainbridge Island, Washington, 1986.

WHILE GAS WORKS PARK REMAINS HAAG'S BEST-KNOWN design, the Bloedel Reserve most cogently synthesizes his interests in landforms and ecological design as well as his aesthetic and poetic response to disturbed sites. The Bloedel Reserve is internationally recognized for its evocative beauty as a landscape of environmental rehabilitation as well as a place that constructs an aesthetic experience "bound to, and enmeshed in, [its] specific cultural and ecological context."[1] The experience is choreographed in a design language that merges Japanese philosophies with the nature of the Pacific Northwest while grappling with the challenges of a logged and disturbed landscape. As argued by landscape architect and scholar Elizabeth Meyer, Haag's designs "open up connections between both the environmental and cultural histories of a particular place—Seattle and the Pacific Northwest and phenomenological response and ecological thinking."[2]

PRENTICE AND VIRGINIA BLOEDEL'S VISION OF A RESERVE

The Bloedel Reserve comprised 150 acres of forest and gardens created by Prentice (1900–1996) and Virginia Merrill (1902–1989) Bloedel, intended to "capture the essence of the Japanese garden—the qualities of naturalness, subtlety, reverence, tranquility—and construct a Western expression of it."[3] The reserve featured gardens, ponds, meadows, and wildlife habitats covering sixty-six acres while another eighty-four acres remained in second-growth forest. Prentice Bloedel had been at the helm of the MacMillan Bloedel Timber Company, founded by his father. When he retired in 1950, he turned his attention to nurturing a forest preserve on a once-logged landscape on Bainbridge Island, a forty-minute ferry ride away from downtown Seattle.

The site of the Bloedel Reserve had been given to the Washington Territory in 1855 for the purpose of developing a territorial university. It was subsequently logged, and the logs were sent to the Port Madison Mill on the southern shore of the island.[4] The land was then platted in 1904, when Angela Collins purchased it to create a beach retreat. She planted a collection of rhododendrons but otherwise allowed a second-growth forest to develop. The Bloedels purchased the forested landscape in 1951 and over the next thirty years created the Bloedel Reserve that is today open to the public.[5]

Bloedel described his first response to the land as one inspired by the beauty of the Pacific Northwest: "We found single plants and colonies of fragile woodland species, mosses, ferns, a world of incomparable diversity. . . . One feels the existence of a divine order. . . . One realizes that we humans are trustees in this world, that our power should be exercised in this context."[6] He set out to create a landscape that would simultaneously reveal the disturbance of the site and the potential of a different relationship between cul-

10.2 Japanese garden by Fujitaro Kubota, with Kubota on rock, The Bloedel Reserve, Bainbridge Island, c. 1963

ture and nature, not necessarily a healing but a differencing. He wanted to express the spiritual and philosophical powers of the place as a landscape layered in natural and cultural histories. In addition, as collectors of Asian art, he and Virginia wanted to draw on an Eastern sensibility while retaining an appropriately Western character. To realize this complex vision, Bloedel sought advice from landscape architects and garden designers including Thomas Church, Fujitaro Kubota, Richard Yamasaki, and Richard Haag. Bloedel invited Church to join a board of advisers for the reserve.

One of the first garden designs to be implemented by Bloedel was designed by Church in 1954. It was a long reflecting pool in the woods that once extended through what is now the Japanese Garden. Neil Twelker, a geotechnical engineer in Seattle, identified the site for its high water table and suggested that Church just dig the pool and reveal the standing water. Bloedel oversaw construction in order to ensure that the least damage was done to existing trees and underbrush and the character of the forest environment would be retained. The pool was constructed by digging to the water table and then inserting a concrete rim that give it a definite shape. Little else was done around the pool, and the site remained an unfinished garden over the next decade.

With the desire to express a more Asian character in the reserve, Bloedel turned to Fujitaro Kubota, a Japanese American who owned Kubota Garden, a nursery and garden design business in south Seattle. They had met through efforts in 1960 to establish a three-and-a-half -acre teahouse and strolling garden for the Washington Park Arboretum. Japanese garden designer Juki Iida was designing and constructing the garden and brought Kubota in to provide plants. Bloedel hired Kubota in 1961 to create a Japanese pond garden at his estate as a part of the reserve. In 1964, Paul Hayden Kirk would design the guesthouse, which would be situated just above the garden, described as an expression of both the Japanese character of the site and the regional interest in Native American longhouses.[7]

10.3 Aerial view of the Reflection Garden, designed by Thomas Church and Richard Haag, The Bloedel Reserve, Bainbridge Island, 1986.

10.4 Reflecting pool with hedge, The Bloedel Reserve, 1982.

HAAG'S CONTRIBUTIONS

Haag's introduction to the Bloedel Reserve occurred in 1969, when Bloedel contacted him on the recommendations of architects Paul Kirk, Ibsen Nelsen, and Fred Bassetti to address the "canal pond" that Church had designed.[8] Bloedel found the pond murky and gloomy, contradicting his vision for the landscape. There was also the problem of the high water table throughout the reserve gardens, including the area around the pool. The Bloedels wanted to retain the pool as a place of retreat but make it better integrated with the rest of the landscape and easier to reach. Virginia Bloedel appreciated the flatness of the reflecting pool and did not want any rocks put in the water.[9] They did not want a water garden but a quiet place in the forest.

Haag worked on the project in his office with John Ullman. They developed alternative versions of how they might refine the pool's design. What appealed to Bloedel was the concept of a glade or opening in the woods. Haag suggested creating a glade by means of a ten-foot-high yew hedge that would completely surround the pool, making a clearly delineated room in the thick forest. The dark pool, nearly two hundred feet long and forty feet wide, would be edged with a natural stone lip that would "make the apparent water surface closer to the top of the pool."[10] Between the pool's edge and the hedge would be lawn. It was a simple refinement of Church's design, letting the pool define the ground plane as it reflected sky and trees above. The space would be literally carved out of the ground and forest.

Once the concept was agreed upon, Haag suggested finding small yew plants that would mature into the ten-foot-high hedge. Bloedel quipped that he might not live long enough to see it, and so they needed to find full-grown yews to transplant. Plants of the appropriate size were identified in an Oregon nursery in the summer of 1969, and Bloedel selected the specimens he wanted. In 1970, ten-foot yews were planted, giving formal definition to the forest room, and their reflections in the pool seemed to contain the breadth of the full sky above. The hedges were left untrimmed on the exterior side so that they merged with the forest texture, while on the interior side, they were trimmed, emphasizing the clear geometry of the space. The hedge opened into narrow slits at the corners that were almost invisible due to the overlapping of the vertical plane.

Once within the narrow threshold, the view of the hidden glade opened to an immense breadth of sky and water. For Haag, the point of entrance reflected a Japanese sense of arrival, one of juxtapositions, change, and surprise. The visitor moved through the thick hedges, wild places, and dark shadow and then broke into the open space and sunlight of the reflecting pool. This experience would be heightened later when Haag designed the Moss Garden, in essence creating the sequence of gardens that was beginning to coalesce in his head as he designed the Reflection Garden. Departure from the secret garden was where the visitor then left through the thick hedge and descended a flight of stone steps leading to a path that wound through the woods to return to the center of the estate and the main road. After the pool was completed in summer 1971, Haag designed woodland trails throughout the forest that were enhanced and thickened with native plants.

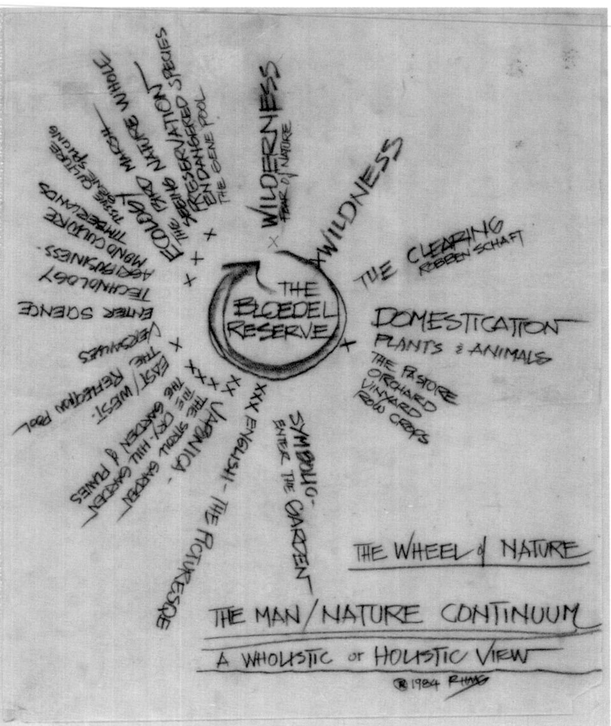

10.5 The Man/Nature Continuum, drawing by Richard Haag, 1983.

While Haag was redesigning the pool, the Bloedels were in the process of transferring the reserve to the University of Washington, an agreement that came to fruition at the end of 1970, with the Bloedels maintaining a lifetime interest.[11] With a board of directors (later called the Arbor Fund)[12] to oversee the reserve, by 1973 there was discussion of developing a master plan. The reserve was to serve as a site for research and study as well as a place of retreat.[13] By 1978, the board of directors, with Bloedel at the helm, were ready to move forward, though Bloedel remained skeptical of any plan that might be set in stone. He described the role of the designer as being more of a consultant who would help direct the philosophical dimension of the gardens. The selected designer would address the treatment of four undeveloped parts of the reserve while creating stronger connections between the main residence, the Japanese Garden, and the Reflection Garden. The prospectus identified the four areas as an extension of the "oriental feeling of the Japanese Garden but modified, more western," the creation of paths around the water resource basin, the steep slope and prospect from the main residence to the sound, and the northern glen, an extension perhaps of the Rhododendron Glen.[14]

Four respected Pacific Northwest firms, including Richard Haag Associates, were invited to submit proposals to serve as a "landscape design and development consultant." In contrast to the designs offered by Arthur Erickson Associates, Jones and Jones, and Jongejan and Gerrard, Haag presented a minimal scheme. Having proposed that his "emerging vision of the future of the Bloedel Reserve is tilting more to the transcendental than to the professional, more to the metaphysical than to the scientific, more to the timeless bondage of man to savannah and forest, than to timeful over-dominion,"[15] Haag laid out his philosophy as a spiral that reflected the man/nature continuum, a framework that likely appealed to Bloedel. Haag drew his proposal on trace laid over a hundred-scale map of the reserve. As director of the reserve Richard Brown recalled, "he painted his plans right in front of us much as an artist would make a painting."[16] Haag thought that because Bloedel was partially color-blind, the primarily black-and-white pencil drawings would be easier to grasp. Brown believed that Bloedel's response was also due in large part to Haag's "artistry, creativity, knowledge of plants and that he [Haag] would be personally involved with the changes at the reserve."[17] Bloedel likely appreciated the process-oriented approach, as he did not believe in a rigid master plan. He also may have felt that Haag's aims were attuned to his and Virginia's visions for the reserve—not to return the disturbed landscape to an idealized nature but to acknowledge the accretions of history, natural and cultural, and to create gardens from these layers of time and place. A committee of four trustees was to judge the proposals, but Bloedel had the last word in the decision. He selected Haag as the consultant.

10.6 View from the main house to the water, The Bloedel Reserve, Bainbridge Island, May 1979.

As the two men, Bloedel and Haag, worked closely together between 1978 and 1984, Haag documented their discussions with plans, sketches, and notes that reveal the design as it unfolded.[18] Haag visited the reserve every Thursday for months, walking the site in the morning with Bloedel, often having to push through underbrush in the forest. In the afternoon, they would set about designing areas in response to their discussions of the morning. In the process, Haag came to view Bloedel as a godfather figure, a patron who shared his view of the world, of culture, and, most important, of the role of design in the landscape.[19] As Haag described the process, the final design was "a reflection of the garden rather than a document that led to the garden."[20]

Haag began realization of this shared vision with the prospect from the main residence on the east bluff. From where the house stood, the Bloedels enjoyed a magnificent view of the sound and distant mountains. However, the slope down to the water was dangerously steep and overgrown, so Haag regraded the land and created a more graceful descent to the waterfront. On the east bank, an existing orchard was removed and the bluff was lowered thirty inches, broadening the view from the main house. This vista was flanked by earth mounds meant to be planted with wildflowers, although grasses were eventually planted for ease of maintenance. The central axis was planted with fescue, and a Hinoki cypress hedge on the north side balanced the woodland to the south, together framing the view. The project was figured out on the ground rather than in drawings, a process Bloedel appreciated, as it assured a site-specific response. This approach reflected Haag's non-striving principle emphasizing an economy of effort and repurposing of resources. Designing on site was by this time Haag's preferred creative process.

Circulation was the second focus of Haag's design, as there was a need to better connect the parts of the reserve and to improve the roads themselves. Most important for Haag, however, was that the circulation would determine the speed

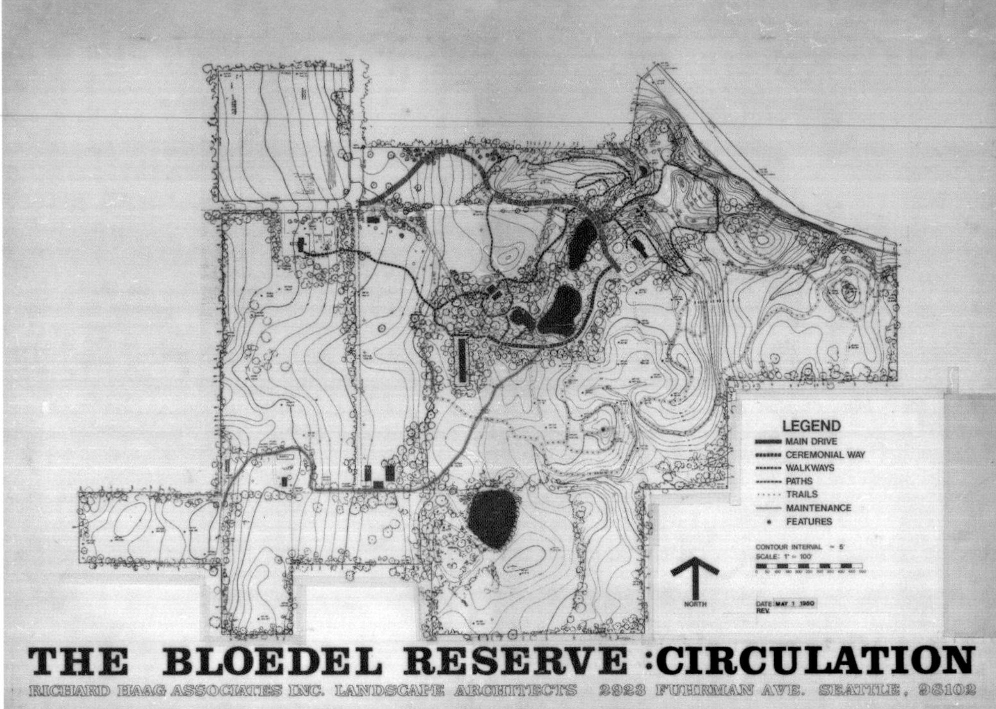

10.7 Main residence, with view corridor evident, The Bloedel Reserve, Bainbridge Island, May 1989.

10.8 Circulation plan for the Bloedel Reserve, 1980.

at which one experienced the landscape. As he noted in his "Policy on Circulation," "A direct relationship exists between slowing movement through an environment and enriching the quality of the sensory perception of that environment."[21] He then argued that this was more true in the Pacific Northwest forest, where the detail and nuances of the woods suggest an intimate and slow experience. He had learned from his experiences in Japan that a finite space might seem larger if one moved through it more slowly. In response he designed a series of roads and paths that would be visually subtle, even hidden from view if possible, functional without being overly engineered, and flexible enough to respond to the "natural and cultural form-givers discovered along the routes as well as to the larger esthetic context."[22]

The final circulation plan revealed a hierarchy composed of the main road, the ceremonial drive, service roads, and walking trails (major path, minor path, innermost path, and subliminal trail, as Haag labeled them on the plan). These paths and roads were woven into the existing bogs and random rambles, a pond for cattails and red-winged blackbirds, and a grove of evergreen and deciduous trees. They were designed to first fit into their natural context, then to serve as circulation routes for humans, and finally to heighten the experience of the landscape itself.

Haag began construction by realigning the existing main drive that also served as a service road so that it would "most creatively reveal the essence and yet strengthen the myriad landscape qualities and moods from the most fragile, ephemeral to the most hardened and fixed."[23] It was moved north in order to avoid cutting through the middle of the landscape, as it had originally. Much of the grading was done on-site, with Haag directing the bulldozer. Brown recalls this as rather harrowing, as Haag would keep altering the contours as the driver, sometimes his son, tried to keep up. Eventually, the road was graded to follow the natural contours and minimize its visibility and intrusions.

The Ceremonial Drive was created as a separate path offering visitors a graceful path through the gardens and landscape. It was not intended for regular automobile traffic, except in the case of a ceremonial visitor such as a president or governor, so Haag narrowed it from twenty feet to twelve feet in width, diminished the crown of the middle, and created earth mounds in the pasture to make the road less visible, assuring that it would not "fracture the view from the guesthouse deck or from the Japanese garden."[24] Walking paths were minimally marked in the woodlands and meadows. One senses a synthesis of Haag's topographic interest in landform and his ecological knowledge and curiosity.

The design details also contributed to Haag's and Bloedel's commitment to a site-specific response. When a bridge was being built on the main drive, it was initially designed to curve with the topography, as did the rest of the road. Haag knew that it was difficult to make a concrete bridge curve gracefully and instead engineered the bridge to emphasize its straightness, in contrast to the road. The bridge was relatively short, and yet it provides a pause, a straight element in a curving line that called attention to the nature of the road and the land's topography.

While, on the one hand, the circulation system appears as a functional element of the Bloedel Reserve, on the other, Haag's design choreographed movement to reflect the purpose and function of the landscape as a reserve, a place of retreat, meditation, and deep engagement with nature. Haag intended a poetic landscape but simultaneously heeded the natural processes. Included in his conceptual plan were diagrams of water, climate, and flora and fauna, all in relation to experience. His "Talking Working Plan" laid out topographic forms and their associated phenomena as a whole. It identified the spaces for meadows, the Great Plain, prime second-growth areas, test bogs, and views that opened to the water and distant landscapes. He labeled observation zones, including a meadow reserve and a forest reserve that would be stewarded within the bird preserve. It was a conceptual plan, intended not to be built exactly as drawn but to suggest the potential of landscape experiences that would foster human and environmental health.

THE GARDEN SEQUENCE

Among Haag's designs for the Bloedel Reserve, the most extraordinary was the garden sequence that would win him his second ASLA President's Award of Excellence (1986). The sequence was a response to Bloedel's desire to construct a more unified series of gardens in the reserve that might engage visitors in the nature of the landscape and environment. Haag started the design of the gardens as a sequence in 1981 and continued working through 1985.

To experience this sequence, the visitor entered the site from the northwest corner and followed the main drive and then a path through the meadow and then forest to arrive at the threshold of the first garden room. The garden was enclosed by a series of mounds, with the guesthouse by Kirk as a backdrop. The earth mounds were constructed with the soil from regrading the east bluff, a visual reminder of Haag's creed to recycle existing resources. To determine the height of each mound he used orchard ladders with tape draped from one to the other. He covered the largest mounds in blue fescue, a color that resonated with the grayish blue of Seattle's sky and echoed his earlier Wong garden mounds. Erratic boulders were emerging from the mounds were retained. Small shrubs echoed the forms of the boulders and mounds in an abstract manner that suggested the regional landscape of mountains and valleys, a site within a site. This abstraction was particularly evident in Haag's drawing of the project in which the mounds, boulders, and even the trees appear like a miniature version of the Cascade mountains visible on the eastern horizon.

In the garden, Haag altered the ground plane by removing one-foot square pieces of the concrete terrace and replacing them with grass and moss, abstractions of the surrounding meadow and forest. Likely remembering his visits to the Hojo garden at Tōfuku-ji in Kyoto, Haag manifested his theory of fusion, the merging of human or cultural and natural materials, in the ground design. It was a one he had initially used for the Wong garden: a checkerboard arrangement of pavers alternating with the lawn. A large cedar tree with roots that swelled into the terrace defined the corner nearest the guesthouse entrance, breaking up the geometry of the ground and thus again fusing one design with the character of yet another element in the garden. The garden's surface was a hybrid of the meadow that visitors passed through on their way to the garden, the forest that lay ahead, and the architectural character of the guesthouse, as well as a palimpsest of the former uses of the garden itself. This ability to layer multiple readings of a site imbued Haag's designs with a thick narrative.

Haag proposed creating the Garden of Planes in an empty swimming pool in the center of this garden room.[25] The garden was based on a concept he had been thinking about since the 1950s, drawing on his proposal for the use of sand pyramids in his Case Study House. He considered other ideas for the pool, including a garden of bamboo and sand, an aquatic garden, and a mound garden. In these proposals, he sought to define the garden room through the scale of the pool and its central position, to catch the visitor's eye. This was, after all, to be the first in a series of gardens, and so Haag needed to establish a clear character and mood.[26]

Bloedel remained tentative but agreed to a full-scale model of Haag's concept for transforming the pool by adding two unequal pyramids made of white pea gravel, one ascending and the other descending. As Haag described it:

> Here you would come upon a pure rectangle of 2 balanced but unequal pyramids, one larger and inverted, the smaller being positive. The pyramids rose and fell from a horizontal plane of checked squares of stone and moss. As originally envisioned, the moss would have escaped and covered all. The pure pyramids are composed of seven moss-covered planes of four differing sizes but all with an identical angle of repose.[27]

An inverted pyramid placed at the deep end of the pool contrasted with the second pyramid that rose from the shallow end. The design echoed the guesthouse plan, suggesting that the garden and guesthouse were of a piece. Whereas the

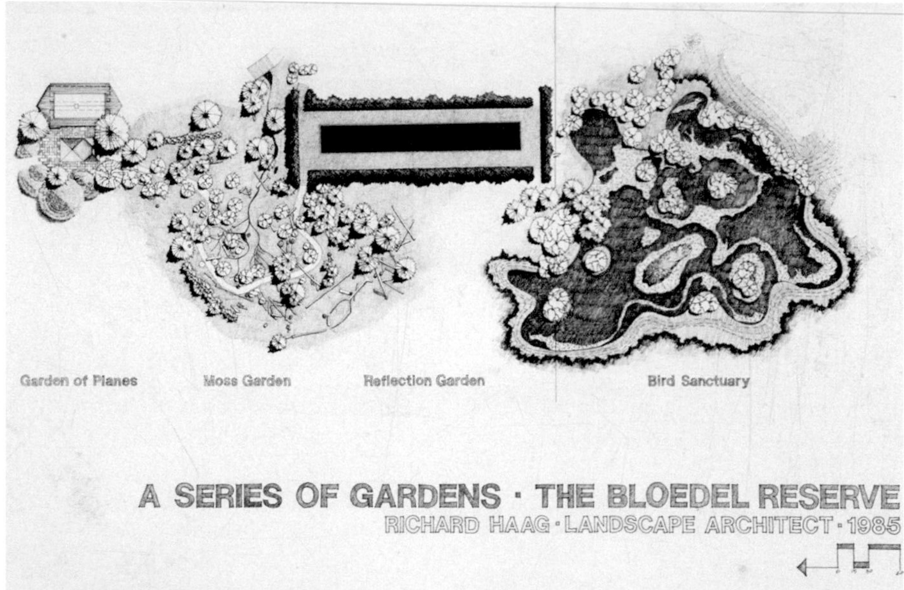

10.9 Garden sequence design for the Bloedel Reserve, 1985.

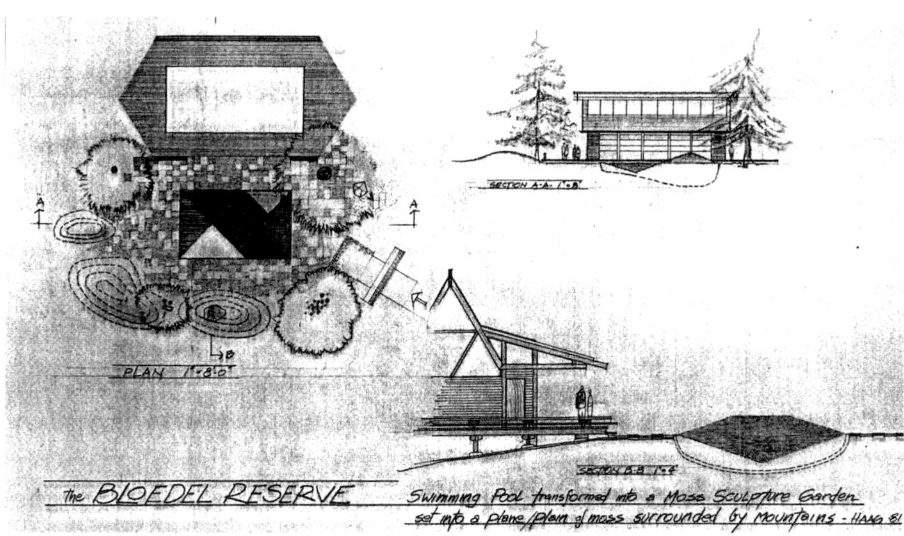

10.10 The Garden of Planes plan, with guesthouse, The Bloedel Reserve, 1981.

10.11 The Garden of Planes ground plan with checkerboard pattern, The Bloedel Reserve, 1985.

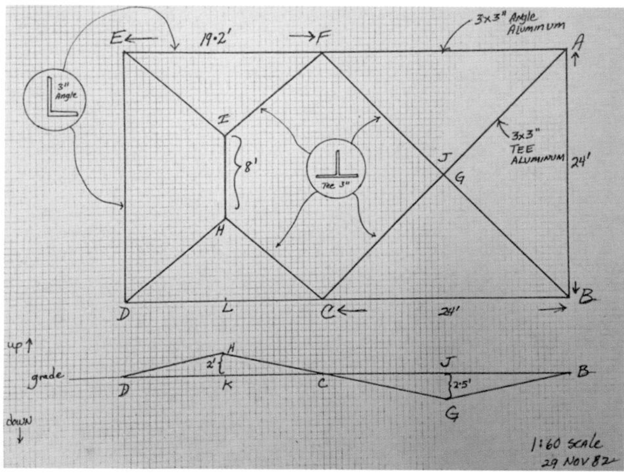

10.12a Plan for pyramids in the Garden of Planes, The Bloedel Reserve, drawn on graph paper, 1981.

10.12b Garden of Planes, The Bloedel Reserve, 1981. Caption reads "The Garden of Planes Swimming pool transformed into a Moss Sculpture Garden, set into a plane of Moss & surrounded by mountains for the plain."

10.13 The Garden of Planes under construction, The Bloedel Reserve, Bainbridge Island, February 1983.

10.14 The Garden of Planes as constructed, The Bloedel Reserve, Bainbridge Island, 1984.

10.15 The Garden of Planes, looking toward the guesthouse designed by Paul Hayden Kirk, The Bloedel Reserve, Bainbridge Island, 1984.

guesthouse enclosed an interior with its outer boundaries visually if not physically (due to the overhanging terrace) open, the Garden of Planes central piece was bounded only on the ground plane, with its edges physically and visually bounded by mounds and vegetation. Although they were designed at different times, Haag's attention to the compelling geometry and lines of the guesthouse offers an example of how architecture and landscape architecture could be designed in close dialogue with one another.

Haag, Bloedel, and the trustees discussed the pyramid idea and the construction of the mock-up. The idea was to the test the concept before realizing a final project. The pyramids were composed of white gravel set into an aluminum framework. The slopes were set at exactly the right angle to hold. Haag had proposed covering the mounds in moss to mute the sharpness of the geometry, but the clarity of the white gravel against the gleaming aluminum in the green and gray garden worked without the moss. The photographs suggested an enigmatic garden, reminiscent in character of Zen meditation gardens, which did not reveal themselves in one sitting but invited contemplation. It was, in Haag's opinion, the most explicitly intellectual of all his gardens, establishing a meditative framework for the garden sequence.

As the first of the gardens in the designed sequence, the Garden of Planes created an experience that was essential to Haag's concept. It was in this garden that he gave form to the first of the seven steps of Buddhism by getting the attention of the visitor and then focusing it inward. The garden referenced Zen practice in a language that Westerners could understand—the language of objects, geometry, and mathematics.[28] Haag explained to landscape architect Patrick Condon:

> The first step is . . . [here Haag loudly clapped his hands]; just get the attention of the person. From that point you try to set up, and I tried to set up, one end of the yin-yang; or one end of the "min-max continuum." . . . In my master plan, the people would arrive by bus, unload, and come down through the meadow—through an orchard. You have the human order of the orchard. The you have to come around the big mound and [here Haag paused, eyes wide, mouth open] . . . here's this space! It's sort of like going to the garden of Ryōan-ji, where you get off the train with your group, go up the path through the woods—all go up together. Then you go in and . . . here's this thing! So that's just to get your attention, to break this conviviality of the group.[29]

10.16 Gateway between the Garden of Planes and the Moss Garden, The Bloedel Reserve, Bainbridge Island, 1981.

In this way, Haag drew on Western geometry to express an Eastern concept of balance. The swimming pool's form and the architecture of the guesthouse were expressed in a Western design language. The sand was a traditional Eastern element, and the framework was aluminum, a modern Western material. In a larger context, the geometry of the planes also balanced the rounded earth mounds, the sand and the soil, the reflective nature of the sand with the absorbent nature of the blue fescue grass.

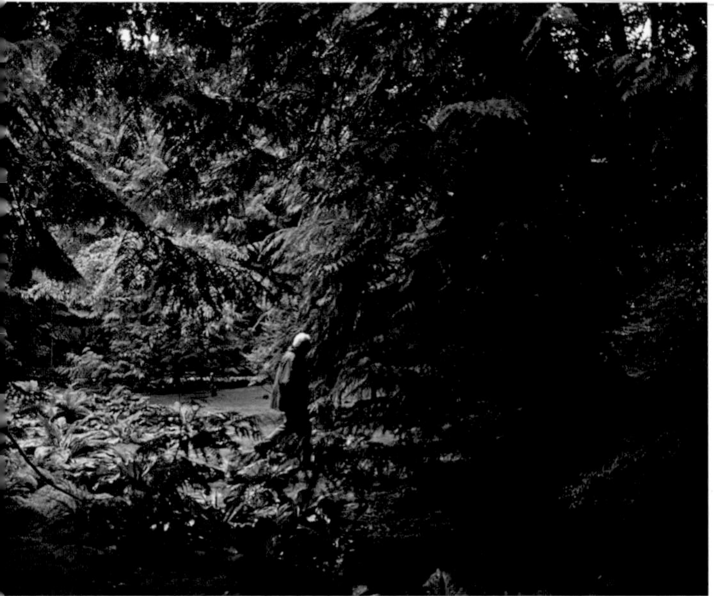

From this first garden, the visitor passed through a wooden gateway and across a stone path, edged with black mondo grass that echoed the geometry of the squares of grass and concrete around the pool and past the large katsura tree marking the intersection with a driveway. The visitor followed the path to enter the forest, or so it would seem. The second garden, the Anteroom or Moss Garden, was both forest and bog, "created by selective subtractions of the nuances of nature from the chaos of a tangled bog."[30] It was here that the forest referenced its natural form and logged history.

Cleared of its understory, the large stumps of harvested trees and fallen trunks, some with the roots still visible, stood out as if they were sculpted works. Originally, forest surrounded the garden, enclosing it with the vertical reach of the giant native arborvitae, western hemlocks, and larches mixed with alders and mountain ash, with elderberries and blueberries forming a middle story. More than two thousand plugs of chartreuse moss, extensive plantings of devil's club (*Opolopanax horridus*), and native ferns heightened the

10.17 Entering the Anteroom, The Bloedel Reserve, Bainbridge Island, 1993.

10.18 Moss Garden, The Bloedel Reserve, Bainbridge Island, May 1992.

10.19 Moss Garden, detail of plant in dappled sunlight, The Bloedel Reserve, Bainbridge Island, May 1992.

enchanted nature of the forest. The wet ground of the bog lay beneath this forest. The garden revealed a diverse landscape emblematic of the Pacific Northwest. Haag inserted a narrow path, meandering past stumps, moss, trees, skunk cabbage, and pools of water, guiding both water and visitors to the garden's far end. To design the path, he laid visqueen along the ground, again designing on site.

Bloedel described the garden as "an extension of the oriental feeling of the Japanese Garden. . . . Mood-inducing plantings, i.e., those producing light and shadow." Stumps, uprooted trees, logs carpeted in moss, fungi, and ferns decayed into the earth, while seedlings grew from nurse logs and along the water's edge. Although Bloedel had been hesitant about the use of stumps, as it was reminiscent of former logging practices, he appreciated how the garden became a primordial place, wet, thick, and beautiful with standing trees providing shelter and intimacy. It was a garden that recalled the mossy forest in the Cascades just hours from Seattle, a part of nature reimagined by an artist. It was also a primordial landscape, in which visitors could imagine discovering a dinosaur or other prehistoric remains. Whether the idea for the Moss Garden came from Haag's trips to Saihō-ji, the Japanese moss garden, Bloedel's interest in such gardens, or images of the rain-forest landscape of the Olympic Peninsula is unimportant, except for how these images established a legacy that might fuse the garden into its site.

At the end of the Moss Garden path, the visitor discovered a narrow opening in a tall hedge and, upon entering, found the formal garden space of the Reflection Garden, the first space Haag had designed. Haag described it as "an empty space until your spirit instills a total unity."[31] The garden was composed of ground, water, and sky enclosed by forest. Here again, Haag fused the languages of Western and Eastern thought. The formal geometry of the Western garden manifested by the rectangular form of both the glade and the Reflection Garden met the poetic simplicity of the Japanese Garden revealed in the material palette, the enclosed nature of the garden, and the stillness of the experience. In

10.20 The Reflection Garden in snow, The Bloedel Reserve, Bainbridge Island, 1996.

an interview with Barbara Swift, a local landscape architect and former student of Haag's, Haag's response to a question about the pool was "Not the pool, the space, the room."[32] This carving out from the forest was reminiscent of the Ise shrine, which also formed an opening in the cryptomeria forest. It was a garden without any objects, "clear and figured."[33] The garden seemed open, and the gardeners were often tempted to add benches or sculpture; however, as Haag remarked, "If you put a sculpture in there, it better be unbelievable. It better be the Venus de Milo. In the original! Not the copy!"[34]

Visitors following the path from the Reflection Garden through deep woods discover the Bird Refuge, a place given over to nature that Haag referred to as a bird sanctuary. By design, this was a space where visitors communed with nature and birds by remaining at the edge, as they were not allowed to enter. For the Bird Refuge, Haag imagined an experience similar to that of the Reflection Garden, with the visitor following a forest trail through the woods and then, upon coming into the sunlight, discovering a reflecting pool carved out of the bog, this one at the scale of a pond with islands. He again worked with what existed, highlighting, for example, an alder grove that marked the site of a 1910 fire. He understood the hydrological systems of the specific place and strengthened the role of water by making it more visible to humans and more functional for the birds. Haag allowed the ecological systems already in place to trace the history of the site, sometimes merely clearing the underbrush to expose found conditions and processes.[35]

After considering alternatives, Haag proposed a plan for bird ponds that drew on his abstraction of the stone garden of Ryōan-ji. He used the pond itself as the setting for a series of islands that were reminiscent of the stones at Ryōan-ji. By excavating a large free-form pond just south of the existing irrigation pond, he created a sanctuary with plants for nesting and feeding. The ponds originally included seven interconnected and vegetated "safe" islands that birds could use for resting and nesting. Ironically, given its references to Ryōan-ji, one of the islands sank after being built and remains out of sight. Working with ornithologists at the University of Washington, Haag determined which plants and what requisite sizes and which varieties of islands and small coves would provide habitat for birds and waterfowl. As at Ryōan-ji, people would not enter but would contemplate the sanctuary from a place of refuge and prospect on the small peninsula, where a bench was concealed from behind by an earth mound and from the front obscured by plants.

Unfortunately, the trustees later added a new pathway that allowed visitors to circumnavigate the pond and, by thinning out the vegetation, opened up multiple views in and across the water. As visitors did not generally appreciate the cattails and other "weedy" plants, the trustees replaced them with plants of "greater visual interest."[36] While this remains a beautiful area, the nature of Haag's bird sanctuary as a place apart from humans has been turned upside down by the increased access and the focus on the scenography instead of on its role as a bird preserve.

Haag's garden sequence was an experience that moved visitors through space and time. It relied on a simple path through a series of spaces that were composed simply and with a limited palette of materials and plants, and yet, as one ASLA juror noted,

> The thing I keep coming back to is . . . how simple the means are and how much has been achieved, . . . [yet the gardens] are simple in different ways. For instance the great water court is nothing but two rectangles one inside another, but it is magical, . . . [the anteroom] uses fallen logs, things are called up that normally one would clear away, . . . but they . . . are brought in and made a part of a composition. . . . You can't see the hand that made it. . . . The last one is nature and yet by the time you're there, you're set up to see it as something special. It would be invisible if you came upon it without this preparation and without this sequence.[37]

Haag has written about his work as a synthesis of the natural and the cultural in gardens such as the Bloedel Reserve. "The gardens are extracted principles from our

10.21 Bird Refuge sketch plan, The Bloedel Reserve, 1981.

10.22 The bird pond under construction, The Bloedel Reserve, Bainbridge Island, November 1982.

10.23 The Bird Refuge, with alders along shoreline, The Bloedel Reserve, 1982.

10.24 Bird Refuge islands, The Bloedel Reserve, Bainbridge Island, April 1983.

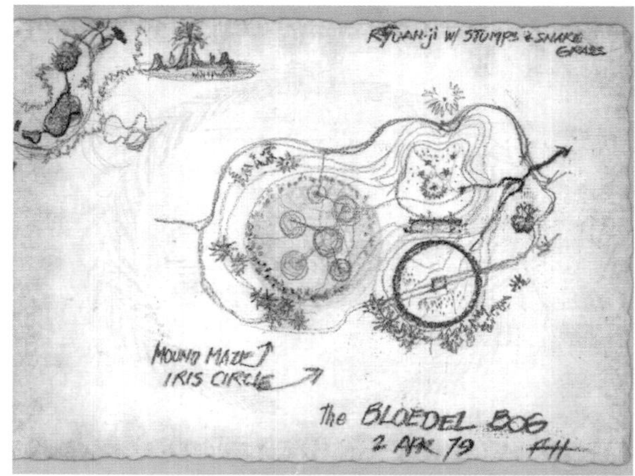
RYUAN-ji W/ STUMPS & SNAKE GRASS
MOUND MAZE
IRIS CIRCLE
the BLOEDEL BOG
2 APR 79

rich heritage of landscape form—providing living proof that man can be the steward of the land and can design with nature. To arouse latent emotional and aesthetic instincts and feelings, and to reaffirm man's immutable and timeless bond with nature, is implicit in its primary purpose."[38] A visitor who observed carefully might see the water move through the landscape, the katsura tree bloom, the mosses and ferns grow and die and reemerge. It was a landscape without clear interpretative programs, and yet it served the purposes of eco-revelatory design.

Haag had come to brilliant realizations for some parts of the reserve and struggled with other parts. It was a landscape created through explorations and experiments, designed on the ground. Haag explored geometric ideas, including uses of the circle as an archetypal geometry that contrasts with the architectural square and rectangle. Early on, he designed a circle of water grasses that then became an iris circle joined by a mounded maze. He played with the idea of a stump garden with native perennial grasses set within the natural depression of the landscape to the east of the main house in the Bird Refuge. Bloedel was not enthralled by the idea of a stump garden, however, something that, given his background, had different connotations for him. So instead, Haag planted a circle of beech trees set twenty feet apart with a seventy-foot diameter that he described as a "living Stonehenge."[39] This, too, was eventually removed. Other ideas were never fully proposed or were rejected. The design process for the Bloedel Reserve clearly enchanted Haag, which is perhaps why the gardens there are some of his most spiritually and aesthetically provocative designs. He continued his work on the reserve until 1984, when Bloedel retired and put the leadership of the landscape in the hands of Arbor Fund directors and the trustees.

In 1986, Haag, with his partner, Cheryl Trivison, submitted the Bloedel Reserve project for an ASLA Award. The project was honored with the ASLA Presidential Awards for Design Excellence" given for work which makes an outstanding professional advancement and which exemplifies the stewardship ethic."[40] Nonetheless, the reserve's trustees had already adopted a new plan in May that included alterations in the circulation routes and Bird Refuge and the destruction of the Garden of Planes. They had determined that the white gravel pyramids did not work for them, and these were soon altered to form a level plane where a more common Japanese-style garden was installed. The trustees viewed the reserve as a place for nature and all things natural and considered Haag's design too sculptural.[41] Haag and the ASLA jury found the Garden of Planes evocative and moving, a way of engaging with nature, but the reserve trustees did not. They would, however, retain other parts of the garden sequence.

UNDERSTANDING THE GARDEN

Designers and scholars have sought to understand the complexities of the Bloedel Reserve gardens. Susan Rademacher Frey's description of of Haag's landscape as a "poem" resonates with visitors. She identifies an ABAB pattern in the sequence of gardens.[42] The Garden of Planes and the Reflection Garden were the reflective, highly crafted, elegant spaces (A), while the Anteroom and the Bird Refuge are the complex, highly crafted spaces that nevertheless appear natural (B). Poetry is found in the placement of plants, in the use of scale and proportion, and in the play of materials to engage contrasts.

What is most often written about the Bloedel Reserve design is its Japanese essence, although Haag initially pointed to the Chinese stroll garden as a framework, indicating on his first master plan that the concept was "stolen from the Tao philosophy & China, the mother of gardens."[43] And yet the plan includes a building labeled "Ise Experience," referencing his mixing of Chinese and Japanese sources. As a whole, the Bloedel Reserve gardens focus as much on transition, a critical intersection of Chinese and Japanese gardens, as on moments of listening, seeing, and reflection. Haag was clear that he was not imitating a Japanese garden but rather adapting, rewriting, and translating it through the lens of the specific site. He described his designs as reflecting an abstraction of principles and approaches he had learned in Japan.[44] Patrick Condon has suggested that the design expressed a series of reciprocal relationships in order to help "the visitor experience something of *satori* (roughly translated, 'an awakening'), in which the gap between the mind and the material world is bridged."[45] Drawing on Bloedel's "Statement of Nature and Purpose," Haag remarked in his essay "Contemplations of the Japanese Influence on Bloedel Reserve" that the gardens and landscape "represent a synthesis of humankind's immutable bond with nature, a bond that transcends time, language and culture."[46] He elaborated further by suggesting that the garden experience is a "cerebral exercise that paid a special tribute to Jay Appleton—it was the ultimate distillation of his prospect/refuge theory: its geometry was the essential counterpoint to the Anteroom, the Reflection Room and the Bird Sanctuary—each space interpreting Nature in a different but complimentary way."[47]

The Japanese character of the design becomes apparent in the relationships of the parts of the garden, both within and between rooms. As prescribed by Haag's principle of reciprocity, the parts of each garden were to be experienced in relation to the other parts. There was no single focal point or intended moment within the gardens; instead, each "offers multiple foci, and more importantly, a set of shifting patterns and relationships—even if the field appears to be static."[48] The relationship between the meadow, the earth mounds or landforms, and the original sand pyramids constructed an experience that was a prelude to the Moss Garden and beyond. It was the eye that moved and scanned the view and thereby enhanced a sense of the place by seeing relationships between the parts.[49] The Garden of Planes, the Moss Garden, the Reflection Garden, and the Bird Refuge were not meant as singular objects but as parts of a larger and more complex whole—like elements of a musical fugue. Altering a note or phrase would change the entire fugue.[50]

In the Bloedel Reserve design, Haag brought his use of land-sculpting techniques to their most complex and elegant He drew on his horticultural knowledge and growing ecological awareness to develop a design that appeared to be as much about cultural inscriptions as about natural systems. The role of growth and decay in landscape, the concept of a healing landscape, both spiritually and ecologically, and the emphasis on native plants came together in this design, which remains iconic in his career.[51] Haag treated the Bloedel Reserve like a great earth sculpture. Such a sculptured landscape offers a space for thoughtful seeing, listening, and reflecting, in other words, the exquisite experience of careful thought, for as Robert Pogue Harrison wrote, "Thinking needs place to take place in."[52]

The Bloedel Reserve as a landscape architectural project in many ways synthesized design ideas Haag had developed over the previous decades of practice. The design reflected his time in Japan as well as his tenure in the Pacific Northwest. The landscape manifested ideas about reuse and recycling of space and elements. It was a disturbed site reinterpreted to acknowledge its past and, at the same time, suggest an alternative future as a place of meditation and a celebration of ecological processes and natural beauty.

In 2003, Haag received the ASLA Medal, the highest honor the ALSA awards a landscape architect for lifetime achievements and contributions to the profession that have had a unique and significant influence on both the public and the environment. This acknowledgment of his legacy was grounded in his designs for Gas Works Park and the Bloedel Reserve, as well as his ongoing advocacy for the important role of landscape architecture in the public realm, specifically, in the urban sphere. The award also recognized the leading role of Haag and his students, employees, and clients in changing the practice of landscape architecture, all from the far corner of the Pacific Northwest, from the modernism of mid-century to the urban ecological design of the twenty-first century.

the legacy

IN 2014, AT THE AGE OF NINETY, RICHARD HAAG CONTINues to practice in Seattle and around the globe. With more than fifty years of practice, however, it is appropriate and timely to consider his substantial body of work. This narrative began with Haag's introduction to practice and the establishment of Richard Haag Associates in 1957 and ends by 2000. The review was not comprehensive but selective, intended to describe the breadth and depth of Haag's work that continues to inform how landscape architecture is understood and practiced. This legacy is evident in the Pacific Northwest, in Haag's students, in the department he founded, and, finally, across the globe.

While internationally recognized, the vast majority of Haag's projects have been built, planted, and stewarded in the Pacific Northwest, most particularly in and near Seattle. Accordingly, his designs have been deeply grounded in the Pacific Northwest and have, in turn, shaped a regional approach to design shared with landscape architects, architects, artists, and even writers. His designs draw on the character and qualities of the region's landscapes, its habitats, ecology, and environments. The designs also draw on and enrich the cultural character of the region, in particular, urban narratives and identities. In the Emerald City, as some have called Seattle, Haag's landscapes offer an abstraction of nature in the city, an urban nature that is closely woven into the tapestries of urban culture.

Haag's teaching inspired a generation of practitioners and civic activists. The landscape architect and writer Gary R. Hilderbrand described how, for "a group of idealistic young people rebelling against architecture, Haag, with an almost religious zeal, delivered an epiphany: the landscape is the site for urgent and meaningful work."[1] Initially teaching in the architecture department, he had a legendary hold on his students, including Laurie Olin, Grant Jones, Frank James, Robert Hanna, Jerry Finrow, and Jerry Diethelm, as well as those who came to teach and design with him, such as Don Sakuma. They learned from Haag not only to hold true to a set of values but to take on the roles of mentor and master. Each of these individuals developed his own design milieu; there is no Haag school, but as teachers, they disseminated Haag's lessons and approaches to subsequent generations of students and practitioners across the country. Generations of designers continue to be inspired by Haag's belief in the potential of landscape architecture to shape the world.

The same legacy can be assigned to the Department of Landscape Architecture that Haag established. In 2014, it is committed to urban ecological design as that which "integrates site, landscape, and people in a design practice that is functional, artful, and engaging."[2] The focus of current faculty and students builds on the strengths of more than fifty years of practice in a city and metropolitan region that are increasingly recognized for their efforts to address environmental challenges, from clean water to climate change.

Haag's broadly exploratory practice has also extended his legacy beyond Seattle, reflecting the profession as it struggled to move away from its identity as a luxury-oriented practice of garden design to that of urban-oriented and ecologically grounded design. His work fostered alternative ways of thinking about landscape architecture and ecological design in the city. His experiments in landscape remediation and reclamation opened areas of inquiry into the adaptive reuse of postindustrial sites for researchers and practitioners in diverse fields including ecology, environmental science, microbiology, cultural studies and geography, and, of course, design. Haag's investigations helped reorient the balance of art and science in the practice of landscape architecture and subsequently shaped the emerging theoretical foundations of what has come to be called urban ecological design.

Since Haag began his practice in Seattle, urban ecological design has emerged as a leading framework for landscape architectural practice in the twenty-first century. A practice focused at the mid-twentieth century on modernist approaches emphasizing architecture is now oriented to the complexities of the urban landscape and its cultural and natural ecologies. Haag played a critical role in this transformation. At a celebration of the Harvard University Graduate School of Design in 1991, Haag was awarded an Alumni Council Achievement Award. In honor of the event, John O. Simonds wrote the following:

> In the decades that have followed the tumultuous HGSD "revolution," the practice of landscape architecture has progressed by quantum leaps. . . . We have reoriented public thinking from the indoors to the out; from the backyard to the planned community; from suburban sprawl to restructured and more agreeable cities; from cities to the open countryside and the realm of nature beyond. We, more than any other group, have spearheaded the world crusade for environmental protection and improvement. In this vitally important evolution it would be hard to find four individuals who have done more to lead the way. Let's hear it, then, for Garrett Eckbo, Larry Halprin, Richard Haag, and Hid Sasaki![3]

Finally, Haag continues to challenge the system and each of us to live by our values, as expressed in his own words:

HAAG CREDO

the cosmos is an experiment
the universe is a park
the earth is a pleasure ground
nature is our theater
the landscape is our stage
let us write the script
direct the play
and embrace the audience
with compassion and joy
for LIFE!

PERSONALITI VANITATUM JAPONICA.

Richard Haag as the Zen master, 1963. Sketch by Laurie Olin

afterword

AN APPRECIATION OF RICHARD HAAG, AN INSPIRATION AND MENTOR TO US ALL

In memory of Frank James and Robert Hanna

> Once someone has been your teacher, and truly an influential one, he remains your teacher. He has gone ahead, breaking trail so to speak, and in a way will always remain so, like one's parents.

RICH HAAG HAS BEEN A FORCE IN MY LIFE, AT DIFFERENT times a teacher, role model, father figure, employer, hostile critic, loyal and generous supporter and advocate, colleague, and both cranky and affectionate friend. He has been an inspiration and a caution to me about our profession, landscape architecture. I am one of a group of his diverse students who went off in different directions to do battle with the world and to make landscapes of ambition or to teach. The following are selected memories about a few years when we both spent a lot time in the same environment. Like all memoirs, my understanding has been filtered through my life and experience.

Richard Haag is a low-key, but arguably seminal figure in American landscape architecture. As anyone who knows Rich could explain, Gas Works Park and the Bloedel Reserve are two high points, but there are other designs and moments of great subtlety, intelligence, and delight in his oeuvre. Personal favorites are the clear structure of the Seattle Center planting and bold fountain square, his work at Western Washington State College (now Western Washington University) in Bellingham, and Steinbrueck Park at the Pike Place Market in downtown Seattle. There was a recessive, quiet, almost invisible hand at work in his handling of the steps, stairs, walks, paths, and native plantings at Bellingham, as well as his quiet handling of a group of talented, strong-willed, somewhat contentious architects at work there throughout his tenure. Likewise, the simple and clear, even amusing park he executed with his longtime friend and colleague Vic Steinbrueck, after our stunning victory in saving the market, rivals Aldo Rossi's work in its employment of fundamental typologies, bold elemental forms, and cultural resonance, with its one hill, big tree, council ring, totem pole, shelter, and railing. This park is a brilliant response to the needs of Skid Road and its situation within the region.

Rich Haag has surveyed the range and territory of our landscape heritage in his own work in terms of meaning, values, and experiment, leaving us with built examples to envy and think about. That is an achievement. But for me, before the work, there was Rich as a teacher in the classroom.

I entered the University of Washington's School of Architecture and Urban Planning in the autumn of 1957 as a transfer student from the Civil Engineering program at the University of Alaska, near my hometown of Fairbanks. Approximately eighty undergraduate students were thrown together that year in two adjoining basement studios in the old architecture building. We were a mixture of interior design, industrial design, and architecture undergraduates at the beginning of the studio sequence. It was a rigorous basic design course, and in the next three years, we would be whittled down to seventeen survivors of the original group, graduating in 1961, along with three others who joined us, having been in the army or on a leave for a year or more. Out of that class of twenty, several later were selected for Fulbright grants, several moved into art history, many later taught in one place or another, some left the field for development or government service. Four won the Rome Prize, three in landscape architecture and one in urban design. One won a Guggenheim Fellowship. Several became prominent teachers or practitioners of landscape architecture: Jerry Diethelm, first at Arizona State University and then as chairman at the University of Oregon, Frank James at the University of Washington and then Harvard University and Hideo Sasaki's office, and myself, first at the University of Washington, then at the University of Pennsylvania, for a time chairman at Harvard, later teaching at Virginia, Texas, and again at Penn. Others, such as Grant and Ilze Jones in the class immediately behind ours, also went on to distinguish themselves in landscape architecture, Grant also having taught at various places off and on. Others in a class ahead of me, Robert Hanna, my former partner, and Gary Okerlund, taught for decades at the University of Pennsylvania and University of Virginia respectively.

Why this shift by so many would-be architects to landscape architecture, and why so dedicated to proselytizing for the field? The short answer is Richard Haag and the power of a great teacher to give direction to people's lives. In the mid-1950s, the University of Washington possessed an unusually good architecture school. If design schools at Cornell University, the University of Michigan, the University of California, Berkeley, the University of Pennsylvania, and Harvard University all had departments of landscape architecture, the reasoning went, so should the University of Washington. It would be progressive. For the old guard, it was a proper adjunct to city and estate design. For those recently arrived, it bespoke the new motopia, the design of suburbs, housing developments, highways, campus planning, and a new emerging indoor-outdoor western style of postwar living. How to get started?

Luckily, Haag was hired by the University of Washington College of Architecture and Urban Planning in the summer of 1958. That autumn, as my class of nascent architects moved upstairs for the first year of solid architecture courses with all of our requirements for humanities and sciences behind us, we settled in for structures, architectural history, and the backbreaking, endless, all-consuming studio. Rich had been engaged to develop a landscape program, but he also was expected to do something to earn his keep. The college put him in our studio for the year as a design critic along with a handful of rotating architects drawn from the faculty and local offices. Although we were aspiring to become architects with a series of projects that concerned mostly buildings and their construction, we were his only students. He had just moved to the area and had no clients to speak of as yet who might have been outlets for his thought and energy.

Rich threw himself into teaching us, spending by far the most time of any of our critics. That spring he added a landscape appreciation and theory course that my class was required to take. Later there was a site-planning course also. By the next year, when we entered Grade III (the fourth-year studio), he was a familiar soul to our class, having become something of an uncle or family retainer, as well as an interesting foil to the rest of the faculty.

In the summer of 1960, I talked my way into working at Bassetti & Morse, one of the most distinguished firms in the region and at the time a virtual clearinghouse for talented young designers. I shared an annex down the hall from the main drafting room for three months with Folke Nyberg, who had just graduated from Yale after studying under Paul Rudolph, and who was later to become a respected intellect and beloved teacher at the University of Washington. My main topics for the summer were a group of dormitories for Western Washington State College in Bellingham and the furnishings of a library at Central Washington State College in Ellensburg. The dorms were to be located on a steep, heavily wooded hillside. Haag was the landscape architect. Jerry Diethelm (my roommate the following year) and Frank James were working for Rich, who now had an office, that summer. Our two offices agreed to try to keep as much of the native vegetation on the site as possible and to insert the buildings, walks, service drives, and site elements in place carefully. It was difficult, and despite the usual tensions and difficulties of coordination between two design offices, the project was a triumph as built. It was my baptism into what collaboration can be, in terms of the psychodynamics of individuals and the dilemmas of subconsultants, as well as how much a landscape architect can do for an architectural project.

From that summer until I left Seattle for the third time in 1972, I maintained what might be described as a loose orbit around Haag's office, occasionally working within or without on projects and schemes. Probably the last of these was in 1969, when I was living in Betty Willis's guesthouse at Agate Point on Bainbridge Island and maintaining a studio in the Globe Hotel south of Pioneer Square. On the heels of the battle to save the Pike Place Market, which we seemed to have won for the moment, Rich and I learned that there was a move afoot to demolish the skeletal frame of a remarkable and no-longer-used gasometer immediately north across the street from a long-abandoned gasworks plant on the north shore of Lake Union. Nearly every architecture student in our college had drawn and painted these blackened artifacts in an attempt to obtain a few desperately needed last-minute sketch points in the annual schoolwide spring watercolor contest. My friends and I had become fond of these hulking relics. At the time, I was also concerned about the fate of an enormous neon sign adjacent to them, which spelled out "Grandma's Cookies" and could be seen from several districts of Seattle: the Denny Regrade and Queen Anne and Capitol Hills. Rich and I began to brainstorm about the threatened gas tank as well as the cracking towers across the way.

Rich asked me to sketch up something for the threatened gasometer. Over a weekend in the cabin on Bainbridge Island, I produced a stream of free-association images on a long, continuous scroll of paper that might suggest social and recreational uses and thereby justify the site's preservation. We lost the gasometer battle, and the cookie sign was torn down; however, under pressure from the Seattle Design Commission, a couple of city council members, and the Forward Thrust bond issue, a park on the gasworks site became a real project. Then, unexpectedly, in the bizarre public politics of Seattle, which more than occasionally went wrong, Rich miraculously landed the commission.

Again, several years later in 1971, while Haag and a couple of assistants were slowly coaxing various community groups and agencies along as they developed a master plan, I became involved, helping with sketches of kids playing on the pipes and equipment in one of the sheds. Rich and I speculated about the cracking towers over a few beers. "Why not a camera obscura? Is there some way one could actually get inside such potentially creepy but stimulating things safely?" I asked. Or might there be a way the towers could become a great jungle gym, some sort of bizarre and exciting climbing apparatus for adults? I knew nothing about toxic chemicals, nor did I care about any of the issues of liability, safety, and accessibility in those days, and Rich, always one to say "Why not?" came up with other innocent suggestions for these particular ruins. These ideas and issues would bubble to the surface in the profession over the next two decades. In any case, I wandered off to England and back the next year and became immersed in a wonderful project and terrible political battle over a zoo, which led to its eventual radical transformation at the hands of Grant Jones and David Hancocks. Finally, I left town in 1972, with little more to do with the gasworks project that was tough going for Rich at the time.

TEACHING

People often ask me where I studied landscape architecture. When I tell them nowhere, that I have only a bachelor's degree in architecture, they are surprised. It is true, however, that I did become a landscape architect. I usually mumble something about studying with a very distinguished landscape architect named Haag when I was in architecture school, later gaining practical experience in his office and elsewhere, and eventually, through work, self-study, travel, and teaching, somehow metamorphosing into a landscape architect. Sometimes I tell them that it's probably related to growing up in Alaska, that I started out in one of the greatest landscapes in the world, which satisfies them. All of this is true, but it hardly tells the story. I was learning more about landscape architecture from Haag than I knew, by osmosis and inference.

Rich introduced us, first as students and then as his assistants, to a wealth of reading not found in any architectural curriculum at the time. He had us read widely in easily accessible works on natural history and land use: Aldo Leopold, Joseph Wood Krutch, and Loren Eisley. He introduced us to *Landscape*, a slender new magazine edited and often largely written by someone named J. B. Jackson. He got us to read Henry David Thoreau's *Walden*. Clearly it was something like a holy text to him. It would be years before I finally got the hang of some of its implications, and only after reading Stanley Cavell's *The Senses of Walden* in 1981 did I fully realize how deeply radical it was and that the underlying message went beyond environmental hortatory—namely, that Thoreau was calling for Americans to remake the nation spiritually as well as physically. It wasn't just about understanding, care, and preservation of wilderness—although that was an important part—it was also a call to nurture the wilderness in ourselves and a call to move beyond European ancestry and perceptions, to remake ourselves in particular ways more suited to a new society in a new land.

My generation was raised on liberal democratic civics classes that were a common feature in public schools across the United States following World War II. Stimulated by the sudden outburst of rock and roll while in high school, through college, and after, we hung out in bars and coffeehouses listening to jazz and American folk music and began participating in civil rights demonstrations that included picketing Woolworth's in downtown Seattle in support of blacks whose struggle for equality was gaining momentum. At the urging of our professors, we joined in attempts to document the rich, historic urban fabric that was being blown away by a new interstate highway (I-5 and its various ramps and interchanges) as it plowed through the city from north to south. We were also just old enough to notice how extensively the new suburban development was reshaping the world. The development of the Vietnam War was the final straw and loosened whatever remaining hold traditional and entrenched authority had on our allegiances. The literature Haag directed us toward in school and after was as provocative as it was appropriate and helpful.

From Rich, I came to understand that one of the chief duties of a teacher is to challenge students from first acquaintance throughout their academic careers, to get them to reexamine and test any and all assumptions, beliefs, and habits they may have. The purpose isn't to destroy their confidence or purpose but rather to have them develop considered and informed views and principles. Rich's students were led to broader, more synthetic, and evolving ideas and theories about the physical and cultural worlds. His methods were both subtle and direct. A master of the Socratic method, Rich rarely directed students to do anything in a particular manner or method. At times it surely was that he hadn't a clue what to tell us anyway (something I frequently encountered later in my own teaching). He would hint at things, tease, make jokes, and leave us with something to think about. *We* were supposed to do the work. It is a superb approach, and harder to do than many realize, for it requires restraint. Unlike several other famous and powerful teachers I have known and watched at work, he didn't produce a group of followers whose work looks alike and is really more the teacher's than the students'.

What sort of performance did he give as a beginning teacher faced with a group of architecture students those first years at the University of Washington? For one whole semester he talked about nature, plants, water, stones, and an odd combination of design elements. We sat in the dark spellbound by one beautiful photograph after another taken in Japan when he was there as a Fulbright fellow. They were projected to an enormous size in the main auditorium, often in voluptuous color, although some were in startling silhouette, nearly black and white, and graphically striking. I am certain that it was Rich who asked Betty Wagner, the librarian, to order a new book for the library, *Form and Space in Japanese Architecture* by Norman Carver. It became something of a private handbook of forms and images. Unbeknownst to us, Carver and Rich had traveled together in Japan as Fulbright fellows, at times standing side by side, trading places for the same views and photographs of garden, temple, stairway, rock composition, roof, and shadow. Twenty-five years later, when I reached those locations myself, I maneuvered and lined up carefully to see the very images that I'd memorized that year and after, to make my own versions, which I now share with another generation of students.

Rich's slide shows were a great bath of color, texture, and form. Rich is a hedonist and a modernist of the first order. His unabashed embrace of sex and death in nature and therefore in people aligns him with all great artists, but not with the nervous and squeamish upper middle class of the Eisenhower era or in Seattle as it was at the time. On the one hand, this earthiness has lost him scores of commissions, public and private. On the other hand, it has meant that many of those things he has actually gotten built are truly beautiful, and at times sublime (I say this with full knowledge of how art historians use these terms). It has also endeared him to hundreds of students who are at a point in their lives where they are struggling to maintain or develop their own personae and are seeking some way to make beautiful things in a world that seems particularly resistant. He seemed to be achieving a life and work that embraced aspects of the enormous yearnings of many of his students.

OFFICE PRACTICE

The notion that a professional office could be in an abandoned storefront next to a Chinese mom-and-pop grocery in a quiet residential neighborhood was certainly a revelation. Rich opened up shop on Fuhrman Avenue, conveniently down the street from Sam's Red Robin, a tavern that was a favorite hangout of faculty and students. Compared to the academic side of a world recently reprised visually in the TV series *Madmen*, one of button-down collars, crew cuts, knit ties, horn-rims, woven webbed belts with brass buckles, suntan slacks, narrow-lapel tweed jackets, and Clark's desert boots—the culture of architecture and design in the late years of Eisenhower's America—Rich's office was bohemia.

Rich needed assistants. There really wasn't a supply of landscape architects in Seattle from which he could select and hire assistants for his office. At the same time, my class had already been through a year of drawing from plaster casts, as well as from life and nature, plus a year of mechanical drafting and perspective construction, exercises in hand lettering, and a semester of watercolor painting. Plus we'd had some training and exposure to landscape from Rich. Some of us began to work for him part-time and occasionally to help out with his first commercial projects and to have beers with him at the Red Robin Tavern. It was fun. It was new and stimulating. It was a world of real (if stingy) clients, of deadlines (nothing new there), of contractors, construction, and a little spending money. Also it was endless hours of talking about design, books, travel, ideas, and life. Rich had professional victories and defeats. Those who were around shared them. A building committee had approved a project! Go next door to Wong's and get some beer—let's celebrate! A client has decided not to go ahead. Some dentist's wife disapproved, or a councilman insisted we be let go! You mean fired?! Go next door to Wong's. Get some beer for the wake! It was the ups and downs of a talented young purist in what was a wilderness for landscape architecture.

And so the work came, and eventually real employees. Aside from his own students, the best ever was probably Don Sakuma, a Californian who'd gone to Harvard to study and work under Hideo Sasaki. Rich had written to Hid asking him to send someone of talent whom he could hire to help him turn the corner and have a more professional enterprise. Sakuma turned up one day outside the office to take the job, having driven across the country in a delicious little Porsche coupe. He was a gracious, handsome, ebullient Nisei product of southern California. He was also a natural and facile designer, as well as one of the best talents at grading I've ever known. He was to become a pillar of the practice for more than a decade, teaching as well at the university in the new Department of Landscape Architecture until his untimely death.

Richard Haag Associates (RHA) embraced a diversity of individuals in those early years. There was Frank Lockfeld, a thoughtful, pipe-smoking, somewhat introverted eastern urban sort, the product of left-wing Jewish Brooklyn, tortured and intellectual, the best read of us all at the time. Another was my sorely missed prickly and emotional dear friend and classmate Frank James, whose father was an important federal judge in Seattle. James, balding, small and wiry, recently returned from army service in Korea with a strong young Korean wife, envied my drawing skills and willed himself into becoming a graphic powerhouse—strong, fast, bold, and with a wicked, almost demonic sense of humor. Grant Jones—a product of the most exclusive prep school in Seattle, with parents who were pillars of the establishment in Portland, Oregon, and Seattle, had already burned through a marriage and had established a relationship with Ilze Grinbergs, a Latvian refugee and gifted, challenging designer in his architecture class—had begun a lifelong quest for a deeper connection to the land, its creatures, and indigenous peoples. There was my roommate Jerry Diethelm, whose parents owned a general store in the sleepy burg of La Conner, on the coast north of Seattle. A sharp-witted intellectual who'd been an all-state high school basketball star, he was an obsessive chess player who took pleasure in endless debate in a style that could shift from Jesuitical to Talmudic. Miles Yanick, a passionate and hot-headed, folk-singing, madman skier from a tough working-class background who approached design the way he approached a mountain, in a full headlong rush that as easily produced results that were at times awkward and ugly and at other moments clear, strong, and graceful. Another was Ken Rupard. In large part a Pacific Northwest Native American (we used to say "Indian"), he drew more beautifully than any of us, had the softest voice and the dreamiest, most poetic thoughts. Like myself, Ken would wander off and disappear, doing something else for months or years at a time, and then reappear as if nothing had happened. Judy Fleniken, an accomplished folk singer and superb guitarist (whether steel, gut, six- or twelve-string, in all manner of fingering styles) was the secretary and bookkeeper for several years. She was a good strong performer who helped hold the office together while keeping Rich sorted out, for the most part. It was an interesting bunch, dreamers in search of themselves or direction, of which I was one, who came and passed through RHA in the 1960s.

I went straight into practice, skipping graduate school as a luxury that I couldn't afford. But the web of precedents and examples spun by Rich had its effect. I worked in superb architectural offices in Seattle and New York, then Seattle again, and London, before coming to Philadelphia. In one office after another, I gravitated toward the site-planning phase of projects, often producing the first grading and road plans whether or not there were engineering or landscape subconsultants. I coordinated landscape architects and civil engineers on the projects. There were detours along the way, whole years at a time when I lived in a cabin and painted or wrote or lived and studied in Europe. The insecurity of not having gone to graduate school, the sense of being uneducated on the one hand and not a good enough artist or professional of whatever sort on the other, spurred me onto a course of ceaseless reading, looking, traveling, and working that has yet to abate. Nevertheless, it was Rich who invited me to give my first academic lectures and Grant Jones who asked me to participate in a design studio.

In the autumn of 1970, I returned to Seattle from my first visit to England, a trip that was to have a strong influence on my subsequent career. By then, Haag had created a spirited Department of Landscape Architecture and turned the chairmanship over to Robert Buchanan. In the spring of 1971, Grant Jones offered a studio concerned with the development and preservation of Bainbridge Island, where I was living at the time, and asked me to join him as a critic. The next autumn, I was asked to teach a drawing course for the landscape department, which was fun to do. It felt odd to have one of Rich's sons, Zach, in the class. One couldn't help noticing this transmission of knowledge and information between alternating generations.

By 1969, when I left New York and returned to live in Seattle, Don Sakuma and Frank James had left Rich to form their own office in a storefront farther up on Capitol Hill. There had been a near-Oedipal struggle on Frank's part in his need to have Rich's approval and to break away that at times manifested itself in wild and emotional outbursts. The office he and Don produced was truly an offspring of Richard Haag Associates on Fuhrman Avenue. Their practice was taking off with a series of small parks funded by Forward Thrust, a landmark public bond initiative in Seattle, as well as several educational institutions and small commercial projects. Rich wisely hired them both to teach despite ongoing fractious personal relations, and they proved to be inspirational and effective in the classroom.

Two years later, after I'd returned to the Pacific Northwest and was living at Agate Point on Bainbridge, in the cabin where Theodore Roethke had been staying when he died, Grant and Ilze visited from Hawaii. His parents were ailing, and he was feeling homesick for the Pacific Northwest. Frank James and I pitched Grant to return. We were convinced that the gang of Rich's protégés could effect some sort of renaissance of design and environmental planning in the region. Shortly thereafter, the Joneses moved back, renting the cabin next to mine on Bainbridge. I had also located a boat, a Poulsbo fishing boat with a lovely wooden hull that I thought might interest Grant, which he bought and still owns. Grant didn't feel he could return to Rich, who was without sufficient work to hire him anyway. He and Ilze set out looking for space to open an office. Earlier, I'd created a studio on the second floor of the old Globe Hotel Building owned by Dick White, whose gallery around the corner exhibited and sold work by most of the younger artists in the region, including mine. It was on south Main Street, below Pioneer Square, above a ceramics gallery and what became the Elliot Bay Book Company. Several other architects, such as Ralph Anderson, and painters, such as Frank Okada, had studios in nearby buildings. So it seemed natural to suggest to Jones that they join us there. They were able to rent and renovate the top floor, where the office of Jones and Jones continues to flourish. A landscape community that Rich had been incubating for a decade was beginning to hatch.

Bob Hanna, who had been in the architecture class two years ahead of mine, was also one of Rich's early devotees and full-time employees. He'd moved from Bob Small's, a respected architectural office where he'd been designing and documenting private residences and commercial buildings, to Haag's office after an impulsive visit and spur-of-the-moment interview around 1962. He worked there for a couple of years before following Diethelm, James, and Jones to the Harvard Graduate School of Design for an MLA. A couple of years later, Ian McHarg recruited Bob to join the University of Pennsylvania Department of Landscape Architecture faculty; Bob was working at the Boston Redevelopment Authority, where he'd gone after Harvard. At Penn, Peter Shepheard, the dean of the Graduate School of Fine Arts, noticed Hanna's broad background and skills in landscape, urban design, and architecture, qualities that characterized Haag's students and employees, and in the summer of 1974 put him in charge of reorganizing the undergraduate Design of the Environment major. Three years after my first teaching experience at Washington, Hanna, in turn, thought another Haag protégé would be helpful and coaxed me back to the States from England, where I had begun working in Derek Lovejoy's London landscape architecture and planning office after two years at the American Academy in Rome.

So it was that seventeen years after Haag opened his office in Seattle, Bob Hanna and I opened ours in Philadelphia on a vacant floor over a rowdy tavern next to a live burlesque house across from the Greyhound bus station. Like Rich in his early days, the only capital we had was our wits and energy. We supported ourselves as he had on our teaching salaries, working full-time at both Penn and the office. Naturally, our first employees were part-time and drawn from among our students. A couple of recent graduates of Bob's moonlighted for us while working at day jobs in local firms. Like Rich, we picked those who could draw well and seemed keen. One student who was supporting himself through college as a carpenter helped build the office, desk by desk, partition by partition, one piece of wallboard and floor tile at a time. Hollow-core doors on sawhorses for desks, Luxo lamps, and one phone had worked for Rich, so it would do for us. As in the early years at Haag's when there were no secretaries or bookkeepers, we had none. I did the typing and bookkeeping, such as it was. The emphasis was totally on design and service. It was a late-night (often all-night) and weekend affair. It was a diet of cheeseburgers and beer, fried chicken and wine, on paper plates and in plastic cups, for several years.

Like Rich's, our first clients were architects who'd been to Harvard, Princeton, Penn, and Berkeley, who knew about landscape architecture and believed in the idea if not the fact of collaboration. Like Rich, we often had to teach them the advantages and pleasures of real collaboration and that trying to tell us what to do with a site wasn't really their best use of us as a resource. We won a competition. We went to New York to work with architects who had tons of projects, needed help, and were looking for fresh faces. We worked extremely hard, placing great emphasis on how we drew things and how well made they were in terms of materials and details. And, as with Rich, the work came in.

Grant Jones once told me that he didn't think Rich really knew much about running a practice in those early years and that the young people around him just had to figure it out as they went along and do it for him. There is some truth in this, but one shouldn't underestimate Rich's ability to get others to do things for him and to put up with any awkwardness that might result from problems created. Since I was really never a full-time employee for any extended period of time, I can't say. I do know that Don Sakuma, Frank James, and the others really did worry about the business, the contracts, the fees, the deadlines and despaired at times at how little Rich seemed to respond to their sense of what he should do. But then, it was his office, and eventually they went off to have it their own their way, having learned how to do the work and run a practice, and Rich kept on going.

All of us learned a lot about our craft and how to work on the spot in a very short period of time in the crowded and confusing clutter in which Rich held forth. Despite the fact that I hadn't taken any courses in landscape design, I learned a lot about grading, planting, circulation, and form, not to say attitude and values, there. Grant decided to teach himself plants so successfully that it astonished us all, including Rich. Haag's office was a graduate school of sorts for some of the things that I needed at the time, part club, part seminar, part workhouse, part bedlam, but always instructive in one way or another. Later, in a long, roundabout, and at times painful way, in New York, London, Rome, and Philadelphia, I learned things that I might have acquired more quickly in an educational setting, although probably not with such depth and intensity. Much of what I went off to see and study, however, such as the life and work of Thoreau and Olmsted, ecology and gardens, Rich introduced to us as important topics in his office as much as in class.

Rich taught us to respect materials in our work and methods in the office and in our designs. He hounded us to make certain we always had enough of whatever and not to be stingy. He would get exasperated with me if I developed a drawing or sketch on some scrap of paper or flimsy (which he called "bumwad"), or if I tore it off with a ragged or diagonal edge. "Jeeee-zzzuz Christ, Olin!" he'd say. "Look what you've done!" I'd stare at him, stunned, having done what I thought was a pretty nice study of something. "You've gone and done a lovely drawing on a goddamned, half-assed piece of paper. How am I supposed to show that to a client?" I learned that studies are often the best drawings, the most thoughtful, rich, and persuasive, and that one must be prepared in the tight schedules and crazy life of practice to turn every gesture to use, that everything counted. All of it was serious despite the horseplay. One's work was always on trial. Every meeting with a client or agency, no matter how informal the setting or topic, was always a presentation, a performance. One was constantly on trial, being judged. Life might be a game, but the game mattered.

Another lesson was that having an idea and drawing it up wasn't design. It was the start. We studied things over and over, went through mountains of paper, boxes of pencils and markers, bottles of ink, pens and pen points. It took a lot of work to get things boiled down, to find simpler, better, clearer solutions. It took effort to make things look simple and obvious or natural. Later, when Bob and I opened our office, one thing we insisted on was that there always be more that enough supplies, and of the best sort. Design is hard enough as it is; one doesn't need to fight the materials or for supplies as well.

So we drew a lot. Because of our architectural training and graphic skills, we placed a lot of emphasis on drawing. And yet, Rich always cautioned us not to fall in love with the drawings. Nice or bold as they might be, fun to do, beautiful to look at and savor (and this went for working drawings as well), they were only a means to an end, to the real world of rain and sun, trees and earth, men and women, food and plants. Drawings were tools, roadmaps, instructions, and not reality. He referred with pleasure and pride, but not-so-veiled suspicion, to my drawings as "visual swindles."

The office Rich presided over struggled to make ends meet. This was because of his values, his methods, and his life. At this moment I can say that after nearly forty years in practice myself, the same has been true for my own offices. We have almost gone out of business twice and continue every so many years to struggle financially. Landscape architecture as I learned it from Rich is a great calling but, if it remains design driven, a terrible business.

Rich's practice was and continues to be design driven, and our office has been also. It allows me to sleep well, knowing that I really have tried to do everything possible that I know how to do for a design, project, or client while staying true to my values. It has allowed me to put up with an awful lot of ill-informed and hostile criticism or political reversals. It didn't help me sleep on occasions when bills were coming due and clients weren't paying their bills. Nevertheless, when I consider what we have been able to achieve by following Haag's example of running a practice that, while seeming a bit chaotic, is totally devoted to design, its ideas, physical and social results, what such a practice can achieve—I wouldn't trade it for the world.

RICH HAAG AND FREDERICK LAW OLMSTED

One day in 1967, while I was living and working in New York as a young architect, Rich turned up on his way to Europe to see something or other with some City of Seattle officials. It's the sort of junket I've suggested to clients on several occasions, which they've then embarked on without bothering to include me. I obviously didn't learn all of the lessons Rich could teach. He showed up carrying a suitcase in his arms like a baby. The airport baggage handlers had somehow managed to drop it in such a unique way that they'd shattered the handle without hurting the bag. I knew of a place uptown near Harlem where a man in a basement could fix just about anything. After leaving the bag there for the afternoon, we walked over to Central Park. Rich had introduced Olmsted and his work to us in a combination of classroom, office, and tavern discussions when I was still in Seattle. Rich pointed out how the Olmsted office had utilized natural systems, especially drainage and river corridors, as a basis for urban structure and open space and noted the social attitudes regarding health and class, along with specific built works and their features, especially Central Park.

After living in New York for a couple of years, I had learned my way around the park and took pride in my knowledge of its organization and design principles. I led us into the park at Engineers Gate. After about ten minutes in the park, I noticed that he looked perturbed, even sad. "You know," he began, his voice rising with the hint of a question as he began in his wheezy soft Kentucky twang, even though what is about to follow is almost never something his listener does know or yet fully appreciate, "it's worn out." He paused. "Look at how the ground is compacted, scraped, beaten! The soil has been washed away, the walks are crumbling, the roots of the trees are all exposed." His voice fell. "It's dying." He meant the park. I was stunned. While I'd been happily coming to the park for several years and had studied its parts, design, circulation systems, and built elements and reveled in its social vibrancy, I'd missed this all-pervasive fact! How could I be so informed and so ignorant at the same time? Rich was delivering a lesson about life and natural processes, which I'd somehow missed. He went on to observe that the park was too heavily used, that nothing could sustain the pressure of so much need and love, especially considering its age. The concept of human erosion through use (not mere vandalism) and the analogy to concepts of carrying capacity in habitats that had begun to appear in ecological texts hadn't dawned on me until that moment. As we wandered along, Rich casually remarked that the whole park would have to be rebuilt, and soon, or it would disappear. The Central Park Conservancy was formed to tackle this problem under the leadership of Elizabeth Barlow Rogers, and forty years later, it has nearly completed exactly the task of reconstructing the park. So many things that Rich has foreseen and pointed out to those who were listening have come to pass, for better and for worse.

Rich and I concluded our walk and retrieved his bag, which had acquired a peculiar spiral brass handle such as might have once graced the top of a large teakettle or been one of those gizmos used to lift a stove lid. It looked incongruous on the zippy, premolded, hard-sided Tourister suitcase, but it was serviceable and cost only a couple of bucks. The next day Rich went off to Europe, unconcerned about how it (or he) looked. I took note of the manner often attributed to absentminded professors as epitomized by images of Einstein. Rich was keeping his priorities straight regarding what really mattered and what didn't. For a designer, he seemed at times oblivious to some aspects of design, the sort of details that those in other fields fuss over. Consider the Eurocentric black T-shirt crowd or even the average designer of that decade. Such a cobbled-together solution as his suitcase would have bothered them. The great dictum "God is in the details" was as often as not parodied by Rich, who would say that "the Devil is in the details" and "less is a bore." Conversely, he was deeply interested in minimal solutions that achieved the most with the least gesture or material.

He'd obviously gotten to a point that I've reached only in the past few years, which is to accept that in landscape design there is so much that one can't effectively control. Things break down, evolve, and other people and professionals put in their oars. As an architect, I had designed hardware, fine cabinetry, and doorknobs and specified the locations of light switches, doors, windows, wall sections, roofs and metalwork, foundations and drains. As landscape architects, we lay out and design stream corridors, ponds, lakes, highways, groves of trees, habitats and walkways, pavements, roads, stairs, railings, shrub beds and curbs, grading and drainage systems, seating and lighting, pavilions, shelters, and fences. Partly because of the early experience that Bob Hanna and I had in architectural practice, our office from time to time has been able to design and detail some things that have gone together like a watch (the Sixteenth Street transit/mall in Denver comes to mind, or aspects of Battery Park City, Bryant Park, and the Getty Center). Conversely, there is no question that my partners and I have also worked in much broader and less precise or fussy ways. The suitcase handle incident with Rich was an early message about relaxing, and focusing on things that matter.

ZEN HAAG

There is an important aspect of Rich, his personality, design, and life, that defies logic, order, or reason. It is instinctual, visceral, guttural, at times veering from downright goofy to demonic. He often manifests pure feeling and spirit. It can be beautiful and inspiring or disturbing. While many of us may occasionally possess the potential for aspects of these characteristics ourselves, in Rich it is close to the surface and often courted, extolled, and willfully brought into action. This is when Rich displays some of the most characteristic (even notorious) attitudes and mannerisms of a Zen monk. Not the gentle sort of religious figure seen in TV documentaries, sitting calmly in saffron robes, all smiles, looking peacefully into space, but rather the wild and violent one who dashes out into a storm holding a sandal over his head while shouting koans, or who scowls and breaks the beautiful thing he has just made with his hands after years of training and practice.

Rich had more than an affinity for particular aspects of Japanese culture, and he was drawn toward aspects of Buddhist thought. Seemingly, the sort that most attracted him, at least as he presented himself to us in those years, were particular aspects of the Zen (or Chan) sect. Idiosyncratic, and powerful, this order has produced at a number of its monasteries in Japan some of the most abstract and powerful gardens and paintings in history. Placing emphasis on years of training, study, discipline, and work, whether in pottery, calligraphy, painting, poetry, or gardening, members of this order seek a form of heightened sensibility that Westerners might compare to a trance or divinely inspired state. Under the right circumstances, this allows them to act with sudden, effective, powerful, and rapid action, producing work that is extraordinary in its form and content. One might say about such an activity, whether it is writing a poem or making a painting, that the hand, eye, and brain act together in a way akin to lightning in its rush from cloud to ground. It happens as pure event. To my knowledge, Rich never formally embraced any organized religion and was not particularly involved with any conventional form of worship, including Buddhism. Nevertheless, the man and what he does at times seem deeply spiritual and very much in such a tradition.

Rich made it clear that he expected us to purify ourselves in nature, to go to the source, and learn directly for ourselves. In another person, this could be a basis for naïveté, suspect romanticism, or anti-intellectualism. Not with Rich. It was different. It was wise and spiritual, not self-indulgent or mushy. The need for concentration, silence, emptiness before we could be full was part of the message. We had to rid our profession and ourselves of the rubbish and habits of society, of much of our training. The influences from West and East that he proposed we take up ranged from Thoreau on one side to Sesshū on the other, from Jens Jensen to Kobayashi Issa. It was and continues to be powerful stuff. A young person (or, for that matter, a person of any age) cannot seriously engage these individuals, their thought and creative work, without being affected.

The homogeneity of all creation, the linked quality of events and creatures, the eternal flow of energy through the universe must be seen and joined before we can accomplish anything. The yoking of absolute calm and pure action was the goal. Consider Matsuo Bashō:

THE WAY OF ZEN
Well then, let's go—
to the place where we tumble down
looking at snow!
"Near the Great Shrine, Ise,
From what tree's bloom
it comes, I do not know,
but—this perfume!"[1]

Essences were to be learned and felt and become the foundation of our work. In recent years I have realized that it was Rich who introduced us to the appreciation and use of typology and that he habitually employed a distillation of archetypal forms. The work he produced is both atavistic and modern, often employing prime forms and shapes and elemental materials directly expressed. Vegetation, whether unusual or overly familiar and common, is isolated and presented so that one encounters it as if for the first time in life. He is a master.

There is also another side to his character. Those who know Rich Haag will at some point be likely to use the word "cranky" to describe him. There is a consciously frustrating, even perverse streak in him, which we have all encountered at some time. Oddly enough, it is related somehow to his great generosity and passionate love for life and others. This could be seen as one of his most monklike and Zen aspects. I firmly believe it results from self-will and is a conscious choice on his part, not some mere joke of biology. While it may seem at times that Rich is being willful and contradictory, he is frequently courting analogies to natural forces and processes. I was conscious of a perpetual contest in his work between balance and imbalance, between dynamic forces and rest. I genuinely believe that this is not an accident. Like John Cage and others who have been influenced so deeply by Asian art and thought, he frequently invokes the necessity of accident. A favorite attitude of his in my years around him was the search for *shibui*: the imperfection without which a thing (or design) would not be perfect. This is also known as *wabi-sabi*, the beauty of things impermanent, imperfect, incomplete, yet somehow inevitable, right. This sense of contradiction can inform and enhance both work and life. While striving to create balance or harmony in a project, Rich would come in and rough it up, deform it, and then "center" it again. It was the aesthetic of the bent pot, the ugly burned tea bowl, of Shoji Hamada's beautifully awkward, strong, yet humble ceramics.

PASSING THE TORCH

Aspects of Richard Haag's ideas and influence have to a degree been transmitted through subsequent professional offices and projects of his students and through their involvement in teaching. It has now been more than forty years since I last lived in Seattle. In that period, Haag has known and influenced many other students I don't know. It is probably safe to say that the collective work executed by the various offices formed by Haag's protégés encompasses the scope of topics and ambitions he had for us. The projects of the now extinct office of Sakuma and James and of the very much alive ones of Jones and Jones, and OLIN (formerly Hanna/Olin and the Olin Partnership), those I know best, are truly varied in kind and scale. However, the large regional plans, conservation, recreation, and zoological schemes, highway and corridor projects, urban parks and plans of Jones and Jones, when added to the urban design, civic parks, squares, waterfronts, transportation and campus plans, institutional, corporate, and private landscapes of our office, really were all anticipated in the work we rehearsed and aspired to accomplish under Haag's direction and encouragement.

I believe that I first heard the phrase "reflective practitioner" from Harry Cobb, I. M. Pei's partner.[2] I knew immediately what he meant. While many people have become practitioners of architecture, landscape architecture, planning, and engineering, and many others have become academics, few have been equally successful at both. Rich Haag is one of the rare examples, and several of his students have been as well. Professional design education frequently located within great research-based modern universities commonly suffers distrust and lack of understanding among other faculty and administration. As a result, design schools often go through contortions and frequently put on pseudoscientific airs in order to seem intellectually adequate or comparable to other disciplines and university administrators. It is only in recent years that we have begun to understand and be able to articulate the extraordinary amount of information and skills needed to be a successful designer, and the nature and differences of the intelligence at work in doing so.[3]

We don't look and act like social and natural scientists; we don't smell like bona fide scholars or artists. We are designers and professionals. Educating others is not a science but a hands-on, lengthy, experimental, and experiential thing. It is labor intensive and costly. It is intellectual. It is physical and manual. It is reflective. It is also intuitive. It is hard work. And Rich Haag is all of those things. He always taught and always practiced. He thought about what he practiced, and he practiced what he thought about. He has been a powerful and inspiring example of an engaged and reflective practitioner as well as a great artist and teacher.

LAURIE OLIN
Philadelphia, January 2014

notes

FOREWORD

1 Haag, "Landscape Architecture."
2 Haag, "Garden on Lake Washington," 31.

1 GROWING UP IN A KENTUCKY LANDSCAPE

1 Olin, "Reflections on Richard Haag," 45.
2 Fabris, *La Nattura Comme Amante.*
3 Sprowl, "Jeffersontown, Ky."
4 Ibid., 7.
5 Johnson and Lewis Publishing Company, *A History of Kentucky*, 812.
6 He is known for the Rudy Haag variety of *Euonymus alata*, introduced into cultivation in 1963.
7 Family lore says that he was; however, no confirming evidence has been identified.
8 Of the children, Virginia and Louise would graduate from the University of Kentucky, Lexington, and John from Morehead College (now Morehead State University) in Morehead, Kentucky.
9 Hurt, *American Farm Tools.*
10 Staff Reporter, "Kentucky Boy, 4, Attains Fame."
11 Howett, "Ecological Values," 80.
12 Marsh, *Man and Nature.*
13 Sargent, "Notes."
14 The term "ecology" was coined by German scientist Ernst Heinrich Haeckel (1834–1919) in 1866 but was most clearly described in Henry Chandler Cowles's dissertation of 1899, generally considered the beginning of ecology as a science.
15 Editor, "Review of *Flowers and Their Friends*, 437.
16 Ganong, " Botanic Garden of Smith College," 512.
17 Spirn, "Constructing Nature."
18 Grese, *Jens Jensen*, 10.
19 Howett, "Ecological Values," 83–84. See also Tishler, "Frederick Law Olmsted."
20 Cleveland, *Landscape Architecture*; Waugh, *Landscape Gardening.*
21 Other nurseries in the region as of 1929 included Dixie View Nursery in Covington, the Donaldson Nursery in Sparta, the Highland Place Nursery in Versailles, the Hillenmeyer Nursery in Lexington, and the Louisville Nurseries in St. Matthews. See "University of Kentucky Botanic Gardens."
22 Way, *Unbounded Practice*; "Annette Hoyt Flanders," 197–218.
23 Haag, "From Casablanca to Tripoli," 1.
24 As his birthday was in October and the cut-off date in Kentucky at that time was September 1, he started first grade in 1930 and would have graduated high school in June 1942.
25 Haag, "From Casablanca to Tripoli," 3.
26 Jackson, "The Need of Being Versed."
27 Haag, "Edible Landscape," 635.

2 A LANDSCAPE EDUCATION

1 The Morrill Act, or Land-Grant College Act, was passed by Congress in 1862. Landscape gardening and landscape design were included at many of these land-grant colleges from 1862 to 1900.
2 Hoddeson and Herman, "Florence Bell Robinson,"; "College of Fine and Applied Arts, University of Illinois at Urbana-Champaign, College Historical Timeline" accessed January 23, 2010, http://www.faa.illinois.edu/Timeline.
3 Robinson, *Planting Design*; Alpert, Kesler, and Harris, "Florence Bell Robinson.
4 Kessler and Cairns, "Stanley Hart White."
5 See Way, *Unbounded Practice.*
6 As quoted in Kessler and Cairns, "Stanley Hart White," 448.
7 Simo, "Conversation with Hideo Sasaki," 18.
8 White's commonplace books, or daybooks, in which he wrote his thoughts, notable quotes, and copies of letters, offer more than forty-five years' worth of his insights, recorded from 1925 to 1972, Stanley White Papers, 1925–1977, University of Illinois Archives.

9 Feld, “Landscape Architects.”
10 Stanley White, commonplace book, summer 1948, Stanley White Papers, 1925–1977, box 3, journal 26: 3972, University of Illinois Archives.
11 Ibid.
12 Stanley White, “A Primer of Landscape Architecture” (unpublished manuscript, 1957–58, 1974), Stanley White Papers, 1925–1977, box 7, University of Illinois Archives.
13 Melanie Simo, “Biography of Hideo Sasaki, 1919–2000,” in *Shaping the American Landscape: New Profiles from the Pioneers of American Landscape Design Project*, ed. Charles A. Birnbaum, Stephanie S. Foell, and Cultural Landscape Foundation (Charlottesville: University of Virginia Press, 2009), 301–4.
14 Stanley White, commonplace book, 1948,Stanley White Papers, 1925–1977, box 3, journal 26: 3971, University of Illinois Archives.
15 Ibid.
16 Richard Haag, Sasaki Lecture, University of Illinois, 1995, Richard Haag Papers, 1992–1999, Special Collections, University of Washington Libraries, Seattle.
17 Treib, *Thomas Church, Landscape Architect.*
18 Laurie and Streatfield, *75 Years of Landscape Architecture*, 34–36.
19 “Is There a Bay Area Style?” 92.
20 Rozdilsky, “Landscape Art,” 14.
21 Don Carter, interview by John Rozdilsky, Seattle, 1997.
22 They eventually had seven children: Zachary, Aaron, Miyaka, Derek, Gordon, John, and Fred.
23 Rozdilsky, “Landscape Art,” 14.
24 Stanley White, “New Eyes for Old,” (unpublished manuscript, 1952), Stanley White Papers, 1925–1977, box 7, University of Illinois Archives.
25 Alofsin, *Struggle for Modernism.*
26 Ibid.
27 Eckbo, Kiley, and Rose, “Landscape Design in the Urban Environment”; Eckbo, Kiley, and Rose, “Landscape Design in the Rural Environment”; Eckbo, Kiley, and Rose, “Landscape Design in the Primeval Environment.”
28 Anderson, *Women, Design, and the Cambridge School.*
29 Simo, *Coalescing of Forces and Ideas*, 41.
30 Ibid., 42.
31 Cornelia Hahn Oberlander, a graduate of the Graduate School of Design, worked in the office during summer 1951. Her employer at the time, architect Oscar Stonorov, sent her to Kiley's office to learn to make detail drawings, something she had not fully mastered yet. See Herrington, *Cornelia Hahn Oberlander.*
32 Rozdilsky, “Landscape Art,” 15.
33 See notes from Laurie Olin, interview by John Rozdilsky, Seattle, 1997; Frank James, telephone interview by John Rozsdilsky, March 12, 1996.
34 Kiley, letter to Haag, March 18, 1992, Richard Haag Papers, 1934–1985, Special Collections, University of Washington Libraries, Seattle.
35 Richard Haag, interview by author, Seattle, January 30, 2014.

3 “KEEP YOUR EYES OPEN!”

Epigraph from an interview by the author, July 23, 2010.
1 Rozdilsky, “Landscape Art,” 16.
2 Recordings of many of these lectures are held in Richard Haag's private collection.
3 “Description of the Japanese Exhibition House on View at the Museum of Modern Art During the Summers of 1954 and 1955,” Museum of Modern Art press release, May 1956, Museum of Modern Art Press Archives, http://www.moma.org/momaorg/shared/pdfs/docs/press_archives/2084/releases/MOMA_1956_0065_57a.pdf?2010.
4 Kuck, *One Hundred Kyoto Gardens.*
5 Crowe, Jellicoe, and International Federation of Landscape Architects, *Space for Living*; Association for Planning and Regional Reconstruction, Colvin, and Trywhitt, *Trees for Town and Country.*
6 Haag, “Review.”
7 Bruno Taut's publications on Japan were not yet readily available, although they would become important to later readings of modernism in architecture. Haag did not read them until well after his Japan trip.
8 See Nakamura, “Jobo Nakamura in Tokyo”; quoted in Rozdilsky, “Landscape Art,” 18.
9 See Oshima, *International Architecture in Interwar Japan.*
10 Eitaro Sekiguchi was a Japanese landscape scholar who graduated from the Tokyo Imperial University, School of Agriculture. In 1923, he was appointed an associate professor in the School of Agriculture, Kyoto Imperial University, and became a professor in 1936. In 1959, he retired and was named professor emeritus.
11 Simonds, *Landscape Architecture.*
12 Carver, *Form and Space of Japanese Architecture.*
13 Haag's address in Japan was Higashi-ichi-jo-dori, Kawabata, Higashi, Iru, Ichibanchi-no-ichi, Sakyo-ku, Kyoto.
14 Richard Haag, interviews by the author, 2009–12.
15 Norm Carver, telephone interview by author, May 8, 2010.
16 Quoted in Rozdilsky, “Landscape Art,” 18.
17 Richard Haag, Lectures on Japan for L.A. 361, University of Washington, Seattle, 1991, lecture tapes in Richard Haag's private collection.

18 Norm Carver, telephone interview by author, May 8, 2010.
19 Richard Haag, interview by Charles Birnbaum for The Cultural Landscape Foundation, Pioneers of American Landscape Design Oral History Series, Seattle, November 2004.
20 Ibid.
21 Lippit, "Distillations."
22 Gropius, "Architecture in Japan."
23 See, for example, "Eagleson Hall."
24 Rozdilsky, "Landscape Art," 19.
25 Haag, "Review," 302.
26 Richard Haag, Lectures on Japan for L.A. 361, University of Washington, Seattle, 1991, lecture tapes in Richard Haag's private collection
27 Clay and Johnson, "Tireless Teacher, Civic Preacher."
28 Futagawa and Itō, *Rural Houses of Japan*; Ito, *Traditional Domestic Architecture of Japan*.
29 Carver, *Japanese Folkhouses*.
30 Richard Haag, Lectures on Japan for L.A. 361, University of Washington, Seattle, 1991, lecture tapes in Richard Haag's private collection
31 "Memo to Japanese Designers," *Sinkentiku*, 1955.
32 Ibid.
33 Futagawa and Itō, *Traditional Japanese Houses*; Ito, *Traditional Domestic Architecture of Japan*; Ito and Futagawa, *The Classic Tradition in Japanese Architecture*.
34 Kobayashi, *Japanese Architecture*, cover image.
35 Gropius, "Architettura."
36 Richard Haag, interviews by John Rozdilsky, Seattle, 1986–91.
37 While there was a twelfth-century garden, around 1339, it was likely redesigned by the Zen priest Musō Soseki, who also designed the garden at nearby Tenryu-ji.
38 Treib, "Reduction, Elaboration and Yugen," 95.
39 Richard Haag, interview by author, Seattle, August 2012.
40 Ibid.
41 Treib, "Converging Arcs on a Sphere," 291.
42 Ibid.
43 Richard Haag, interview by author and Ken Oshima, University of Washington, Seattle, October 18, 2012.
44 Richard Haag, Lectures on Japan for L.A. 361, University of Washington, Seattle, 1991, lecture tapes in Richard Haag's private collection.
45 Ibid.
46 Ibid.
47 Ibid.
48 Haag had read Sigfried Giedion's *Space, Time and Architecture: The Growth of a New Tradition*.
49 Haag, "Space."
50 Ibid., 6.
51 Ibid., 7.
52 Draft of request to Fulbright committee, 1954, in Richard Haag's private collection.
53 Ibid.
54 Ibid.
55 Stanley White, letter to R. Haag, October 18, 1957, Stanley White Papers, 1925–77, box 4, journal 41: 5877, University of Illinois Archives.

4 DESIGNING THE HOME GARDEN IN CALIFORNIA

1 Treib, "Axioms for a Modern Landscape Architecture."
2 Initially, the firm included a third partner, Gibson, who had left by 1949. See Helphand, "Il Paesaggio 'Pastorale.'"
3 Church, *Gardens Are for People*.
4 Treib, *Modern Landscape Architecture*, 166.
5 Halprin garnered numerous awards, including the Thomas Jefferson Medal in Architecture and the National Medal of Arts given by the president of the United States.
6 Don Carter, telephone interview by John Rozdilsky, 1997.
7 Halprin, *Cities*; Halprin, *Freeways*.
8 Stanley White, commonplace book, July 9, 1957, Stanley White Papers, 1925–1977, box 4, journal 41: 5924, University of Illinois Archives.
9 Stanley White, commonplace book, July 10, 1957, Stanley White Papers, 1925–1977, box 4, journal 41: 5925, University of Illinois Archives.
10 In the same building where Peter Walker would set up his office for Sasaki Walker and Associates in 1959.
11 Editor, "Case Study House Program."
12 Knorr makes no reference to Richard Haag as landscape architect but does describe Haag's design, particularly the earth mounds. Knorr, "Case Study House No. 19."
13 Ibid.
14 Don Carter, telephone interview by John Rozdilsky, 1997. That mound was oriented to the movement of the sun and created an effect that Carter described years later as brilliant.
15 Rozdilsky, "Landscape Art," 32.
16 Robert B. Marquis Collection, Environmental Design Archives, University of California, Berkeley.
17 Rozdilsky, "Landscape Art," 36.
18 "Young Style Setters," 105.
19 Association for Planning and Regional Reconstruction, Colvin, and Tyrwhitt, *Trees for Town and Country*.

20 "Young Style Setters," 104.
21 Rozdilsky, "Landscape Art," 36.
22 Ibid., 38.
23 Richard Haag Associates Records, 1956–1992, Wong, box 9, Special Collections, University of Washington Libraries, Seattle.
24 Eichler homes were residential subdivisions of Mid-Century Modernist tract housing in California.
25 Richard Haag, "University of Washington Publications of the Faculties: For the Year July 1, 1952, to June 30, 1961." As this was Haag's first report, he was to include all his work since graduating from Harvard's Graduate School of Design.
26 "Young Style Setters"; "Nine Marin Homes."
27 Richard Haag Associates records, 1956–1999, Zollinger, box 9, Special Collections, University of Washington Libraries, Seattle.
28 Rozdilsky, "Landscape Art," 43.
29 Ibid., 44.
30 Richard Haag Associates records, 1957–1994, Dux Corporation box 2, Special Collections, University of Washington Libraries, Seattle. DUX was located at 1633 Adrian Road.
31 "Design for Furniture Distribution," 158.
32 "Factory Showroom Project."
33 Rozdilsky, "Landscape Art," 48.
34 Unfortunately, no photographs could be found, although poor reproductions of original photos were identified, documenting the design.
35 Appendix 20C-1 Downtown Linkage System Construction Specifications, Redmond Community Development Guide, http://www.codepublishing.com/wa/redmond/cdg/RCDGAppx/RCDGAppx20C-1.html.
36 One notable project is the 1963 design for St. Francis Square in San Francisco by Marquis and Stoller, with landscape architect Lawrence Halprin.
37 Tamura, *Art of the Landscape Garden*, 8.
38 Hudnut, "The Modern Garden," 178.

5 A TEACHER'S TEACHER

1 Richard Haag, interview by author, July 23, 2010.
2 Haag was hired as of September 16, 1958.
3 Johnston, *College of Architecture and Urban Planning*, 6–7.
4 By 1957, the programs in architecture and planning were sufficiently substantial for President Henry Schmitz to announce the creation of the College of Architecture and Urban Planning.
5 *Bulletin of the University of Washington*, course catalog, 1961–1963 (Seattle: University of Washington, 1961), 19.
6 The college launched a program in building and technology; in the 1970s, this became the Department of Building Construction (predecessor to the Department of Construction Management).
7 Letters between Sasaki and Dietz, February 24, March 25, 1958. Note that Dietz promised that the new faculty would be given the opportunity to practice, a feature Sasaki mentioned to Haag. Richard Haag Papers, 1952–1999, Correspondence, box 2, Special Collections, University of Washington Libraries, Seattle.
8 Richard Haag, in Richard Haag's personal collection.
9 Richard Haag, letter to Arthur Herrmann, May 19, 1958, Richard Haag Papers, 1952–1999, correspondence, box 2, Special Collections, University of Washington Libraries, Seattle.
10 Jeffrey Ochsner, "Victor Steinbrueck Finds His Voice."
11 See College of Architecture and Urban Planning Yearbook, 1960–1961 (Seattle: University of Washington, 1961).
12 Johnston, *College of Architecture and Urban Planning*, 55. Edstrom graduated in 1964, Rice in 1967; there are no records of graduation for Beardsley.
13 Elizabeth Meyer, "The Post–Earth Day Conundrum," 57.
14 Rozdilsky, " Landscape Art," 55.
15 As quoted and discussed in Jeffrey Karl Ochsner, *Lionel H. Pries*, 278.
16 The contract to serve as an associate is for fall 1957. Richard Haag Papers, 1952–1999, Correspondence, box 2, Special Collections, University of Washington Libraries, Seattle.
17 See the various notes and drafts of course descriptions included in Stanley White, commonplace books, Stanley White Papers, 1925–1977, University of Illinois Archives.
18 Stanley White, "A Primer of Landscape Architecture" (unpublished manuscript, 1957–58, 1974), Stanley White Papers, 1925–72, box 7, University of Illinois Archives,.
19 Richard Haag, "Proposal for Landscape Architecture in the College of Architecture and Urban Planning," 1959, Richard Haag Papers, 1952–1999, box 1, Special Collections, University of Washington Libraries, Seattle. See also Richard Haag to Dean Dietz, "proposal," Richard Haag Papers, 1952–1999, box 2, Special Collections, University of Washington Libraries, Seattle.
20 Sasaki, "Thoughts on Education."
21 Ibid., 158.
22 Richard Haag, "Proposal for Landscape Architecture in the College of Architecture and Urban Planning," 1959, 2, Richard Haag Papers, 1952–1999, box 1, Special Collections, University of Washington Libraries, Seattle.
23 Ibid., 3.
24 Crowley, "Helix."
25 Notes and letters, Richard Haag, personal collection.
26 Richard Haag, "Proposal for Landscape Architecture in the

College of Architecture and Urban Planning," 6–7, 1959, Richard Haag Papers, 1952–1999, box 1, Special Collections, University of Washington Libraries, Seattle.

27 Ibid., 7–8.

28 The course catalog for 1959–61 announced that the program in landscape architecture was to be launched in fall 1959; however, no curriculum was published. The 1961–63 catalog included the full curriculum.

29 See Richard Haag, 1963–1964 Annual Report on Landscape Architecture Program, 1964, College of Architecture and Urban Planning, University of Washington.

30 "Landscape Architecture," *The Daily*, February 23, 1960.

31 Grant Jones, in discussions with author, 2009–10; Laurie Olin, "Reflections on Richard Haag" (unpublished manuscript, 2010), personal collection.

32 Richard Haag, LA 361 lecture notes, in Richard Haag's personal collection

33 Richard Haag, lecture notes for LA 361, 1980, in Richard Haag's personal collection.

34 For graduate students in architecture, Haag offered a version of the course as ARCH 450 Landscape Seminar as of the 1961 course catalog.

35 In 1972, the course was renamed "Landscape Architecture 361/ Theory and Perception."

36 *Bulletin of the University of Washington, 1961–1963* (Seattle: University of Washington, 1961), 46.

37 Students were regularly required to submit a one- or two-page extension on a selected topic. It was not to be a research paper but an argument or reflective consideration of a topic discussed during lecture.

38 Richard Haag, LA 361 lecture notes, in Richard Haag's personal collection.

39 Richard Haag, Arch. 106 lecture notes, 1965, 1, in Richard Haag's personal collection.

40 Richard Haag, LA 361 lecture notes, January 1989, unpaginated, in Richard Haag's personal collection.

41 Jackson and Zube, *Landscapes*.

42 In 1950, Phil Thiel, then a student at MIT, and Haag collaborated with Gyorgy Kepes on an exhibit on the work of Walter Gropius.

43 He was a lecturer in the Center for Asian Studies from 1963 to 1965 and taught in the College of Architecture and Urban Planning in 1963–64.

44 Quoting Oswald Spengler, *The Decline of the West*, 11:39, in his 1965 Arch. 106 notes.

45 Studio and course syllabi are in the author's personal files, with more in Richard Haag Papers, 1952–1999, Teaching Files, box 1, Special Collections, University of Washington Libraries, Seattle.

46 Kenichi Nakano, in discussion with author, Seattle, 2009–2010; Grant Jones, in discussion with author, Seattle, 2010; Laurie Olin, interview by author, Seattle, August 2009, and Philadelphia, June 2011.

47 Students Grant Jones and Ilze Jones (of Jones & Jones), Laurie Olin, and Robert Hanna would take this approach as a core value in their practices.

48 The sketch problem was given about every seven to fourteen days. The problems were assigned at 2:00 PM, and students' single-sheet presentations were due the same day at 10:00 pm. Each sketch problem handout included about a half page of descriptive text indicating a few limiting parameters of the problem and usually a suggestion on what was expected in the drawing. Jeffrey K. Ochsner, e-mail to author, January 23, 2014.

49 Richard Haag, "Trees in the City" (unpublished manuscript, 2008), in Richard Haag's personal collection.

50 Descriptions of the content of Haag's courses are from tapes of lectures, 1980–94, in Richard Haag's personal collection.

51 *Bulletin of the University of Washington, 1961–1963* (Seattle: University of Washington, 1961), 20.

52 Richard Haag, "Course prospectus for Landscape Design Studio," 1975, in Richard Haag's personal collection.

53 Louis I. Kahn, "1973: Brooklyn, NY," *Perspecta* 19 (1982): 92.

54 This quality is evident in the work of Laurie Olin as well as designers of another generation, such as Gary Hilderbrand.

55 Haag, "Space."

56 Ibid., 6.

57 Richard Haag, "Advanced design studios (Grades III and IV) and planting design course (LA 465)," in Richard Haag's personal collection

58 Richard Haag, "Lecture 4.16.91 for LA 361," in Richard Haag's personal collection .

59 The actual quote reads "Things that cannot be used possess something negative in their beauty." Soetsu Yanagi, "The Way of Tea" (lecture, Honolulu Academy of Arts, Honolulu, January 1953), Themista, http://www.themista.com/freeebooks/wayoftea.htm.

60 Richard Haag, teaching slide, 1983, LA 361, in Richard Haag's personal collection.

61 Richard Haag, letter to Bruce Walker, Architect, Walker & Mcgough, Spokane, Wash., July 24, 1963, Richard Haag Papers, 1952–1999, Special Collections, University of Washington Libraries, Seattle

62 Richard Haag, interviews by author, Seattle, 2009–12.

63 Raver, "Creative Collaboration," 68.

64 Sakuma joined Frank James to form Sakuma & James, which became Sakuma James & Peterson in 1971.
65 Kenichi Nakano, in discussion with author, Seattle, 2009–10
66 Crowe, *Tomorrow's Landscape.*
67 Frank James, "Thoughts, Written in Response to Questions by John Rozdilsky," October 17, 1996, in personal collection.
68 He was appointed acting chair in September 1969 for just the one academic year.
69 Don Sakuma was appointed assistant professor in 1963 and promoted to associate professor in 1971. Frank James served as acting associate professor from 1968 to 1971.
70 Haag, "Landscape Architecture."
71 Exam copy in Richard Haag Papers, 1934–1985, Teaching Files, Special Collections, University of Washington Libraries, Seattle.

6 GARDENS OF THE PACIFIC NORTHWEST

1 See Klingle, *Emerald City*, 166.
2 See ibid., 163–64.
3 See Jeffrey Karl Ochsner, "Regionalism and Modernism," in *Shaping Seattle Architecture: A Historical Guide to the Architects*, ed. Jeffrey Karl Ochsner, 2nd ed. (Seattle: University of Washington Press, 2014), 18–19, 30; and Grant Hildebrand, "The Context: The Northwest School," in *Gene Zema: Architect, Craftsman* (Seattle: University of Washington Press, 2011), 29–39.
4 The history of the early landscape architects has not been thoroughly documented. The best resource is *Shaping Seattle Architecture: A Historical Guide to the Architects*, ed. Jeffrey Karl Ochsner, 2nd ed. (Seattle: University of Washington Press, 2014).
5 On October 17, 1959, eleven landscape architects adopted the constitution of the Pacific Northwest Chapter of the American Society of Landscape Architects. In 1961, the Washington and Oregon sections of the chapter were authorized. Elizabeth Rivers and Dan Gilchrist, "Our History," American Society of Landscape Architecture, accessed January 25, 2014, http://www.wasla.org/about-us/our-history/.
6 This would become the Red Robin in 1969 and, later, the franchise Red Robin hamburger restaurant.
7 Haag also employed Ken Rupard, George Bartlet, William E. Wrede, and John Ullman in the first twenty-five years.
8 After almost twelve years with Haag, Nakano launched his own firm in Seattle and was in practice until he passed away in 2012.
9 Office managers were Judy Fleniken in the 1960s, Betty Sinderman in the 1970s, Deborah Natelson until 1983, and Cheryl Trivison after 1986.
10 Hildebrand, "Little Wooden Buildings." See also Jeffrey Karl Ochsner, *Lionel H. Pries*, 279.
11 Hildebrand, "Little Wooden Buildings." Leading Northwest regional modernists, including Fred Bassetti, Paul Kirk, Roland Terry, Gene Zema, Wendell Lovett, Ralph Anderson, and Arne Bystrom, worked with landscape architects.
12 Maybeck and Maybeck, "Programme."
13 Hildebrand, *Gene Zema*; Fred Bassetti, interview by author, Seattle, July 10, 2012.
14 Fred Bassetti, interview by author, Seattle, July 10, 2012.
15 Fred Bassetti, note to Richard Haag, June 12, 1992, Richard Haag Associates Records, 1956–1992, correspondence, box 1, Special Collections, University of Washington Libraries, Seattle.
16 Frank James, letter to John Rozdilsky, October 17, 1996, in personal collection.
17 Richard Haag, "Arch 216, 1968," Richard Haag Papers, 1952–1999, Special Collections, University of Washington Libraries, Seattle.
18 Richard Haag, interview by Charles Birnbaum and Nancy Slade, Pioneers of American Landscape Design Oral History Series: Richard Haag Interview Transcripts, Seattle, November 2004 and May 3–5, 2013, The Cultural Landscape Foundation, 47.
19 Haag, "Plants."
20 Frank James, letter to John Rozdilsky, October 17, 1996, in personal collection.
21 Kenichi Nakano, in discussion with author, 2009–10.
22 Phillips, "Home of the Month."
23 Richard Haag, "Preliminary Master Plan for Edgar Residence, July 1966," Richard Haag Associates Drawings, Architectural Records, Special Collections, University of Washington Libraries, Seattle.
24 Small was a member of the architecture faculty at the University of Washington.
25 Kreisman, "Inside Out."
26 Haag, "Garden on Lake Washington."
27 Kreisman, "Inside Out."
28 Richard Haag Associates Records, 1957–1994, Merrill Court, box 3, Special Collections, University of Washington Libraries, Seattle.
29 Elana Chan, "Harvard Belmont District: The Rich Life on Capitol Hill," accessed January 25, 2014, Seattle Architecture Foundation, http://www.seattlearchitecture.org/tour_harvard_more.html (site discontinued).
30 See Richard Beyer, "Rich Beyer Sculpture."
31 Haag, "Eco-Revelatory Design."
32 Haag, "Edible Landscape," 637.
33 Way, "Haag's Edible Estate."
34 Lucia Pirzio-Biroli and Michelle Marquardi of Studio Ectypos were the architects.

7 FROM MODERNISM TO URBANISM

1 Thiel and Haag interviewed the public and compiled ideas that included sinking the highway to just above the high waterline; however, the elevated highway was constructed for the most part as planned, although a more concerted Freeway Revolt would eventually lead to small changes in the plans. Ironically, when the Embarcadero Freeway was torn down after suffering significant damage in the 1989 Loma Prieta earthquake, Haag recalled that Thiel e-mailed him "We have won after all!"

2 Ochsner, "Victor Steinbrueck Finds His Voice."

3 Forward Thrust notes, Gas Works Park files, Richard Haag Associates (RHA) office collection, Seattle.

4 Others involved include Don Frothingham, Ibsen Nelsen, Lee Copeland, Norm Johnston, Richard Hobbs, Clayton Young, Don Myers, A. W. Bumgardner, Mary Randlett, and Laurie Olin. Hancock, "History Link."

5 Hancock, "Bassetti, Fred."

6 Sanders, *Seattle*, 83.

7 Ibid. See also Brown and Morrill, *Seattle Geographies*.

8 Richard Haag, course notes, Design Gr. III, spring quarter, 1961, in Richard Haag's personal collection.

9 Richard Haag, "LA 498 A. Recycle Landscapes, Spring 1982," Richard Haag Papers, 1934–1985, Special Collections, University of Washington Libraries, Seattle. Groshart, "Develop Sammamish Project."

10 Lawrence Halprin, interview by Charles Birnbaum, Pioneers of American Landscape Design Oral History Series: Lawrence Halprin Interview Transcript, San Francisco, March 2003 and December 2008, The Cultural Landscape Foundation, 44–45.

11 Haag, "The Landscape."

12 For the history of this important organization, see King, *The Central Area Motivation Program*.

13 See files and correspondence with W. Hundley, July 7, 1967, in Richard Haag Associates Records, CAMP, box 6, 4405-001, Special Collections, University of Washington Libraries, Seattle.

14 Bassetti commented: "I doubt anybody knows about that one, but I feel pretty good about the artistic quality achieved while addressing a utilitarian purpose and serving public safety." Fred Bassetti, interview by author, Seattle, July 10, 2012.

15 Becker, "Seattle Voters."

16 Richard J. Brooks, letter to the editor, *Seattle Times*, January 24 1992.

17 All of these records may be found under the project names with correspondence in Richard Haag Associates Records,1956–2004, Special Collections, University of Washington Libraries, Seattle; the drawings are in Richard Haag Associates Drawings, Architectural Records, Special Collections, University of Washington Libraries, Seattle.

18 Richard Haag Associates Records, 1957–1994, US Embassy, Lisbon, Portugal, box 5, Special Collections, University of Washington Libraries, Seattle.

19 Richard Haag Associates Records, 1957–1994, Steinbrueck Park/Market Park, box 4, Special Collections, University of Washington Libraries, Seattle.

20 Brown and Morrill, *Seattle Geographies*, 145.

21 Ochsner, "Victor Steinbrueck Finds His Voice."

22 Steinbrueck, *Market Sketchbook*.

23 Sketches are in Richard Haag Associates Records, 1957–1994, Steinbrueck Park, box 4, Special Collections, University of Washington Libraries, Seattle.

24 Ibid.

25 Cantor, *Contemporary Trends*, 263.

26 They provided a detailed maintenance manual for the park, noting that it would need to be stewarded carefully. Richard Haag Associates Records, 1957–1994, Maintenance Manual, Market Park Construction Bidding in Process file, box 4, Special Collections, University of Washington Libraries, Seattle.

27 Jordan Bell, an MLA student at the University of Washington, did the research on this park in 2009.

28 "An Arboreal Adventure," *Landscape Architecture Magazine* 58, no. 10 (October 1968): 42.

29 The Department of Housing and Urban Development (HUD) awarded the project in 1966; see "Seven Win HUD Design Awards; 350 Entries," *Journal of the American Institute of Architects*, 46:5, 13,16 (November) 1966, https://digital.lib.washington.edu/architect/publications/5768/.

30 On the dorms and master plan, see Richard Haag Associates Records, 1971–1997, Western Washington College, Ridgeway dorms, box 2, and Master plan, box 3, Special Collections, University of Washington Libraries, Seattle. For the later work at the school, see Richard Haag Associates Records, 1992–1999, Western Washington College, 1999 updates, box 3, Special Collections, University of Washington Libraries, Seattle.

31 Cantor, *Contemporary Trends*, 263.

32 "About the Magnolia Branch: Architecture," The Seattle Public Library, http://www.spl.org/locations/magnolia-branch/mag-about-the-branch.

33 Hackett, "$12 Million Renovation." In 2009, SHKS Architects, with Swift Landscape Architects, renovated the project, adding a small extension to the back of the library.

34 Wilma, "Magnolia Branch."

35 Haag, Teaching notes for LA 330, in Richard Haag's personal collection.

8 THE ART OF THE LANDFORM AS LANDSCAPE ARCHITECTURE

1 Richard Haag, interviews by author, Seattle, 2009–12.
2 Smithson, "Frederick Law Olmsted."
3 Chambers received a BLA from the Ohio State University in 1929 and an MLA from Harvard's Graduate School of Design in 1932. He taught at the GSD from 1933 to 1955.
4 Clay, "Dirt Art."
5 Baird, "Herbert Bayer."
6 Clay, "Dirt Art."
7 Findlay, " Seattle World's Fair of 1962," 239–44.
8 Rozdilsky, " Landscape Art," 66.
9 Ibid., 68.
10 "Battle of Bulge."
11 "Hundreds of Trees."
12 Virginia Anderson, Director, Seattle Center, letter to Richard Haag, August 28, 1992, Richard Haag Papers, 1934–1999, Seattle Center Awards, box 1, 3774–003, Special Collections, University of Washington Libraries, Seattle.
13 Richard Haag Associates Drawings, Architectural Drawings Collection, Battelle Science Research Center, box 2, 4405–002, Special Collections, University of Washington Libraries, Seattle.
14 The Landmarks Preservation Board voted to designate the Battelle/Talaris Institute campus as a Landmark on November 7, 2013.
15 Richard Haag Associates Records, 1957–1994, Jordan Park, Everett, box 1, Special Collections, University of Washington Libraries, Seattle.
16 Rozdilsky, "Landscape Art," 77.
17 Richard Haag, "Public Earth Sculpture, Jordan Park, Everett, Washington," Richard Haag Associates Records, 1957–1994, Jordan Park, box 1, Special Collections, University of Washington Libraries, Seattle.
18 Ibid.
19 Cantor, *Contemporary Trends*, 261.
20 Daniel U. Kiley, letter to R. Haag, March 18, 1992, in Richard Haag's personal collection.
21 Specifically, Haag argued for a redesign of the standard riser-tread relationship to match that of the Spanish Steps, which has a six-inch riser and a fourteen-inch tread. This made for a comfortable stroll up the stairs.
22 Fabris, *La Nattura Comme Amante*, 112.

9 "IT WAS A GAS!" AT GAS WORKS PARK

1 Newell, *Westward to Alki*, 84.
2 Olmsted Brothers Records, 1903–1915, correspondence, box 1, Special Collections, University of Washington Libraries, Seattle.
3 Passamani, *Paul Troger*, 6.
4 "Dr. and Mrs. J. L. Kinslow."
5 McAllister, "Seattle Landmarks."
6 West, "Dead Gas Plant."
7 "A Tight Little Island," "Filling in Lake Union Stopped," "Islet Rises," and "Lake Union Isle."
8 Raymond, "Lake Union Virtual Museum."
9 Richard, "Seattle's Gas Works Park," 15.
10 "Park Models to Be Displayed." The Committee of 33 was a group of "private wealthy women" who were patrons of the arts.
11 Bailey, Judy, Assistant News Editor, undated, box 2, folder 71 C73, Richard Haag Associates Records, 1971–2000, Special Collections, University of Washington Libraries, Seattle. Rod Knipper, Rod Clarke, and Paul Pierce made a film about Gas Works Park that was featured on the cable television series *People of Seattle* on September 25, 1976.
12 Glen Hunt, letter to Edward J. Johnson, Superintendent, 1966, folder 27/9, Gas Works Park 1916–1975, Don Sherwood Parks History Collection, 5801–01, Seattle Municipal Archives.
13 E. J. Johnson, Superintendent, Memorandum: Lake Union Park to Members of the Board of Park Commissioners, 1962, Gas Works Park 1916–1975, Don Sherwood Parks History Collection, 5801–01, Seattle Municipal Archives.
14 Margaret W. Beyer, *The Art People Love*.
15 Johnson, Memorandum: Lake Union Park to Members of the Board of Park Commissioners, Gas Works Park 1916–1975, Don Sherwood Parks History Collection, 5801–01, Seattle Municipal Archives.
16 Copies of the surveys are included in "Gas Works Park," box 2, folder 71 C73, Richard Haag Associates Records, 1971–2000, Special Collections, University of Washington Libraries, Seattle.
17 Rozdilsky, "Landscape Art," 82.
18 Steve Cowan, Lightship Relief Guild, letter to Councilman Wing Luke, 1963, folder 27/9, Gas Works Park 1916–1975, Don Sherwood Parks History Collection, 5801–01, Seattle Municipal Archives.
19 Mrs. Frederick M. Mann of the Citizens' Planning Council and Elizabeth Pendleton Miller of the Seattle Garden Club, letter to Superintendent of Parks Edward J. Johnson, Gas Works Park 1916–1975, Don Sherwood Parks History Collection, 5801–01, Seattle Municipal Archives.
20 In 1970, Richard Wagner, founder of Seattle's Center for Wooden Boats, developed a plan to create a marine-oriented park with the towers. See University District Herald, Maritime Design

Proposal for Park, 1969, folder 27, Gas Works Park 1916–1975, Don Sherwood Parks History Collection, 5801-01, Seattle Municipal Archives.

21 Notes on Joint meeting of Park Board and Design Commission, Gas Works Park 1916–1975, Don Sherwood Parks History Collection, 5801-01, Seattle Municipal Archives.

22 Hans A. Thompson, letter to Mr. W. P. Woods, President of Washington Natural Gas Company, with c/c to Frank R. Ray Administrative Planning, Gas Works Park 1916–1975, Don Sherwood Parks History Collection, 5801-01, Seattle Municipal Archives.

23 Rochester, *Lakelure*.

24 Alf Collins, "Park Art of Cluttered Confusion or . . ." Puget Soundings, Environmental Designs West, box 2, folder 71 C73, Richard Haag Associates Records, 1971–2000, Special Collections, University of Washington Libraries, Seattle.

25 Okamoto/Liskamm, a firm based in San Francisco, was working in Seattle on the design of a mass transit system for the city.

26 Frank R. Ray, memo to Mr. John Vibber, 1970, box 2, folder 71 C73, Richard Haag Associates Records, 1971–2000, Special Collections, University of Washington Libraries, Seattle.

27 On April 22, 1970, the city approved Richard Haag Associates to be part of the Lake Union Park development project; on June 25, the Department of Community Development approved RHA for the project; the Design Commission approved on July 2; and the Board of Public Works approved on August 31, 1970. A formal contract for landscape architecture services for developing the program and the design was awarded on September 9, 1970.

28 Rozdilsky, "Landscape Art," 83.

29 Richard Haag, letter to Mr. Robert Griffith, Staff Assistant for Environmental Matters, Office of the Mayor, 1970, box 2, folder 71 C73, Richard Haag Associates Records, 1971–2000, Special Collections, University of Washington Libraries, Seattle; Bassetti, *Action*.

30 Richard Haag, interview by author, Seattle, 2009–12.

31 The *Wawona* sailed in Puget Sound from 1897 to 1947 and was berthed at South Lake Union until 2009, when it was dismantled.

32 Richard Haag, Master Plan for Gas Works Park, 1971, Gas Works Park Project files, 24, Richard Haag Associates, Special Collections, University of Washington Libraries, Seattle.

33 Bassetti, *Action*.

34 Haag, "Master Plan," 24.

35 Becker, "Seattle Voters ."

36 Collins, "Edwards Park Plan Wins Support."

37 Joining the efforts were students and colleagues including Lottie Eskilsson, Kenichi Nakano, William Wrede, and Don Sakuma, as well as Victor Steinbrueck, Ibsen Nelsen, John R. Ullman, Michael Ainsley, Douglas H. Tuma, Stephen Ray, and Fred Bassetti.

38 Steinbrueck took AIA architects on a tour that resulted in a letter of support in 1971 for the park design from AIA Seattle. "Stone in Landscape." Hull, "Profitable Projects."

39 See Richard Haag Associates Records, Gas Works Park folders and drawings, Special Collections, University of Washington Libraries, Seattle.

40 Lane, "Gas-Plant Towers."

41 Wilding and Del Balso, "T&C's Guide."

42 Halprin, *Freeways*, 4.

43 While exploring alternatives, Miller hired two engineers who suggested that for $850,000 they could drive steam pipes through the site and "cook" it. It was not clear that this procedure would eliminate the toxins.

44 In testing the plots, some originally measured a pH of 2.8, while other plats showed a pH of 9.8. They not only mixed the soils within the pits but across the site, adjusting the pH levels.

45 Rozdilsky, "Landscape Art," 84.

46 See files and notes on remediation testing and experimentation in Richard Haag Associates Records, 1956–1992, Remediation/ Soils, boxes 2, 3, and 4, 4405-007, Special Collections, University of Washington Libraries, Seattle.

47 "Not at Gas Work"; "Gas Work Park."

48 The sinks were later removed, however, when they attracted homeless individuals, and it was claimed that neighborhood families did not feel safe.

49 Halprin, *Freeways*, 2.

50 For further details on the remaining structures, see National Register of Historic Places, Gas Works Park, Seattle, King County, Washington, National Register no. 0200862, listed January 2, 2013.

51 "National Register of Historic Places Listings," National Park Service, January 11, 2013. http://www.nps.gov/nr/listings/20130111.htm. Archived from the original on September 22, 2013; retrieved February 20, 2014. The year of nomination is indicated by the first two digits of the ID number. Also see National Register of Historic Places, Gas Works Park, Seattle, King County, Washington, National Register no. 0200862, listed January 2, 2013.

52 March 14, 1996, at the RHA office, 2335 Eastlake Avenue, E. Patricia and Don Fells along with Tom Gran joined later that same year. See Friends of Gas Works Park, http://fogwp.org/.

53 Cheryl Trivison leads the management of the office as she has since the mid-1980s. Anne James, senior associate, joined in March 2006 after studying with Haag's students Laurie Olin and Robert Hanna at the University of Pennsylvania.

10 LAND SCULPTING AND ECOLOGICAL DESIGN AT BLOEDEL RESERVE

1 Elizabeth Meyer, "The Post–Earth Day Conundrum," 188.
2 Elizabeth K. Meyer, "Seized by Sublime Sentiments," 24.
3 Bloedel, "The Bloedel Reserve," 5.
4 See The Bloedel Reserve, "The Bloedel Reserve."
5 Virginia remained intimately involved in the garden and landscape designs until her death; however, it was Prentice who worked directly with architects, artists, landscape architects, and garden designers.
6 Bloedel, "The Bloedel Reserve," 3.
7 Richard Brown, "The Japanese Garden."
8 Frank James, telephone interview by John Rozdilsky, March 12, 1996. Also see drawings for the canal and notes from meetings with the Bloedels in Richard Haag Associates Records, Bloedel Misc., box 1, 4405-003, Special Collections, University of Washington Libraries, Seattle.
9 Notes by Haag of the first meeting with the Bloedels, Richard Haag Associates Records, 1965–1995, Bloedel Misc., box 1, Special Collections, University of Washington Libraries, Seattle.
10 John R. Ullman, Landscape Architectural Services/Bloedel Reserve, September 16, 1970, Richard Haag Associates Records, 1965–1995, Bloedel Misc., box 1, Special Collections, University of Washington Libraries, Seattle.
11 Bloedel, "The Bloedel Reserve."
12 "The Arbor Fund was formed to have as its exclusive purpose, the development, maintenance, management and financial support of the Reserve," 9/26/1974, agreement between UW Board of Regents and P. Bloedel. Richard Haag Associates Records, 1965–1995, Bloedel Misc., box 1, Special Collections, University of Washington Libraries, Seattle.
13 The history of this relationship is not fully written but can be gleaned from the Bloedel Reserve newsletters; Prentice Bloedel, "The Bloedel Reserve"; and Richard A. Brown, "The Bloedel Reserve Annual Report."
14 Richard A. Brown, "The Bloedel Reserve: Prospectus."
15 Richard Haag, letter to Mr. Bloedel, October 10, 1978, Richard Haag Associates Records, 1965–1995, Bloedel Misc., box 1, Special Collections, University of Washington Libraries, Seattle.
16 As quoted in Rozdilsky, " Landscape Art," 95.
17 As quoted in ibid.
18 These notes are found in Richard Haag Associates Records, 1965–1995, Bloedel Misc., box 1, Special Collections, University of Washington Libraries, Seattle.
19 Richard Haag, interview by Charles Birnbaum and Nancy Slade, Pioneers of American Landscape Design Oral History Series: Richard Haag Interview Transcripts, Seattle, November 2004 and May 3–5, 2013, The Cultural Landscape Foundation, 72.
20 Richard Haag, interview by John Rozdilsky, Seattle, October 10, 1990.
21 Richard Haag, "A Policy on Circulation," Richard Haag Associates Records, 1965–1995, Bloedel Misc., box 1, Special Collections, University of Washington Libraries, Seattle.
22 Haag, "A Policy on Circulation."
23 Ibid.
24 Pennypacker, "1919–2001."
25 It was in this pool that the poet Theodore Roethke drowned in 1963.
26 Plans for the swimming pool conversion can be found in Richard Haag Associates Records, 1965–1995, Bloedel Swimming Pool Conversion, box 2, Special Collections, University of Washington Libraries, Seattle.
27 Haag, "A Policy on Circulation."
28 See "Contemplations of Japanese Influence," 4, Richard Haag Associates, files, author's collection.
29 As quoted in Condon, "The Zen of Garden Design," 48.
30 Ibid., 49.
31 Frey, "A Series of Gardens," 58.
32 Haag, "Contemplations of Japanese Influence," 5.
33 Rozdilsky, "Landscape Art," 117.
34 Condon, "The Zen of Garden Design," 56.
35 Ibid.
36 Elizabeth K. Meyer, "Seized by Sublime Sentiments," 8.
37 Notes from the Design Jury, ASLA 1986, Richard Haag Papers, 1934–1999, ASLA Awards, President's Medal, Garden of Planes, box 1, 3774-003, Special Collections, University of Washington Libraries, Seattle.
38 As quoted in Richard Haag, "Contemplations of Japanese Influence on Bloedel Reserve," Richard Haag Papers , 1965–1995, Bloedel Reserve, box 2, Special Collections, University of Washington Library, Seattle.
39 Frey, "A Series of Gardens," 54.
40 Rozdilsky, "Landscape Art," 105.
41 As recorded in the minutes of the May 17, 1983, A.F. Directors Meeting and discussed in Frey, "A Series of Gardens."
42 Rozdilsky, "Landscape Art," 112.
43 Richard Haag, Master plan for Bloedel Reserve, sketch, Richard Haag Associates Drawings, Architecture Records, Special Collections, University of Washington Libraries, Seattle; Frey, "A Series of Gardens."
44 Elizabeth Meyer, "The Post–Earth Day Conundrum," 188.
45 Condon, "The Zen of Garden Design," 46.

46 Quoted in ibid.

47 Haag, "Contemplations of Japanese Influence," 4.

48 Frey, "A Series of Gardens," 56.

49 Treib, "Silence Condensed," 27.

50 My thanks to composer Carter Pann for noting the musical relevance.

51 The Bloedel Reserve is featured in more than sixty-seven publications in multiple languages as of 2013.

52 Treib, "Silence Condensed," 29.

11 THE LEGACY

1 Gary R. Hilderbrand, "A Teacher's Teacher," in *Richard Haag: Bloedel Reserve and Gas Works Park*, ed. William S. Saunders (New York: Princeton Architectural Press, with the Harvard University Graduate School of Design, 1998), 75.

2 Landscape Architecture, Features, Urban Ecological Design, http://larchwp.be.washington.edu/features/urban-ecological-design/.

3 John O. Simonds, letter to Stuart Dawson, September 11, 1991, personal collection.

AFTERWORD

1 Harold Gould Henderson, *Intro to Haiku: An Anthology of Poems and Poets from Basho to Shiki* (Garden City, N.Y.: Anchor, 1958), 38.

2 Donald A. Schon, *The Reflective Practitioner, How Professionals Think in Action* (New York: Basic Books, 1983).

3 For a good bibliography and thoughtful discussion of what designers really do and know, see Peter Rowe, *Design Thinking* (Cambridge, Mass.: MIT Press, 1987).

bibliography

Alofsin, Anthony. *The Struggle for Modernism: Architecture, Landscape Architecture and City Planning at Harvard*. New York London: W. W. Norton, 2002.

Alpert, Natalie, Gary Kesler, and Dianne Harris. "Florence Bell Robinson and Stanley Hart White: Creating a Pioneering School of Landscape Architecture." In *No Boundaries: University of Illinois Vignettes*, edited by Lillian Hoddeson and Richard Herman, 113–23. Urbana: University of Illinois Press, 2004.

Anderson, Dorothy May. *Women, Design, and the Cambridge School*. West Lafayette, Indiana: PDA Publishers Corp., 1980.

"Annette Hoyt Flanders: A Biographical Minute." *Landscape Architecture Magazine*, October 1946, 29–30.

Association for Planning and Regional Reconstruction, Brenda Colvin, and Jaqueline Tyrwhitt. *Trees for Town and Country; a Selection of Sixty Trees Suitable for General Cultivation in England*. London: L. Humphries, 1947.

Baird, Timothy. "Herbert Bayer and the Art of Reclamation." The Official Website for the City of Kent. Accessed June 20, 2014. http://kentwa.gov/content.aspx?id=5956&terms=baird.

Bassetti, Fred. *Action: Better City*. Seattle: AIA Seattle, 1968.

"Battle of Bulge—Many Protest Mounds at Center." *Seattle Times*, August 27, 1963.

Becker, Paula. "Seattle Voters Reject the Seattle Commons Levy on September 19, 1995." August 8, 2007. HistoryLink.org. http://www.historylink.org/index.cfm?DisplayPage=output.cfm&File_Id=8252.

Beyer, Margaret W. *The Art People Love: Stories of Richard S. Beyer's Life and His Sculpture*. Pullman: Washington State University Press, 1999.

Beyer, Richard. Rich Beyer Sculpture: Art for the People. http://www.richbeyersculpture.com/.

Birnbaum, Charles A., and Robin Karson, eds. *Pioneers of American Landscape Design*. New York: McGraw-Hill, 2000.

Bloedel Reserve. *The Bloedel Reserve: Self-guided Tour*. Bainbridge Island, Wash.: Bloedel Reserve, 2003.

Bloedel, Prentice. "The Bloedel Reserve—Its Purpose and Its Future." *UW Arboretum Bulletin* 43, no. 1 (Spring 1980): 2–6.

Brooks, Richard J. "Seattle Commons—Metro Needs Public Direction on Plan to Cleanse Storm Water." *Seattle Times*, January 24, 1992.

Brown, Michael, and Richard L. Morrill, eds. *Seattle Geographies*. Seattle: University of Washington Press, 2011.

Brown, Richard. "The Japanese Garden: An Evolution in Time." *The Bloedel Reserve*, no. 2 (1990): 1–2, 5–6.

Brown, Richard A. "The Bloedel Reserve Annual Report of Progress 1986." Bainbridge Island, Wash.: Bloedel Reserve,1986.

———. "The Bloedel Reserve: Prospectus for Appointment of Design Consultant." Bainbridge Island, Wash.: Bloedel Reserve , 1978.

Cantor, Steven L. *Contemporary Trends in Landscape Architecture*. New York: Van Nostrand Reinhold, 1997.

Carver, Norman F. *Form and Space of Japanese Architecture*. Tokyo: Shokokusha, 1955.

———. *Japanese Folkhouses*. Kalamazoo, Mich.: Documan Press, 1984.

Church, Thomas Dolliver. *Gardens Are for People: How to Plan for Outdoor Living*. New York: Reinhold Pub. Corp., 1955.

Clay, Grady. "Dirt Art." *Landscape Architecture Magazine* 60, no. 1 (October 1969).

Clay, Grady, and Norman Johnson. "Tireless Teacher, Civic Preacher: Rich Haag." *Landscape Architecture Magazine* 71, no. 9 (September 1981): 544–48.

Cleveland, H. W. S. *Landscape Architecture, as Applied to the Wants of the West: With an Essay on Forest Planting on the Great Plains*. Chicago: Jansen McClurg & Co., 1873.

"History" College of Fine and Applied Arts, University of Illinois at Urbana-Champaign. Accessed June 20, 2014. http://faa.illinois.edu/About+FAA/History.

Collins, Alf. "Edwards Park Plan Wins Support." *Seattle Times*, March 2, 1972.

Condon, Patrick M. "The Zen of Garden Design." In *Richard Haag: Bloedel Reserve and Gas Works Park*, edited by William S. Saunders,

45–60. New York: Princeton Architectural Press, with the Harvard University Graduate School of Design, 1998.
Crowe, Sylvia. *Tomorrow's Landscape*. London: Architectural Press, 1956.
Crowe, Sylvia, Geoffrey Alan Jellicoe, and International Federation of Landscape Architects. *Space for Living: Landscape Architecture and the Allied Arts and Professions*. Amsterdam: Djambatan, 1961.
Crowley, Walt. "Helix, Seattle's First Underground Newspaper, Debuts on March 23, 1967." June 15, 2000. HistoryLink.org. http://www.historylink.org/index.cfm?DisplayPage=output.cfm&file_id=1990.
"Description of the Japanese Exhibition House on View at the Museum of Modern Art during the Summers of 1954 and 1955." Museum of Modern Art Press Archives, 1950–1959. http://www.moma.org/momaorg/shared/pdfs/docs/press_archives/2084/releases/MOMA_1956_0065_57a.pdf?2010.
"Design for Furniture Distribution." *Architectural Record* 127, no. 1 (January 1960): 157–61.
Gas Works Park 1916–1975, Don Sherwood Parks History Collection, 5801–01, Seattle Municipal Archives.
"Dr. and Mrs. J. L. Kinslow, 10758 Riviera Place N.E." *Seattle Times*, September 14, 1959.
"Eagleson Hall, University of Washington, Seattle, Wash." *American Architect* 127, no. 2471 (1925).
Eckbo, Garret, Daniel U. Kiley, and James C. Rose. "Landscape Design in the Urban Environment." *Architectural Record* 85 (May 1939): 70–77.
Eckbo, Garrett, Daniel U. Kiley, and James C. Rose. "Landscape Design in the Primeval Environment." *Architectural Record* 87 (February 1940): 73–79.
———. "Landscape Design in the Rural Environment." *Architectural Record* 86, no. 8 (August 1939): 68–74.
Eckbo, Garret, Daniel U. Kiley, and James C. Rose. "Landscape Design in the Urban Environment." *Architectural Record* 85 (May 1939): 70–77.
Editor. "The Case Study House Program." *Arts & Architecture* (1945): 37–41.
———. "Review of *Flowers and Their Friends* by Margaret Warner Morley." *Garden and Forest* 10, no. 506 (November 3, 1897): 429–38.
Fabris, Luca M. F. *La Nattura Comme Amante: The Lover of Nature*. Rome: Maggioli Editore, 2010.
"Factory Showroom Project by Knorr-Elliot Associates, Richard Haag, Landscape Architect." *Arts & Architecture*, April 1959, 24–26.
Feld, Marvin S. "Landscape Architects I Have Known." *Landscape Architecture* 70, no. 11 (1980): 643.
"Filling in Lake Union Stopped." *Seattle Times*, May 24, 1962.
Findlay, John M. "The Seattle World's Fair of 1962: Downtown and Suburbs in the Space Age." In *Magic Lands: Western Cityscapes and American Culture after 1940*, 214–64. Berkeley: University of California Press, 1992.
Frey, Susan Rademacher. "A Series of Gardens, Bainbridge Island, Washington." *Landscape Architecture* 76 (1986): 54–61.
Futagawa, Yukio, and Teiji Itō. *The Rural Houses of Japan*. Seattle: University of Washington, 1963.
———. *Traditional Japanese Houses*. New York: Rizzoli, 1983.
Ganong, William. "The Botanic Garden of Smith College: A Study of an Educational Adaptation." *Garden and Forest* 10, no. 514 (December 29, 1897): 509–18.
"Gas Work Park." *Seattle Times*, October 31, 1972.
Giedion, S. *Space, Time and Architecture; the Growth of a New Tradition*. The Charles Eliot Norton Lectures for 1938–1939. Cambridge, Mass.: Harvard University Press; London: H. Milford, Oxford University Press, 1942.
Grese, Robert E. *Jens Jensen: Maker of Natural Parks and Gardens*. Baltimore: Johns Hopkins University Press, 1992.
Gropius, Walter. "Architecture in Japan." In *Katsura Imperial Villa*, edited by Arata Isozaki and Virginia Ponciroli, 349–86. Milan: Electa Architecture, distributed by Phaidon Press, 2005.
———. "Architettura, Tenchica Ed Industria Edilizia / Il Giappone Visto Da Walter Gropius." *Architettura Cantiere* 23 (March 1960): 16–17.
Groshart, Craig. "Develop Sammamish Project." *The Daily*, June 27, 1963, 13, 16.
Haag, Richard. "Eco-Revelatory Design: The Challenge of the Exhibit." *Landscape Journal* 17, no. 2 (special issue 1998): 72–79.
———. "Edible Landscape." *Landscape Architecture* 70, no. 11 (November 1980): 634–37.
———. "From Casablanca to Tripoli." *The Green Caldron* 16, no. 2 (December 1946): 1–3.
———. "Garden on Lake Washington." *Pacific Horticulture* 53, no. 4 (Winter 1992): 31–35.
———. Interview by Charles Birnbaum and Nancy Slade, Seattle, November 2004 and May 3–5, 2013. Pioneers of American Landscape Design Oral History Series. Richard Haag Interview Transcript, The Cultural Landscape Foundation. http://tclf.org/sites/default/files/Richard-Haag-Oral-History-Transcript.pdf.
———. "The Landscape." *Seattle Post-Intelligencer*, January 2, 1966.
———. "Landscape Architecture." *The Daily*, February 23, 1960.
———. "Memo to Japanese Designers." *Shinkechu*, February 1955.
———. *1963–1964 Annual Report on Landscape Architecture Program*. University of Washington, College of Architecture and Urban Planning Records, Special Collections, University of Washington Libraries, Seattle.
———. "Plants the Very Essence and the Life Blood of the Garden." Keynote lecture for Great Garden Vision Symposium, 1993.

———. "A Policy on Circulation—Bloedel Reserve." *Washington Landscape Architecture*, October–December 1988, 17–19.

———. "Review: Japanese Gardens by Jiro Harada." *Journal of Asian Studies* 17, no. 2 (1958): 302–3.

———. "Space." *Space Magazine, University of California* (1956): 7.

Haag, Richard, Papers. Special Collections, University of Washington Libraries, Seattle.

Hackett, Regina. "$12 Million Renovation Trumpets New Day at Frye Art Museum." *Seattle Post-Intelligencer*, January 23, 1997.

Halprin, Lawrence. Interview by Charles Birnbaum, San Francisco, March 2003 and December 2008. Pioneers of American Landscape Design Oral History Series. Lawrence Halprin Interview Transcript, The Cultural Landscape Foundation. http://tclf.org/sites/default/files/pioneers/halprin/videos/pdf/halprin_transcript.pdf.

———. *Cities*. Cambridge, Mass.: MIT Press, 1972.

———. *Freeways*. New York: Reinhold Pub. Corp., 1966.

Hancock, Marga Rose. "Bassetti, Fred (B. 1917–2013), Architect." Last modified December 5, 2013. HistoryLink.org. http://www.historylink.org/index.cfm?DisplayPage=output.cfm&file_id=8959.

Helphand, Kenneth I. "Il Paesaggio 'Pastorale.'" *Ville giardini*, no. 222 (December 1987): 40–45.

Herrington, Susan. *Cornelia Hahn Oberlander: Making the Modern Landscape*. Charlottesville: University of Virginia Press, 2013.

Harold Gould Henderson. *Intro to Haiku: An Anthology of Poems and Poets from Basho to Shiki.* Garden City, N.J.: Anchor Books, 1958.

Hildebrand, Grant. *Gene Zema: Architect, Craftsman*. Seattle: University of Washington Press, 2011.

———. "Little Wooden Buildings; the Puget Sound School." Unpublished manuscript, last modified August 12, 2012. Microsoft Word file.

Hoddeson, Lillian, and Richard Herman. "Florence Bell Robinson and Stanley Hart White: Creating a Pioneering School of Landscape Architecture." In *No Boundaries: University of Illinois Vignettes*, 113–22. Urbana: University of Illinois Press, 2004.

Howett, Catherine. "Ecological Values in Twentieth-Century Landscape Design: A History and Hermeneutics." Special issue of *Landscape Journal* 17, no. 2 (1998): 80–98.

Hudnut, Joseph. "The Modern Garden." In *Gardens in the Modern Landscape*, edited by Christopher Tunnard, 175–78. [London]: The Architectural Press, 1948.

Hull, George. "Profitable Projects: Civic Plantings Aid Business and Public." *New York Times*, March 12, 1961.

"Hundreds of Trees, Plants Stockpiled for Center Debut." *Seattle Times*, April 28, 1963, 10.

Hurt, R. Douglas. *American Farm Tools: From Hand-Power to Steam-Power*. Manhattan, Kans.: Sunflower University Press, 1982.

"Is There a Bay Area Style?" *Architectural Record* 105 (May 1949): 92–97.

"Islet Rises, Sinks Again in Lake Union." *Seattle Times*, May 17, 1962.

Ito, Teiji. *Traditional Domestic Architecture of Japan*. New York: Weatherhill, 1972.

Ito, Teiji, and Yukio Futagawa. *The Classic Tradition in Japanese Architecture: Modern Versions of the Sukiya Style*. New York: Weatherhill, 1972.

Jackson, John Brinckerhoff. "The Need of Being Versed in Country Things." *Landscape: Human Geography of the Southwest* 1, no. 1 (Spring 1951): 4.

Jackson, John Brinckerhoff, and Ervin H. Zube. *Landscapes: Selected Writings of J. B. Jackson*. Amherst: University of Massachusetts Press, 1970.

Johnson, E. Polk, and Lewis Publishing Company. *A History of Kentucky and Kentuckians; the Leaders and Representative Men in Commerce, Industry and Modern Activities*. Chicago: Lewis Pub. Co., 1912.

Johnston, Norman J. *The College of Architecture and Urban Planning, Seventy Five Years at the University of Washington: A Personal View*. Seattle: printed by author, 1991.

Kessler, Gary, and Michael Cairns. "Stanley Hart White." In *Pioneers of American Landscape Design*, edited by Charles A. Birnbaum and Robin S. Karson, 447–49. New York: McGraw-Hill, 2000.

King, Ivan. *The Central Area Motivation Program, a Brief History of a Community in Action*. Seattle: CAMP, 1990.

Klingle, Matthew W. *Emerald City: An Environmental History of Seattle*. The Lamar Series in Western History. New Haven: Yale University Press, 2007.

Knorr, Don. "Case Study House No. 19, the Landscape Plan." *Arts & Architecture* (December 1957): 21.

Kobayashi, Bunji. *Japanese Architecture*. Tokyo: Sagami Shobo, 1957.

Kreisman, Lawrence. "Inside Out—This Medina Home Is a Marriage of House and Garden." *Seattle Times*, May 21, 1995.

Kuck, Loraine E. *One Hundred Kyoto Gardens*. London: K. Paul, Trench, Trubner & Co.; Kobe, Japan: J. L. Thompson & Co., 1937.

"Lake Union Isle Was Long Developing." *Seattle Times*, May 22, 1962.

Lane, Polly "Gas-Plant Towers Get Reprieve in Pla." *Seattle Times*, December 12, 1971.

Laurie, Michael, and David C. Streatfield. *75 Years of Landscape Architecture at Berkeley*. Berkeley, Calif.: M. Laurie, 1989.

Lippit, Yukio. "Distillations: Gropius_Japan_1954." Harvard University Graduate School of Design, Exhibits. http://www.gsd.harvard.edu/#/projects/distillations-gropius-japan-1954–1.html.

Marquis, Robert B. Collection, Environmental Design Archives. University of California, Berkeley.

Marsh, George Perkins. *Man and Nature; or, Physical Geography as Modified by Human Action*. New York: Scribner, 1864.

Maybeck, Bernard R., and Annie Maybeck. "Programme for the Development of a Hillside Community" Bernard Maybeck Collection, Environmental Design Archives, College of Environmental Design, University of California, Berkeley.

McAllister, Parker. "Seattle Landmarks, Sketches by Times Staff Artist." *Seattle Times* January 20, 1946.

Meyer, Elizabeth. "The Post–Earth Day Conundrum: Translating Environmental Values into Landscape Design." In *Environmentalism in Landscape Architecture*, edited by Michel Conan, 188–244. Washington, D.C.: Dumbarton Oaks Research Library and Collection, 2000.

Meyer, Elizabeth K. "Seized by Sublime Sentiments." In *Richard Haag: Bloedel Reserve and Gas Works Park*, edited by William S. Saunders, 5–44. New York: Princeton Architectural Press, with the Harvard University Graduate School of Design, 1998.

Nakamura, Jobo. "Jobo Nakamura in Tokyo." *San Francisco Chronicle*, January 1957.

Newell, Gordon R. *Westward to Alki: The Story of David and Louisa Denny*. Seattle: Superior Pub. Co., 1977.

"Nine Marin Homes Win Architectural Awards in AIA-Sunset Contest." *Independent-Journal*, September 27, 1957, 4.

"Not at Gas Work: Edwards Park? No Says Family." *Seattle Times*, June 7, 1972.

Ochsner, Jeffrey. "Victor Steinbrueck Finds His Voice: From the Argus to Seattle Cityscape." *Pacific Northwest Quarterly* 99, no. 3 (2008): 122–33.

Ochsner, Jeffrey Karl. *Lionel H. Pries, Architect, Artist, Educator: From Arts and Crafts to Modern Architecture*. Seattle: University of Washington Press, 2007.

———. *Shaping Seattle Architecture: A Historical Guide to the Architects*. Seattle: University of Washington Press in association with the American Institute of Architects Seattle Chapter and the Seattle Architectural Foundation, 1994.

Olmsted Brothers records, 1903–1915, Special Collections, University of Washington Libraries, Seattle.

Oshima, Ken Tadashi. *International Architecture in Interwar Japan: Constructing Kokusai Kenchiku*. Seattle: University of Washington Press, 2009.

"Park Models to Be Displayed at Art Commission Meeting Newspaper." *Seattle Times*, October 29, 1961.

Passamani, Bruno. *Paul Troger, 1698–1762: Novità e Revisioni*. Mezzocorona, Italy: Comune di Mezzocorona, 1997.

Pennypacker, Eliza, with contributions by Janis Hall. "1919–2001: Biography of Arthur Edwin Bye Jr." November 12, 2012. The Cultural Landscape Foundation: Pioneers. http://tclf.org/pioneer/arthur-edwin-bye-jr/biography-arthur-edwin-bye-jr.

Phillips, Margery R. "Home of the Month: Two-Level Contemporary Residence." *Seattle Times*, October 30, 1966, 31.

Raver, Anne. "Creative Collaboration: Hideo Sasaki, 1919–2000." *Landscape Architecture Magazine*, March 2001, 65–75, 96.

Raymond, Vaun. *The Story of Gasworks Park with Richard Haag*. "Gas Works Park," Lake Union Virtual Museum. http://www.lakeunionhistory.org/Video,_Gasworks_Park.html'.

Richard, Michael. "Seattle's Gas Works Park: The History, the Designer, the Plant, the Park, Map & Tour." Seattle: Tilikum Place Printer, 1983.

Richard Haag Associates records. Special Collections, University of Washington Libraries, Seattle.

Richard Haag Associates Drawings. Architectural Records, Special Collections, University of Washington Libraries, Seattle.

Richard Haag Associates Landscape Architects (RHA). Office files, Seattle, 1956–2000.

Rivers, Elizabeth, and Dan Gilchrist. "Our History." ASLA Washigngton: Our History. http://www.wasla.org/about-us/our-history/.

Robinson, Florence Bell. *Planting Design*. Champaign, Ill.: Garrard Press, 1940.

Rochester, Junius. *Lakelure: A Tale of Medina, Washington*. Seattle: Tommie Press, 1993.

Rozdilsky, John. "The Landscape Art of Richard Haag: Roots and Intentions." MLA thesis, University of Washington, 1991.

Sanders, Jeffrey C. *Seattle and the Roots of Urban Sustainability: Inventing Ecotopia*. Pittsburgh, Pa.: University of Pittsburgh Press.

Sargent, Charles S. "Notes." *Garden and Forest* 1, no. 41 (1888): 492.

Sasaki, Hideo. "Thoughts on Education in Landscape Architecture: Some Comments on Today's Methodologies and Purpose." *Landscape Architecture Magazine* 40, no. 7 (July 1950): 158–60.

Simo, Melanie. *The Coalescing of Forces and Ideas: A History of Landscape Architecture at Harvard*. Cambridge, Mass.: Harvard University Graduate School of Design, 2000.

———. "A Conversation with Hideo Sasaki." *Pacific Horticulture* 49, no. 4 (Winter 1988): 16–25.

Simonds, John Ormsbee. *Landscape Architecture: The Shaping of Man's Natural Environment*. New York,: F. W. Dodge Corp., 1961.

Smithson, Robert. "Frederick Law Olmsted and the Dialectical Landscape." *Artforum* 11, no. 2 (1973): 62–68.

Spirn, Anne Whiston. "Constructing Nature: The Legacy of Frederick Law Olmsted." In *Uncommon Ground: Rethinking the Human Place in Nature*, edited by William Cronon, 91–113. New York: W. W. Norton & Co., 1996.

Sprowl, Edwin Ruth. "Jeffersontown, Ky. The Coming Suburb." Jeffersontown, Ky.: Jeffersonian Press, 1908.

Staff Reporter. "Kentucky Boy, 4, Attains Fame as Tree-Grafter." *Kentucky Times Start*, August 22, 1928.

Steinbrueck, Victor. *Market Sketchbook*. Seattle: University of Washington Press, 1968.
"Stone in Landscape—Japanese Garden." *Stone Magazine*, March 1962, 10–12.
Tamura, Tsuyoshi. *Art of the Landscape Garden in Japan*. Tokyo: Kokosua Bunka Shinkokai, 1938.
"A Tight Little Island Pops Up in Lake Union." *Seattle Post-Intelligencer*, May 17, 1962.
Tishler, William H. "Frederick Law Olmsted, Prophet of Environmental Design." *American Institute of Architects Journal* 44, no. 6 (December 1965): [31]–35.
Treib, Marc. "Axioms for a Modern Landscape Architecture." In *Modern Landscape Architecture: A Critical Review*, edited by Marc Treib, 36–67. Cambridge, Mass.: MIT Press, 1993.
———. "Converging Arcs on a Sphere: Renewing Japanese Landscape Design." In *The Architecture of Landscape, 1940–1960*, edited by Marc Treib, 270–99. Philadelphia: University of Pennsylvania Press, 2002.
———. *Modern Landscape Architecture: A Critical Review*. Cambridge, Mass.: MIT Press, 1993.
———. "Reduction, Elaboration and Yugen: The Garden of Saiho-Ji." *Journal of Garden History* 9 (1989): 95–101.
———. "Silence Condensed: Thoughts from the Japanese Garden." *Arkkitehti* 86, no. 3 (1989): 24–33.
———. *Thomas Church, Landscape Architect: Designing a Modern California Landscape*. San Francisco: William K. Stout Publishers, 2004.
Ullman, John R. September 16, 1970. University of Washington College of Architecture and Urban Planning Records, Special Collections, University of Washington Libraries, Seattle.
"The University of Kentucky Botanic Gardens." *Science*, September 6, 1929, 233.
Walter, Gropius. "Architecture in Japan." In *Katsura Imperial Villa*, edited by Arata Isozaki and Virginia Ponciroli, 349–86. Milan: Electa Architecture, distributed by Phaidon Press, 2005.
Waugh, Frank A. *Landscape Gardening; Treatise on the General Principles Governing Outdoor Art; with Sundry Suggestions for Their Application in the Commoner Problems of Gardening*. New York: Orange Judd Co., 1899.
Way, Thaisa. "Haag's Edible Estate: You May Have Heard of Artist Fritz Haeg's Edible Landscapes, but What about Rich Haag's Delicious Home Garden?" *Landscape Architecture Magazine* 99, no. 9 (2009): 102–9.
———. *Unbounded Practice: Women and Landscape Architecture in the Early Twentieth Century*. Charlottesville: University of Virginia Press, 2009.
West, Karen. "Dead Gas Plant Looks toward Life as a Park." *The Outlook*, October 13, 1971, 1, 6.
White, Stanley, Papers, 1925–77. University of Illinois Archives.
Wilding, Suzanne, and Anthony Del Balso. "T&C's Guide to the Art of Landscaping." *Town & Country*, June 1980, 81–84.
Wilma, David. "Magnolia Branch, the Seattle Public Library." July 7, 2002. HistoryLink.org. http://www.historylink.org/index.cfm?DisplayPage=output.cfm&file_id=3879.
"Young Style Setters." *House & Garden*, May 1961, 104–6 .]

illustration credits

AIA Seattle
Fig. 7.1

CBE Visual Resources Collection
Figs. 8.7, 9.2, 9.19, 10.14, 10.15

Thomas D. Church Collection, Environmental Design Archives, University of California, Berkeley
Fig. 2.4

Collection of Richard Haag
Figs. 1.2–1.4, 1.5, 2.1, 2.3, 2.5, 2.6, 3.1, 3.7–3.22, 4.5, 4.6, 4.8, 4.9, 4.11, 4.12, 4.14, 4.15, 5.4, 5.5, 5.7, 6.4–6.7, 6.13, 6.15, 6.22, 6.24, 6.26, 6.27, 7.3, 7.4, 7.12, 7.13, 7.17–7.20, 7.23, 7.24, 7.26, 7.30, 7.31, 8.8, 8.12–8.14, 8.16, 8.17, 8.19, 8.24, 9.3–9.7, 9.10–9.12, 9.14, 9.16, 9.20, 9.21, 9.24, 10.1, 10.4, 10.6, 10.7, 10.9, 10.11, 10.13, 10.18, 10.19, 10.22–10.25

Photo by David Hall
Figs. 6.10, 6.12

Friends of Kubota Garden
Fig. 10.2

Photo by Anne James, RHA
Fig. 6.28

Photo by Frank James
Fig. 6.1

Kentucky Times Start
Fig. 1.3

Jeffersontown Historical Society
Fig. 1.1

Collection of Laurie Olin
Figs. 5.1; p. 189

Photo by Bob Peterson, © Bob Peterson
Fig. 5.2

Photo by Mary Randlett
Figs. 7.5, 8.9, 8.10, 8.20, 8.21, 10.3, 10.17, 10.20

Photo by Julius Schulman. © J. Paul Getty Trust. Used with permission. Julius Shulman Photography Archive, Research Library at the Getty Research Institute (2004.R.10)
Fig. 8.22

The Seattle Public Library
Figs. 7.28, 7.29

Photo by Buster Simpson
Fig. 7.9

Sinkentiku
Fig. 3.6

Photo by Ezra Stoller, © Ezra Stoller / Esto
Fig. 4.3

© Tighe Photography
Figs. 6.19, 6.21, 7.8, 7.25, 8.15, 8.18, 8.25, 9.1, 9.23

Photo by Marc Treib
Fig. 6.16

University of Washington Libraries, Special Collections

1961–1963 Bulletin of the College of Architecture and Urban Planning, UW Special Collections: fig. 5.3

Alfred R. Rochester Papers, UW 30034z, Acc. No. 3048-2, box 4: fig. 8.5

Richard Haag Associates records, 4405: figs. 4.1, 4.2, 4.4, 4.7, 4.10, 4.13, 5.6, 6.36.8, 6.9, 6.11, 6.14, 6.20, 6.23, 6.25, 7.2, 7.6, 7.7, 7.10, 7.11, 7.14–7.16, 7.27, 8.2–8.4, 8.6, 8.11, 8.23, 9.8, 9.9, 9.13, 9.15, 9.17, 9.18, 10.5, 10.8, 10.10, 10.12, 10.16, 10.21

MSCUA, Dearborn-Massar, DM 487: fig. 6.2

UW Campus Photograph Collection, Davis Freeman, UW 18028: fig. 7.21

Collection of Thaïsa Way and Natasha Way
Figs. 6.17, 6.18, 7.22, 9.22

Wikimedia Commons
Frontispiece; figs. 1.6, 8.1

index

A

Action: Better City, 106–7, 207n4
aging process, gardens, 34, 54. *See also* Bloedel Reserve
agricultural activity, Japan, 31–33, 40–42*f*. *See also* nutrimental landscapes
Ahvakana, Lawrence Ulaaq R., 113
AIA Seattle, 106, 110, 120, 127, 153, 209n38
Ainsley, Michael, 164, 209n37
Alex, Will, 26
American Institute of Architects (AIA), 59, 90
American Society of Landscape Architects (ASLA): Bloedel Reserve award, 175, 182, 184; early nursery relationships, 8–9; Haag's lifetime achievement award, 185; Haag's preservation proposal, 109; Haag's service, 127; during Haag's student years, 19; program accreditations, 13; White's service, 14
American Tar Company, 149
Anderson, Guy, 70
Anderson, Ralph, 84, 87, 195
Anteroom (Moss Garden), Bloedel Reserve, 36, 172, 177*f*, 179*f*, 180–81, 184
Appleton, Jay, 78, 142, 185
Arbegast, David, 52
Arbegast, Mae, 51
Arboreal Adventure playground, Mercer Island, 117–18
Arbor Fund, 172, 184, 210n12
Architectural Record, 18–19, 21
Argus newspaper, 106
armory building, Seattle, 112
art exhibition, San Francisco, 18
Arthur Erickson Associates, 172
art movement, counterculture, 69–70
Arts & Architecture magazine, 54
Ashley, Bob, 155
ASLA. *See* American Society of Landscape Architects (ASLA)
Aspen Center, 129
Asplund, Gunnar, 133
Association of Landscape Architects, 18

B

Back Bay Fens, 130
Bain, Connie, 165
barns, Gas Works Park, 163*f*, 164
Bartlet, George, 206n7
Bascom, Willard, 166–67
Bashō, Matshuo, 199
Bassetti, Fred: Action program, 105, 106–7; in architectural community, 51, 84; Bloedel Reserve project, 171; college campus projects, 120–21, 190; Embassy project, 110*f*, 111; Gas Works Park project, 159; Haag relationship, 87; Hilltop community, 83–84; Jackson Federal Building, 142; Seattle City Light substation project, 109–10, 207n14; Seattle Commons project, 110
Battelle Memorial Research Institute, 63, 137–40, 208n14
Bayer, Herbert, 129
Bayliss, Douglas, 51
Beardsley, Cassius, 84, 119, 152
Beardsley, Jean, 68
Bebb, Charles H., 67
Beijing Olympics, Peoples Park Competition, 126*f*, 127
Bell, Jordan, 207n27
Bellevue projects, 84, 119, 127
Bellingham projects, 119*f*, 120–21, 190–91
bench placements: Bloedel Reserve, 182; college campuses, 121; corporate facilities, 63, 138*f*, 139; parks, 113, 115, 117; residential gardens, 89, 98*f*
Bender, Jim, 114
Bengal, Haag's gardening experiment, 10–11
Bernardi, Theodore, 54
Betty Bowen Park, 115

Beyer, Richard, 100
Big Bend Community College, 123
bioremediation. *See* Gas Works Park, Seattle
bird attractions, Merrill Court Townhomes, 97, 100
Bird Refuge, Bloedel Reserve, 182, 183*f*, 184, 185
Blackburn, Margaret, 68
blacksmith shop, gasworks site, 154*f*, 155
Blaine projects, 111
Block Island project, 23
Bloedel, Prentice, 169–70, 171, 172–73, 210n5
Bloedel, Virginia Merrill, 169, 171, 210n5
Bloedel Reserve: overview, ix, 37, 169, 184–85; circulation system development, 173–76; Garden of Planes, 168–69*f*, 176–79, 184; garden sequence planning, 175–76, 179–84; house vista changes, 173; Japanese Garden, 170, 172, 181; master plan proposals, 172–73; Moss Garden, 36, 172, 177*f*, 179*f*, 180–81, 184; Reflection Garden, 171*f*, 172, 181–82, 184; site history, 169–70
Blue Green Park competition, 127
bog garden, Sommervilles', 95, 96*f*. *See also* Bloedel Reserve
Booth, Mary (earlier Edstrom), 68, 85, 90, 91
Boston competitions, 127
Bothell, college campus project, 123
bridge design, Bloedel Reserve, 175
Brockman, Frank C., 122
Brooks, Richard J., 110, 160–61, 166–67
Brown, Richard, 173, 174
Broz, Mr. and Mrs. James (and garden), 36, 59–60
Buchanan, Robert, 80
Bumgardner, Al (A. W.), 153, 207n4
Burke Building, 142, 143
business landscapes. *See* corporate/commercial gardens

C

California: corporate gardens, 62–64, 204n36; freeway landscapes, 102; Haag and UC Berkeley, x, 17–18, 68, 206n16; landscape exhibition, 18–19. *See also* residential gardens, California
California Landscape Architects, 54
Callahan, Kenneth, 70
Camp, Harry (and garden), 55–57, 130
Campbell, Craig S., 85, 140
CAMP (Central Area Motivation Project), 109, 115, 117
Cane, Percy, 25–26
Capitol Hill, gardens, 97, 102–3
Capitol Hill Viewpoint Park, 115, 207n27
Capitol Lake Recreation Plan, 110
Carkeek Park, Seattle, 119
carry capacity studies, Fulbright proposal, 26
Carter, Don, 20, 52, 203n14
Carver, Joan, 26, 27
Carver, Norman: book by, 28, 193; Japan visit, xi, 25, 26, 27–28, 32–33, 39
Case Study House, xi, 36, 54–55, 130, 203n12, n14
CAUP. *See* College of Architecture and Planning (CAUP)
Cedar Croft farm, 3
Center Park, Seattle, 109
Central Area Motivation Project (CAMP), 109, 115, 117
Central Park, New York City, 197–98
Central Washington State College, 120, 190–91
Century 21 Exposition, 53, 84, 87, 105, 106, 132–33, 134*f*
ceramics, Japan, 30–31, 34
Ceremonial Drive, Bloedel Reserve, 174–75
Chambers, Walter Louis, 23, 130, 208n3
Chapman, Bruce, 159
Cheney, college campus project, 123
Cherokee Park, Louisville, 9
Chiarelli & Kirk, 83–84
Chinese elements, Bloedel Reserve, 184
Chittock, Robert, 84
Christian Science Church, Berkeley, 79
Church, Thomas: Bloedel Reserve, 170, 171; book by, 52; Haag's relationship, 19, 52, 67; influence of, x, 21, 51; Martins' garden, 18; San Francisco garden, 18; White's comments about, 53
civic engagement philosophy, Haag's, 53, 73–74, 108–9, 192. *See also* urban development, Seattle's strategies
Clarke, Rod, 151, 208n11 (Ch. 9)
Clay, Grady, 130
Cobb, Harry, 200
Cohan, Peter, 165
Cole, Dale, 160, 161
college campus projects, 120–23, 190–91
College of Architecture and Planning (CAUP): brochure, 73*f*; curriculum expansion, 67–68, 204n3, n6; faculty listed, 67, 80; Haag's legacy, 187; hiring of Haag, 67, 204n2, n7; landscape accreditation, 80. *See also* teaching approach, Haag's
Collins, Angela, 169
Collins, Lester A., 23, 25, 26
commercial landscapes. *See* corporate/commercial gardens
Commodore Aviation, 64
commonplace books, White's, 14, 15–16, 201n8
community gardens, 102
competitions, student, 15, 23, 126–27
Condon, Patrick, 179, 185

cookie sign, 191
Copeland, Joyce, 165
Copeland, Lee, 207n4
Copley Square competition, 127
corporate/commercial gardens: California, 62–64, 204n36; Pacific Northwest, 86*f*, 87–88, 137–40, 208n14. *See also* urban development, Seattle's strategies
Cougar Mountain Park, Bellevue, 119
Council Ring, Century 21 Exposition, 132–33, 134*f*
countercultures, in Haag's curriculum development, 69–70
courtyards: Battelle facility, 138*f*, 139; California gardens, 55, 57–58, 63; Japan, 28*f*; Seattle museum, 124
Cowle, Henry Chandler, 201n14
crafts, Japan, 30–31
Cramer, Ernst, 129, 130*f*
credo, Haag's, 79, 188
cultural landscapes, Japan, 31–32

D

The Daily, 72
Danny Woo Community Garden, Seattle, 102
Darwin, Charles, 9–10, 74, 76
Dean, Francis, 84
DeLong, Eric, 165
de Maria, Walter, 130
Denes, Agnes, 166–67
Dennis, Dale, 85, 140
design philosophy, Haag's. *See specific topics, e.g.,* Japan *entries;* land forms; trees *entries;* urban development, Seattle's strategies
Dickinson, Calhoun, 153–54
Diethelm, Jerry, 80, 85, 120, 130–31, 190–91, 194
Dietz, Robert, 67, 76, 204n7
Dimmich garden, 87
Dixie View Nursery, Kentucky, 201n21
Donaldson Nursery, Kentucky, 201n21
dormitories, college, 119*f*, 120–21
Double Negative, Heizer's, 130
Dumbarton Oaks, 79
DUX project, California, 62–64, 65

E

Eames, Charles, 54
Earth Day, 70
earth forms. *See* land forms
Eastern Washington State College, 122*f*, 123
East Pine Street Substation, 109–10, 207n14
Eckbo, Garrett, 21, 51, 52, 53, 58
Eckbo, Royston and Williams, 18, 51
ecological design, beginnings, 6, 8. *See also specific topics, e.g.,* Bloedel Reserve; residential gardens *entries;* teaching approach, Haag's; trees *entries;* water *entries*
Ecology Building, Washington State Department of, 127
Edgar, Mr. and Mrs. Richard B. (and garden), 89–90, 91, 100
"Edible Landscape" (Haag), 101–2
Edstrom, Mary (later Booth), 68, 85, 90, 91
Edwards, Myrtle, 150, 153
Eichler houses, 57, 204n24 (Ch. 24)
Eisley, Loren, 74
Ellensburg, dormitory project, 120, 190–91
Elliot, Charles, 130
Ellis, James R., 106, 147
Ellwood garden, 130
Embarcadero Freeway project, 105, 207n1
Embassy and Consultate project, Lisbon, 110*f*, 111
Emmons, Donald, 54
England: Olin's period, 191, 194, 195; Rudy Haag's visit, 3
entrance designs: California gardens, 57–58, 60, 63; Japan's gardens, 34; Portugal embassy project, 111; Roosevelt Memorial, 131
entrance designs, Pacific Northwest: corporate facilities, 87; residential gardens, 89, 94, 97, 101*f*; Seattle projects, 124, 126
Entsu-ji, 34
Environmental Concern firm, 140
Eskilsson, Lottie, 85, 159
Evening Terrace, Jackson Federal Building, 142–43
Everett Community College, 123
Everett projects, 111, 140–42
Exhibition of Landscape Design, 18
The Experience of Landscape (Appleton), 142
Experiments in Environment, Halprin's, 53

F

Fairhaven College of Interdisciplinary Studies, 120*f*, 121–22
Farrand, Beatrix, 79
Farrar, Corice, 167*f*
Fein, Benjamin, 22
Fells, Don, 209n52
Fells, Patricia, 209n52
Fike, Sherry, 85
Findlay, John, 132

Finrow, Jerry, 85
Firehouse Mini Park, Seattle, 115–17
Flag Plaza, Century 21 Exposition, 132–33
Flanders, Annette Hoyt, 9
Fleniken, Judy, 194, 206n9
Flowers and Their Friends (Morely), 8
Foley, Robert, 93, 167*f*
Form & Space (Carver), 28, 193
Fort Lawton Military Reservation, 108, 127, 153
Forward Thrust initiative, 106, 153, 165, 195
"Four Freedoms, Four Courts" design, 131–32
Freeway Park, Seattle, 53
freeways: California landscapes, 102; Seattle conflicts, 105–6, 108–9, 207n1
Frey, Susan Rademacher, 184
Frey garden, 87
Friends of Gas Works Park, 165, 209n52
Friends of the Market, 112–13
Frothingham, Don, 207n4
Frye Art Museum, 123*f*, 124–25
Fulbright-Hays Exchange Program, 25, 38–39
Fuller, Buckminster, 16
Fuller, Carole, 165
fusion concept: Bloedel Reserve, 175; California gardens, 57; development of, xi, 32, 93–94; Pacific Northwest projects, 95*f*, 99*f*, 122*f*, 123, 124; Roosevelt Memorial design, 131

G

Gananong, William, 8
Garden and Forest, 8
Garden of Planes, Bloedel Reserve, 168–69*f*, 176–79, 184, 185
Gardens Are for People (Church), 52
Gardens in the Modern Landscape (Tunnard), 19
The Gardens of Japan (Harada), 25–26
Gas Works Park, Seattle: overview, 147–48; design stage, 151–56, 191; naming of, 162; opening of, 163–65; project approval, 107, 159, 209n27; public engagement strategies, 154–59, 209n37; remediation activity, 159–63, 209nn43–44; significance, ix, 165–67; site history, 148–50; visions for, 150–51
Gaynor, Peggy, 113
Geller, Abraham, 131–32
Gibson garden, 21
Gilman Village, 102
Gould, Carl F., 67
Gran, Tom, 209n52
Grand Shrines at Ise, 34–35, 45–46*f*
Grassy Common, Merrill Court Townhomes, 97, 98*f*
gravel story, Haag's childhood, 6. *See also* stones
Graves, Morris, 70
Great Garden Vision Symposium, 88–89
Great Mound, Gas Works Park, 162, 163, 164–65
Great Pyramid, Jordan Park, 141
Greening, Charles (Chuck), 95, 164–65
Grieg Garden, Seattle, 122*f*
Grinbergs, Ilze (later Jones), 63, 190, 194
Grohs, Edwin, 84
Gropius, Walter: exhibition of, 205n42; Haag's photograph, 35; during Haag's student years, 22, 23; Japan visit, 29–30, 33, 34, 307; teaching position, 21
guesthouse, Bloedel Reserve, 175, 176, 178*f*, 179

H

Haag, Gertrude, 3
Haag, John, 201n8
Haag, Louise, 201n8
Haag, Luthera Owings, 3–7
Haag, Philip, 4*f*
Haag, Richard: childhood/youth, ix–x, 3–6, 9–10, 201n24; college years, 13–23; drawings of, 68*f*, 189*f*; legacy, 187–89, 198–200; military service, 10–11; photos, 70*f*, 87*f*, 103*f*. *See also specific topics, e.g.,* Gas Works Park; Japanese elements *entries;* teaching approach, Haag's; trees *entries*
Haag, Rudy (and Nursery), 3–6, 7*f*, 9, 11, 201n6
Haag, Virginia, 201n8
Haag, Zach, 194–95
Haag Nurseries, R. L., 3–6, 7*f*, 201n6
Haeckel, Ernest Heinrich, 201n14
Hall, David, 91–93
Halprin, Anna, 53
Halprin, Lawrence, xi, 51, 52, 122, 132, 203n5, 204n36
Halvorson, James, 93
Hamada, Shoji, 30–31
Hanna, Robert: Battelle facility, 137; Century 21 Exposition, 132–33; dormitory project, 120; employment with Haag, 85, 195; Olin partnership, 195–96; teaching positions, 80, 190
Harada, Jiro, 25, 32
Harmon, James, 113
Harvard University, Graduate School of Design: award to Haag, 188; Haag's attendance, 20–23, 88, 130; program development, 14, 71
"Heinz 57" courses, White's, 15, 69
Heizer, Michael, 73, 130

Hendrickson, Robert, 113
Henry Klein Partnership, 91–92
Henry M. Jackson Federal Building, 87, 142–44, 208n21
Hermann, Arthur, 67, 76
Highland Place Nursery, Kentucky, 201n21
Highlands development, Olmsted design, 83
Highline Community College, 123
High Noon Plane, Jordan Park, 141, 142
High Noon Terrace, Jackson Federal Building, 142–43
Hildebrand, Grant, 85, 187
Hillenmeyer Nursery, Kentucky, 201n21
Hilltop community, 83–84, 87
Hinterberger, John, 110
Hobbs, Richard, 207n4
Hodemaker, Dave, 139
Holl, Steven, 143
Holt, Nancy, 130
Holtman, Robert E., 68
homes, Japan, 28–29*f*, 32–33
Horiuchi, Paul, 87
housing developments, Seattle, 83–84, 106, 107, 109
Howett, Catherine, 6, 8
Hoyts, Eric W., 122
Hudnut, Joseph, 21, 65
Hunt, Glen, 51, 84, 152

I

Iida, Juki, 170
The Immense Journey (Eisley), 74
Indian Shell Mound Park, Seattle Center, 135
industrialization impact, Lake Union, 147–48. *See also* Gas Works Park, Seattle
International Bridging the Gap competition, 127
internment camps, 16, 20, 26
Isaac residence, 86*f*
Ise Shrine, 34–35
Island Park Elementary School, Mercer Island, 117–18
Issaquah gardens, 89–90, 102–3
"Is There a Bay Area Style?" (Royston), 18–19
Ito, Teiji, 75, 205n43

J

Jackson, Henry M., 106
Jackson, J. B., 10
Jackson Federal Building, 87, 142–44, 208n21
James, Anne, 209n53
James, Frank: characterized, 194; college campus projects, 120, 190–91; employment with Haag, 85; on field trips, 88*f*; formation of own company, 195, 206n64; Gas Works Park, 152; on Haag's business skills, 91; medical building project, 87; Roosevelt Memorial design, 130–31; Sprague garden, 89, 90*f*; teaching activity, 80, 206n69
Japan, Haag's visit: exploratory approach, 27–29, 31–32; garden experiences, 27, 34–38; Gropius' visit, 29–30, 33; immersion experience, 26–27; importance of, x–xi, 38–39; photographs from, 28–31*f*, 33*f*, 35*f*, 40–42*f*, 44–46*f*; preparations for, 23, 25–26
Japanese Architecture (Kobayashi), 35
Japanese elements: corporate/commercial gardens, 62, 87–88, 139; in curriculum, 75, 79, 192–93, 205n59; as Haag foundation, 198–200; Roosevelt Memorial design, 131. *See also* Bloedel Reserve
Japanese elements, residential gardens: California, 57, 58, 59–62, 64–65; Pacific Northwest, 85, 87–88, 89, 94
Japanese Exhibition House, New York City, 25
Japanese Folk Crafts Museum, Kanazawa, 31
Japanese Garden, Bloedel Reserve, 170, 172, 181
Japanese Gardens (Harada), 32
Jefferson Terrace, Seattle, 109
Jeffersontown, Kentucky, 3–4, 9, 23, 201n21
Johanson, Perry B., 83–84
John Graham & Associates, 142
Johnson, Edward, 152
Johnson, Philip, 25
Johnson, Samuel, 101
Johnson, William J., 68
Johnston, Norm, 207n4
Jonegan and Gerrard, 172
Jones, Grant: Century 21 Exposition, 132–33, 134*f*; characterized, 194; dormitory project, 120; on field trips, 88*f*, 89; Haag's hiring of, 84–85; Haag's impact, 187, 190; plant knowledge, 84, 87; studio participation with Olin, 194, 195; teaching activity, 80; zoo project, 191
Jones, Ilze (earlier Grinbergs), 63, 190, 194
Jones and Jones, 172
Jordan Park, Everett, 22, 37, 140–42
Jorgensen, Patti, 85
Junjokan (Pure View Hall), Japan, 33

K

Kahn, Louis, 78
Kaiser Center Roof Garden, 52
Katsura Rikyū, 34, 48*f*

Kawai, Kanjirō, 30
keblis design, 63, 121, 139
Kenmore Park, Bellevue, 119
Kentucky Nurseryman's Association, 4
Kentucky Times-Star, 5–6
Kepes, Gyorgy, 205n42
Kiley, Dan: and DUX design, 63; Ford Foundation Building, 79; Fort Lawton project, 127; Gas Works Park project, 153; Haag's internship, x, 22; on Jordan Park, 142; Oberlander's employment, 202n31; teaching approach, 21
kimonos, Japan, 30
Kirk, Paul Hayden, 84, 87, 125–26, 170–71, 175
Kirk, Wallace, McKinley & Associates, 109
Kirkland projects, 127
Kite Hill, Gas Works Park, 147, 163, 164–65
Klein, Henry, 91–92
Klingle, Matthew, 83
Knipper, Rod, 151, 208n11 (Ch. 9)
Knorr, Don, 54, 203n14
Knorr-Elliot, 54, 62
Kobayashi, Bunji, 35, 79
Kolb, Keith, 67
Kruckeberg, Arthur R., 72, 122
K Street Farmers Market, 110
Kubota, Fujitaro, 170
Kuck, Loraine, 25
Kukes, Dina and Wilbur (and garden), 91–93, 100

L

Lacey, Ecology Building project, 127
Lake Sammamish, 91, 100
Lake Union, 118, 147, 148–49. *See also* Gas Works Park, Seattle
Lake Washington: location, 83; pollution, 106, 147; Sommerville garden, 93–95, 97; Steinbrueck Park, 112–14, 119–20
Lake Whatcom, Kukes garden, 91–93, 100
land art movement, 129–30, 140
land forms: Battelle facility, 137–40; Bloedel Reserve, 175, 176–79; California gardens, 55, 57, 58, 60, 203n14; Century 21 Exposition, 132–33; Haag's evolution, 144–45; Jackson Federal Building, 143; Japan's gardens, 36–37; Jordan Park, 140–42; Roosevelt Memorial designs, 131–32; Seattle Center project, 133–36; Seattle parks, 113, 115, 117, 162, 165; Stern garden, 100. *See also* sculptures *entries*
land grant colleges, origins, 201n1 (Ch. 2)
Landmark Preservation Board, Seattle's, 125, 208n14
Landscape Accreditation Review Board, 80
Landscape Architecture, Department of. *See* College of Architecture and Planning (CAUP)
Landscape Architecture Magazine, 101–2, 118
Landscape Architecture program, UW. *See* College of Architecture and Planning (CAUP); teaching approach, Haag's
Landscape Architecture (Simonds), 26
landscape design philosophy, Haag's. *See specific topics, e.g.,* Japan *entries;* land forms; trees *entries;* urban development, Seattle's strategies
Landscape Exchange Program, 15
Landscape for Living (Eckbo), 52
"Landscape Gardening—A Definition" (van Rensselaer), 8
Landscape of Time (Noguchi), 143
Latourell, Elaine Day, 130–31
Lazare, Kim, 164–65
LCD list, Haag's classes, 79
Leach, Bernard, 30
Lebo, Willis, 160–61
Lehner, Roy, 91, 121–22
Leland, Larry, 160
Lewerentz, Sigurd, 133
library projects, 121, 123, 190–91, 207n33
lighting, 57, 115
Lightship Relief Guild, 153
Little Goose Dam, 111
Litton, Burton J., 19–20
Lockfield, Franklin, 130–31, 152, 194
Loehner garden, 60*f*
Lohmann, Karl B., 13, 14
Lost Wilderness, field trip explorations, 88*f,* 89
Louisa Boren Park, 115
Louisville Nurseries, Kentucky, 201n21
Lovejoy, Derek, 195
Lovett, Wendell, 67, 84, 87
Luders, J. Edward, 17
Luke, Wing, 111, 153
Lynnwood, medical building project, 86*f,* 87–88

M

MacMillan Bloedel Timber Company, 169
magic theme, landscape design, 73
Magnolia Branch library, 125–26, 207n33
Magnuson, Warren G., 106
Maiden Lane home, Bassetti's, 87
Manzanar internment camp, 20, 26

Marin Professional Center, 64
maritime theme, gasworks site, 153, 208n20
Marquardi, Michelle, 206n34
Marquis and Stoller, 52, 55, 64, 204n36
Martins' garden, San Francisco, 18
Marymoor Park, Redmond, 118*f*, 119
Maybeck, Bernard, 79
McHarg, Ian, 51, 53, 67, 195
Memorial Glade, University of California, 122*f*, 123
"Memo to Japanese Designers" (Haag), 33
Mercer, Thomas, 148
Merrill Court Townhomes, 97–101
Mesoamerican land forms, 129
Metro, establishment, 147
Meyer, Elizabeth, 169
Midway, college campus project, 123
Mies van der Rohe, Ludwig, 19*f*, 33
Miller, Elizabeth Cary Pendleton, 153, 161, 209n43
Miller and Whiry, 23
minka, building of, 32–33
min-max approach, 77, 78, 80, 123, 179. *See also* non-striving theory, Haag's
Mithun, Omar, 67
"Mixed Pickles" course, White's, 15, 69
Model Cities program, 107, 109
Modern Gardens, British and Foreign (Cane), 25–26
modernist ideas: during Haag's student years, 16, 18–19, 21; in Northwest architecture, 84, 85, 86*f*. *See also specific topics, e.g.,* residential gardens, California; teaching approach, Haag's
Mohl, Marvin and Ruth, 102
Morely, Margaret Warner, 8
Morning Plane, Jordan Park, 141, 142
Morning Terrace, Jackson Federal Building, 142–43
Morrill Act, 201n1 (Ch. 2)
Morris, Robert, 130, 140
Morse, John, 153
Moses Lake, college campus project, 123
Moss Garden, Bloedel Reserve, 36, 172, 177*f*, 179*f*, 180–81, 184, 185
moss gardens, Japan, 28, 34, 36
Mulligan, Brian O., 122
Municipal Arts Commission, Seattle, 53, 153
Museum of Modern Art, 25, 26
museum projects, 123*f*, 124–25
Myers, David, 67
Myers, Don, 207n4
Myrtle Edwards Park, 156, 158*f*, 159, 162. *See also* Gas Works Park, Seattle

N

Nakamura, Jobo, 26, 27
Nakano, Kenichi, 80, 85, 91, 151, 159, 206n8
Nakashima, George, 25, 87
Napa Medical Dental Building, 64
Naramore, Bain, Brady, & Johnson, 139
Natelson, Deborah, 206n9
National Landscape Exchange program, 151–52
native plants, microclimate considerations, 79. *See also* plants *entries*
Natorp, William A., 6
Natsuhara, Maryo, 20, 26, 27
nature-oriented visions. *See specific topics, e.g.,* Bloedel Reserve; Japanese elements *entries;* residential gardens, Pacific Northwest; trees *entries*
NBBJ (Naramore, Bain, Brady, & Johnson), 139
"The Need of Being Versed in Country Things" (Jackson), 10
Nelsen, Ibsen, 87, 97, 159, 171, 207n4
Neutra, Richard, 54
New England tours, 15–16, 25
Nijō-jō, 34
Nishita, Satoru, 52
Noguchi, Isamu, 37, 143
Nolen, John, 14
non-striving theory, Haag's: and Bengali farming experiment, 11; Japan's influence, 32, 35, 37–38; teaching approach, 68, 76, 78, 80. *See also* Bloedel Reserve; Gas Works Park, Seattle
North Cascades Environmental Center, 93
North Passage Point Park, Seattle, 117*f*, 118–19
North Waterfront Park, California, 166–67
Northwest regional modernism, defined, 84, 86*f*
Northwest School, architectural philosophy, 84, 85, 86*f*
Northwest School, art culture, 70
nursery, Haag's, 87*f*, 88–89
nutrimental landscapes, 5, 32, 58, 101–3
Nyberg, Folke, 190

O

Oberlander, Cornelia Hahn, 21, 22, 202n31
Observatory at Ijumiuden (Morris), 140
Ochsner, Jeffrey Karl, 111–12
Ohlsson, Folke, 62
Okada, Frank, 195
Okamoto/Liskamm, 153, 209n25
Okerlund, Gary, 190

Olin, Laurie: afterword by, 189–200; Better City study, 207n4; with colleagues, 85*f*; college campus projects, 120, 190–91; drawings of Haag, 68*f*, 189*f*; on field trips, 88*f*, 89; Gas Works Park project, 156, 159, 191; hiring of, 80; Pike Place Market preservation, 112; Roosevelt Memorial design, 130–31; scrap paper story, 90, 196; teaching activity, 80, 194–95
Oliver, Marvin, 114
Olmsted, Frederick Law, 8, 9, 129–30
Olmsted, John C., 149
Olmsted Brothers, 14, 83, 84
Olson Sundberg Kundig Allen, 124
Olympia projects, 110
Olympic Games, Peoples Park Competition, 126*f*, 127
One Hundred Kyoto Gardens (Kuck), 25
Osmundson, Theodore, 51, 79
Osmundson and Staley, 52
Owings, Luthera (later Haag), 3–7
Owings, Luther Clay, 3

P

Pacific Horticulture, xi, 93–94
Pacific Science Center, Seattle Center, 134*f*
Panorama Park, Kirkland, 127
paper story, Olin's, 90, 196
Parc de la Villette competition, 127
park projects: Bellevue, 119; California, 166–67; Everett, 22, 37, 140–42; Redmond, 118*f*, 119; Seattle, 112–19, 135. *See also* Gas Works Park, Seattle
Pearson, Esther, 84
Peets, Elbert, 23
Peoples Park Competition, 126*f*, 127
Philadelphia housing project, 22
Picardo Farm community garden, 102
Pierce, Paul, 151, 208n11 (Ch. 9)
Pike Place Market, 108, 111–13
Pioneer Square, Seattle, 107
Pirzio-Biroli, Lucia, 206n34
Planting Design (Robinson), 13
plants: early ASLA-nursery relationships, 8–9; Everett's Jordan Park, 141–42; in Haag Nurseries, 4, 201n6; Haag's philosophy, 78–79, 88–89; Japan's gardens, 32, 34; Philadelphia housing project, 22; Portugal embassy project, 111; Seattle City Light substation project, 110
plants, California gardens: Broz residence, 60; Camp residence, 55, 57; Case Study House, 54–55; DUX business, 62–63, 64*f*; Wong residence, 57–58; Zollinger residence, 60
plants, Pacific Northwest gardens: Edgar residence, 91; Haag/Trivison residence, 101–3; Merrill Court Townhomes, 97, 98*f*; Sommerville residence, 95, 96; Sprague residence, 89; Stern residence, 100. *See also* trees, Pacific Northwest projects
playgrounds, Seattle parks, 113–14, 116*f*, 117–18, 164
"playing landscape architects" game, 21
Plaza Plane, Jordan Park, 141, 142
"Poetic Response," Olin's drawing, 68*f*
poetry comparison, Bloedel Reserve, 184
Poet's Garden (Cramer), 129, 130*f*
Point Parks, Seattle, 117*f*, 118–19
pollution problems, Seattle, 147, 149–50, 151*f*. *See also* Gas Works Park, Seattle
pools. *See* swimming pools; water *entries*
Portage Bay home, Bassetti's, 87
Port Townsend project, 111
Portugal, Embassy and Consultate project, 110*f*, 111
pottery, Japan, 30–31, 34
P-Patch Community Gardens, 102
Pries, Lionel, 67, 75, 84
"A Primer of Landscape Architecture" (White), 69
Princess Louisa Inlet, British Columbia, 88*f*, 89
Prow, Gas Works Park, 164
Puget Consumer Cooperative, 102
Puget Sound Maritime Historical Society, 153
Pullman, college campus project, 123
pyramid forms, Bloedel Reserve, 176–78, 184

R

R. H. Thomson Expressway, Seattle, 105
Randlett, Mary, 142, 155, 156, 165, 207n4
Ray, Stephen, 209n37
Raymond, Antonin, 37
Reader's Digest building, Tokyo, 37
reading habits, Haag's: childhood/youth, 4–5, 9–10; teaching materials, 74–75, 192, 193
recycled landscapes, in Haag's teaching, 108. *See also* Gas Works Park, Seattle
Reflection Garden, Bloedel Reserve, 171*f*, 172, 181–82, 184, 185
remove-and-reuse strategy, Haag's. *See* Gas Works Park, Seattle; Jordan Park, Everett
residential gardens, California: Camp house, 55–57; Case Study House, 54–55, 203n12, n14; Haag's approach summarized, 64–65; Halprin office approach, 52–53; modernist context, 51–52; professional recognition/awards, 58–59; temporary housing community, 53; Wong

house, 57–59
residential gardens, Pacific Northwest: Edgar family, 89–91; Kukes family, 91–93; Merrill Court Townhomes, 97–100; nutrimental types, 101–3; region-based visions, 83–84, 85, 87, 100–101; Sommerville family, 93–97; Sprague family, 89, 90*f*; Stern family, 100–101
Reynolds, Harris, 14
RHA. *See* Richard Haag Associates (RHA)
Rice, William, 68
rice production, Japan, 31–32, 40–42*f*
Richard Haag Associates (RHA): business management skills, 91, 196; design process, 90–91, 196–97; field trip explorations, 88*f*, 89; personnel approach, 80, 84–85, 165–66, 193–94; San Francisco opening, xi, 54; Seattle launching, xi, 65, 84–85. *See also specific topics, e.g.,* Bloedel Reserve; Gas Works Park, Seattle; teaching approach, Haag's; urban development, Seattle's strategies
Ridenour & Cochran, 89–90
Ridgeway dormitories, 119*f*, 120–21
Riley, Russ, 62, 65
road projects, opposition, 105–6, 108–9, 207n1
Roberts, John, 166–67
Robinson, Charles Mulford, 13
Robinson, Florence Bell, 13
Roche and Dinkeloo, 79
rocks. *see* stones
Roethke, Theodore, 210n25
Rogers, Elizabeth Barlow, 198
Rohrer, John, 67
roof gardens, 52, 79, 97
Roosevelt Memorial designs, 130–32
Root, Ralph Rodney, 13
Rose, James, 21
Rottle, Nancy, 167*f*
Royston, Robert, 18–19, 51, 53
Rozdilsky, John, 63, 140, 165
RSVP cycle, Halprin's, 53
Rupard, Ken, 85*f*, 194
Ryōan-ji garden: agrarianism aesthetic, 32, 47*f*; and Bloedel Reserve, 179, 182; in Haag's "Space" article, 38; impact on Haag, 27, 34, 35–37

S

Saarinen, Eero, 54
Saihō-ji garden, 28, 34, 35*f*, 36, 49*f*
Sakanashi Construction, 62
Sakuma, Don: college campus projects, 121–22; formation of own company, 195, 206n64; Gas Works Park project, 209n37; on Haag's business skills, 91; hiring of, 85, 193–94; teaching positions, 80, 85, 194, 206n69
Sam's Red Robin, 84, 193, 206n6
Sanbō-in, 34
Sanders, Jeffrey, 108
sand gardens, California, 55
San Francisco Museum of Art, 18
Sarkowsky, Herman (and garden), 97, 99*f*
Sasaki, Hideo: background, 16; college teaching, 16–17, 21–22; curriculum development advice, 68, 69, 80; during Haag's student years, x, 14, 17, 21; Nakamura friendship, 26; recommendation of Haag, 67, 204n7; UW master landscape plan, 122
Sasaki Walker and Associates, 203n10
Schwägerl, Edward Otto, 84
Scott, Geraldine Knight, 19, 20
sculpture, Roosevelt Memorial design, 131
sculptures, Seattle projects: college campuses, 121; Gas Works Park, 164–65; Jackson Federal Building, 143; museum, 124–25; parks, 115; residential gardens, 95, 97. *See also* land forms
Seablom, Herb, 130–31
Seattle. *See specific topics, e.g.,* Gas Works Park; urban development, Seattle's strategies
Seattle Arts Commission, 106, 159
Seattle Board of Park Commissioners, 152–54
Seattle Center project, 79, 133–36
Seattle City Light, 109–10, 207n14
Seattle Cityscape (Steinbrueck), 106
Seattle Commons, 110
Seattle Design Commission, 153, 209n27
Seattle Garden Club, 153
Seattle Gas Light Company, 148–49
Seattle Post-Intelligencer, 109, 125
Seattle Tilth, 102
Seattle Times, 90, 110, 135, 150, 159
secret garden assignment, in Haag's teaching, 77
Sekiguchi, Eitaro, 26, 27, 202n10 (Ch. 3)
Shepard, Paul, 74
Shepheard, Peter, 195
Shepherd, Harry W., 19, 20
Sherlock, Smith, and Adams, 23
Shifflet, Professor, 14
Shigemori, Mirei, 37
shrines, Japan, 31, 32, 34–35, 44–46*f*
Siegler, Frederick Adrian, 154
Simonds, John O., 26, 188
Simpson, Buster, 113

Simpson, Diane, 165
Sinderman, Betty, 206n9
sketching style, Haag's, 38
Skidmore, Owings & Merrill, 16
Small, Robert, 93, 206n24
Small, Tom, 95
Smithson, Robert, 73, 129–30, 140
social space: California gardens, 55, 58, 63, 65; Century 21 Exposition, 132–33; Halprin's approach, 52–53; Pacific Northwest gardens, 91, 94, 102–3; park projects, 112, 115–20. *See also* Gas Works Park, Seattle; land forms
Solar-Assisted Low-Income Housing, 109
Sommerville, Mimi and Vinton (and garden), 93–95, 97
Soseki, Musō, 203n37
South Passage Point Park, Seattle, 117*f*, 118–19
space concept. *See specific topics, e.g.,* Japanese elements *entries;* land forms
"Space" (Haag), 38
Spanish Steps design, Jackson Federal Building, 143, 208n21
Spectacle Island competition, 127
Speed Memorial Museum, 4
Spiral Jetty (Smithson), 130, 140
Spirn, Anne Whiston, 8
Sprague, D. L. (and garden), 89, 90*f*
Sproule, Jack, 67
St. Francis Square, San Francisco, 204n36
Staley, John H., 51
Stamey Medical Clinic, Lynnwood, 86*f*, 87–88
Steele, Fletcher, 14
Steinbrueck, Victor: Gas Works Park project, 155, 156, 159, 209n38; house of, 87; Japan visit, 75; Pike Market Place project, 111–12; teaching position, 67; visions for Seattle, 105–6, 107, 108
Steinbrueck Park, Seattle, 112–14, 119–20
Stern garden, 100–101
stones: Bloedel Reserve, 171, 175, 179; California gardens, 57, 58, 60, 62, 64–65; Japan's gardens, 32, 34, 37, 47–49*f*
stones, Pacific Northwest gardens: corporate facilities, 87, 88, 137; Jackson Federal Building, 143; residences, 89, 91, 93–95, 96*f*, 97, 102–3
Stonorov, Oscar, 22, 202n31
Streatfield, David C., 80
streetscaping projects, Seattle, 109, 115
Streissguth, Daniel, 67
Studio Ectypos, 127, 206n34
substation project, Seattle City Light, 109–10, 207n14
suitcase story, Olin's, 197, 198
Sundberg, Rick, 124
sundial, Gas Works Park, 164–65
Sunset magazine, 52, 59
Swanson, Sally, 85
Sweden visit, Haag's, 133, 134*f*
Swift, Barbara, 182
Swift Landscape Architects, 207n33
swimming pools: Bloedel Reserve, 175–77, 179, 210n25; California gardens, 55, 58, 65; Forward Thrust initiative, 106; Gas Works Park, 152, 163
symbiomsteading problem, 76–77

T

Tacoma projects, 110–11
Talaris Institute (Battelle Memorial Research Institute), 63, 137–40, 208n14
Talley, William, 119
Tange, Kenzō, 39
tatami, 32–33, 63
Taut, Bruno, 202n7
teaching approach, Haag's: overview, xi; creativity emphasis, 77–78; curriculum development, 68–72, 122–23, 205n28, nn34–35; design problems, 21, 75–79, 76, 88, 205n48; drawing about, 68*f*; essay requirements, 74, 205n37; field trips, 89; hiring/promotions, 67–68, 80, 204n2, n7; influence summarized, 187, 189–93; lecture components, 28–29, 74–76, 79, 192; mentorship role, 80; partnering lecturers, 79–80; part-time approach, 79–80; public projects, 108; reading materials, 74–75, 192, 193; services of landscape architecture, 72–74; unorthodoxy of, 80–81
teaching philosophy, White's, 14–15
teahouse, Zollinger garden, 60, 62, 64
technologies, in Haag's curriculum development, 69, 70
Temko, Allan, 105
The Tender Carnivore (Shepard), 74
Teufel, William G., 51, 84
"Theory and Perception" courses, 15, 74, 75–76, 205nn34–35
Thiel, Phil, 105, 205n42, 207n1
Thiry, Paul, 121, 132
Thomas Jefferson Award, 203n5
Thompson, Hans A., 153, 154
Thoreau, Henry David, 74
Thorson, Lloyd F., 68
"Thoughts on Education in Landscape Architecture" (Sasaki), 69
time elements, gardens, 34, 54. *See also* Bloedel Reserve
Tobey, Mark, 70

Tōfuku-ji, 37
Torres, Roman E., 114
totem poles, Steinbrueck Park, 114
Treasure House, Japan, 35, 45*f*
trees: California freeway landscapes, 102; in Haag's curriculum, 78–79; Philadelphia housing project, 22; Portugal embassy project, 111; Roosevelt Memorial designs, 131
trees, California gardens: Camp residence, 55, 57; Case Study House, 54; DUX business, 63, 64*f*; Wong residence, 57, 58; Zollinger residence, 60
trees, Pacific Northwest projects: Bloedel Reserve additions, 175–76, 184; Century 21 Exposition, 132–33; college campuses, 120–21, 122, 123; corporate facilities, 88, 139–40; Jackson Federal Building, 143; library, 126; museum, 124, 125; parks, 113–14, 115, 117–19, 142, 163; Seattle Center, 134*f*, 136; streetscaping, 109, 115
trees, Pacific Northwest residences: Edgar garden, 91; Kukes garden, 93; Merrill Court Townhomes, 97, 98*f*; Sommerville garden, 93, 94, 96*f*; Sprague garden, 89; Stern garden, 100
Trees Nursery, 87*f*, 88–89
Treib, Marc, 36
Trivison, Cheryl, 102, 127, 165, 167*f*, 206n9, 209n53
Tschumi, Bernard, 127
Tsutakawa, George, 87
Tucker, Shields, & Terry, 84
Tuma, Douglas H., 160, 209n37
Tunnard, Christopher, 18, 19
Twelker, Neil, 170
Tyler, Varro E., 122

U

Uhlman, Wes, 107, 155, 157*f*
Ullman, John R., 165, 171, 206n7, 209n37
United Nations Pavilion, Century 21 Exposition, 133
University of California, Berkeley, x, 17–18, 68, 204n16
University of Illinois, Haag's attendance, x, 10, 13–17
University of Kyoto, 26–27
University of Pennsylvania, 51, 195
University of Washington, master landscape plan, 122–23. *See also* College of Architecture and Planning (CAUP); teaching approach, Haag's
Untermann, Richard K., 80
urban agricultural movement, Seattle, 102
urban development, Seattle's strategies: overview, 105–9; park projects, 112–19, 135; Pike Place Market preservation, 111–13; public projects, 109–11. *See also* Gas Works Park, Seattle
urban ecological design, Haag's legacy, 185, 187–88. *See also specific topics, e.g.,* Bloedel Reserve; Gas Works Park, Seattle

V

van Rensselaer, Mariana Griswold, 8
Vaughan, H. L., 19
Veblen, Thorstein, 101–2
vegetable gardens, 5, 32, 58, 101–3
vernacular architecture, Japan, 32–33, 43*f*
Victor Steinbrueck Park, Seattle, 112–14, 119–20
Vignola, Richard, 52
Volunteer Park, Seattle, 119

W

Waddell, Patrick, 165
Wagner, Betty, 193
Wagner, Richard, 208n20
Walden (Thoreau), 74
Walker, Peter, 65, 68, 203n10
Walla Walla, dam project, 111
Walla Walla Community College, 123
Washington State National Guard Armory, 112
Washington State Society of Landscape Architects, 84
Washington State University, 67, 123
Watanabe, Edward, 84
Watchtower, Jordan Park, 141, 142
water: California gardens, 55, 58, 62–63, 64*f*; Fein's fountain, 22; Japan's gardens, 36, 37, 48*f*; Portugal embassy project, 111. *See also* Bloedel Reserve; Gas Works Park, Seattle; swimming pools
water, Pacific Northwest gardens: Battelle facility, 137–40; residences, 89, 93–94, 95, 97, 100
water pollution, management strategies, 110. *See also* Gas Works Park, Seattle
Wawona, 155, 209n31
Westcrest Park, Seattle, 119
Western Washington State College, 119*f*, 120–22, 190–91
Whelan Professional Building, Palo Alto, 64
White, Dick, 195
White, E. B., 16
White, Katherine, 16
White, Stanley Hart: background, 14; California visit, 53–54; curriculum development advice, 68–69; faculty position, 13, 14; Haag's Japan photographs, 39; during Haag's student years, x, 14–15, 32
Whitesburg Memorial Hospital, Kentucky, 52
Wightman, Roberta, 84
Williams, Edward, 51
Willis, Betty, 191

Wong, Mr. and Mrs. Elwood (and garden), 37, 57–59, 130, 175
Woodland Cemetery, Sweden, 133, 134*f*
Wrede, William E., 206n7, 209n37
Wurster, William, 18, 54

Y

Yamasaki, Richard I., 84, 170
Yanagi, Sōetsu, 31, 37, 79, 205n59
Yonick, Miles, 85, 137, 194
Young, Clayton, 207n4

Z

Zema, Gene, 75, 86*f*, 87
Zen elements. *See* Japan, Haag's visit; Japanese elements *entries*
Zollinger, Mrs. Lee (and garden), 36, 37, 60–62